Railroad Ferries of the Hudson

And Stories of a Deckhand

Railroad Ferries of the Hudson

And Stories of a Deckhand

By
Raymond J. Baxter
and
Arthur G. Adams

LIND Publications
Woodcliff Lake, NJ 1987

COVER ARTIST

WILLIAM G. MULLER

Marine artist William G. Muller created the impressive paintings and cover design for this book. He has a long and intense artistic interest in the majesty and romance of the classic American steamboat.

He has been particularly close to the steamboats of the Hudson, a now extinct species, having served as Quartermaster pilot of the ALEXANDER HAMILTON, last of the side-wheelers, while a youth in the mid-1950's.

Widely known today for his carefully-researched, lively paintings of historic and contemporary shipping, Bill Muller's work is sought by collectors and commissioned by publishers and maritime companies.

He is a founding director and academician-member of the American Society of Marine Artists, and founding director of The Hudson River Maritime Center Museum. He resides with his family in Briarcliff Manor, N.Y.

Lind Publications
188 Broadway
Woodcliff Lake, New Jersey 07675

Library of Congress Cataloging-in-Publication Data

Baxter, Raymond J.
  Railroad ferries of the Hudson.

  Bibliography: p.
  Includes index.
  1. Ferries—Hudson River (N.Y. and N.J.)—History—
20th century.   2. Local transit—New York Region—
History—20th century.   I. Adams, Arthur G.   II. Title.
HE5774.B39   1987   386'.2234'097473   87-2278
ISBN 0-910389-01-2

Printed in the United States of America
10 9 8 7 6 5 4 3 2 1

CONTENTS

ABOUT THE AUTHORS

RAYMOND J. BAXTER

Raymond J. Baxter was born in the Northern Valley community of Englewood, New Jersey in 1928, and was a lifelong resident of New Jersey until moving to East Stroudsburg, PA in 1974. He has had a lifelong interest in the Erie and the Delaware, Lackawanna & Western Railroads—especially in the New Jersey/Pennsylvania area. His late grandfather was a conductor on the Lackawanna for almost fifty years during the interesting "steam" era of railroading.

It was this association that led Ray to getting his first job with the Erie Railroad on their ferryboats. Over the years he grew to want to know more about the various ferry operations of the lower Hudson. His desire to write a book about the railroad ferry operations increased with the rapid decline and ultimate abandonment of the last such ferry operation on November 22, 1967.

Baxter worked for almost forty years on, or around, the New York Harbor waterfront, first as a railroad ferryboat deckhand and railroad police officer, then for twenty-six years in the Jersey City Police Department. A graduate of Tenafly High School, Seton Hall University and Rutgers University, Ray presently lives in East Stroudsburg, PA with his wife Catherine and youngest son Thomas. He is a member of the Erie-Lackawanna Historical Society and the Railroadians of America.

ARTHUR G. ADAMS

Arthur G. Adams was born in the Hudson River community of Englewood, New Jersey in 1935 and, like co-author Ray Baxter, has been a lifelong resident of New Jersey. Adams' consuming interest in the Hudson River and the surrounding region has stirred his constant exploration of its highways, byways, waterways, and foot trails from the Atlantic Coastal inlets to the Catskill and Berkshire Mountain peaks. Deeply interested in regional history, he has been active in preservation and conservation movements.

Adams is the Founding President of the Hudson River Maritime Center at Roundout Landing in Kingston, NY; a fellow of the Carl Carmer Center for Catskill Mountain and Hudson River Studies, at the State University at New Paltz; and, in 1981, the recipient of a special Award of Merit for outstanding achievement in Regional Studies by the State University of New York. Additionally, Adams is a member of the Steamship Historical Society of America and a Vice President of the Steamer Alexander Hamilton Society. His other books on related subjects include: *The Hudson Through the Years; The Hudson: A Guidebook to the River; The Hudson River in Literature; Guide to the Catskills and The Region Around;* and *Guide to the Catskills with Trail Guide and Maps* (in conjunction with Harriet and Leon Greenman and cartographer Roger Coco). Arthur Adams has had many articles published in various journals and lectures widely on regional subjects. A graduate of Brown University, he resides in Mahwah, NJ, in the foothills of the Ramapo Mountains, with his wife Daryl and children Cynthia and Christopher.

With the passing of the last steam-powered double-end ferryboat, a graceful and romantic period in American history ended. Someone had to leave a written and pictorial record for our grandchildren. For this reason, Ray Baxter and Arthur Adams decided to produce this volume.

Adams and Baxter have been associated for approximately six years. Both men have been very active in local transportation issues, realizing the need for improvements and a greater dependence on mass transit. As they worked on various projects, they became aware of the need for a history of the North River ferry. The North River was truly the birthplace of the double-end ferryboat.

ACKNOWLEDGMENTS

A very special appreciation must be expressed to Arthur's wife Daryl and my wife Catherine for their gracious understanding, patience, and postponed meals while Art and I discussed this book and the many problems that arose during its creation.

Mr. R. Thomas Crew, Jr. and the Staff of the Mariner's Museum, Newport News, Virginia for their help during the many hours spent in the Museum's Research Library doing the necessary research, I am most appreciative.

To our friend *Jack Emerick* who pulled his negative and photograph files apart looking for photographs of the Lackawanna Terminal and ferryboats. He came up with a couple of Official Company photographs which have been used in this volume.

Dan Biernacki, a fellow rail enthusiast, who has very freely availed his collection of Official Erie Railroad Company photographs. I must say that this volume would have been at a loss without them.

Mr. Benjamin Kline, Archivist of the Railroad Museum of Pennsylvania, Strasburg, Pa., who granted me permission to examine the photographs and negative files of the Museum, then printed all the photographs supplied by the Museum for this book.

The Lee Brothers, James and Warren who both came to my rescue with many old photographs of the Central Railroad of New Jersey boats. Warren called Jim and within a couple of days I had all the photos that they had.

The Staff of the National Archives who provided vessel documents on many of the Erie Railroad Ferryboats.

Ms. Mildred C. Poole, Archivist of the Sun Company Inc. for providing most of the technical data and drydock photo of the *Meadville.*

Mr. Richard T. Speer, Ships Histories Branch, Naval Historical Center, Department of the Navy, Washington Navy Yard, Washington, D.C. for the data supplied on various ferryboats while in Government service during World War II.

Mr. James Ransom, For the knowledgable input and suggestions of an experienced historian and former ferry commuter.

Mr. Richard Whiting, Director of Engineering, Skinner Engine Co., Erie, PA, for providing all the material and engine drawings of the Skinner Unaflow Engine used on the Ferryboat *Meadville.*

To the many people who are too numerous to mention who went that one or two steps beyond, which is necessary to complete a volume of this nature, you have my heartfelt thanks. For without you this book would never have been completed.

To my Co-Author *Arthur G. Adams,* I will be forever grateful for inspiring me to undertake the writing of this book and the much appreciated help and many long hours of sacrifice that he put into its completion. Art's guidance and direction helped me to fulfill a lifelong ambition to write the history of a vanishing dinosaur, the double-end ferryboat. A boat on which people from all walks of life strolled upon and became friends for a few brief minutes each morning and evening as they came to and from their daily tasks. People who shared the adventures of fog, mist, falling snow, and heavy rainstorms. This adventure has been replaced by the sardine-like subway cars of the Port Authority Trans-Hudson trains.

And last, but not least, a little remembrance of the many passengers who came aboard the vessels of the Erie Railroad and the Delaware, Lackawanna & Western Railroad that I worked on. You were a friendly and cheerful group of people, in most cases, and I hope that someday your sons, and daughters and grandchildren may see the double end ferryboat, which helped put that cheer in your daily trek to and from work.

This book is dedicated to three people without whose help and guidance I would not have been able to accomplish many of my goals: my mother, Jennie Mae Baxter, for her gentle manner and ability to make the hardest task simple by her loving ways—I am forever grateful to have been her son; my grandfather, Jacob Walters, who inspired me to work on the railroad, and to whom I owe many happy days of a life on the river with men who knew hard work and enjoyed it; and last, Thomas A. Hogan, the man who took an eighteen-year old "wise guy" and taught him so much about the real way life is.

Although these people are no longer with us, they will go on living in the hearts of all who knew them and were inspired by their ways and manners.

RAYMOND J. BAXTER

To Ray Baxter and all the other men who built and operated these great steamboat lines.

ARTHUR G. ADAMS

Mid-town Manhattan, on a sunny morning in the 1940's as seen across the hurricane deck of the Lackawanna ferryboat *Elmira* docked at Hoboken. — Lackawanna Railroad Photograph, RJB Collection

PART I

THE RAILROAD FERRIES OF THE HUDSON

REMINISCENCES OF A FERRY PASSENGER

While Ray Baxter spent many years working on the boats, I can lay claim to a widely diverse ridership of the North River ferries. In fact, I can claim considerable prenatal ridership, since my mother was living in Ridgefield, New Jersey and working at the National City Bank in Wall Street until shortly before my birth. She commuted by trolley car, ferryboat, and rapid transit. She had two favorite routes. One was to use the Hudson River Line car to Palisades Junction and Edgewater and then take the 125th Street Ferry to Manhattan and the West Side IRT subway downtown.

The other route was to change cars at Palisade Junction and continue by trolley car in New Jersey to Weehawken and take the West Shore's Cortlandt Street boat to downtown Manhattan. I thus logged many miles of ferryboat travel before I was ever aware of the fact.

Like Ray, I was born in Englewood and spent about ten childhood years in Tenafly, before my family moved to Bergenfield, over on the West Shore line near the West Englewood station.

My father was a manufacturer's representative and traveled a great deal, both locally and throughout the United States, visiting factories he represented. He also owned a convertible automobile during my early days—first an Auburn Roadster and, later, Fords, Packards, and Mercurys, before my mother finally convinced him to purchase a four-door sedan. When not in school, I frequently joined my father on his business travels by automobile, Pullman, interurban, trolley, steamboat, and ferryboat and was fortunate to see a great deal of our beautiful and interesting country in an age when America still had a great public transportation system. This travel by means of such unheard of things today as clean subway stations, upper- and lower-berth sleeping

cars, nightboats, high-speed electric interurbans in Illinois, Indiana, Missouri, Pennsylvania, and California made a very deep and lasting impression. Ferryboats were accepted in due stride as natural features of San Francisco Bay, Puget Sound, Chesapeake Bay, the Delaware River, and, of course, all the waters around New York City—most especially, the North River.

Gasoline rationing certainly accounted for much of the non-automobile travel by rail and long-distance boats. However, the desire to save gas also led my father to ferret out unusual ferryboat routes in his random-patterned saleswork throughout the metropolitan area. Living in New Jersey, and with a Manhattan office, he had frequent occasion to use such routes as 23rd Street Manhattan to Jersey City, 69th Street Brooklyn to St. George Staten Island, and other offbeat routes that a "kid from Jersey" would otherwise never find occasion to ride. Also, the ferryboat toll for a private automobile across the Hudson was 25¢ and the George Washington Bridge and Holland and Lincoln Tunnels was 50¢. A half-dollar saving on a round trip meant a lot in the 1940s, and I can remember sitting in ferry lines reaching from Cliffside Park to Edgewater and from atop the Palisades to the Weehawken ferry and on 125th Street Manhattan from Broadway to the river. Unlike today, the big vehicular traffic jams were on weekends, when people went for pleasure rides to the country and suburban people visited relatives in the city. It was on weekends that the ferry lines took the old sidewheelers out of retirement to handle the overloads—boats that would otherwise have been scrapped long ago—and this is how I became familiar with archetypal steamboats at first hand. Most of these boats had been retired from such major lines as the Hoboken Ferry to the likes of the Yonkers-Alpine and the Englewood to Dyckman Street lines—but run, they still did.

For a New Jersey boy, going to the city with one's father for the day was a great experience. First, a ride on an open-windowed steam train, with the choking smoke in the Palisades Tunnels—awful, but at the same time, strangely pleasing. Alternatively, you might have a ride on a big yellow Public Service trolley car and then down the cliffs along Pershing Avenue with the safety-switch and sand pit. Finally, the old, looming, wooden ferry terminals with the ingrained odor of softcoal smoke and crowds of rushing people. At the Erie Terminal in Jersey City, you also saw long-distance equipment which was uncommon at the West Shore's Weehawken Terminal in those days. The Lackawanna Hoboken Terminal and Jersey Central's Communipaw Terminal were somewhat more modern and offered a great deal of glamorous, long-distance passenger equipment to view. Generally, I only frequented those terminals preliminary to departing on a longer trip on the *Lackawanna Limited, Royal Blue, Capitol Limited,* or *Crusader.* Usually we would have left Tenafly or West Englewood on the Northern Railroad to Jersey City or the West Shore to Weehawken and taken the Chambers Street or Cortlandt Street boat to Manhattan and then carried our baggage to either Liberty Street or Barclay Street to recross to Jersey City or Hoboken. It *sounds* frightfully slow and inefficient, today. However, I doubt if you could drive there directly as rapidly, comfortably, or economically today—and the trip was exciting and refreshing. To get back to our day trip to New York City . . . .

After getting off your suburban train, you got aboard the ferryboat and were treated to a shoeshine by a professional bootblack on the boat, while your father smoked a cigarette and read his paper. You could also go onto the upper deck and, if you were fortunate, see either a large ocean liner sailing or a battleship or aircraft carrier. You often saw sailors in uniform in Manhattan on leave. In the morning, it was not unusual to see a large Day Liner such as the *Hendrick Hudson* or *Alexander Hamilton* departing on its trip upriver with crowded decks, flags flying, and band playing. There were always hundreds of tugboats, carfloats, lighters, barges, barge tows pulled by maroon-colored Cornell Steamboat Company tugs from Kingston, upriver, and occasional Coast Guard and smaller Navy vessels and ubiquitous freighters and many lesser oceangoing passenger ships. A trip across the river was an exercise in broken-field running. People today, who do not actually remember this epoch, can have little conception of how crowded the river was. During WW II, everything was painted a drab gray and lights were kept low—the amount of movement was unbelievable. After the war, the activity continued for a while with the added glamour of refurbished ocean liners with gleaming black hulls and red smokestacks and departure parties. The Hudson River waterfront is indeed a dull and depressing place these days for those who remember the glory years.

If it was wintertime, the ferry crunched its way through fields of large icefloes, leaving a temporary channel behind itself. The deckhands threw sand or rock salt on deck to counteract the freezing spray and the air on deck was exhilarating and icy sharp. In the morning, you always had the smell of roasting coffee from the Maxwell House and Hills Brothers plants in Hoboken and Edgewater. The Cortlandt Street four-mile trip was a particular treat, as you also saw all the other ferry lines. It sometimes seemed that you could build a pontoon bridge out of ferryboats.

Foggy days were scary, with the tooting of whistles and ringing of bells and gongs, and the dismal scream of horns and sirens—no radar or ship-to-shore telephone—but few accidents, either. Life was living—on the line. You COULD get run over by the *Queen Mary!* There was some thrill to life. The threat was not getting mashed by an eighteen-wheeler while riding in a Japanese-made tin can Toy-Auto, but being annihilated by the world's greatest oceanliners while riding yourself on a handsome steamboat of no mean size: If you were killed, at least you would go out in style!

Once you reached Manhattan, further adventures awaited. At 42nd Street, you then took an open-sided electric streetcar across town and then possibly a subway or elevated train uptown or downtown. Your father might take you to Rogers Peet or Brooks Brothers for a new suit for school, or for lunch at the University Club where the big Captains of Industry sat reading their papers in the solemn clubroom. After sitting for several hours trying to keep busy in your father's office while he opened his mail (these trips were most frequent on Saturday mornings), the two of you would set off on adventure: possibly the Museum of Science & Industry at Radio City or the Museum of Natural History or the Metropolitan Museum of Art; or St. Patrick's Cathedral or the Cathedral of St. John the Divine or Grant's Tomb. The Statue of Liberty with its endless winding circular staircase might attract. Always, there was lunch: Needicks with its icy-cold orange drinks that stabbed your sinuses if taken too rapidly; the truly "heavenly smell" of Chock-Full-O'-Nuts coffee and donuts; or the fascinating Horn and Hardarts Automat with its then-unique coin-vending machines. On a more upbeat day, you might visit a German Rathskeller, French Restaurant, or "Spaghetti Palace"—none of which were then standard suburban fare.

Possibly you might go to a stage show matinee or a department store—the purchases would be sent home by UPS a few days later. Then, back to the boat and the trip home—tired and happy and still with the chance of seeing an early evening sailing of an oceanliner. The ferry and train were integral to all this excitement. Taken for granted, but loved. The Hudson River was part of our lives, both suburbanite and city dweller. It belonged to all of us, rich and poor alike. Everyone could afford the

3¢-ride across the 42nd Street Ferry. Now, Mr. Imperatore is talking about $10 fares on a hi-tech express! Maybe I don't recognize progress.

I grew up in a small town, but the World's Greatest City was also part of my hometown—and it was safe. The universal use of good public transportation helped to make it so.

On a quieter note, during the war years of gas rationing, a frequent outing would be to drive to the Hudson River shoreline at Englewood or Alpine and watch the steamboats passing by in the evening. Maybe your father would spring for a round trip across on the ferryboat to Dyckman Street or Yonkers in the cool of the evening, with the itinerant accordionist and violin players offering a serenade and passing the cup. It certainly was not sophisticated, but you did see the great steamboats passing by. The ferryboat was a window on the greater world.

Later, when I was at Brown University, the 42nd Street crosstown bus from Grand Central Terminal, the 42nd Street Ferry, and the West Shore trains became a well-beaten route on my frequent trips back and forth to school and home for holidays. In those days, the New Haven Railroad sold tickets for New York Broadway shows, including the round-trip excursion train fare from Providence, for as low as $20. Many students saw a great many Broadway plays in this way. Frequently, the students also availed themselves of a trip to New York to ride the Staten Island or other ferries to see the harbor and great liners.

After graduating from college, I worked in New York City and became a daily commuter on the Cortlandt Street ferry until it was discontinued. Even after that, I had occasion to use the Jersey Central, Erie, and Lackawanna ferryboats while living in Washington Township, served by the Erie Railroad and later by the Erie-Lackawanna. Business trips to Philadelphia served as excuse to ride the Reading Railroad and the B & O to visit factories in St. Louis and Parkersburg, West Virginia, not to mention visits to the North Jersey shore by train. Yes, Virginia—not all young married couples in the New Jersey suburbs owned cars in those days—but we still went to the beach—by train and boat. When first married and working in Manhattan, we were frequently very impecunious, but we regularly attended concerts and the opera. My wife would get out of work in West Englewood at 5 P.M. and go back to our apartment to make up several sandwiches. I would leave my own downtown Manhattan office about 5:30 and take the Cortlandt Street boat up to Weehawken. My wife would take a 5:30 local from West Englewood and meet me at Weehawken at 6:15. We would then both get on the 42nd Street boat and go to the top deck to eat our sandwiches and enjoy the early evening. We might cross back and forth several trips and then take the crosstown bus to Carnegie Hall, the old City Center, or the Old Met for an 8 P.M. curtain. After the show, we would frequently walk back crosstown for the 12:10 A.M. boat or the 1:30 A.M. boat connection for the *Albany Milk Train*. It was safe and you were not alone. It was also quite inexpensive. Now they charge $15 per night to just park at Lincoln Center.

I miss the ferries.

ARTHUR G. ADAMS

Manhattan, the North River, and the Lackawanna Railroad yards, as seen from the Palisades in Jersey City. — Lackawanna Railroad

CHAPTER 1

THE NORTH RIVER

~~~~~~

If you were to ask someone from outside the New York Metropolitan area where the North River is, you would probably get a variety of answers. So, for those of you who have never set foot on the shores of the Lower Hudson River, allow us to introduce you to the North River.

The North River is that section of the mighty Hudson River which runs from the tip of Manhattan Island, at the Battery, northward to approximately beneath the George Washington Bridge—a distance of 11.3 miles. The Hudson River serves as the boundary line between New York and New Jersey for twenty-two miles; the southern half of this stretch is, properly speaking, the North River. It is always called North River by people in the shipping industry, with the name Hudson generally reserved for that stretch above Yonkers where Hudson River pilots are taken on board.

This stretch of river was originally given this name to distinguish it from the South River (what we today call the Delaware River) and the East River, a strait connecting Upper New York Bay and Long Island Sound. At its southern end, the North River flows into Upper New York Bay at the Battery. Below the Upper Bay, the shores of Brooklyn and Staten Island converge, forming a bottleneck known as the Narrows. Further south, the Narrows again open up into Lower New York Bay, which opens directly into the Atlantic Ocean at Sandy Hook.

New York Harbor is considered one of the finest natural harbors on the Eastern Seaboard. For many years, the North River, from the Battery to 57th Street, was known as Luxury Liner Row. All the world's major shipping powers had berths for their ships on the North River, either in Manhattan, Jersey City, or Hoboken.*

---

*Famous American shipping lines and passenger liners which regularly sailed the North River:

The *S.S. United States*, holder of the transatlantic speed record, both eastbound and westbound; the *S.S. America*; and the earlier *Leviathan, Washington,* and *Manhattan*—all operated by the United States Lines from piers in Hoboken and Manhattan.

The steamships *Constitution, Independence,* and *Excaliber* of the American Export Lines, which docked at Pier 84 Manhattan and Harborside Terminal in Jersey City.

The famous President Class cargoliners of the "Around the World" service of the American President Lines: *President Polk, President Monroe, President Harrison,* and *President Cleveland*. They sailed from Pier 9 in Jersey City, offering the world's longest regularly scheduled service—around the world.

Famous more recent foreign flag lines and vessels which graced the North River were:

The British Cunard Line steamships: *Queen Mary, Queen Elizabeth, Brittanic, Mauretania, Parthia, Franconia,* and *Sylvania*. Originally, Cunard liners docked near Exchange Place in Jersey City. Later, they used the old Chelsea Piers be-

tween Manhattan's 13th and 23rd Streets; still later, Piers 85-86-87; and, most recently, the new Port Authority Passenger Ship Terminal.

France's contribution of gracious ladies of the sea were the French Line's *Normandie, Ile de France, Liberté,* and *France* (the last, still operating in the Caribbean for other owners under the name *Norway*).

The Italian Lines made an excellent showing with the *Rex, Conte di Savoia, Cristoforo Colombo, Andrea Doria* (lost in a tragic collision with the Swedish Liner *Stockholm* on July 25, 1956), *Leonardo Da Vinci, Rafaello,* and *Michaelangelo*. The French and Italian lines first operated from the Chelsea Piers and later from Piers 85, 86, and 87.

Other famous lines operating from Manhattan were the Swedish Line (whose *Gripsholm* became famous as a prisoner-of-war exchange ship during WW II), the Norwegian-American Line, North German Lloyd Line, Hamburg-American Line, Holland-American Line, and Furness Line, which operated its stately *Queen of Bermuda* and smaller *Ocean Monarch* on almost a weekly ferry schedule to Bermuda.

For many years, the Hamburg-American and Holland-

S.S. United States receiving the traditional harbor welcome on her maiden voyage, July 3, 1952. Erie tug *Olean* with float in foreground and F/B *Arlington* has just crossed bow of the *United States*.

From 1900 to 1960 every Friday evening, starting at about 4 P.M., the North River witnessed a parade of famous "name" ships slowly steaming out to sea and the notable, exotic ports of the world. One might say that the North River was America's showplace of passenger luxury liners. This was a just tribute to the North River, for it was on this famous river, almost 180 years ago, that modern steamboating began. In December 1806 Robert Fulton returned to New York from London and commenced construction of the great-great-grandfather of the modern steamboat, the 150-foot-long *North River Steamboat*, (sometimes erroneously called the *Clermont*), which made its first successful commercial voyage to Albany in 1807, inaugurating the age of steam navigation. This early vessel, propelled by a single-cylinder engine driving two side paddlewheels, has developed into the mighty ocean steamships of the 1950s, driven by large turbines and multiple propellers. Even these mighty vessels have now become obsolete as the large jet airplanes of the 1980s have reduced the multiday Atlantic Crossing to only a few hours.

Over the years, many changes have taken place on the North River. Most of them have been costly to the people who have depended on the river for a living. This book is about one phase of river life—the railroad ferryboat.

The Northeastern railroad industry played a major role in the rise and fall of the North River dynasty. New Jersey cities such as Jersey City, Hoboken, and Weehawken were greatly affected by the railroads, as the steamboat and railroad men of the mid-1880s purchased the majority of the waterfront acreage of these cities. In fact, they even purchased land *in* the river. The banks of the North River have been so changed by landfills, upon which railroad terminals, yards, and warehouses were built, that Henry Hudson would no longer recognize the beautiful river he discovered way back in 1609.

The once-great Northeastern railroads have so deteriorated that now, after a series of mergers, of the eleven great roads that once converged on the North River, only one, the Consolidated Rail Corporation (Conrail),

American Lines operated from Hoboken, but more recently moved operations to Manhattan. The Holland-American Line can claim the unique distinction of corporate descent from the Dutch West India Company, whose predecessor, the Dutch East India Company, employed a certain Henry Hudson— discoverer of the river.

Famous Holland-American ships have been the *New Amsterdam*, *Rotterdam*, and *Veendam*, and this line still operates its cruise ships from Manhattan. Famous German vessels were the *Europa*, *Imperator*, *Kaiser Wilhelm II*, *Kronprinzessin*

Cecilie, *Vaterland* (later, the *Leviathan*), *Hamburg*, and *Bremen*.

The great coastal liners of the Fall River Line, the *Puritan*, *Priscilla*, and *Commonwealth* and the *Yarmouth*, *Evangeline*, and *St. John* of the Eastern Steamship Lines, docked in lower Manhattan on the North River, as did the large and luxurious Hudson River Night Liners, *Adirondack*, *Berkshire*, and *C. W. Morse*, and the giant Iron Palace Day Liners, *Hendrick Hudson* and *Washington Irving*.

S.S. America tied up at Todd Shipyard, Hoboken, N.J. after being replaced by the *S.S. United States.*

Tug has let go from the American President Lines *President Polk* after backing her from her berth at Pier 9, Jersey City.

Hudson River Day Liner the *Hendrick Hudson* largest of the Day Line fleet, which was named in honor of the famous explorer of the Hudson River. Her last year of service was in 1947 the same year that Ray Baxter (co-author) started working on the Erie Railroad. – Hudson River Day Line Photo Alfred V.S. Olcott Collection

survives. Gone are the Baltimore & Ohio, the Central Railroad of New Jersey, the Philadelphia & Reading, the Lehigh Valley, the Pennsylvania Railroad, the Erie Railroad, the Delaware, Lackawanna & Western, the New York, Susquehanna & Western, the New York, Ontario & Western, the West Shore Railroad, and the New York Central – and their once extensive marine operations. The empires of the mighty moguls are no longer and, in the wake of their deterioration, they have left a mass of abandoned wharves, floatbridges, burned-out piers, collapsed terminal buildings, and rusty rails. The river was left to choke in filth, raw sewage, and chemical waste. During the last two decades, river traffic has dwindled to a mere trickle as port activities have moved to Brooklyn, Staten Island, Elizabeth, and Newark. Passengers cross the river through road and rail tunnels and on vehicular bridges. Only occasionally do a few cruise ships use the magnificent, large, new Passenger Ship Terminal. A lone Day Liner, direct descendant of Robert Fulton's first steamboat, makes its lonely way daily upriver during a short summer season. There are no ferryboats.

Both the states of New Jersey and New York have undertaken projects to clean up the river and its shores and far-sighted developers are acquiring the abandoned rail facilities and building new homes and offices along the shores. Maybe someday the beauty of the North River will return.

The North River and the lordly Hudson have a history and heritage second to none. Many things were developed on this river – not the least important and interesting of them, the double-ended ferryboat. It is twenty years since the last one operated on the North River. Today, there is considerable interest in bringing the ferryboats back to serve the shoreline redevelopment. Possibly a close study of their history and development will help to rebuild upon the ruins, avoid the pitfalls of the past, and return this wonderful river to the people who dwell along its banks.

CHAPTER 2

EARLY FERRIES — PRE-STEAM ERA

The first ferries were simple canoes, dugouts, and rafts, manned by Indian traders. They accommodated foot passengers in a casual manner, but never made ferrying their principal business. The first organized ferry operated by a white man was that of Cornelius Dirckman, in 1642, across the East River. It was a flat-bottomed row boat. He placed a loud horn at both landings and performed service upon the "trumpet's clarion call." This soon proved to be a profitable business and Governor Peter Stuyvesant considered the possibility of government regulation. Some authorities say that the original Brooklyn Ferry was operated by Cornelius Hooglandt, in 1642. However, it is certain that in 1661 the New Netherlands Council granted authority to William Jensen to operate a ferry to Communipaw for one year.

As far as history tells us, there was no question regard-

The first ferryboats were flat-bottomed boats propelled by an oarsman. From an old print.

Painting of a periauger. Artist unknown.

ing the right for every man to paddle his own canoe. That veracious chronicler, Diedrick Knickerbocker, refers to the thrifty village of Communipaw as the "egg from whence was hatched the mighty city" of New York. "It is within but a half-hour's sail of the latter place, provided you have a fair wind, and may be distinctly seen from the city." He further informs us that "the Dutch negros, being infinitely more adventurous and more knowing than their masters, carry on all the foreign trade, making frequent voyages to town in canoes loaded with oysters, buttermilk, and cabbages" (Irving, 1862, p. 84).

Jensen became the first licensed ferryman and, in December of 1661, was authorized by the governor-general and council to charge certain established rates for the service. Jensen managed to get in trouble with his patrons for exercising his exclusive right to transport persons and goods across the river. Persons who owned their own boats asserted that they had the right to carry over whomever they so desired.

The authorities of Bergen (Communipaw was under the jurisdiction of Bergen) took the popular side in the controversy, and the sheriff advised the people that every man could keep his own "schuyt" and carry over whom he pleased.

Jensen complained to the authorities of New Amsterdam, and then the sheriff was summoned before the governor-general and council to answer to the charge of interference with a right held under license.

Countercharges were brought against Jensen by the sheriff, claiming that he refused to carry passengers across. Defending himself, Jensen claimed that the only persons he refused to transport were those who declined to pay for his service. The council decided that an equitable agreement could be reached. Their decision was that it was the sheriff's duty to assist Jensen in the collection of fares when a person refused to pay and that the ferryman must do his duty or be dismissed. Thus was established the right of ferriage on the North River.

Jensen's successor was Pieter Hetfelsen, who received his license from Governor Carteret in 1669. Carteret's grant had a clause stating that all persons were prohibited from carrying over "any persons, goods, corne, or cattle without ye consent or license of said ferry-man," under a penalty of "tenn shillings sterling," to be paid to the ferryman, "and also to pay to him the fraight for such persons, corne, or cattle as shall be so illegally transported to the prejudice of said ferryman. But a man may keep a canoe or boate of his owne for transporting such goods as belong to himselfe." And the following important privilege early on was appended to the right of ferriage – "always provided the Governor and his family are to be freed from paying anything for their transporting as aforesaid." Thus, at the very outset, did some of the important stipulations connected with the exercise of this franchise find settlement, and so they continue to the present day.

As later charters were issued, the ferryman was further required to maintain one or more good boats for the transporting of passengers and be prepared to supply transportation to the inhabitants of Bergen and Communipaw at least three days a week, mainly Mondays, Wednesdays, and Fridays, unless some extraordinary occasions prevented this.

It was reported that Samuel Bayard was the operator of the ferry in 1717. He complained that several persons without permit from the crown were making it their business to keep boats for the transporting of cattle, horses, and country produce to New York.

In 1713, King George II issued a charter to Archibald Kennedy for a ferry from Pavonia to Manhattan, although this charter was never operated by Kennedy.

For approximately 100 years, the only ferry operating from the communities which comprise present-day Jersey City was the Communipaw Ferry. Around 1760, the Powles Hook or Paulus Hook Ferry was placed into operation. The *New York Mercury* announced the establishment of this ferry. Titled "Good News for the Public," the story reported that "the long-wished-for ferry is now established, and kept across the North River, from the place called Powles Hook, to the city of New York; and

boats properly constructed as well for the conveniency of Passengers as for carrying over Horse and Carriages, do now constantly ply from one shore to the other."

Cornelius Van Voorst was operating this ferry in 1767. The next downriver ferry was established in 1774 when a charter was granted to Hermanus Talman to operate a ferry to Manhattan from Horsimus or Hoboken. This ferry connected with Andrew Van Buskirk's stage line which ran to New Bridge, near Hackensack; the Powles Hook Ferry connected with the stage line to Newark and Philadelphia; and the Communipaw Ferry continued to serve mainly Communipaw and Bergen. The Horsimus, or Hoboken, ferry was operated by both sailboats and rowboats. Another early ferry was at Bull's Ferry, north of Weehawken.

John H. Morrison, in his 1903 *History of American Steam Navigation,* gives an interesting picture of Hudson River ferry navigation just prior to the introduction of steam navigation:

In 1810 there were propositions before the Legislature for improvements in the ferries, which required the owners of ferry boats to have their names painted with white letters on the stern of the boat, and the words "Ferry Boat," on the inside of the stern. It was furthermore proposed that the owners of ferry boats should at all times in the months of May, June, July, August and September, have their boats ready for passage from half an hour before sunrise until 9 o'clock in the evening, and in all other months from sunrise until 8

The need for faster boats developed as more people started to cross the river and the flat boats were replaced by sailboats known as Periaugers. From an old print.

Team boats were used for many years on the rivers throughout the United States. Location of this boat is unknown.

o'clock in the evening; and that no passenger should be detained more than five minutes. It was proposed that a sufficient number of barges for passengers should be kept at all of the ferries, upon which barges no baggage or lumber should be carried. Four men were to be employed to row every barge, and in every horse boat two men. The passenger barges should not be less than 22 feet long and 7 feet wide, and no more than fourteen passengers should be ferried in them at one time. (p. 515)

The sailboats used were known as "pirogues" or "periaugers." They were very wide, flat-bottomed, sailboats about fifty feet long, with the mast quite near the bow, so as to leave the deck unencumbered. Horses and carriages first had to be unhitched and lifted onto the boats in order to be ferried.

The stage was now set for the dramatic improvements to be brought by steam power.

CHAPTER 3

COMING OF THE STEAMBOAT

EARLY EFFORTS

It can truly be said that commercial steam navigation had its birth on the Hudson River. Robert Fulton's *North River Steamboat of Clermont,* in making its first successful commercial trip from New York to Albany on September 4, 1807, can be said to have begun the steamship industry. However, prior to this, Fulton and others had done considerable experimentation with steamboats—some of it in local waters.

The earliest record of an attempt at steam navigation can be credited to Blasco de Garay, a Spanish naval officer under King Charles V. In 1543, de Garay constructed a paddle-wheel vessel to be moved by steam. It is not recorded if he had any success with his experiments. In 1630, an English patent was granted to David Ramseye, "to make shippes and barges goe against strong wind and tide."

In France, a similar patent was granted to Denys Papin of Blois, in 1690, and he constructed a boat in 1707 which had some limited success. However, nothing more came of these early attempts, for steam-engine development was not yet far enough along.

In the early eighteenth century, Thomas Newcomen, John Smeaton, and James Watt made important contributions to steam-engine design and construction. In 1769, James Watt joined Matthew Bolton in a steam-engine manufactory in Soho, a suburb of Birmingham, England. They specialized in pumping engines. Benjamin Franklin visited the Bolton works and contributed some improvements of his own. The time was now ripe for further nautical development.

In 1764, William Henry of Lancaster, PA, operated a small steam vessel on the Conestoga River. This experiment was noted at first hand by John Fitch. In 1774, Perier Freres built a small steamboat for operation on

the Seine, and, in 1783, the Marquis de Jouffray operated one on the Rhone at Lyons. In 1786, James Rumsey built a small steamboat operated by hydraulic jets at Shepherdstown, WV, on the Potomac River. Much of this early experimentation was desultory and was made without knowledge of similar experimentation going on elsewhere.

The first individual to make serious sustained efforts towards the development of a steamboat in America was John Fitch (1743–1798). Fitch was born in Windsor, CT, served as apprentice to a clockmaker, and eventually set up a brass shop. He served briefly in the Continental Army and as a sutler selling tobacco and beer. After the war, he took his profits and purchased land grants along the Ohio River. These proved to be valueless, and he drifted back to Pennsylvania, where he became interested in steamboat development. He obtained exclusive steam navigational rights from the states of New Jersey and Pennsylvania for the years 1786–1787 and, in the latter year, successfully operated a steamboat on the Delaware River at a speed of 3 to 4 mph. This was followed by other boats, in 1788 and 1790, which achieved 7 mph and operated regularly for a time between Trenton, Bordentown, Bristol, and Burlington. Despite his rapid advance, Fitch's backers were timid and did not support his further efforts, which suffered a great setback when a fourth vessel was wrecked by a storm. He experimented further with miniature vessels on Collect Pond on Manhattan Island and with a screw propeller in 1796.

Another early steamboat builder was Samuel Morey, who operated a boat on the Connecticut River in 1790. He built a second paddle-wheel boat in 1793 and in 1794 made a voyage in it from Hartford to New York City. In 1797, he had a side wheeler operating between Philadelphia and Bordentown on the Delaware River, in which travelled Chancellor Livingston, Robert Fulton, and Colonel John Stevens. Morey's main contributions were the design of stern and side-type paddle wheels.

In 1791, Nathan Read developed a vertical, multiple-tube, firebox boiler which best suited early steamboat designs. In 1792, Elijah Ormsbee operated a small steamboat on Narragansett Bay. The reason that nothing much came of these early experiments seems to have been lack of capital, rather than of inventive genius. Meanwhile, much practical knowledge was being gained.

Back in England, Patrick Miller, James Taylor, and William Symmington were doing much experimentation around 1788, and there was considerable interest in applying steam propulsion on the extensive network of canals. The British, with great good reason, claim that the first successful commercial steamboat was William Symmington's *Charlotte Dundas,* which was successfully tried on the Forth & Clyde Canal in 1801. She had a paddle wheel, a Watt-built engine, and pulled two 70-ton barges. Henry Bell, an associate of Symmington's, built a successful oceangoing steamboat, *The Comet,* in 1812, which had two paddle wheels on each side! But we are anticipating . . . .

Back in America, these experiments were being closely observed by some wealthy capitalists. Chancellor Robert R. Livingston (1746–1813), of the great Hudson River patent-holding family founded by Robert Livingston (1654–1728), was particularly interested in the possibilities of steamboats. He resided at his estate *Clermont,* opposite Saugerties. He attended Kings College (now Columbia University), was admitted to the bar, and became a partner of John Jay. Livingston was a member of the Continental Congress and served on the committee to draft the Declaration of Independence. In 1781, he was appointed the first secretary of the Department of Foreign Affairs (Secretary of State). From 1777 to 1801, he was the chancellor of New York State and administered the presidential oath of office to George Washington. In 1801, Thomas Jefferson appointed him minister to France, where he conducted the negotiations leading to the Louisiana Purchase.

Prior to leaving for France, Livingston travelled in Samuel Morey's Delaware River steamboat in 1797. In 1798, he participated with Colonel John Stevens, John Stoudinger, and Nicholas Roosevelt in the construction and operation of a small steamboat, the *Polacca,* on the Passaic River at Belleville, NJ, and is reputed to have made a trip in it from there to New York City.

While in France, Chancellor Livingston met the man who was to bring his steamboat interests to fruition. Robert Fulton (1765–1815) was born in Little Britain, PA. He first learned the trade of gunsmith and was accomplished in this business at the time of the American Revolution. He next turned to landscape and portrait painting and, in 1786, went to England to study with Benjamin West. Little Britain is near Lancaster, and it is likely that,

as a boy, Fulton knew of William Henry's steamboat experiments on the Conestoga. In 1794, Fulton's interests turned to engineering and he was engaged by the Duke of Bridgewater as engineer on his system of private canals, particularly on a project to replace locks with incline planes. In 1796, he was invited to Paris by the American merchant, poet, and diplomat, Joel Barlow (1754–1812), who was interested in steamboat development and had brought the plans of the *Polacca* to France with him. Fulton resided with Barlow for seven years, during which time he occupied himself with developing submarines and other destructive naval weaponry for the French and British governments.[1] It was during this time that he became acquainted with Chancellor Livingston.

In 1803, Fulton, Barlow, and Livingston pooled their talents and resources to build a steamboat for operation on the Seine. This successful experimental vessel was 86 feet long and 8 feet wide. As Livingston held a monopoly from the New York State Legislature for steamboat operations in that state, the success of the experiment led him to contract with Fulton to build a steamboat for operation on the Hudson River. Before returning to America, they ordered a steam engine from Boulton & Watt, to be sent to New York in 1806; upon returning home, they ordered a hull to be built by Charles Browne, of New York City, whose yard was on the East River.

Before continuing with the story of Robert Fulton, it is useful to consider the work of the Stevens family of this same period, as it was soon to come into conflict with the Fulton-Livingston combination.

This illustrious engineering dynasty was founded by Colonel John Stevens. He studied law at Kings College and, shortly thereafter, joined his father, a wealthy land-owner, in Jersey politics. During the revolution he served as treasurer of the State of New Jersey, and from 1782 to 1783 was surveyor general of that state. In 1784, Stevens purchased extensive tracts at Hoboken. Upon his father's death in 1792, he inherited a vast estate. For the moment we will ignore his steamboat activities to note that, from 1810 on, he became interested in railroad development and, in 1815, received from the State of New Jersey the first railroad charter in the United States for construction of the Camden & Amboy Railroad. In 1825, he operated a small steam locomotive on a circular track on his Hoboken estate. This little locomotive had a vertical steam boiler which activated a cog wheel that engaged a ratchet rail between the running rails — as in the Mt. Washington Cog Railroad.

His son, Robert Livingston Stevens (1787–1856) carried on his father's interest. He became chief engineer for the Camden & Amboy, imported the early steam locomotive *John Bull* from England for operation on that

---

[1]Who were then at war. The "destructive" weaponry technology was to go to the higher bidder.

Colonel John Stevens (1749–1838) from a portrait painted around 1812.

line, and invented the famous Stevens, or American-type steel rail, which came into general use in railroad construction.

In the marine field, Robert L. Stevens invented the spring piling used in ferry-slip and steamboat-wharf construction and made the following important contributions to steamboat development: He invented the high-pressure boiler, tabulated the laws of variance of resistance of water to vessels at various speeds, and developed the graceful "hollow water line," which was later used on clipper ships. This was known as the "wave line" form of vessels. He anticipated Ericsson with the "feathering" paddle wheel and developed the sponson, or strut guards, used on sidewheel ships. He was a pioneer in the use of anthracite as fuel, and first to mount boilers on the guards. He developed the "skeleton" style of walking beam, two-part wheel floats, hog frames, artificial blast for furnaces, spring bearings under paddle shafts, double poppet valves, metallic packing rings, and the "Stevens Cutoff" valve gear. Anticipating future events, he also drew up plans for a vehicular tunnel under the Hudson River!

John Steven's nephew, Francis B. Stevens, worked with Robert L. Stevens in developing the "Stevens Cutoff." Robert's brother, Edwin Augustus Stevens (1795–1868), worked closely with the father and brother in all their enterprises. Edwin initiated the construction of the first railroad from New York to Philadelphia, was a pioneer builder of ironclad warships, and invented the "Stevens plow." He also founded the Stevens Institute of

Technology in 1871, which was created as a bequest in his will.

Returning to the marine activity of Colonel John Stevens, let us note that he owned the Hoboken Ferry franchise from 1789 to 1794. In 1794, he became president of the Bergen Turnpike Company and, in 1811, reacquired the franchise for the Hoboken Ferry; at that time, he undertook to furnish a steam ferry to Vesey Street (later to Barclay Street), Manhattan, from Hoboken. This was the world's first franchised steam ferry route and operated continously until November 22, 1967 – a total of 156 years. Colonel Stevens could undertake this ambitious commitment because he had sufficient experience in steamboat construction. In 1802, he had built a small single-screw steamboat 25 ft. long by 5 ft. wide called the *Little Juliana*. Made twin-screw in 1804.

In 1807, John Stevens built the *Phoenix,* a paddle-wheel vessel for the Hoboken-to-New Brunswick run. However, this venture ran into trouble with the Fulton–Livingston monopoly, and the *Phoenix* was brought around by sea to operate on the Delaware River in 1808. This was the first open sea voyage by any steamboat. Captain E. S. Bunker was in command. Captain Bunker had very advanced ideas and had previously operated a high-class line of passenger-only sloops on the Hudson. This sea voyage was completed successfully despite en-

Robert L. Stevens (1787–1856) who along with his father Colonel John Stevens did much for the development of ferryboats on the North River.

Edwin A. Stevens (1795–1868) founder of Stevens Institute in Hoboken, N.J. also worked on the development of the modern ferryboat.

Col. John Stevens twin-screw vessel the *Little Juliana* of 1804. Originally built with single-screw in 1802.

countering a strong gale. The *Savannah* made her epochal transatlantic voyage in 1818.[2]

In 1811, Colonel Stevens introduced the new *Juliana*, with twin screws, on the Hoboken Ferry. The last steam ferry to close out the service in 1967 was the *Elmira*,[3] which was still equipped with reciprocating steam engines and burned anthracite.

Before turning to the epochal voyage of the *North River Steamboat of Clermont*, let us finally note a few later Stevens vessels: *Philadelphia*, of 1813; *Passaic*, also of 1813 (first steamboat to burn coal); *Hoboken* (first with skeleton walking-beam); *Trenton* (first with boilers on guard); *North America*, all of 1822; and the *Pioneer* of 1823. These ships were all important in the development of the standard ship types that were to handle the bulk of traffic for almost a century.[4]

Despite all the important engineering developments of the Stevens family, popular interest was first strongly caught by the endeavors of Chancellor Livingston and Robert Fulton. In 1807, their creation, originally called simply *North River Steamboat*, was launched at Charles Browne's shipyard near Corlears Hook on the East River. Later, she became known simply as *Clermont*, after Chancellor Livingston's Hudson River estate. There is a persistent, and erroneous, story that she was built at North Bay, near Clermont. In her second season of operation, she was registered under the name *North River Steamboat of Clermont*, which might be how the error arose. Clermont was merely her home port, or port of registry—but the name *Clermont* stuck, although it never was her official name.

---

[2] It is of interest to note that the last passenger liner equipped with reciprocating steam engines to sail from New York Harbor was the *Stavangerfjord* of the Norwegian-American Line, in November 1964.

[3] Built in Newport News, VA in 1905, the *Elmira* was 232 ft. long, 43 ft. breadth, and had 1400 horsepower. The other surviving vessel was the *Lackawanna*, built as the *Hamburg* in Newburgh, NY in 1891. She measured 222 ft. long, 40 ft. breadth, and had been dieselized in 1950 when she was renamed *Lackawanna*. She was the third Hoboken ferry to bear that name. George Eastland, public relations officer for the Erie Lackawanna Railway, which then owned the Hoboken Ferry Company, said that fewer than 3,000 daily passengers were still using the ferries, compared with 100,000 daily at the turn of the century. Let it be noted that the railroad contrived this development largely through service cutbacks to avoid operating the boats which were expensive to run.

[4] Of all these vessels, only the *Hoboken* of 1822 and *Pioneer* of 1823 were ferryboats; all the others were steamers.

Steamboat *Phoenix*, built by John Stevens, 1807.

The engines were built by Boulton & Watt of Birmingham, England. As originally built, the *North River Steamboat* measured 130 ft. × 16 ft. × 7 ft. deep. She had a square stern, as was common with all early Fulton–Livingston steamboats, and carried masts and sails. She had two paddle wheels—one on each side—15 ft. in diameter, and of the radial type. They were unenclosed in any housing. The cylinder was 24-in. diameter with a 4-ft. stroke. She was equipped with a low pressure boiler 20 ft. long by 7 ft. deep and 8 ft. broad.

There was much cynicism about the claims made for the new ship, and she was called "Fulton's Folly." On Monday, August 17, 1807, she sailed for Albany from the foot of Cortlandt Street, Manhattan, with a list of invited guests, and without using sails against a slight headwind. She arrived at Albany on Wednesday, August 19, after an elapsed sailing time of thirty-two hours, not including landings. There was a twenty-four hour layover at Clermont, not included in the thirty-two hours. Her return trip to New York took thirty hours, with no stops whatsoever, and again without any use of sail.

This first experimental trip was such a complete success that Fulton and Livingston ventured to advertise in the New York papers on September 2, 1807:

The *North River Steamboat* will leave Paulus Hook Ferry on Friday, 4th of September, at 6 in the morning, and arrive at Albany on Saturday in the afternoon. Provisions, good berths, and accommodations are provided. The charge to each passenger as follows:

To Newburg	3	Dolls.—Time 14 hours
To Poughkeepsie	4	Dolls.—Time 17 hours
To Esopus	4½	Dolls.—Time 20 hours
To Hudson	5	Dolls.—Time 30 hours
To Albany	7	Dolls.—Time 36 hours

For places, apply to Wm. Vandervoort, No. 48 Cortlandt Street, on the corner of Greenwich Street. (p. 24) Morrison, 1903

After establishing the *North River* on the Hudson run, Fulton provided two steam ferries, the *Jersey* for the Paulus Hook route in 1812 and the *Nassau* for the East River crossing to Brooklyn in 1813.

A team boat like the ones used on the Hoboken Ferry in the early 1800's prior to the introduction of the steam ferryboat *Hoboken* in 1821. From an old print.

The *Jersey* was a double boat with a paddle wheel between the two hulls. The length of the boat was 78 ft. and the total width was 32 ft. Each hull was 13½-ft. wide, and the space between them was 5 ft. The *York,* which was built one year later, was an exact duplicate of the *Jersey.*

Fulton's plan for the ferry slips or entrance was by two rafts of logs arranged to form the two sides of the slip and chained to the wharf in such a manner as to yield and have motion when struck by the smooth surface of the sides of the double boats, and thus guide the boats to the bridge.

As noted earlier, Colonel Stevens introduced the steam ferry *Juliana* on the Hoboken Ferry in 1811. Because of the Fulton–Livingston monopoly, she was withdrawn and the Hoboken Ferry returned to using "horse" or "team" boats. These horse boats were built at the Hoboken shops for the Hoboken Ferry. These were triple boats connected by the deck beams, having paddle wheels between them. These boats were used for about eight years on the Hoboken-to-Barclay-Street Ferry. Six horses walking in a circle turned a vertical shaft, geared by mitre wheels to the waterwheel shaft.

It was Fulton who brought a successful steamboat to the Hudson River, but it was Colonel John Stevens who brought the first successful steam ferryboat to the North River.

CHAPTER 4

TECHNOLOGICAL DEVELOPMENT OF THE STEAMBOAT AND STEAM FERRYBOAT

Robert Fulton's *North River Steamboat* made its first trip in 1807, and thus secured the New York State monopoly for himself and Chancellor Livingston.

Nonetheless, Colonel John Stevens introduced his *Juliana,* a steam ferryboat, on the Hoboken Ferry in 1811. That same year, the lease on the Powles Hook Ferry expired, and a consortium including Robert Fulton, Elisha Boudinot of Newark, and Nicholas Roosevelt of New York, made application. Steven's boat made its first trip in October 1811—the first steam ferry to operate anywhere in the world. However, Fulton did not get his boat, the *Jersey,* into operation on the Powles Hook route until July 1812. The *Jersey* took 15 minutes for the trip and operated on a half-hourly schedule. Fulton had a complete system of landing bridges worked out as well, which we shall discuss shortly. The Paulus Hook Ferry Company was reincorporated as the York & Jersey Ferry Co. in March 1814.

Also, in 1814, Robert Fulton and his brother-in-law, William Cutting, established the New York & Brooklyn Steamboat Ferry Association to operate from Beekman's Slip Manhattan (now the foot of Fulton Street) to Brooklyn. The first boat on this run was the *Nassau.* The *Jersey,* meanwhile, had been joined by the *York* on the Paulus Hook line. Fare for foot passengers on the Brooklyn Ferry was established at 4¢—twice the rate in row or sail ferries.

Fulton's activity soon led Colonel Stevens to discontinue use of the steam ferry on the Hoboken line and, in 1814, he reverted to use of a horseboat invented by Moses Rodgers. Rodgers's first horseboat had been used on the East River and his second one, on the Hoboken run.

These first horseboats consisted of three hulls of equal length and breadth, placed parallel and firmly connected at a sufficient distance apart so as to leave room on either side of the middle hull for the paddle wheels. A circular platform was constructed in the center hull, which had cleats to give the horses traction. This treadmill was connected by a gear mechanism to the paddle wheels. The boat used 2, 4, or 8 horses or mules. The first boat was single ended, but inconvenience in docking led to building the second one with double ends—a contrivance followed by Fulton in his own first boats, and used on the Hudson scene ever since. Horseboats are known to have been used on the East River, Hoboken Ferry, and at Newburgh. They could not compete after the breakup of the Fulton–Livingston monopoly when steamboating was open to all. Stevens must have come to some royalty understanding with the monopoly as, on November 3, 1821, he incorporated The Hoboken Steamboat Ferry Company and, on April 22, 1822, placed the steam ferryboat *Hoboken* on the Hoboken-to-Barclay Street run. This service ran continuously until the *Elmira* closed out the service at 5:45 P.M. on November 22, 1967—145 years! At that time, it was the last steam ferry on not only the North River, but the entire Hudson River, as it was the first line of steam ferries (if the pioneer *Juliana* is considered the first steam ferry, and the horseboat hiatus is ignored).

The first steam ferries were somewhat similar to the horseboat in design, but consisted of only two hulls. Here is how Fulton himself described them in a letter to Dr. David Hosack in 1812:

First. She is built of two boats, each 10 feet beam, 80 feet long and 5 feet deep in the hold, which boats are distant from each other 10 feet, confined with strong transverse beams, knees and diagonal braces, forming a deck 30 feet wide and 80 feet long . . . . Reflecting on a steam ferry for Hudson River, the waves usually running up or down, I found a great breadth of beam absolutely necessary to prevent the boat rolling in the trough of the sea. This is attained by two boats and one space, giving 30 feet beam.

Second. By placing the propelling waterwheel between the boats, it is guarded from injury by ice or shocks on approaching the wharf, or entering the docks, which operation being performed twenty-four times in twelve hours, allows no time for fending off with boat hooks. To give dispatch and convenience, it is necessary the boat should arrive at the bridge without the possibility of any injury; hence all important parts of the machinery should be carefully guarded, particularly the propelling wheel.

Third. The whole of the machinery being placed between the boats, on the beams over the open space, leaves 10 feet wide on one side on the deck of the boat for carriages, horses, cattle, etc., the other having neat benches and covered with an awning, is for passengers. On the latter side, there is a passage and stairs to a neat cabin, which is 50 feet long and 5 feet clear from the floor to the beams, and furnished with benches for passengers in rainy or bad weather. In the winter there will be a stove in this cabin, which will add much to the comfort of the passengers while navigating through the ice.

Fourth. Although the two boats and space between them give 30 foot beam and proportionate stability, yet they present sharp bows to the water, and have only the resistance in water of one boat of 20 foot beam, which diminution of resistance gives speed in crossing.

Fifth. The space from stem to stern is 20 feet wide, which gives ample room at each end for carriages or persons to enter or go out of the boat.

Sixth. Both ends being alike, and each having a rudder, she never puts about. At New York the horses and carriages enter at one end of the boat, the horses' heads toward Jersey. On arriving, they go out at the manner at the other end of the boat without changing the line of direction; in like manner, when coming from Jersey to New York. Thus the shortest possible and quickest movement of all that is to pass is made to save time and secure convenience. Her rudders are equipollent—the iron shaft which serves as a rudder-post standing in the middle of each, equal on each side of the centre, it can go either end foremost. With yokes and parallel bars, the movements of the rudders are carried to the helms, the only position where the helmsmen can have a full view of all around the boat, and see how to steer her into the dock. (P. 518–519) (Morrison, 1903)

The double hulls were dispensed with in 1836. A double-ended ferry is practical only when terminal facilities permit of running into special slipways out of the sweep of the current. Such terminal facilities are expensive and are possible only where large traffic exists.

In 1833, when Brooklyn citizens had purchased a controlling interest in the ferry to that city, an attempt was made to meet the public demand by separating the traffic, and the *Relief* (1836) was built to carry passengers and freight, and the *Olive Branch* (1836) for passengers alone. These boats were single hulls, with side wheels; for the double hulls had become so unpopular, and the excitement regarding them ran so high, that peaceable

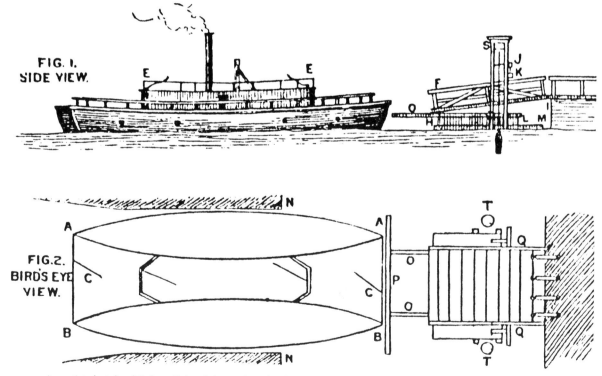

An artist sketch of Robert Fulton's log raft racks, ferry bridge and the ferryboat *Jersey*. From an old print.

Lower slip Erie Terminal, Pavonia Avenue, Jersey City, which was built according to Robert L. Stevens spring rack and floating bridge design.

citizens threatened to join a mob to sink the "old ice-catchers."

In order for the *Jersey* to board and discharge passengers and carriages, it was necessary for Fulton to design a special type loading dock. Fulton describes the dock, as follows (Morrison, 1903):

> It is 180 feet long, 70 wide; the bridge is fastened to the middle of the bulkhead. The boat being only 30 feet wide and the dock 70, leaves 20 feet vacant on each of her sides; in each of these 20 feet spans and in the water are floating stages, made of pine logs, which lie favorable to the boat for 30 feet, and these run diagonally to the extreme end of the wharf, so that the boat when coming in hits within the 70 feet, and the stages guide her direct to the bridge. (p. 521)

> Winfield, in his *History of Hudson County,* as requoted in "The Evolution of the Ferry-Boat" (Harper's Weekly Supplement, January 5, 1889), says "It is said these boats would ordinarily take an hour and a half to make a trip; that when they met in the river passengers could hold quite a conversation before they got beyond talking distance; in fact they were "Like fat green turtles fast asleep On the still surface of the deep." They started on their daily duties every morning at sunrise from each side of the river, and ran all day every hour by 'St. Paul's Church Clock.' "

Fulton's third boat, the *New Jersey,* had a short life; her boiler exploded a short time after completion, killing her engineer and a passenger. Fulton's fourth boat was a total failure. She was known as "Vermilye's folly." *Nassau* was Fulton's fifth center-wheel catamaran vessel.

Fulton's log stage system was the basic concept used for about nine years. In 1822, when the Stevens family reestablished operation of steam vessels on the Hoboken Ferry, with the launching of *Hoboken,* followed in 1823 by *Pioneer,* Robert L. Stevens formulated the general plan of the steam ferryboat and docking facilities of the present-day ferry system. These plans were adopted on the Hoboken Ferry in that year.

Stevens' design for the slips was a spring rack concept. Basically, it is a series of three rows of piles driven into the river bed, running the length of the boat. The piles of each row are of graduated lengths, with the tallest row of piles immediately behind the rack, the second row about two feet shorter and, finally, the third row about two feet shorter than that. Each row of piles was tied together with several horizontal rows of stringers set several feet apart. The stringers were placed between the piles and all bolted together. Finally, the rack, upon which the boat guardrail slid, was added. The rack was a series of 2 × 12 planks placed side by side the full length of the piles, from the side of the bridge to the river end of the row of piles, where a large clump of piles were driven at the end. These were tied together by a series of

Two workmen moving the lines of the workboat, so that the crew can finish greasing the rack, on December 2, 1954. The racks were greased several times a year.

steel cables wrapped around them. The rack was placed sufficiently high so that during all stages of the tide the boat guards would have sufficient area upon which to slide. Since both the rack and boat guardrails were wood, it was necessary to place a heavy coating of grease on the rack in order to reduce friction.

In the summertime, there was always the chance that the racks would catch on fire. The bridgeman had to be vigilant as a boat left the slip; if he noticed smoke, he would either call a tugboat or climb up on the rack, walk out to the fire, and put it out. If a boat was still in the slip, the captain would order the engineer to start the fire pump and then the wheelsman would wet down the rack with the hurricane deck fire hose. The porters were not too happy about this since it got their nice clean windows all dirty.

The two racks were shaped to the contour of the boat, wide on the river end and narrowing at the bridge end.

Of the five railroad ferry companies operating on the North River, only the slips of the DL & W's Hoboken Ferry were smaller than the others. Basically, an Erie boat could operate in a Pennsylvania Railroad or New York Central ferry slip with no problems and vice versa, since their boats' breadth over guards and bow facings

were very close. In fact, in 1861, when the Erie first started operation, two New Jersey Railroad and Transportation Co. boats—the *Philadelphia* and *Hudson*—were chartered to the Erie. It is reported that both the *D.S. Gregory* and *John Darcy* temporarily replaced Erie boats that were in for repair. For many years, the New York Central West Shore Ferry operated their downtown service out of the Pennsylvania Railroad slips at Desbrosses and Cortlandt Streets. Erie boats used to make special trips to the New York Central's 42nd St. ferry slips.

These three railroad company boats could operate out of the Central Railroad of New Jersey slips, but the bridge facing or contour was different and this caused a problem, as the Jersey Central boats had a blunter bow facing. But, because of this, CNJ boats could not use slips of the other roads, whereas the DL & W boats were two feet narrower in breadth, thus only they would fit in their slips. It is said that The Stevens did this intentionally, so they could operate out of their competitors' slips, but not they, out of theirs. In fact, during the Korean Conflict, after the Penn had discontinued its ferries, DL & W boats were chartered to transport troops from Staten Island and Brooklyn to Exchange Place.

Early in the century, Colonel John Stevens abandoned the old idea of carrying the bridge on the boat and adopted Fulton's floating bridge. This floating bridge is independent of the docks, which are built around it. The shore end of the bridge rests in a large cradle running the full width of the bridge. The cradle thus becomes a hinge for the bridge. At the outboard end is a large pontoon; as the tide raises and falls, so does the bridge on the pontoon, while it pivots in the cradle. The pontoon is filled with water to a point where it rests evenly on the bow of the boat. At the shore end, a 1-ft. steel plate running the full width of the bridge is anchored to the dock covering the expansion space between the dock and the bridge. The reason for this space is so that the bridge will have a certain amount of give when the boat slides into the bridge facing and comes against the bridge. Under normal circumstances, this space is sufficient to withstand the normal mating of a 1,600-ton boat to the bridge. In cases when a boat comes in too fast and strikes the bridge, the cradle end raises and then pushes back the dock planks, thus causing only superficial damage. The only part of the bridge that is actually made a part of the dock is the hoisting frame assembly. This assembly supports a large shaft running the width of the ferry-slip opening, in the dock,

on the outboard end of the bridge. The bridge is connected to the shaft by large chains which are anchored to each side of the bridge by large bolts running through the bridge. The actual hoist is on one side of the bridge directly behind the tie-up winch. The hoist is connected to a large drum on the shaft by a smaller chain which runs from the geared drum of the hoist. As the bridgeman turns the large hand wheel connected to a rachet gear, the gear turns the drum and the chain is taken up, which in turn moves the larger drum on the shaft so that the large chains are taken up on the shaft and the bridge is raised. This work can be extremely dangerous on the falling tide; if a bridgeman is not careful, he can be badly hurt by that large hand wheel spinning out of control.

This bridge and rack arrangement, designed by Robert Stevens in the early nineteenth century, is still used today, with only minor modifications, such as electric hoists replacing hand-operated ones, no need for the pontoons, and steel replacing wood in some of the structural parts.

In early January 1986, co-author, Ray Baxter, was invited to tour the International Boiler Works in East Stroudsburg, PA by its president, Fred Taylor. There he saw, first hand, large industrial boilers in various stages of construction. IBW has been building boilers for 100

Ferry bridge looking from apron toward the river, immediate center is the hog frame structure, bridge hoisting cables and structure can be seen at right edge and left center.

years. They did manufacture marine boilers during the marine steam era. IBW entered the boiler business in 1886, a few years after the first high-pressure boiler was designed.

Prior to his tour of IBW, he knew that the steamboat inspectors, and their counterpart on land, inspected boilers and placed whatever restrictions were necessary upon them for safe operation. There is, he found, much more to it than just that inspection. Each boiler built for a steam vessel has to have its plans approved by the U.S. Steamboat Inspection Service, a part of the United States Coast Guard, before any work could be started on it. Each piece of metal used in the construction of a boiler is documented. Starting with the first piece to enter the pattern shop, right on through the erecting shop, to the final installation in the vessel, all boiler parts and construction are documented. Two copies of this documentation are prepared. One copy is retained with the boiler and the other is forwarded to the American Society of Mechanical Engineers. If the boiler manufacturer goes out of business, the boiler parts can be made by another

company even if the original documents are lost, just by contacting the ASME.

Safety is the critical factor or standard in production of high-pressure boilers. Each marine boiler built to Lloyd's Register or the American Bureau of Shipping Requirements standards is inspected by their inspectors during construction and the final test is made in their presence. This final test is a hydrostatic pressure test 50% greater than the prescribed working pressure of the boiler.

Engines and boilers of early steam vessels were a simple unit operating at very low steam pressure, as little as 3 to 5 psi above atomospheric pressure. A nineteenth-century steam engine and boiler arrangement was basically a unit burning wood or coal in proximity to water in a square boiler. The water came to a boil, causing steam, which formed under pressure. The pressurized steam passed to the cylinder of the steam engine, where it applied pressure to one side of the piston, causing it to move. As the piston reached the end of the stroke, the steam was allowed to escape to a condenser, where it

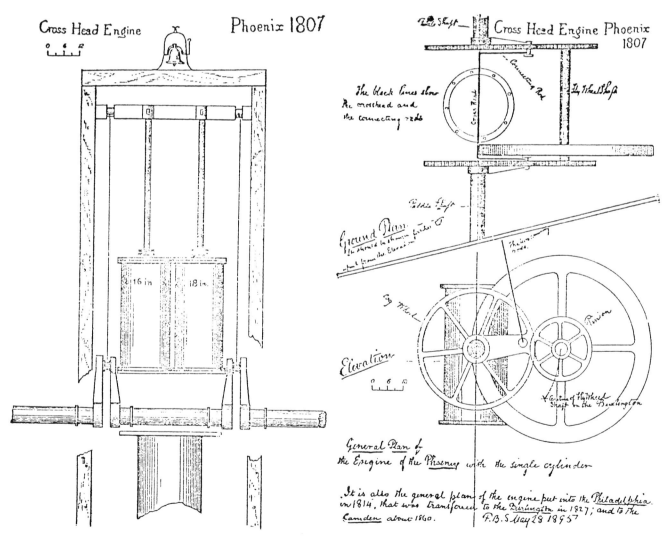

Original engine of the *Phoenix* 1807. — From drawing made by Francis B. Stevens

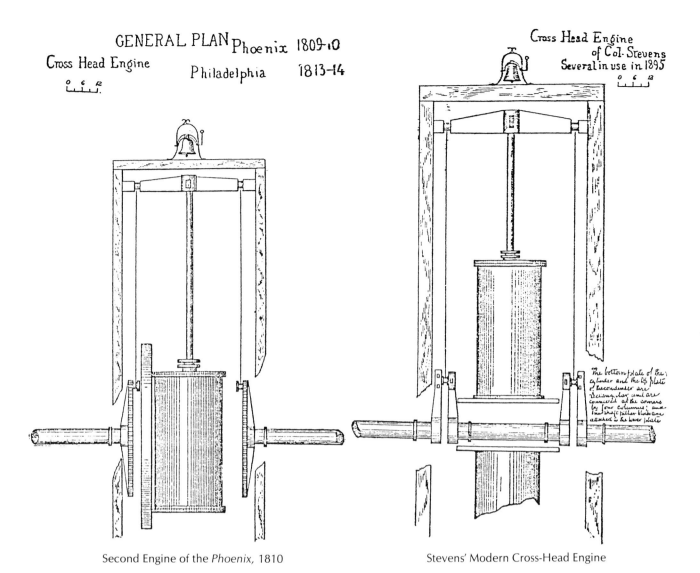

GENERAL PLAN Phoenix 1809-10
Cross Head Engine
Philadelphia 1813-14

Cross Head Engine
of Col. Stevens
Several in use in 1895

Second Engine of the *Phoenix*, 1810

Stevens' Modern Cross-Head Engine

was returned to a liquid state and fed back into the boiler to complete the cycle. All of these boilers were simple, as were the engines.

The fuel of the early boilers was pine wood. The engine's piston rod was guided by a parallel motion, rather than slides. Fulton's first boats used a bell crank engine. He later discarded this type of engine for the Stevens crosshead engine, like that used in the *Phoenix* of 1807. For the next fifty years, these simple single-cylinder engines saw modification and improvements, such as crossheads and slides, improved throttle and valve linkage, the skeleton walking beam, and so on. With the modifications, came larger engines and paddle-wheel improvements.

After fifty years of steamboats, maximum possible steam pressure was about 30 to 50 psi. The largest single-piston engine could deliver only up to 1,000 hp. By 1860, this boxlike low-pressure boiler had reached its limit of potential.

In the 1870s, the British warship *HMS Iris* was equipped with a boiler built in the form of a cylinder.

This experiment was so successful that a much higher steam pressure was achieved without structural failure to the boiler.

With the development of the gunboat boiler and higher steam pressure, came new engines and methods of propulsion for maritime use.

By 1886, side-wheel ferryboat engines had reached cylinder diameters of 50 in. with a piston stroke of up to 11 ft. in length, which developed 800 hp, yet operated on only 50 psi boiler pressure.

The industry was in the mood for change. This change came about with the successful development of a high-pressure boiler.

The design of the double-end ferryboat remained unchanged, except that it kept getting larger and larger as its engine's size increased. The ferryboat of the mid-1880s had reached about 215 ft. in length, over 1,000 gross tons in weight. Side-wheel ferryboats could be seen on the North River well into the twentieth century.

Steel hulls are used today, but lightweight wooden su-

Boiler built for the tug-boat *Robert Rogers,* owned by the Taylor Dredging Co., Jersey City, New Jersey.

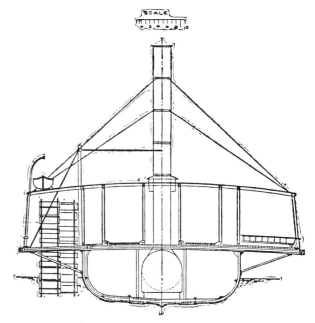

Ferryboat *Baltimore,* amidship section.

perstructures survived until quite recent times. Longitudinal strength is a factor of great importance on account of the heavy deck loads caused by the vehicular traffic — alternately of a static and a rolling nature. For this reason, frame and reverse-frame construction is used in conjunction with truss girders spaced at varying distances from the centerline of the ship in accordance with the size. Other important features of modern Hudson River ferryboats were the double hulls of the DL & W boats, with compartmentalized sections and watertight bulkheads, and provision for direct passenger loading to the second deck.

Many Hudson ferries, in addition to side passenger cabins, had a large passenger saloon on the upper deck. Interior stairways, often crafted of elaborately carved and paneled rare woods, connected the two decks amidships, or at each end on both sides, in the Men's and Women's cabins. These stairways were plentifully bespattered with signs warning passengers not to descend when the boat was entering her slip — a wise precaution, because the inevitable bump as the vessel Fetched-up against the racks of the slip was more than likely to precipitate passengers to the bottom of the stairway with more speed than dignity. Stairways were open during daylight hours and roped off only at night. Although used infrequently when top-deck loading arrangements were provided at terminals, these stairways were desirable for ready access from deck to deck in the event of fire or collision. Hudson River ferries usually provided seating accommodations, lavatories, and

washrooms[1]. Coffee and buns were available on the Hoboken boats, and there are snack bars on the present-day Staten Island boats.

Proper metacentric height must always be provided to ensure a "stiff ship" under all conditions of loading, heeling, and trim. It must be noted that human freight, when transported in bulk, either in ferryboats or excursion ships, has all the bad characteristics of a bulk cargo such as grain or coal, in addition to the danger of panic. A mad rush of passengers from one side of a ferryboat to the other may easily put the deck edge under water. For this reason, the flared section has much to recommend it, since the heeling would gradually increase the load water-plane area. As a specific example, a ferry with a 48.5 ft. extreme breadth has a metacentric height of 11 ft.

When a ship approaches the slips at the termination of a trip, passengers naturally crowd to the unloading end of the ship, tending to put her down by the head. Trimming tanks are not usually operated to counterpart this because the trim by the head so caused is of a relatively temporary nature. Ferryboats were not equipped with trimming tanks.

Upper-deck loading was first perfected in 1891 and put into use on the Pennsylvania Ferry. It was also used on the Lackawanna Railroad, Jersey Central, and Staten Island lines, where it is still in use today.

Approaches to the slips are marked and protected from the current by wooden upright "spring" pilings lashed and bolted together, and thus with plenty of

---

[1]Lavatories and washrooms were only required on runs over 20 minutes.

"give" in the last few yards of her journey, the vessel is practically hemmed in sideways.

In the ferries' heyday, the tops of the face boards and pilings were painted white and contrasted smartly with the black grease. Often, fog bells, with large, round sound deflectors, were mounted at the ends of the bulkheads to guide the ferries into dock in fog. Each dock had its own interval of bell stroke. A few lines also used fog horns. By keeping their engines turning slightly ahead, the ferries, when berthed, could keep their nose hard up to the dock. This could be a dangerous practice if the deckhands and dockmen were too lazy to fasten the lines as well. On several occasions, boats drifted out from the dock while loading, dumping vehicles and passengers into the water with fatal results. The author (AGA) remembers seeing such an accident on an electric ferry as a child at the Edgewater ferry terminal, in which several lives were lost. This particular incident led to strict enforcement of proper berthing rules in subsequent years.[2] Often, a strong tide or wind would bring the ferry into the slip partially sideways, causing the ship to bounce back and forth from side to side several times—often quite roughly. Good pilots could minimize this, however.[3]

On modern ferryboats, propulsion was by screw propellers, the paddle wheel having rapidly disappeared after the 1920s. The last railroad operated side-wheel ferry on the Hudson was the DL & W's *Montclair,* which ran on the Christopher St. line. The Lackawanna's old *Musconetcong* also operated on the Yonkers-Alpine line under the new name *F. R. Pierson* into the 1940s.

In the 1920s, diesel-electric boats, called "electric ferries," made their appearance on the Hudson. The last one, *The Tides,* remains in service to Governor's Island. They had originally been used on the Staten Island-to-69th Street Brooklyn line, 125th St, and 34th St. to Weehawkin line (Baldwin Ave.) line, which specialized in vehicular, rather than passenger, traffic. On the primarily passenger lines, the traditional steamboats proved more suitable. A typical steam ferry, such as was used on the railroad-owned routes, might have engines developing 1,400 hp at 125 rpm, and driving two four-bladed cast steel or bronze propellers, 8-ft. diameter by 12-ft. pitch, or larger. There were usually two steering engines, one at each end at engine-room level, rod and cable controlled from the bridge or pilothouse.

An important requirement of a ferryboat was that it have longitudinal stability to resist burying its nose; that it had good maneuvering power when forereaching with engines stopped; and that it was able to fight ice and steer well when trimmed by the head.

In many innovations, the Hoboken Ferry was the leader: In 1823, it had the first steamboat ferry with a "ladies cabin" below decks—carpeted and with fireplaces and large mirrors; in 1856, it operated the first night service; in 1888, it used the first screw propellers.

Boats of the different lines had distinctive paint schemes. In the early days, white was the most popular color on all lines, and remained so on the upriver lines for many years. Downriver, white was longest in use on the Hoboken Ferry, to be superseded in later years by brown with white pilot houses and gold-leaf lettering. The Fort Lee and Edgewater ferries were red; West Shore Railroad used mustard buff, with gold and red trim; Erie used green with white pilot houses and black trim and gold lettering on the sides. Pennsylvania Railroad used Tuscan red with gold trim; whereas the Central Railroad of New Jersey favored a two-tone green scheme with white pilot houses and trim. The various lines of electric ferries favored a dark, or dull, green, with black and gold trim. Gilded lanterns, known as range lights, sat atop the pilot houses on all ferry boats, usually with a gilded ball as finial.[4] Stacks were almost always painted black, with the insignia of the operator displayed thereon.

A distinctive feature of some terminals was the location of the waiting-rooms and accessory conveniences for passengers in the second story of the building to afford easy communication with the upper-deck cabins of the ferry boats. Many terminals had steel frames sheathed with copper resting on pilings, and the roof projecting over the slips suffi-

---

[2]The electric ferries, a privately operated line, had much less strict safety rules than the railroads. Most railroad companies required a deckhand to remain on the inboard end while loading and the wheelsman to stand by in the pilothouse next to the engine telegraph.

[3]There were times when the wind would affect the manner in which a captain had to steer his vessel. A counteracting wind, coming up under the ferryboat's overhang from the opposite direction of the tide, could turn the stern up-/or down river, thus causing the bow to head into the rack. A good captain could overcome this by backing the boat and turning the wheel into the rack, then quickly turn the wheel away from the rack, as he rang for full speed ahead. It was a very quick move and a fast one, but it worked.

One thing the captain had to be concerned about was that if he rode the rack and bound against the opposite clump, the boat's guard had a tendency to climb the rack, causing the vessel to tilt sharply towards the clump. If this tilt became too sheer, the clump would go through the side of the boat on a high tide, breaking cabin windows and injuring passengers.

---

[4]These white lights were 32-point light to be seen all around the horizon and to be visible for a distance of 5 miles.

All vessels were required to carry running lights, which consisted of a red light on the port or left side, and a green light on the starboard or right side. These port and starboard lights were to face from directly ahead to 2 points aft the beam and to be protected with inboard screens so that one light cannot be seen across the vessel's opposite bow.

The superintendent of a district might also prescribe certain special designation lights, to be carried on a mast amidships and to be seen from all points of the compass. New York Harbor Railroad ferry designation lights were: CNJ & West Shore none; Erie, white; Penn, red; DL & W, green.

Lackawanna's *Montclair*, the last sidewheel ferryboat to operate in the North River. – Railroad Museum of Pennsylvania

ciently to protect the passage to and from the boats. Buffer platforms were placed in the floor at the head of the slips to diminish the shock to the terminal structures from impact. As the ferries were also used for local street traffic, driveways to the boats and passenger accommodations were necessarily required on the ground floor, separated from the railroad terminal. Such construction was used on the Staten Island Ferry terminals at Whitehall Street, Manhattan and St. George, Staten Island, and by the Pennsylvania Railroad at Exchange Place, Jersey City, the DL & W at Hoboken and on the CNJ. Smaller scale versions were at 23rd Street, Barclay Street, Cortlandt Street, and Liberty Street, in Manhattan. Several Manhattan terminals had footbridges across West Street, prior to construction of the West Side elevated highway.

The Whitehall Street Terminal of the Staten Island Ferry had direct access to elevated trains on the upper level. In later years, Steven's float-bridge technology for lower-deck loading was superseded by using truss or girder bridges, hinged on the wharf side, that could be raised or lowered to accommodate the varying tides. They were suspended by chains or strong steel cables, were raised or lowered by either ratchet wheels or electric motors, and were counterweighted. The arch-truss type of bridge predominated, and for some strange reason, were almost universally painted red and made of wood. The girder-type construction was used at the West Shore Railroad's Weehawken Terminal. The vehicle gangways were usually cavernous and dark, but provided capacious protection from the elements.

INBOARD WORKINGS OF THE STEAM ENGINE

In view of the central importance of this technology to the development of ferryboats and in consideration of the fact that few of our readers will have had firsthand experience of them, let us describe the workings of a steam engine as used on board a steamboat or early period ferryboat.

The prime moving force in a steam engine was the terrifically powerful expansive force of steam, which takes up roughly 1,600 times the space of the water required to generate it. The force is measured in terms of the pressure this steam exerts in a closed vessel, expressed in pounds per square inch (psi) on the surface of the vessel. The steam was generated in boilers which were fired, first by wood, later by coal and oil. If the fire was hot, steam formed quickly and the piston moved rapidly. If the fire was low, steam formed slowly and the piston moved less rapidly. There were two basic types of boilers. In firetube boilers, hot gases from the firebox exhaust passed through convoluted tubes inside a large vessel containing water, before passing up the stack. The steam was generated inside the boiler shell before being drawn off to the manifold and cylinders. This type of boiler was subject to terrific internal pressures and often led to terrible boiler explosions in the early days. In the watertube boiler, more commonly in use in later years, the hot exhaust gases passed through the boiler shell on their way to the stack. Water circulated through convoluted tubes inside the boiler shell which were heated by the passing hot gases. As the water inside the tubes turned to steam, it was drawn off to the manifold and cylinders. The reason wood was abandoned as a fuel in favor of coal was that coal has a higher caloric value per pound and does not pass sparks through the stacks. Consequently, less weight of fuel had to be carried. The early coal burners were fired by hand shovels and were known as "hand bombers." It is interesting to note that the last coal-burning steamboats on the Hudson, the ferryboats *Binghamton* and *Elmira,* were both "hand bombers," which used anthracite coal. This innovation was introduced by Robert Stevens, one of the founders of the Hoboken Ferry. It was a cleaner burning fuel than soft coal, or certain "dirty burning" oils. Oil was used on the newer New York Central boats.

The name "reciprocating" steam engine came from the fact that, in this type of engine, a piston moved back and forth inside a cylinder. This was accomplished by admitting live steam into the cylinder through a valve to push the piston. The inlet of steam was stopped about halfway through the piston's stroke so as to take full advantage of the expansive force of the steam. At the end of the stroke, another inlet valve was opened on the other side of the piston, which pushed it back in the opposite direction. Spent steam was exhausted through outlet valves which were mechanically activated in synchronization with the steam inlet valves. This mechanism was known as the valve gear or eccentrics. On more modern engines, it was very complex, and differed in design on vertical and inclined beam engines[5]. The critical factors in describing ship's steam engines are the diameter of the cylinder bore and the length of stroke of

---

[5]It should be noted that incline beam engines were not popular on double end ferryboats in N.Y. Harbor. Only a couple of boats the Staten Island Ferries *Robert Garrett* and *Erastus Wiman,* both built 1888 used them.

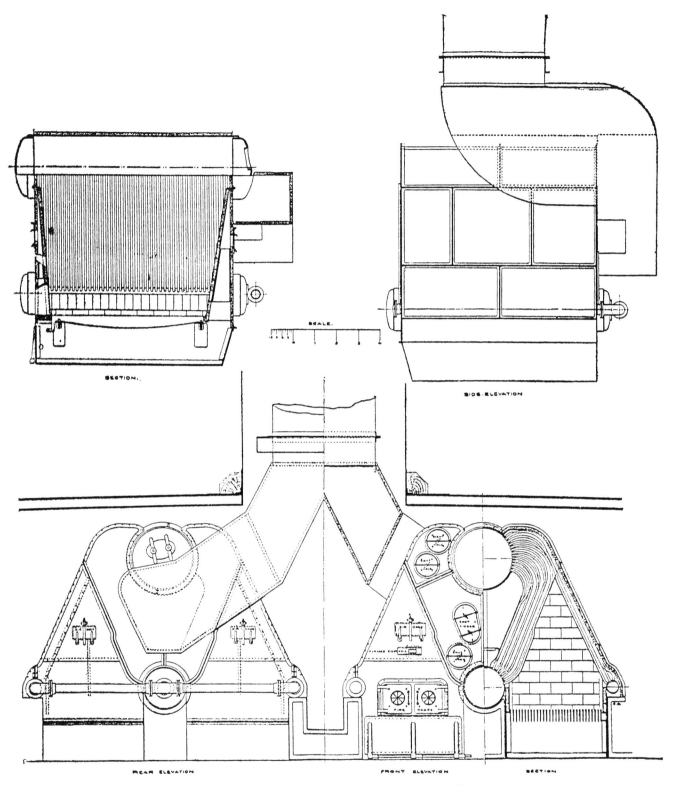

SCALE.

SECTION.

SIDE ELEVATION

REAR ELEVATION

FRONT ELEVATION

SECTION

Ferryboat *St. Louis*, section and elevation of boilers.

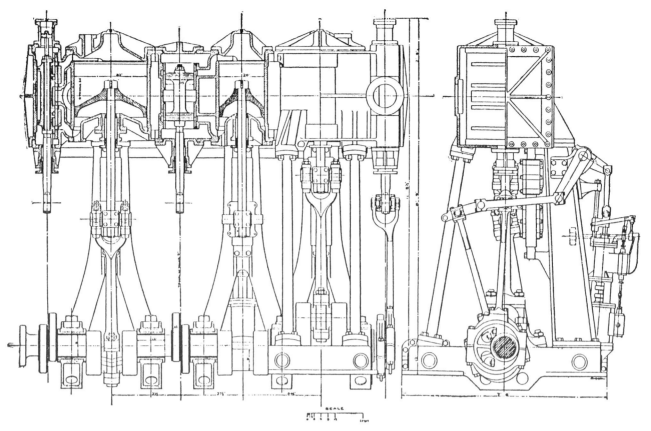

Engines of the ferryboat *St. Louis.*

the piston. In later years, it was found that much of the exhaust steam retained expansive force; therefore, engines were designed with second, third, and fourth cylinders, of increasing diameter, into which the exhaust steam from the next smallest cylinder was utilized as inlet steam. These were known as compound engines. The later large day boats, such as the *Hendrick Hudson* and *Alexander Hamilton,* had triple-expansion engines, as did many post-1900 railroad ferries. The dayline's *De Witt Clinton* had two triple-expansion engines, like the Pennsylvania Railroad's *St. Louis*-class ferryboats. The most popular engine among the various marine architects who designed the propeller ferryboats after 1888 was the double compound engine. These were two-two cylinder compound engines placed back to back. The low pressure or larger cylinder in the middle and the high pressure or small cylinder on the ends.

The next problem of steamboat design was to change the reciprocating, or back-and-forth, movement of the pistons into rotating movement to turn either a paddle wheel or a propeller. In the early steamboats, the cylinder was mounted vertically, so that the piston worked up and down out of the top of the cylinder. Usually there was only one very large-diameter cylinder on the early day boats. This piston was connected by a flexible joint to a connecting rod which ran up to the top of the boat where it was fastened to one end of a balanced beam, similar to a seesaw, known as a walking beam. As the

piston rod and connecting rod pushed one end of this walking beam up, the other end would go down, and vice versa.

At a relatively early date, a beam *per se* was replaced by a diamond-shaped metal frame known as a skeleton beam. This was both stronger, lighter, and less subject to breaking from sudden jars to the machinery. The end of the walking beam, opposite to that end connected with the piston, was connected to another rod which ran

Skeleton walking beam of the Hudson River Day Line steamer *Albany.* Outside of the Mariner's Museum, Newport News, Virginia.

down through the body of the ship to a crank rod on the paddle-wheel shaft, which, in turn, ran through the hull, or, on some boats such as the *Robert Fulton,* was supported on bearings slightly above the waterline. On Hudson River steamboats, there was usually only a single monolithic paddle shaft, and both paddle wheels always turned in the same direction. On America's Western rivers and in Europe, it was not unusual to have two smaller engines, two paddle shafts, and paddle wheels which could operate independently in opposite directions. This aided in maneuverability, but was used only rarely, generally on towboats, on the Hudson.

The second connecting bar, which joined the walking beam and the paddle shaft, was also connected to a "rocker bar" which automatically activated the valve gear. On older, vertical-beam boats, the steam was let into the cylinder by manual valving, using a "starter bar." Once a certain velocity was attained, linking hooks would be attached from the connecting rod and rocker bar to activate the valve gear automatically. This was known to steamboaters as "dropping the hooks," and is the action from which the popular cant phrase "hook her up," is derived.

In later steamboats, the cylinders were frequently mounted horizontally, or on a slight slant, and a single connecting rod, or set of rods in the case of a compound engine, connected the pistons with crank shafts on the paddle shaft. This was known as an inclined-beam engine. The *Alexander Hamilton* was a well-known example. Passengers could easily view the workings of this magnificent machine as the ponderous revolutions of its great crank shafts acted much as does a flywheel.

In sidewheel ships, the paddle shaft passed through the lubricated bearings, supported by springs, on either side of the vessel. In early sidewheelers, large paddles radiated out from the hub and slapped the water. This created much wasteful turbulence, and when a paddle blade first hit the water, it exerted a downward force against the water which would tend to raise the ship up in the water. Near nadir of its revolution, it exerted maximum forward thrust. In the ascending phase of its revolution, the paddle lifted water from the level of the river and thus wasted energy. Maximum efficiency was attained for each blade only when near nadir in its revolution. This early type of wheel was known as a radial wheel.

John Ericsson is credited with an improvement in paddle-wheel design, although there is some good evidence that the Stevenses preceded him in this matter. He perfected what is known as the "feathering," or

View of the Commodious Barge provided by the Erie Railway Company for the transfer of Emigrants and their Luggage from Castle Garden to the Erie Railway Depot. — Courtesy of James M. Ransom

Detail of feathering wheel of steamer *Ticonderoga*.

Ericsson, wheel. (in Europe, called the Morgan Wheel). In this type of wheel, the blades, or buckets, as they are sometimes called, are mounted on a circular cage similar to the frame of a ferris wheel with swinging cars. They are hinged on one end, and the other end is connected to a radius arm fastened to an eccentric crank on the hub of the paddle shaft. The paddle blades thus always move in a plane nearly perpendicular to that of the surface of the water. Entering the water, they cut right into it, exerting neither downward thrust nor tending to lift the vessel from the water, so as not to waste energy. On rising from the water, they lift no heavy splash. Because the paddle blade is perpendicular to the surface of the water from first entry, it is placed so as to exert maximum horizontal thrust throughout its entire submerged revolution. It thus conserves power, increases speed, and minimizes splash. The first large Day Boats to be fitted with feathering wheels were the *Albany* and *New York* of the Hudson River Day Line. They were used on most of the later ships.

To protect the wheels from damage, often of a deliberate and malicious nature, and to contain the splashing water, the early radial wheels were enclosed in semicircular paddle housings, often ornately decorated. Just as with locomotive drive wheels, large-diameter sidewheels were designed for speed and smaller ones, for power. The wheel on such early steamboats as the *St. John*, *City of Troy*, and *Kaaterskill* would extend to the third and fourth decks. The wheel of the *St. John* had a diameter of 48 ft., whereas the average railroad ferryboat paddle wheels were 22-ft. diameter and 9 ft. wide. The paddle housings were often called paddle boxes.

On vertical-beam ships, the walking beam was supported on a heavy wooden or steel framework called the "gallows frame," from its obvious resemblance to the structure of that same name.

On screw-propelled steamships, the cylinders were usually mounted vertically over the propeller shaft – or shafts, if on a twin-screw vessel. The pistons came through the bottom of the cylinders and were linked to

connecting rods by a flexible crosshead. The connecting rods were attached to cranks on the propeller shafts. The valve gear was actuated by another set of rods motivated by the propeller shafts. Some ships had as many as four engines, driving two shafts. These could be simple or double, triple or quadruple, expansion machines.

In the earliest steamboats, the boilers were mounted on the deck. Later, they were mounted down in the hull. However, after some disasterous boiler explosions, people became afraid of injury, and it became common practice to mount the boilers outboard "on the guards" to lessen injury to both passengers and ship in case of explosion. The *Mary Powell* was the last important Hudson River passenger steamboat with boilers on the guards. This arrangement also made it easier to store the fuel and made for cooler working conditions for the firemen who had to feed the large fires manually.

On ships with boilers on the guards, the stacks were usually on the sides, above the boilers. On some larger ships, with four separate boilers (one forward and one aft of the paddle on either side), there were four separate stacks. Later, with the boilers in the hull, it became common to use a third boiler and mount the three stacks athwartship, as in the *Chauncey Vibbard*, *Albany*, *New York*, and *Robert Fulton*. Later practice was to place the stacks amidship, one in front of the other. The latter largest modern Hudson River steamboats rarely exceeded the need for two stacks. The *Washington Irving* had a third stack, but the forward stack was a "dummy" used to give an aesthetic design.

Paddle wheels remained in use on the Hudson longer than most other places for a variety of reasons. They were well-suited to shallow-draft vessels and caused a minimum of turbulence in shallow water. They were easily maneuverable in frequent docking and could reverse directions fast and with good power. They also created less vibration, which is important in a large, shallow-hulled, passenger-carrying ship with a light wooden superstructure. They were also very fast when

Excellent example of a wide beam-over-guard vessel with narrow hull.

equipped with feathering wheels. The *Alexander Hamilton,* built by Bethlehem Steel Company in 1924, was the last sidewheeler built for the Hudson. The last sidewheel steam ferryboat built was the *Charles W. Galloway,* built in 1922 for the Staten Island Railroad's Tottenville-to-Perth Amboy line. She operated until October 16, 1948.

The sidewheelers offered another important advantage for a river boat: A rather narrow hull, relative to overall breadth, can be attained by fairing the decks out over the guards to the outsides of the paddle boxes. This provides additional deck or cabin space. The ship thereby had great virtual breadth in proportion to waterline breadth, thus maintaining a beneficial metacentric ratio. This is important in providing stability in passenger ships on which large numbers of persons frequently flock to one side, either for sightseeing or unloading, or to seek or avoid the sun. To help keep these ships in trim and prevent capsizing or excessive tipping over or list, many were equipped with saddle-shaped trimming tanks, with high-speed centrifugal pumps, so that fast adjustments could be made. In the later designs of noted naval architects Frank Kirby, J. W. Millard, and George Sharp, the superstructure was closely bound to the strength hull to minimize vibration and strengthen the superstructure. Earlier ships had to be strengthened by truss frames, known as hog frames, which are prominent in pictures of the older steamboats. There was much use of guy-wire bracing, which had to be constantly adjusted by use of turnbuckles to prevent the ship from either sagging in the middle, or "hogging," or digging her nose into the water.

Although there was considerable variation in details, certain features were fairly standard in steamboat design. Passengers usually boarded from a gangway aft of the paddle wheel. The purser's office and the main dining room were usually on the main deck aft. The saloon and third decks were usually given over either to passenger lounge space or, on night boats, to cabins. The larger day boats had private staterooms, known as parlors, each with its own toilet facilities and, sometimes, outside decks. These were usually located on the saloon deck. Often, crew quarters for the deck officers were located on the hurricane deck abaft the pilot house. Other crew quarters were usually below deck in the forecastle, and the crew mess below deck abaft the boilers and machinery. Originally, steering was done by a large hand wheel in the pilot house. As the ships grew larger, these were superseded by steam-power steering, supplied by a second smaller wheel, with the large hand wheel retained for emergencies. It frequently took up to ten men to steer by hand. (On a recent occasion, for example, when the power steering failed on the *Alexander Hamilton,* it took eight deckhands to man the wheel!) Electricity was generated by steam turbines. Steam

pumps kept pressure in the fire-fighting water lines and for sanitation systems.

Some of the larger boats of later years carried crews of up to 100 men and officers. Fourteen men in the engine room alone was not uncommon. There were usually the captain or master, and a first and second pilot, usually licensed to serve as master in an emergency. There were also the first and second mates, chief and assistant chief engineer, purser, and chief steward, in addition to numerous deckhands, ablebodied seamen, waiters, porters, chefs, cooks, kitchen help, and bartenders and stewards. Passenger loads frequently ran over 4,000 passengers on a busy trip. It was much like a miniature ocean liner. Up until 1949, the better boats were carpeted on the upper decks, elegantly furnished, and decorated with *objects d'art,* oil paintings, and murals. There was much carved fine wood and fancy metalwork and chandeliers. Bands played at sailing time and for dancing, and string orchestras gave concerts and performed in the dining room at luncheon and dinner. Besides the main dining room, the equal of those in the finest hotels, there was usually a separate, lower priced, cafeteria. The day boats offered the height of luxury until after WW II. Naturally, the small excursion boats did not offer the same luxury as the through liners, although some, such as the *Grand Republic,* were impressive in their appointments. On the through Day Line, a gentleman was not allowed aboard without a white shirt, collar, and jacket. It is unfortunate that today's generation, who knowing only the last, sad years of decline with greatly lowered standards of ship operation and passenger behavior, have little knowledge of the magnificence of this operation throughout its heyday.

Some of the large night boats had staterooms arranged around a grand gallery abaft the stack housings, where there was usually a "grand staircase," built of rich woods and decorative metalwork. The gallery was often two or three decks in height, with the cabins opening off circular balconies on each deck level, much like the new Hyatt House in Atlanta or the Brown Palace in Denver. The gallery of the nightboat *Berkshire* was particularly impressive, with large, fluted Corinthian columns, carved corbels, and decorative friezes, the latter, painted white with gilt trim. For many years, the great Hudson River day and night boats were called "Iron Palace Steamers," and they were emulated throughout the world. No trip to America was complete without a voyage up the Hudson on one of these great liners. It is truly unfortunate that some modern version of this magnificent tradition has not survived.

In the early days of railroad ferry service, especially on the Erie Railroad's Manhattan-to-Piermont line, ships as described above were used. The further development of the prototypical, modern, double-end ferryboat will be detailed in the next chapter.

CHAPTER 5

DEVELOPMENT OF THE SCREW PROPELLER FERRYBOAT

Down through the years, engineering improvements and changes reach a point where one definite thing seems to completely revolutionize an industry. For the North River double-end ferryboat, the year 1888 seems to have been that point in time.

In that year, C. L. Delamater Co., in conjunction with T. S. Marvel Shipyard of Newburgh, NY, launched the first screw ferryboat, the *Bergen,* for the Hoboken Ferry Co. *Bergen* had 2 gunboat boilers below decks, which developed 175 lbs. psi pressure. These boilers provided steam for a triple expansion engine, designed by J. Shields Wilson, with the following dimensions—18½ in. × 27 in. × 42 in. with a 24-in. stroke, which developed 800 hp. There were two 8-ft. diameter propellers, one at each end, connected by a continuous shaft to the engine. As the aft propeller pushed, the fore one pulled. The *Bergen* was an experimental craft which, like the first high-pressure boiler, proved herself beyond the expectations of her designers.

On January 28, 1891, Neafie & Levy Shipyard of Philadelphia, PA documented the second new design, the New York Harbor screw-propeller ferryboat, *John G. McCullough,* for the Erie Railway Co. The major differences between the *McCullough* and *Bergen* were in the engines and boilers. *McCullough's* 800 hp was developed by a two-cylinder compound engine 26 in. × 50 in. with a 30-in. stroke powered by two return watertube boilers of 100 lbs. psi pressure.

Within a couple of short years two reciprocating engines were designed which established the standard in the maritime industry for the next seventy five years: respectively, the double-compound and the triple-

expansion engines, both made possible by improved boiler manufacture.

A double-compound engine could be called a double-expansion engine. Hot, high-pressure steam is introduced to the small cylinder—the high-pressure cylinder; after the steam pushes the piston the length of the stroke, it is exhausted into a second cylinder which is approximately twice the size of the first, where it exerts pressure upon the second piston and is, in turn, exhausted upon completion of the stroke. The exhausted steam travels to the condenser where it is restored to a liquid state for reuse or mixed with water and discharged overboard.

In the case of a triple-expansion engine, the steam is used a third time, in which case the two larger cylinders, known as the intermediate and low pressure cylinders, are approximately the same size. In some cases, a fourth cylinder was used and the steam used a fourth time; in these cases, the third and fourth cylinders were the same size, and the second larger than the first but smaller than the third and fourth.

Therefore, when you read an engine statistic for a vessel you could determine the type of reciprocating engine she had by the numerical arrangement.

The Erie ferryboat *Tuxedo* was built in 1904, with two Scotch marine boilers which developed 150 lbs. psi to operate two back-to-back compound engines which developed 1,200 hp. These engines' dimensions were 2- 18 in. × 38 in. × 28-in. stroke, which meant that the high-pressure cylinders were 18 in. in diameter and the low-pressure cylinders 38 in. in diameter, while the stroke of the piston was 28 in. on each engine. These engines

Artist's sketch of the propeller ferryboat *Bergen* of the Hoboken Ferry Co. First of her kind on the North River, in 1888. From an old print.

were placed with the low-pressure cylinders back to back, so one could say her dimensions were 18 in. × 38 in. -38 in. × 18 in. × 28 in.

The Pennsylvania Railroad ferryboat *Newark,* built in 1902, had a triple-expansion engine with a high-pressure cylinder 22 in. in diameter, intermediate- and low-pressure cylinders 32 in. in diameter, and a piston stroke only 24 in. in length. This engine developed 750 hp and its steam was supplied by two watertube boilers developing 225 lbs psi pressure. This engine did not hold true to the double in size for low-pressure cylinders, like a double-compound engine.

The Central Railroad of New Jersey was one of the largest users of triple expansion engines in New York Harbor. All its ferryboats built between 1901 and 1911 had the same basic 4-cylinder engine, with dimensions

of 19 in. × 30 in. × 35 in. × 35 in. × 30 in. developing around 1,400 hp. But these boats all had three return-tube boilers which developed 170 lbs. psi steam pressure.

The double-compound reciprocating engine seemed to be the most widely used engine in New York Harbor. Research shows that the double compound engine developed the most horsepower at lower steam pressures.

Prior to 1905, most compound engines were steeple compound, that is, two solid-frame sides with piston slides affixed to their inward side. After 1905, the open-frame compound engine was adopted. The difference in these two engines was that the open-frame engine had the piston slide affixed to the back frame only. The slide was mounted away from the frame so that one frame could be used. On the up stroke of the piston, the cross-

The late afternoon sun reflects off the freshly painted *Tuxedo* as she heads up river towards Jersey City. — Dan Biernacki Collection

Engineer Chappell stands by the throttles of the Youngstown as he awaits the next command to be rung on the vessels telegraph. The round object with the bell just over his head is the direction indicator, which is pointed toward Chambers Street. His right hand is on the reversing lever while his left is on the throttle. — Dan Biernacki Collection

head guide of the crank slid on one side and the opposite side, on the return stroke. The chief advantage of this type over the solid frame was that it provided better accessibility to the various engine parts for adjustment and repairs. The front column was a smaller, round support column on the open-frame engine. This can be seen on the photograph of Youngstown's engine above.

After WW I, the Skinner Unaflow Reciprocating engine was developed, a multicylinder, double-acting simple expansion engine using the Unaflow principle (central exhaust ports) to obtain uniform direction of steam travel for a constant temperature gradient throughout the steam circuit. Main features of the design are: steam poppet admission valves; dual camshaft valve gear for full reversing capability; duplication of structural elements and running gear components in multicylinder machines.

Characteristics of the Unaflow engine include direct connection to the propeller with reversing valve gear al-

lowing full power ahead or astern. Control of horsepower output is by increasing or decreasing the cylinder mean effective pressure; this produces declining steam rates at partial loads.

The engine is simple and rugged. Its construction is fully enclosed and all running gear is pressure lubricated. The slow-turning speed and absence of shock stresses enable the engine to be operated with low maintenance cost over the life of the ship's machinery. Several tug boats in New York Harbor were powered by Skinner engines, but only one railroad ferryboat, the Erie Railroad's Meadville. Later, in 1950, the City of New York, Department of Marine and Aviation, would purchase three new ferryboats with Skinner engines, to become known as the Merrell class boats.

The numerical statistics for the Erie's Meadville engine were 5-25 in. × 24 in. stroke with steam supplied by two Babcock & Wilcox watertube boilers developing steam at 200 lbs. psi pressure. The engine developed 1,700 hp.

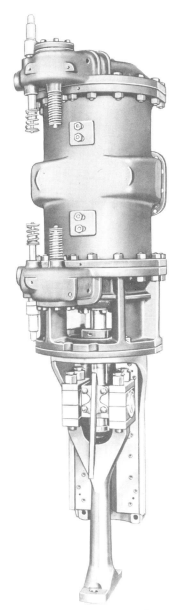

Cylinder assembly of a simple compound Unaflow engine.—
Courtesy of Skinner Engine Co.

The New York City *Merrell* class vessel engines have 6-23 in. cylinders and a 26 in. stroke and develop 4,800 hp.

With the development of more efficient engines, and boilers which allowed higher working pressure, horsepower was increased. With increased horsepower came larger and better ferryboats.

Some seventeen years before the development of the screw-propeller boats, the iron hull made its appearance in New York Harbor with the launching of the *Fulton* and *Farragut* in 1871. Two years later, it appeared on the North River when the Erie Railroad accepted delivery of the ferryboat *Erie,* from the Delaware River Iron Steamboat & Engine Works of Chester, PA, which was launched May 1, 1873. Just like the one-cylinder vertical

beam engine, wood hulls were becoming passé. *Bergen's* hull was of iron. (Use of iron was very short-lived, though, as it was soon replaced by steel.)

These were the major ferry companies of the late 1800s: Hoboken Ferry Co., owned by the Stevens family and operating out of Lackawanna Terminal, Hoboken; the New Jersey Transportation & Ferry Co., by now owned by the Pennsylvania Railroad Co. and operating several routes out of Exchange Place, Jersey City; and the Pavonia Ferry Co., owned by the Erie Railroad Co., operating out of Pavonia Avenue, Jersey City. Each of these companies had a direct effect on the development of the twentieth-century North River ferryboat. Truly, Robert L. Stevens should be considered the grandfather

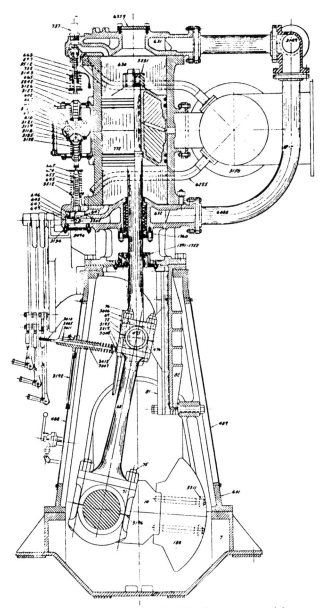

Cross section of a Skinner Marine Unaflow engine, of the type used in the *Meadville* of 1936 and the New York City *Merrell* class boats of 1950.—Courtesy of New York City Department of Marine & Aviation

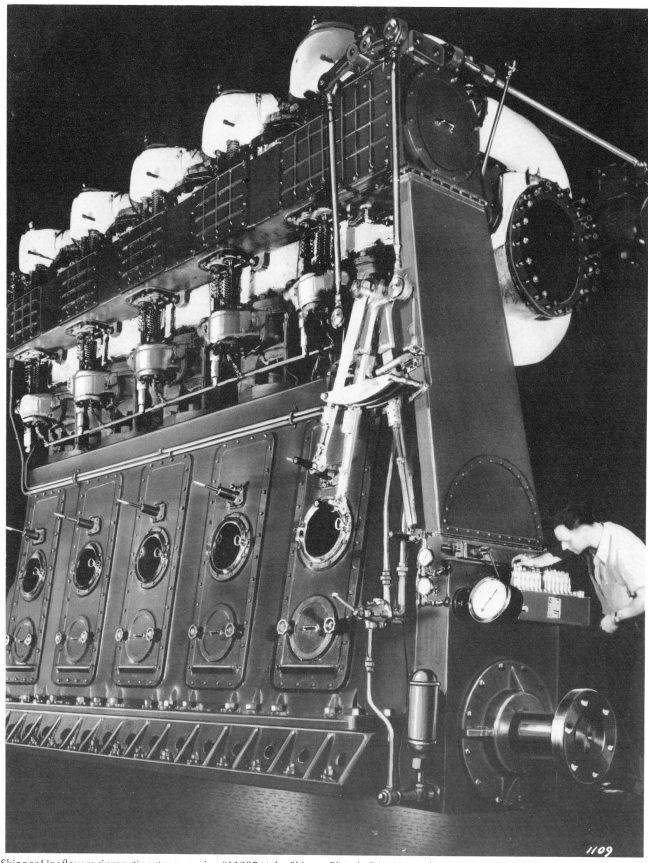

Skinner Unaflow reciprocating steam engine #11287 at the Skinner Plant in Erie, Pennsylvania, in 1935. She was the largest Unaflow engine built at that time and she was placed in the Erie Railroad's ferryboat *Meadville*. — Courtesy of the Skinner Engine Co.

of the North River ferryboat because of his designs of the boats, bridge, and spring rack. Robert Fulton may have launched the first successful steamboat, *North River Steamboat of Clermont;* but Colonel John Stevens launched the first successful ferryboat, *Juliana.* It can be said that the predecessor of the Lackawanna Railroad ferry developed the first successful double-ended screw ferryboat, the single-decked *Bergen;* but engineers and technicians of the other companies also contributed much to the ferryboat development.

Pavonia Ferry Co., which later became the Erie Railroad, built the second screw ferryboat, the *John G. McCullough,* in 1891, again, a single-deck vessel. The Erie also built the first iron-hulled vessel on the North River, the *Erie* of 1873. *McCullough's* main contribution was the first use of the two-cylinder compound engine in a ferryboat. The double-compound reciprocating engine became the most widely used engine in New York Harbor ferryboats. *McCullough* was re-engined to a double compound and double decked in 1906. Forty-five years later, Erie would once again introduce a new engine design to New York Harbor ferryboats, when the *Meadville* was launched with a Skinner Unaflow engine in 1936. But no other railroad would build a new steam ferryboat after *Meadville.*

New Jersey Transportation & Ferry Co., the offspring of Robert Fulton's Jersey Associates, became the Pennsylvania Railroad Company Ferries. It was the first company to double deck its boats. The third screw ferryboat was the Pennsylvania's *Cincinnati* and she had the double-compound steeple engine and double deck which were used in conjunction with the company's new elevated terminal at Exchange Place, Jersey City

and the elevated walkway over West Street at Cortlandt Street, Manhattan. *Cincinnati* was completed in the fall of 1891.

In 1896, Pennsylvania once again came forth with a new dimension in ferryboat design. Its *St. Louis* was the first twin-screw ferryboat. She had two propellers on each end coupled to triple-expansion engines by continuous shafts from bow to stern on each side; she was 1,800 hp.

Unfortunately, only four such boats were built and the model never was used by other ferry companies.

The New York Central System, owner and operator of the West Shore Ferry, was the last railroad ferry operator to enter the transition from sidewheel boats to propeller vessels with the launching of the *West Point* in 1900. Although a latecomer in the design field, the New York Central had, by far, some of the fastest vessels on the river, with the exception of the *Meadville.* All of its boats were converted from coal fired to oil fired, thus requiring only one fireman. This resulted in their ability to maintain a constant steam pressure with very little effort. A visit to the engine- and firerooms of the New York Central *Niagara* on a trip from Cortlandt Street to Weehawken showed a spotless fireroom, in contrast to those same rooms in the coal-fired boats which had a large amount of coal and ash dust in them. The fireroom steel decks were also free of acid corrosion, a major problem with coal.

The ideal steampowered boat—a double-ended, twin-screw, oil-fired vessel using Skinner Unaflow engines—was never developed. There were several factors that prevented this: The Hoboken Ferry Co. had good, well-maintained vessels and no need for a larger

Erie ferryboat *Meadville* launched in 1936 with the first Skinner Unaflow engine in a New York Harbor ferry vessel. Twenty one years later in 1957 she would become the Lackawanna's *Maplewood.* But the Lackawanna Railroad people did not like her as they did not understand the principles of the engine and could not operate her as successfully as the Erie Railroad had done.—Courtesy of Skinner Engine Co.

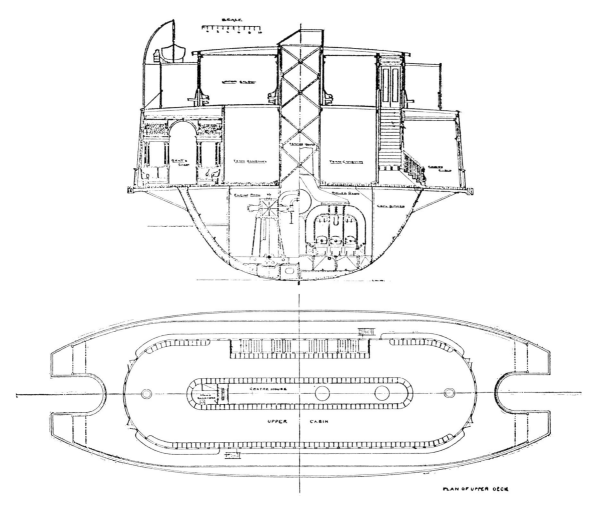

Ferryboat *St. Louis*, 1896. Amidship section and upper deck.

fleet. The Erie, Jersey Central, and New York Central also had well-maintained vessels. The Pennsylvania, on the other hand, no longer had a need for passenger ferries since the opening of Penn Station and the Hudson River tunnels in 1910. Just as boats began to reach the age when companies might consider replacement, the nation was involved in a Depression which was followed by WW II. Only the Erie built one new boat during the Depression. After WW II, rail passenger traffic started to decline and there was a major transition from rail to buses. The ferries then became a costly operation and the building of new boats was a luxury the companies could not afford.

Once again, the Hoboken Ferry Co. took a major step forward. In 1949, it took the *Chatham,* built in 1891 as the *Hamburg,* and rebuilt in 1920, out of service. She was taken to the Brighton Marine Yard where her triple-expansion engine was removed and her boilers stripped and welded closed so that they could be used as fuel tanks. She was rebuilt once again, this time, as a diesel-electric-drive vessel. The marine yard forces and General Motors technicians installed an E.M.D. 1,400 hp diesel. She was renamed the *Lackawanna,* the third ves-

sel to be so named. She returned to active service in 1950. The *Lackawanna* had some problems when she first came out; in fact, on her first trip up from Brighton, Tom Devaney, the Shore Captain, was at the controls and, when he entered the slip in Hoboken, the engine did not reverse and she struck the bridge. So the *Lackawanna* went back to Brighton. The problem was corrected, but it took some time to rebuild the bridge. The *Lackawanna* remained in continuous operation until the closing of the ferry service on November 22, 1967, bringing to a close over seventy-five years of plying across the North River.

Thus, like the railroad locomotive, the New York Harbor ferryboat was destined either to go diesel or become extinct. Unfortunately, with respect to railroad ferry operations, the latter fate prevailed. In 1985, the only remaining ferry operations in New York Harbor are the New York City Municipal or Staten Island Ferry operating from St. George, Staten Island to Whitehall Street, Manhattan; and the U.S. Coast Guard ferry operating from Whitehall to Governor's Island. The City's large vessels are now all diesel since the *Merrell* class boats have been placed in reserve.

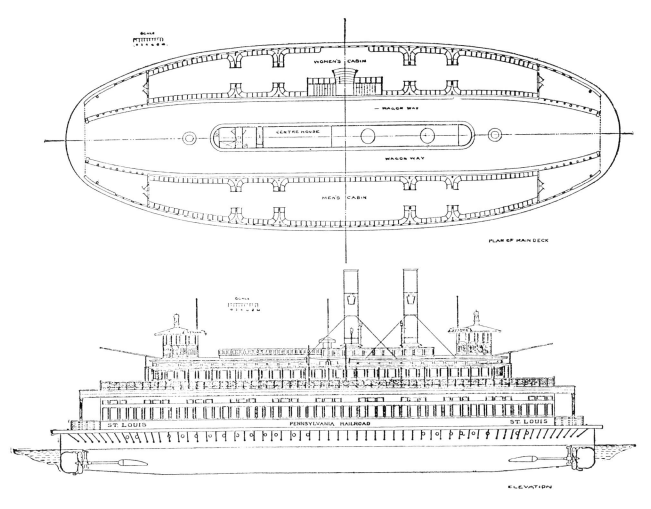

Ferryboat *St. Louis*, Twenty-third Street Ferry, New York, 1896.

The Central Railroad of New Jersey lost the ferryboat *Lakewood* around 1949, when she burned to the guards while in dry dock. The Central chose to rebuild the *Lakewood* with an all-steel superstructure; yet, retaining the steam engine and renaming her *Elizabeth,* she was the third vessel to be so named. *Elizabeth* was the last Jersey Central boat to operate that company's Communipaw route until abandoned April 22, 1967, bringing to a close a ferry route started over 306 years earlier.

During the last decade of the nineteenth century and the first two decades of the twentieth century, the New York Harbor Railroads replaced their entire ferryboat fleets. Prior to the 1888 launching of the Hoboken Ferry Co.'s *Bergen,* the first propeller-driven ferryboat, all ferryboats had been side paddle wheelers. Nine years after the launching of the *Bergen,* the last sidewheel ferryboat was built, for the New York Central Railroad, the *Buffalo.* Nine propeller boats had been built between 1888 and 1897, all proving very successful, yet the Central chose to build another side-wheel, single-deck vessel; this is hard to understand.

The Erie's *John G. McCullough* was the second screw

boat to be launched in the year 1891. Both of these boats remained in active service until after WW II. *McCullough* was renamed twice and finally sold to the Navy, becoming the *YB–48,* and sold in 1946. *Bergen* remained on the North River in service for the Lackawanna Railroad until scrapped in 1953.

The year 1891 was a banner one for ferryboat construction: The *McCullough* was followed by the Pennsylvania Railroad's *Cincinnati,* then the Hoboken Ferry's *Bremen* and *Hamburg.*

In 1892, only one new ferryboat was built, that being the Pennsylvania Railroad's *Washington.* The Hoboken Ferry's *Netherlands* and the Central Railroad of New Jersey's *Easton* and *Mauch Chunk* of 1893 completed ferryboat construction for several years. In 1896, the Pennsylvania Railroad launched the *St. Louis* and *Pittsburgh,* starting another new trend in ferryboat construction, namely, twin-engine and twin-screw boats. Both these boats had two triple-expansion engines and four propellers—two on each end. They also had four watertube boilers. The advantage to having two propellers on each end was that it made the boats more maneuverable, as one engine could be put in reverse and the other run ahead, thus helping the vessel to turn faster. Two more of these boats were subsequently built—the *New Brunswick* in 1897 and the *Philadelphia* in 1899. The odd thing is that no other railroad ever built twin-screw ferryboats. The Pennsylvania's next two boats were single screw.

After the turn of the century, there was a massive rebuilding and new construction program as competitive railroads attempted to outdo one another for the passenger trade. Single-deck boats had a second deck added. Interior design changes were made to improve the passengers' comfort. Separate stairways on the Men's cabin side were installed so that cigar smoke would not travel upstairs. Improvements on the electrical systems providing better illumination, improved heating systems, and many other features were added.

From 1888, with the launching of the first screw-, or propeller-driven, double-end ferry, the *Bergen,* until the last double-end ferryboat, the *Meadville,* was built in 1936 for the Erie Railroad Co., very little change took place in the basic design of the boats.

Most double-end ferry vessels were powered by either double-compound engines (basically, two compound engines coupled back to back) or a triple-expansion engine (combining one high-pressure cylinder, one intermediate cylinder, and one low-pressure cylinder).

The five Erie boats built between 1903 and 1922 all had double-compound engines. The *Meadville* had one Skinner Unaflow engine which had five high-pressure cylinders.

STEAM VERSUS DIESEL

Comparing steam and diesel vessels involves several criteria, as well as whether the viewpoint used is that of management or of worker.

From management's standpoint, a converted vessel is a cost-saving machine. Saving can be measured in several areas:

1. *Fuel*—most railroad steam ferryboats burned expensive anthracite coal; either pea, buckwheat, or a mixture of both. This coal was becoming increasingly expensive as more and more industries discontinued coal use. The railroads themselves were converting to diesel locomotives. They could now buy diesel fuel in bulk and get it cheaper than coal.

2. *Water*—steamboats consumed fresh water. The river below Poughkeepsie had an increasing amount of salt. Therefore, the river at the point where the ferries were crossing was completely salt water, which could be used only for cooling purposes. Ferryboats had either a surface condenser or a jet condenser. The difference is

Construction photo of the Pennsylvania Railroad *Newark* on the ways at T.S. Marvel's yard in Newburgh, New York. From the crowd of people standing around it might suggest that they are getting ready to launch her and the date is June 28, 1902.—Courtesy of The Mariners' Museum, Newport News, Virginia

THE RAILROAD FERRIES OF THE HUDSON

One of the last steam ferryboats in New York Harbor. The *Cornelius G. Kolff* (1951) is 2285 tons and 269 feet long. She is powered by a 6000 hp. Skinner Unaflow engine. She and her sisters, the *Pvt. Joseph Merrell* and *Verrazzano* are the last of a breed, steam power! Say what you want about diesel power, there is nothing like the smell and rhythm of a well running steam engine to someone who worked on boats.

that a surface condenser cools live steam and returns the water via a circulating pump back into the fresh-water tanks for reuse. The jet condenser mixes the steam with salt water and dumps it overboard. Therefore, a vessel with a jet condenser used considerably more water than one with a surface condenser.

Most cities also based sewage rates on the volume of water used. Sewage rates in most cases were four or five times greater than the actual water cost, so for every gallon of water taken aboard a boat a sewage rate was assessed. (Railroads fought this assessment for years in Hudson County.)

3. *Manpower* — the "black gang," as fireroom personnel are commonly called, was reduced by 50% on a diesel boat. Most steamboats on the North River had an engineer, oiler, and two firemen. Since a diesel boat had no boilers to tend there was no need for the firemen.

A second manpower area where management saved was the coal gangs. All of the ferryboats needed coal

Fireman Paul Cainnariado prepares to throw a shovel of coal into the starboard boiler of the ferryboat *Youngstown*. Large hoe like objects hanging just under the ladder are used to pull the fires out of the ash pan just under the firebox door. Each of the Erie ferryboats had two boilers with three fireboxes each. — Dan Biernacki Collection

Fire pump and condenser hot well on the starboard side of the engine room, Ferryboat *Youngstown*.

ashes were removed, in most cases, by the end of one round trip from Jersey City to Chambers Street. The *Lackawanna* did not need ashes pulled, so the railroad cut down on weekend overtime by running the diesel boat nights and weekends.

For the company, it thus was simple economics. From the standpoint of the workers, however, except the captain, a diesel boat could not compare to a steamboat.

Her deck equipment was the same as the steamboat. One good feature of the diesel was that she seldom needed water, which the deckhands had to put in. A boat with a surface condenser usually took water only once a watch.

A diesel boat is much noisier than a steamboat. The *Lackawanna* had a continual whine and was nicknamed "Whinning Winnie" by passengers and crew alike.

The *Lackawanna* was a cold boat. She had forced-air space heaters at each end of the cabins, but they were not sufficient for the area they had to cover.

When you got wet in bad weather you either stayed that way throughout your watch or you found a change of clothes. Extra deckhands had no lockers on the boats; theirs were on the dock. In most cases, you never left a lot of clothing in your locker. Here again, the steamboat was far superior, as you could always duck down in the fireroom and dry yourself and your clothes. On a damp, foggy, cold day it was always a godsend to be able to go in the centerhouse and just stand over the engine on the

brought on and ashes taken off. This problem was simple on tugboats, but not on ferryboats. Tugboats used to pull alongside the coal bunker and the oiler and fireman would open deck hatches and dump the coal in from chutes. Ashes were also handled by the crew. A tug pulled alongside the ash dock and a chute was placed on a steam-powered suction pump in the fireroom. The fireman shoveled the ashes into an opening in the fireroom deck and they were sucked out through the chute to the dock. Ferryboats could not do this. In 1947 when I started to work for the Erie, they coaled the boats at night, with horse-drawn two-wheeled wagons. Several years later, they used a coal truck and the daytime yard gang. Whether horse and wagon or truck, the principle was the same. There was a hatch about 36 in. × 72 in. in the deck, in the gangway near the fireroom hatch. The coal gang would fill the hatch with coal. Once the boat was all coaled up, they would then park their truck over the hatch. The fireroom ladder hatch was large enough for an ash barrel to be dropped through it. There was a large ring attached to the gangway ceiling over the hatch, to which a pulley was attached used to lower the barrels to the fireroom. Ashmen would descend into the fireroom and fill the barrels. Another ashman was in the back of the truck to guide the barrels up through the hatch as the truckdriver handled a power winch on the side of the truck. This operation continued until all the

Engineer P. Chappell makes an entry on the Engineer's Log of the ferryboat *Youngstown*. – Dan Biernacki Collection

grating and let the heat filter up through your clothes. But with the diesel boat, the heat was greatly reduced and the noise would quickly drive you out. In fact, the engineer had a glass-enclosed, soundproofed booth which he stayed in as much as possible. Another undesirable thing about the diesel boats was the inescapable smell of the diesel fuel.

Management looked at the diesels as a way to save money, which became a major factor in later years. However, crewmen who had a choice of working on a diesel or steamboat invariably chose the steamboat. The crew of the diesel *Lackawanna*, for example, always liked it when she was in the shop and the steam *Scranton* ran in her place.

CHAPTER 6

CENTRAL RAILROAD OF NEW JERSEY NORTH RIVER FERRY OPERATIONS

The history of the Central Railroad of New Jersey's Communipaw ferry, like many other North River crossings, can be linked back to services started before the United States became a nation.

The first record of the Communipaw ferry was in 1661, when the New Netherlands Council granted William Jensen a charter to operate a ferry from the settlement of Communipaw, just about a mile inland from the Central Railroad of New Jersey's Communipaw terminal, to New Amsterdam. This ferry was operated for many years by various residents of the Village of Communipaw. It reportedly fell into disuse about 1783, when the British evacuated Paulus Hook.

The History of Forms of Government of the City of Jersey City, published in the municipal codes, indicate that the first settlement in New Jersey was at Communipaw, which stretched roughly from present-day Johnston Avenue south to Caven Point, where an indentation of New York Bay, called South Cove or Communipaw Bay (now filled in by the railroads), reached up to present-day Phillips Street. A house was built there in 1633 for Jan Evertsen Bout, Superintendent of the colony, then called Pavonia. This tiny settlement was destroyed by the Indians some years later after cruel and selfish treatment by Superintendent William Kieft. No other settlement was established until Peter Stuyvesant, Administrator of New Amsterdam, granted permission to Teilman Van Vleck, on March 1, 1660, to build a stockaded settlement behind "Gemoenepaen," the Indian name from which Communipaw is derived.

It was two hundred years later, in 1860, that the New Jersey legislature granted permission to the Central Rail-road of New Jersey to extend its line over Newark Bay to the Hudson River at Jersey City. Prior to this time, the Central entered New York via the Elizabethtown Ferry from Elizabethport on the west side of Newark Bay. It was at this time that the Central of New Jersey filled in South Cove, or Communipaw Bay, upon which it built the massive Communipaw terminal facilities that served it so well for over a hundred years. The terminal and ferry slips were operated from this filled area.

In the year 1863, the Central let the contract for construction of its double-end ferryboat for the Liberty Street line, the *Central,* to Devine Burtis of Brooklyn, NY. Her overall length was 225 ft. with a registered length of 217 ft., breadth of 33 ft., and depth of 12 ft. She was 1,023 gross tons, constructed of wood hull, single deck, with a vertical-beam engine placed on the deck at the New York end. Her engine and boiler were constructed by the Newburgh Iron Works of Newburgh, NY. The *Central* was documented first on May 11, 1865, and remained in active service for the company until taken out of service in 1900. The *Central* became the basic design boat for all future CNJ sidewheelers.

A sister to the *Central,* the *Communipaw,* also built in 1863 and documented the same date, was another Newburgh Iron Works' product. These two boats were the first to operate to Liberty Street terminal, which was completed in 1865. They were the mainstay of the Liberty Street service until 1867, when the third Devine Burtis boat, the *Elizabeth,* was delivered. A fourth boat, the *Plainfield,* came again from the same builder, in 1869. Seven years were to pass before the last CNJ sidewheeler was to be built.

The Statue of Liberty, New York Harbor's most notable and impressive possession. Presently the subject of a legal battle between New York State and some New Jersey residents who believe that she should rightfully be within New Jersey's jurisdiction. Symbol of Central Railroad of New Jersey.

In 1874, the Central of New Jersey decided to expand its ferry service by opening an uptown line to Clarkson Street. For this service, the fifth sidewheel boat was ordered. In 1876, the *Fanwood* was launched and took her place in service. The uptown line opened in September, 1876 and ceased operation on May 10, 1877. *Fanwood* took her place on the Liberty Street line. The *Fanwood* was equipped with electric lights in 1883. This improvement proved so successful that all the other boats were subsequently so equipped.

The Central of New Jersey continued to operate with these five boats for over fifteen years and, during that time, the boats were painted white (for a while, the *Communipaw* was painted cream). In 1892, all the boats were painted dark green.

The Baltimore & Ohio, which had been running its trains into Jersey City for many years, wanted a connection with its ferry service to Whitehall Street, Manhattan, NYC so that its passengers could have a direct connection to the Third Avenue elevated trains. In order to accomplish this new service, the Central let out a contact for its first two propeller-driven ferryboats in 1893. Harlan & Hollingsworth of Wilmington, DE was the successful bidder. Harlan & Hollingsworth built the *Easton* and *Mauch Chunk,* both of whose overall length were 158 ft., with a registered length of 145 ft., breadth of 32 ft., and depth of 14 ft. These two boats were single-deck vessels and only 643 gross tons, much lighter than any of the other Central boats. Both vessels were delivered in 1893, but did not go into service on the Whitehall run until 1896. They were chartered out to other companies for some three years.

The new service was known as The Royal Blue Ferry. This line ran without major incident until June 14, 1901, when the *Mauch Chunk,* about to enter the east slip at Whitehall Street, rammed and sank the outbound Staten Island ferryboat, *Northfield,* which had just pulled out of an adjoining slip with a heavy load of passengers. Only four people were killed, but the *Northfield* was virtually demolished.

In 1901, the City of New York acquired the Staten Island Ferry from the Baltimore & Ohio subsidiary Staten Island Railway, and the Jersey Central was told that it must vacate the ferry slips at Whitehall. The final trip of the Royal Blue Ferry was on Saturday, June 24, 1905.

As the *Easton* and *Mauch Chunk* were too small for the Liberty Street line, it was decided to try them on the newly proposed 23rd Street line. But the lack of sufficient boiler capacity proved their downfall. The *Easton* was sold to the 125th Street Ferry and renamed *Leonia,* while the *Mauch Chunk* was sold and became the *Margate* of the Delaware River Ferry Co., a subsidiary of the Philadelphia & Reading Railroad.

On September 8, 1900, the sidewheel ferryboat, *Plainfield,* was the first of the Central's sidewheelers to be disposed of after she burned at the Communipaw shops.

In 1901, the Jersey Central's first two new double-decked, propeller ferryboats, the *Lakewood* and *Bound Brook,* were delivered by Harlan & Hollingsworth. These boats were steelhulled of a gross tonnage of 1,016, with a registered length of 200 ft., breadth of 44 ft., and depth of 17 ft., powered by an 1,157 hp triple-expansion engine with steam supplied by three return-tube boilers of 170 psi steam pressure.

The ferryboat *Elizabeth* became the next fatality, when she also caught fire and burned at Jersey City on October 22, 1901. New construction once again, in 1902, was evident when Harlan & Hollingsworth delivered a third vessel of the *Lakewood* class—the *Red Bank.* Also in that year, a new joint terminal was established at

Central Railroad of New Jersey's Communipaw Terminal in Jersey City before the facade was built over the ferry house and slips. Sidewheel *Central* built in 1863 and her younger sister *Fanwood* of 1876 await to serve the public. — Warren Lee Collection

Central Railroad of New Jersey's Liberty Street, New York Ferry Terminal in the early days. From an old print.

Elizabeth I built in 1867 by Devine Burtis, Brooklyn, New York. From an old Central Railroad of New Jersey painting.—
Warren F. Lee Collection

Governor's Island Ferryboat *Major General William Hart* leaving her slip at Whitehall. Whitehall was where Royal Blue Ferry route landed.

A 1938 photograph of the *Lakewood* built in 1901 for the Central Railroad of New Jersey. Eleven years later she would burn to the guards while in drydock at Jersey City and rebuilt and renamed *Elizabeth II* in 1950. She would run to the end of the ferry service in 1967 and be sold and renamed *Second Sun*. She is presently moored at Salem, on the Delaware River, as a display vessel. — Warren Lee Collection

Jersey Central's *Bound Brook* heads for West 23rd Street with the downtown Jersey City skyline in the background.

the foot of Johnston Avenue, Jersey City. The present large terminal complex was opened in April, 1914. The train shed measured 818 ft. by 370 ft. and had 18 tracks with Bush train sheds. The train concourse measured 383 ft. by 75 ft., and the upper level, 302 ft. by 50 ft. The upper level provided access between the upper deck of the ferryboat and trains via ramps and escalators. Four double-decked steel buildings adjoined the ferry slips to accommodate the baggage room, mailroom, local ferry waiting room, and stationary department.

This entire enlarged service was operated with great elegance. The main building of the Jersey City terminal resembles a great French chateau, with its Mansard roof, cupola, and gilded steeple. A new, large ferry terminal was also built at Liberty Street in 1902. It was a copper-clad, steel-frame building with Neo-classic motif. Stationmaster Ross Appleton presided, wearing white gloves, a high starched collar, and a swallow-tailed coat, until the 1930s. Two porters handed out face towels in the Men's room and, lest the passengers step in the mire, all horsedrawn vehicles were followed by a porter with a broom and shovel. The outside had fluted Neo-classic pilasters and columns with ornamental cornices. The great two-story waiting room had Rosewood Ionic columns with ornamented cornices and friezes. The brass

door handles were polished daily, and the Tiffany glass skylight was vacuumed twice a week. The Jersey City terminal had five slips, and the Liberty Street, two—all equipped for upper-deck loading and with electric bridge hoists.

With the arrival of the *Red Bank,* the thirty-nine-year-old *Central,* which had been out of service for two years, was scrapped. Modernization still seemed to be the order of the day for the Central of New Jersey and, in 1904, a local shipbuilder, the Crescent Shipyard of Elizabethport, NJ, delivered the *Plainfield.* The *Plainfields'* delivery marked the first boat to be built for the CNJ by a builder other than Harlan & Hollingsworth since the *Fanwood* was built in 1876. She was also the second vessel to bear that name. Her dimensions were somewhat different than the *Lakewood* class. She was heavier, with a gross tonnage of 1,255, her registered length was 200 ft., breadth of 43 ft., and depth of 15 ft., but she was powered by the same type of 1,157 hp triple-expansion engine and three return-tube boilers. Not to be outdone, Harlan & Hollingsworth delivered two new boats that same year, the *Elizabeth II* and the *Wilkes Barre.* The *Elizabeth* was the second vessel to bear that name. Both of these boats had their plans altered for upper-deck loading to accommodate passengers at the new (1905)

On a cold winters day the Jersey Central tug *Newark* works behind the *Cranford,* in a heavy accumulation of ice at Liberty Street.

Central Railroad of New Jersey's F/B *Elizabeth II* taken July 26, 1936 by John P. Scharle. — James Lee Collection

West 23rd Street terminal. They became the regular boats on this line. But the honor of first trip went to the *Red Bank,* on Sunday morning, June 25, 1905, the day after the Whitehall service ended.

The *Elizabeth* and *Wilkes Barre* were slightly smaller than the previous H&H *Lakewood*-class boats. Their dimensions were registered length of 191 ft., breadth of 44 ft., and depth of 15 ft. and a heavier gross tonnage of 1,197, powered again, by an 1,157 hp triple-expansion engine with steam supplied by three return-tube boilers.

The year 1905 saw two more *Elizabeth*-class vessels delivered by Harlan & Hollingsworth, the *Cranford* and the *Somerville.*

With the arrival of these two latest additions to the Jersey Central fleet, the last two remaining sidewheelers, the sixty-three-year-old *Communipaw* and the fifty-nine-year-old *Fanwood,* were towed to Gregory's "bone yard" in Perth Amboy and burned on July 4, 1906. With the disposal of these last sidewheelers, the Jersey Central had a fleet of eight boats all less than six years' old. For several years, there was no need for any further construction.

The *Westfield,* the fifth and last of the *Elizabeth* class, was delivered in 1911. Two years later, in 1913, a totally different boat, the *Bayonne,* was delivered; once again, Harlan & Hollingsworth was the builder. *Bayonne* was 1,334 gross tons, with a registered length of 201 ft., breadth of 44 ft., and a depth of 15 ft. She was powered by a 1,400 hp triple-expansion engine with steam supplied by two single-end scotch boilers. She had a spoon bow, which purpose was to push the water away

from the boat rather than to her side, thus reducing the water taken over the bow in bad weather. Unfortunately, *Bayonne* was a maverick and she acted like a submarine nosing into the water, resulting in more water, not less, being taken over the bow. At times, she took so much water that it went completely through the gangways and off the stern. Once this was corrected, the *Bayonne* gave the Central many excellent years of service. The delivery of the *Bayonne* completed the Central Railroad of New Jersey's new-boat construction. It now had one of the finest fleets on the North River — ten boats and the oldest only thirteen years. The year 1913 also saw the Lehigh Valley transfer its passenger train operation to the Central's Communipaw terminal.

The Jersey Central, like the other railroads of the nation, was taken over by the United States Government on December 28, 1917 and placed under the control of the U.S. Railroad Administration. The USRA changed several procedures on the railroad, but very few on the ferries. Ferryboats were used during WW I to ferry troops from the rail terminals to the embarkation piers. The only major change by the USRA to affect the ferry service was the shifting of the Baltimore & Ohio and the Lehigh Valley passenger operations to New York's Penn Station of the Pennsylvania Railroad, thus reducing some passenger ferry traffic. On February 29, 1920, the USRA officially returned all railroads to the private sector. The Baltimore & Ohio trains, however, did not start using the CNJ's Communipaw terminal until August 29, 1926. The Lehigh Valley through trains never did return to the Johnston Avenue facility, remaining, instead, in

Central Railroad of New Jersey's West 23rd Street Terminal from an old postcard published by the Union News Company. — James Lee Collection

The New York skyline at her stern the Central Railroad of New Jersey's *Cranford* heads for Jersey City's Communipaw Terminal, in July 1939. — Library of Congress

Westfield carrying a small group of people, a United States mail truck and Railway Express trailer and sporting the Central's new Statue of Liberty logo on her stack heads for Jersey City.

Jersey City Communipaw Terminal of the Central Railroad of New Jersey in 1941. The 23rd Street boat *Bound Brook* is in #2 slip, the *Elizabeth II* is in #3 slip and the *Bayonne* is tied up in #4 slip. — James Lee collection

Penn Station until all passenger service was discontinued in 1961 although Lehigh Valley commuter trains operated to Jersey City until June, 1948).

The ferry service continued to operate three major routes during the years between WW I and WW II: the Liberty Street, West 23rd Street, and the Atlantic Highland steamers, *Monmouth* and *Sandy Hook.* These two boats made daily trips between West 40th St., the Battery in New York, and Atlantic Highlands and Sandy Hook. One's regular railroad ticket was valid on these two very fast, twin-screw steamers. The *Monmouth* was built in 1888 by Harlan & Hollingsworth, who also built the *Sandy Hook,* delivering her in 1889. They were 260 ft. long and powered by two triple-expansion engines. Early in WW II, these Highland steamers were discontinued. The *Monmouth* was requisitioned for military use in 1941 and the *Sandy Hook,* in 1943. The Jersey Central never restored this service after the war.

November 14, 1941, saw the second major change take place on the Central ferry service with the abandonment of the West 23rd Street ferry. Realizing the need for vessels to cover wartime needs, the Central retained all its boats until the end of the war.

In 1939, the Central of New Jersey filed a petition in federal court for reorganization under the federal bankruptcy statutes, citing its inability to pay New Jersey real estate taxes and the interest due on its outstanding bonds as the chief factor for reorganization.

After WW II, in 1945, the Jersey Central did not attempt to reopen the West 23rd Street ferry service which it had discontinued in 1941. The *Bayonne* and *Elizabeth II* were laid up at the dock just north of the terminal at the foot of Johnston Avenue. Jersey Central trustee Walter P. Gardner applied to the federal court for permission to scrap the two vessels. On September 8, 1947, Federal Judge Guy L. Fakes signed the order, permitting the scrapping of these two boats, from which the company would realize about $30,000.

In 1949, the ICC approved the Central Railroad of New Jersey's reorganization plan. The Central was finally in the black again. April 23, 1949, was also the one-hundredth anniversary of the company's name and, on August 2, the plan was to take effect. But, all of 1949 was not a happy year, especially for the marine department. The forty-eight-year-old ferryboat *Lakewood* was on dry dock for her annual inspection and repair at the company yard behind the Statue of Liberty when she caught fire and burned totally, destroying her wooden superstructure. Oh! if the Central had only kept the *Elizabeth II* or *Bayonne!* The Jersey Central, like the West Shore, did not have the advantage of a Hudson Tube connection to fall back on. It had only an independent Crosstown bus which ran from its Johnston Avenue terminal through the Lafayette and downtown sections of Jersey City, stopping at the Grove Street tube station and ending at the Erie terminal at Pavonia Avenue. There was no way that this busline could handle CNJ New York-bound commuters. The boat had to be rebuilt.

The rebuilt *Lakewood* returned to service in 1950, a totally new vessel from the guards up, with even her name changed. The all-steel-superstructured *Elizabeth II,* the third vessel to bear this name, was placed in service. She also presented a new, modern look for the future Jersey Central boats to follow. The traditional dark-green paint had been replaced with a new two-tone green paint scheme; the dark-green pilothouses and hurricane deck structures were now painted white, as well as the lifeboats and the former yellow lettering on the boat's sides. The pilothouse nameboards were also lettered white on a red background, and she sported a

Central Railroad of New Jersey steamer *Monmouth* with the New York skyline in the background. Photo by Alexander Grnelin, in 1931. — James Lee Collection

Steamer *Sandy Hook* of Central Railroad of New Jersey's Highland Route fame was snapped by Alexander Grnelin on September 17, 1932 off of the Lackawana Terminal in Hoboken. — James Lee Collection

Plainfield II after her stack had been shortened and radar added in the early 1950's, but still in early Central Railroad of New Jersey dark green. — Warren F. Lee Collection

A single truck and passenger on her deck as the *Wilkes Barre* approaches the slip at Jersey City in 1964 are a good indication how the ferry traffic has declined in the mid 1960's. Aldene Plan will bring an end to all central ferry service in 1967.

Elizabeth II

completely new, low, short-tapered stack, also painted white with the red-and-white Statue of Liberty logo displayed brightly on its side.

Within a few years, the Jersey Central would have given all its boats an updated modern look. It also equipped them with radar, the only railroad to put this equipment on its boats. The only other change was that, in later years, the new, modern stacks were painted black. The DL&W railroad did try radar on its diesel boat, the *Lackawanna,* which was where Ray Baxter saw it operate.

With the end of the Korean Conflict in 1955, the railroads started to feel the effects of reductions in freight revenue, the effects of Hurricane Diane, which took a large toll on fixed structures in the western areas served by the Central of New Jersey, compounded by a decline in coal traffic and the gasoline revolution. Through all this, the Jersey Central ferry operation continued on, while others abandoned them. The river traffic was in decline. The lone Pennsylvania Railroad ferryboat, which had operated between Exchange Place, Jersey City and Cortlandt Street, Manhattan, for so many years, had long since become a memory, having been officially abandoned on December 31, 1949.

The green and white Erie Railroad boats were also no longer plying between Jersey City's Pavonia Avenue terminal and Chambers Street, having been abandoned December 12, 1958, when the Erie completed its consolidation with the DL&W at Hoboken, NJ. This left only three railroad company ferries operating: the New York Central System's West Shore ferry; the Delaware, Lackawanna & Western's Hoboken Ferry Co. from Hoboken, NJ; and the CNJ Communipaw line. Things were not looking good for marine traffic in New York Harbor.

Since the turn of the century, the Baltimore & Ohio, parent company of the CNJ, and its affiliate, the Philadelphia & Reading Co., operated many trains out of the Johnston Avenue terminal, including a deluxe limousine bus service. A passageway on the north side of the terminal allowed direct access for these buses from the ferry to trackside platforms.

The bus would pull up to the platform, discharge its passengers, who had only to walk across the platform to waiting trains while their baggage was transferred from bus to train for them. Arriving passengers would step off the train to awaiting buses, which took them to some six B&O terminals in Manhattan and Brooklyn, including one at Rockfeller Center in midtown Manhattan.

Such famous trains as the *Capitol Limited, National Limited, Shenandoah,* and the *Royal Blues* were just some of the B&O trains using the Central's terminal. The Philadelphia & Reading's crack steamliner, *The Crusader,* seen daily in the Jersey City passenger yard after she made her run from Philadelphia, and the *Wallstreeter* were other famous Reading trains using the terminal. The CNJ also had its share of high-class varnish in trains like the *Queen of the Valley, The Blue Comet,* and *the Harrisburger.*

The B&O buses, at times, would completely fill the ferryboat, and the long lines of vehicles waiting to cross would have to wait for the next boat. One interesting thing was the way the B&O would turn these buses in the trainshed. A turntable was built at the west end of the trainshed between the tracks, and the buses were turned on it so that the passengers could step right from the bus to the platform and then onto the train.

Declining passenger business caused the B&O to discontinue all train service between Baltimore, Philadelphia, and New York in the late 1950s. The loss of this traffic was felt by the Jersey Central.

The Jersey Central itself started to reduce its long-haul service as the *Blue Comet, Harrisburger,* and *Queen of the Valley* were discontinued or cut back, shortening the runs. More and more people started using the modern buses of local transit companies like Public Service, and Somerset Transit, while the long-distance travelers became patrons of Greyhound and others like it. The U.S. Government did not help the situation any with the creation of the Highway Post Office vehicles, or HPOs, as they were known. HPOs were a highway version of the Railway Post Office cars used on long-distance trains. They were built like buses, except that they had fewer windows. The rear part of the unit was where the mail pouches were stored, while the front part had the pouch holders and mail-sorting tables and compartments just like the inside of an RPO car. These units would pick up their mail at the CNJ, Erie, and DLW mail terminals and then travel along the parallel highways to the railroad, stopping at local post offices where they picked up and delivered the mail. Mail was an additional source of revenue to passenger trains and, as it started to be removed from the trains, the cost of operating them went up.

In order to recapture some of its business that was lost to the buses, the Central of New Jersey created the Jersey Central Lines Bus Co. and, for several years, operated a bus line between New York City and Allentown, PA along old U.S. Route 22. I believe this route's franchise was later sold to Public Service and is still operated by New Jersey Transit today.

Early in 1959, the New York Central System departed from the ferry business with approval for total abandonment of both its lines—the Weehawken Ferry (42nd St.) and the West Shore Ferry (Cortlandt St.) The *Stony Point* departed Cortlandt Street, Manhattan, at 6:00 P.M. March 24, 1959, receiving her final salute of three blasts of the whistle from her aging sisters of the Jersey Central and Lackawanna Railroads, who were left to carry on a three-hundred-year tradition of taking persons and goods from one side of the Hudson to the other for a fee.

The financial picture of the Jersey Central grew darker with every passing day, month, and year. In March 1962, Perry M. Shoemaker resigned as Chairman of the Erie Lackawanna Railroad Co. and accepted the presidency of the ailing Central Railroad of New Jersey. The question was, what could the fifty-year-old Shoemaker do for the Central? Shoemaker was a long time New Jer-

B&O Railroad through train connection buses used the Central railroad ferries between Manhattan and the Communipaw Terminal in Jersey City. An old vintage motor coach drives aboard a CNJ boat. Circa 1934.

THE RAILROAD FERRIES OF THE HUDSON

Fairfield Aerial Survey photograph of the Central Railroad of New Jersey's Jersey City Communipaw Terminal Complex taken in the spring of 1949. Black Tom and L.V. Grain elevator is in upper left. – James Lee Collection

sey resident, living in Short Hills on the Lackawanna. He had been an ardent fighter for fairer taxing of the railroads in New Jersey, especially by Hudson County. Jersey City, at one time, derived over 50% of its taxes from the railroads. Shoemaker had threatened to halt and abandon all commuter service, while president of the Lackawanna, if tax relief was not made a reality in New Jersey. New Jersey was just starting to listen, and a bond issue was on the ballot of the November, 1962 general election. He also was cosponsor of the terminal and track consolidation between the Erie and Lackawanna Railroads, in 1956, and also of the merger of the two companies. The big question was, could he pull a rabbit out of the hat for the Central?

As each year passed, the Central's fleet of once-elegant ferryboats was getting older and more costly to operate, boilers were getting weaker and nearing a point of replacement. Should Shoemaker consider converting the boats to diesel as his people had on the Lackawanna? After all options were considered, the bigger money-saver was to do what the Erie had done – consolidate the passenger terminal with that of another railroad – but where and with whom?

In 1962, the Port Authority of New York was ordered to absorb the bankrupt Hudson & Manhattan Railroad into its authority complex. The Port Authority did not like this very much, but "powers that be" – the state legislatures of New Jersey and New York – had spoken. The new company became known as PATH, for Port Authority Trans-Hudson.

What could PATH do for the Jersey Central? Path trains used the same station in Newark as the Pennsylvania Railroad, as the Pennsy owned the Newark-to-Jersey-City part of the line, which was later sold to PATH. There was no way for PATH to be extended down to the CNJ terminal in either Newark or Jersey City. The CNJ had to get to PATH. In 1918, the U.S. Railroad Administration had rerouted the Lehigh Valley passenger trains from the Jersey Central terminal to Penn Station, New York. This was accomplished by building a connection near Meeker Avenue, Newark where the Valley crossed over the Pennsy Mainline below Hunter

Ferry slip gates at the Jersey Central's Communipaw Terminal, Jersey City. Jersey City Police Department photograph.

Tower. That connection was still in place but no longer used, since the Valley had discontinued passenger service. An idea began to take shape; would it materialize? There was a possibility, since the Lehigh Valley and the Central crossed each other, some fifteen miles from Jersey City, between Roselle Park and Cranford. All the connections were possible and the Aldene Plan was put on paper to route CNJ trains to Penn Station Newark via the LV.[1]

Bound Brook and *Westfield,* having long since been retired and scrapped, now left the aging *Red Bank, Plainfield, Cranford, Wilkes Barre,* and the rebuilt *Elizabeth* operating on the Liberty Street line, while the *Somerville* was out of service and being cannibalized for parts to keep the other boats running.

In 1964, the *Red Bank* and *Plainfield* were retired and taken out of service, then *Cranford* and *Wilkes Barre* followed in 1965. This left only the *Elizabeth* running. One boat could not handle all the Central's passengers so, in February 1965, the former electric ferries, *The Tides* and *The Narrows,* were leased from the City of New York. They had been out of service since the closing of the 69th Street Brooklyn-Staten Island ferry in 1964. These two boats now provided the Central the capability of offering ferry service to its passengers. The bad thing about these boats was that they were built to carry cars, rather than passengers, thus they had no lower cabins and were more open to the elements than the old Central boats.

---

[1]A physical connection was built between the Lehigh Valley Railroad and the Central Railroad of New Jersey at Aldene, N.J. Now trains could operate directly from the CNJ to the LV and vice versa.

The Central maintained the three boats' schedule for better than two years, using the *Elizabeth* and the two leased boats. Then, the Aldene Plan was complete: New schedules were worked out; labor agreements and trackage rights were resolved; crew familiarization and qualifications over the new tracks of the Lehigh Valley and the Pennsy that were going to be used were undertaken; and the new storage and yard facilities in Harrison, NJ were completed. All was ready for the Central Railroad of New Jersey to use the Pennsylvania Station in Newark, NJ. Central passengers would actually benefit by the move in that they could now go either to downtown Manhattan via the PATH, direct to midtown via Penn trains to Penn Station, or take the PATH uptown line to 6th Avenue & 33rd Street, with stops in between.

On Tuesday, April 25, 1967, the *Elizabeth,* the last remaining steamboat of the Jersey Central, assisted by the two leased city diesels—*The Tides* and *The Narrows*—finished out their day's work, tying up at Jersey City's Communipaw terminal and bringing to a close a 306-year service started by William Jensen in 1661. On Wednesday, April 26, 1967, all Central trains ran via Aldene to Newark's Penn Station.

The *Elizabeth,* sold to PSE&G (Public Service Electric & Gas Co.), is now serving as a floating energy display at Salem, NJ, having been renamed *The Second Sun.* Both the *The Tides* and *The Narrows* were returned to the City of New York, which later sold them to the U.S. Coast Guard for use on the Governor's Island-to-Whitehall ferry. *The Tides* remains in operation today, while the *The Narrows* was stripped by the Coast Guard for parts and her hull later sold and converted into a restaurant.

The Liberty Street terminal, along with the Cortlandt

Ferry bridge at Communipaw Terminal, taken from the deck of the *Cranford*, showing large hog frame construction. Jersey City Police Department photograph.

The Central Railroad's *Somerville* laid-up at the foot of Johnston Avenue, just above the ferry slips. She was being canabilized for parts to keep her sisters running. Note that her radar is gone and part of her quarterdeck has been knocked off.

Stripped of any useable parts by the Central the *Red Bank* awaits the scrappers torch at Black Tom, Jersey City, in 1964.

Street terminal, used by the Pennsylvania and West Shore, have long since been demolished and the riverfront filled in as part of New York City's new Battery Park City.

The famous Central Railroad of New Jersey terminal in Jersey City is now owned by the State of New Jersey and has been restored as part of the Liberty State Park Complex, which now takes in all of the reclaimed land once known as Communipaw Bay, or South Cove.

Maybe, someday, the State of New Jersey and PSE&G will come to some kind of agreement and let *The Second Sun* return to Jersey City and take her rightful place once again in the ferry slip as the *Elizabeth*.

Of all the Central Railroad of New Jersey boats, the one which I remember best is the *Cranford*. For, on a day early in November 1952, as I returned home on the *U.S.S. General Muir*, which docked at a Staten Island pier, tied to the end of the pier was the *Cranford*. It was she who brought me up, passing by the Statue of Liberty, to the Central terminal for the short train ride to Camp Kilmer, where I would be discharged from the Army — hence, to return home and back to work on the Erie's *Meadville*.

Public Service Electric & Gas Co. still owns a ferryboat named *The Second Sun*. She no longer plys back and forth, but is permanently moored at the Salem, New Jersey Generating Station at the Floating Energy Information Center. *Second Sun* is the former Central Railroad of New Jersey's *Elizabeth* ex *Lakewood*. — Public Service Electric & Gas Co. photograph

CHAPTER 7

PENNSYLVANIA RAILROAD FERRY AND ITS PREDECESSOR COMPANIES

Like the Central Railroad of New Jersey's Communipaw Ferry, the Pennsylvania Railroad Ferry predated the American Revolution. As the villages which comprise present-day Jersey City grew, so did the need for transportation. The Paulus Hook section of Jersey City is about a mile north of Communipaw. It took its name from the patent of Michael Pauw. Later, the English corrupted the name to Powles Hook, and both spellings are in use to this day. The "hook" was an island of relatively higher ground separated from the mainland to the west by tidal marshes that were inundated twice daily. Communipaw Bay lay to the south and Harsimus Cove, to the north. For the early settlers on Paulus Hook, a direct ferry to Manhattan was infinitely preferable to the roundabout route using the Communipaw Ferry, with its New Jersey dock far to the southwest, around Communipaw Bay, and a longer water crossing. Even at an early date, informal ferry services must have been available, as James Fenimore Cooper, in his 1845 novel, *Satanstoe,* set in the year 1757, has the following dialogue concerning this matter:

> "I should have sent Evans to Yale, had it not been for the miserable manner of speaking English they have in New England," resumed my grandfather; "and I had no wish to have a son who might pass for a Cornishman. We shall have to send this boy to Newark, in New Jersey. The distance is not so great, and we shall be certain he will not get any of your Roundhead notions of religion, too." [Author (A. G. A.) notes the early origins of Yale-Princeton rivalry.] "Colonel Brom, you Dutch are not altogether free from these distressing follies."
>
> "Debble a pit!" growled the colonel, through his pipe; for no devotee of liberalism and latitudinarianism in religion could

be more adverse to extra-piety than he. The colonel, however, was not of the Dutch Reformed branch of the Follocks. He was an Episcopalian, like ourselves, his mother having brought this branch into the church; and, consequently he entered into all our feelings on the subject of religion, heart and hand. Perhaps Mr. Worden was a greater favorite with no member of the four parishes over which he presided, than with Colonel Abraham Von Valkenburgh.

> "I should think less of sending Corny to Newark," added my mother, "was it not for crossing the water."
>
> "Crossing the water!" repeated Mr. Worden. "The Newark we mean, Madam Littlepage, is not at home; [England] the Jersey of which we speak is the adjoining colony of that name."
>
> "I am aware of that, Mr. Worden; but it is not possible to get to Newark [from the southern part of the Bronx], without making that terrible voyage between New York and Powles' Hook. No, sir, it is impossible and every time the child comes home, that risk will have to be run. It would cause me many a sleepless night!"
>
> "He can go by Tobb's Ferry [Dobbs' Ferry], Madam Littlepage," quitely observed the colonel.
>
> "Dobb's Ferry can be very little better than that at Powles' Hook," rejoined the tender mother. "A ferry is a ferry; and the Hudson will be the Hudson, from Albany to New York, so water is water."

As these were all self-evident propositions, they produced a pause in the discourse; for men do not deal with ideas as freely as they deal with the old.

> "Dere is a way, Evans, as you and I know py experience," resumed the colonel, winking again at my father, "to go round the Hudson altoget'er. To pe sure, it is a long way, and a pit

in the woods; but petter to undertake dat, than to haf the poy lose his l'arnin'. Ter journey might be made in two mount's, and he none the wuss for ter exercise. Ter major and I were never heartier dan when we were operating on the he't waters of the Hutson. I will tell Corny that roat." As for the Powles' Hook Ferry, it was an unpleasant place, I will allow; though by the time I was a junior I thought nothing of it. My mother, however, was glad when it was passed for the last time. I remember the very first words that escaped her, after she kissed me on my final return from college, were, "Well, Heaven be praised, Corny! you will never again have any occasion to cross that frightful ferry, now college is completely done with!" My poor mother little knew how much greater dangers I was subsequently called on to encounter, in another direction. Nor was she minutely accurate in her anticipations, since I have crossed the ferry in question, several times in later life, the distance not appearing to be as great of late years, as they certainly seemed to be in my youth." (James Femmore Cooper— complete works— *Leather Stocking Edition* 29 Vols. Copy #733, New York, undated (appears mid-19 century) volume entitled *Satanstoe* pp. 23–24)

In 1760, a formal ferry was started from Paulus Hook to Mesier's Dock in Manhattan, at approximately the foot of present-day Cortlandt Street. Cornelius Van Voorst, a prominent resident of the time, operated the ferry until 1767. Van Voorst had purchased the property of Paulus Hook from Abraham Planck, in 1698.

In 1762, Paulus Hook was the terminal point for the Paulus Hook-to-New Bridge, NJ stage line, which served Jersey City and Hackensack. In 1771, a racetrack was established at Paulus Hook, which was popular with the sporting set of Manhattan, as race horses were not allowed in the streets of the metropolis, establishing a tradition later followed by the Guttenberg Racetrack and the present-day Meadowlands Race Track.

During the Revolution, a small redoubt or fort was built at Paulus Hook, commanded by the Patriot general, Hugh Mercer. On September 23, 1776, it was cannonaded by the British, who gained command that day and were to hold it for the rest of the war, except for one brief period. On August 18, 1779, Major "Lighthorse" Harry Lee mounted an attack against the fort at Paulus Hook, routing the British, who used the ferry to retreat across the river to Manhattan. Lee immediately abandoned the fort, as it was to difficult to defend. Thus, the Americans gained a moral victory in the Battle of Paulus Hook.

After the Revolution, Paulus Hook gained prominence as the terminal point for the New York-to-Philadelphia stage line and the ferry became a key link in that route. Early on, the Paulus Hook ferry became an important link in travel to and from Manhattan—a distinction that it would retain until the twentieth century, when the Pennsylvania Railroad opened its massive new terminal in Manhattan.

In 1804, Colonel Richard Varick, Jacob Radclift, and Anthony Dey were instrumental in forming the Associates of Jersey Company, whose charter was drafted by Alexander Hamilton. The Associates governed Jersey City from that time until around 1820.

In March 1811, Robert Fulton and a consortium including the Associates and Elisha Boudinot of Newark, and Nicholas Roosevelt of New York, assumed the lease of the Paulus Hook Ferry.

Both Fulton and Col. John Stevens of Hoboken were granted simultaneous charters to operate steam ferries from New York to New Jersey. Fulton's charter was for the Paulus Hook ferry route, from Cortlandt Street, while Stevens' was from Hoboken to Barclay Street. The Paulus Hook lease was executed on March 25, 1811.

After the success of the *North River Steamboat*, Fulton had built a machine shop at Paulus Hook. Until his death, in 1815, Robert Fulton built engines for his vessels at this machine shop. Fulton's home was located at 77–79 Grand Street, in downtown Jersey City. The first engines used in his boats were of the bell-crank type, which he later abandoned in favor of the crosshead design developed by Colonel John Stevens.

The Jersey Associates were, by their agreement, to complete two boats, but were delayed for nearly a year subsequent to the period at which Stevens' boat was put on his ferry. It appears that Fulton was meantime devising improvements and asked for a time extension on the second boat until experiments were made with the first. The first boat, the *Jersey*, was put in operation in July 1812, on which occasion entertainment was provided at the tavern on Paulus Hook for the members of the Common Council and several other guests. The *Jersey* had a double hull with a center wheel. Her length was 78 ft. Each hull was 13½ ft. wide, with a 5-ft. space in the center, which gave a 32-ft. overall width. She was joined by her twin sister ship, the *York*, in 1813. These boats operated on the line for about fifteen years until the ferry slips were modified and Steven's spring racks were substituted for Fulton's log rafts in 1827.

The York & Jersey Steamboat Ferry Co. was formally chartered in March 1814. However, in 1825, it sublet its charter to a group including Francis B. Ogden, Cadwallader D. Colden, and Samuel Swartwout—all friendly to the Fulton and Livingston interests, but with more progressive views than the members of the Livingston family who directed operations after Fulton's untimely death on February 23, 1815. This progressive group took advantage of new developments. Around 1821, Robert L. Stevens developed the "working" or "walking" beam engine, which rapidly became the engine of common usage. The new operators built two new boats, the *George Washington* in 1826 and the *Jersey City* in 1827, utilizing this new technology, and the new modified slips of 1827, when the *Jersey* and *York* were retired.

Both the *George Washington* and *Jersey City* were

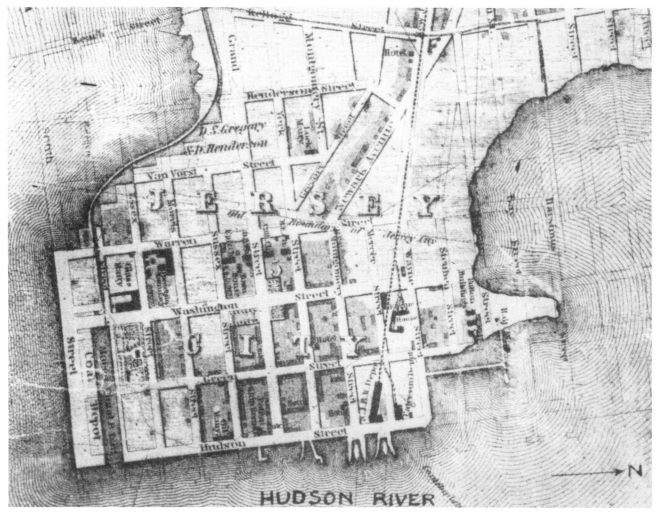

An early map of Paulus Hook, Jersey City. Note that separate passengers stations are shown for the railroads which join east of Greene Street. From an old print.

single-hull boats. They rapidly proved their vast superiority over the old double-hull "ice-catchers" and the advantages of side paddlewheels for ferryboats. The days of the double-hull boats were numbered.

In 1833, the new Associates had the 258-ton *Washington* built. She was followed by the 184-ton *Sussex* in 1834, and the 242-ton *Essex* in 1835 — all also on the new single-hull pattern.

As New Jersey grew, business increased and railroads started to lay track across the state. It was only a matter of time before Jersey City would become one of the greatest railheads of the young nation. Soon a railroad terminal was constructed at Exchange Place at Paulus Hook. On October 14, 1836, passengers of the Morris & Essex Railroad commenced using the new Exchange Place Terminal and the Paulus Hook Ferry. Also in 1836, the City of Jersey City was formally incorporated and the name of the operation changed formally to the Jersey City Ferry. The event was celebrated by the construction that same year of the large 288-ton *New Jersey.*

In 1840, the tracks of the New Jersey Railroad reached from Jersey City to New Brunswick, completing a connection to Philadelphia. At New Brunswick, trains were switched to the Camden & Amboy Railroad to Trenton, and then to the Trenton & Philadelphia to complete the trip.

Jersey City, through the New Jersey Railroad & Transportation Co., had reached its prominence as a railhead and ferry terminus. NJR & T leased the Paulus Hook ferry from the Associates of Jersey Co. in 1841, paying $70,000 for the four boats — *Essex, New Jersey, Sussex,* and *Washington* — and $18,224.99 for the ferry buildings. With increased traffic, the new owners found it necessary to construct a fifth boat and in 1845 the 345-ton *Hudson* was built in Brooklyn, NY. During 1849, *Sussex* was scrapped. Four years later, in 1852, the *Philadelphia,* a product of the Hoboken Yard, was built. In 1853, NJR & T purchased the ferry operation outright and the 578 ton *D. S. Gregory* was added to fleet after the completion in Brooklyn. Three years later, in 1856, the

Jersey City terminal of the New Jersey Railroad and the Paterson and Hudson River, a busy place as early as 1840. From an old print.

Fulton's ferryboat *Jersey*, crossing from New York to Jersey City, 1813.

railroad opened its new terminal at Exchange Place. Along with the new terminal came a new boat: The *John S. Darcy* (13192), built by Devine Burtis of Brooklyn, in 1857, was the latest thing in vertical-beam sidewheel ferryboats. Her overall length was 205 ft., breadth over guards 62 ft., and a depth of hold of 6 ft.; her gross tonnage was 850 with a net of 614 tons. Power was supplied to her 20.1-ft.-diameter, 8-ft.-wide paddles by a 42 in. × 132 in. condensing beam engine.

With *John S. Darcy* taking her place in service, the company decided in 1859 to scrap the second of the Associates' boats and the 24-year-old *Essex* was disposed of. Unfortunately, in June 1859, *Darcy* was burned. She was quickly rebuilt with substantial improvements and was placed back in service in September 1859. When ready for service, *Darcy* was valued at $47,000. With *Darcy* successfully rebuilt, the third Associate boat, the

Washington, was converted to a barge on December 9, 1859.

The ferryboat *John P. Jackson* (12982) was completed in October 1860. Slightly smaller than *Darcy,* the *Jackson* was 777 gross tons powered by a 44-in. × 132-in. vertical-beam engine. On November 6, 1861, *Jackson* was sold to the U.S. Government and her title transferred. The government renamed her *U.S.S. John P. Jackson,* in 1862. She remained in government service until 1865 when she was returned to the railroad on October 3 and redocumented the *J. P. Jackson.*

The sale of the *Jackson* was much regretted by the directors of NJR & T, but application had been made by the War Department and they did not wish to refuse the request.

In April 1861, the *Philadelphia* and *Hudson* were chartered to the New York Lake Erie & Western Rail-

    THE RAILROAD FERRIES OF THE HUDSON

road, for whom they would operate out of that company's new Pavonia Avenue, Jersey City terminal to the new Chambers Street, New York ferry.

The removal of Erie trains from the Exchange Place terminal took away some of the ferry traffic. In 1862, the directors decided to dispose of the last remaining boat originally purchased from the Associates in 1841, so the 26-year-old *New Jersey* was scrapped.

A few months after the Erie opened the Chambers Street Ferry, NJR & T opened the Branch Ferry to Desbrosses Street, New York City, on August 1, 1862. With the opening of the second ferry route came the new and largest ferryboat, the 982-ton *Jersey City* (13159) from the yard of Devine Burtis of Brooklyn in 1862. She was 207-ft. long, 63-ft. breadth over guards and had a depth of 13 ft. Her condensing beam engine was 46 in. × 132 in. stroke and developed 625 hp.

The year 1863 saw the *Philadelphia* sold to the government and the 881-ton *New York* (18277) placed in service, in August 1863, on the Cortlandt Street route. *New York* was another product of Devine Burtis of Brooklyn.

On October 14, 1863, the Morris & Essex Railroad discontinued using the Exchange Place terminal and ferry and started using its own tracks to Jersey City's Western Slope section where the M & E trains were switched on to the Erie and run through its tunnel to the east side, then up to M & E tracks for the run to Hoboken and the Hoboken ferry.

New York's sister, the *Newark* (18278), was completed by Devine Burtis in 1865 and took her place in service.

In 1866, Devine Burtis was once again contracted to build the next NJR & T ferryboat, the *New Brunswick.* Although not as heavy as the *Jersey City,* the *New Brunswick* still weighed in at over 900 tons, 909 to be precise. Her length was 206 ft., and breadth over guards was 65 ft. Like *Jersey City,* she was powered by a 46 in. × 132 in. vertical-beam engine.

The *Hudson City* (11927), the largest of the NJR & T boats to be built to date, was launched in 1867. She measured 212 ft. in length, 64.6 ft. breadth over guards and had a depth of 12.11 ft. with a gross tonnage of 1,008 and 800 tons net. But her 46 in. × 132 in. vertical beam engine developed only 525 hp.

For several years, no new boats were built by the railroad and both the *Jackson* and *Philadelphia* had been returned to NJR & T by the government after the war. With their delivery, the company was operating nine boats on two ferry routes.

Apparently, government service had not done the *Philadelphia* any good as she was scrapped in 1869, after

Early ferryboat of the Associates of Jersey Company, Paulus Hook Ferry. May be either Essex, Sussex, or Washington. From an old print.

Ferryboat, *Jersey City*, built 1827.

The Pennsylvania Railroad acquired the New Jersey Railroad & Transportation Co. and part of the acquisition was the *Jersey City* built by Devine Burtis in 1862. After many rebuildings and improvements the Pennsylvania Railroad scrapped her in 1917, after 55 years of service. — Courtesy of The Mariners' Museum, Newport News, Virginia

The Pennsylvania ferryboat *New Brunswick* built in 1866 before her rebuilding in 1889, after being destroyed by fire. — Courtesy of The Mariners' Museum, Newport News, Virginia

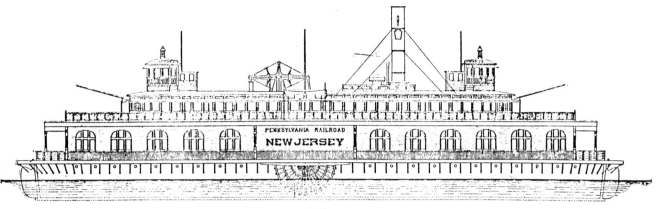

Ferryboat *New Jersey,* Jersey City ferries, rebuilt 1896–97.

PRR *New Jersey* off Pier 13 lower Manhattan as she heads for the Cortlandt Street slips. She was built in 1873 as a single deck boat, the second deck was added in 1896 and she was scrapped in May 1912. — Courtesy of The Railroad Museum of Pennsylvania

only seventeen years of service and two years later the 11-year-old *John P. Jackson,* the other vessel sold to the Government, was scrapped.

September 3, 1869, saw the trains of New York & Oswego/Midland Railroad start using the Exchange Place terminal and ferries. The holdings of the New Jersey Railroad & Transportation Company were acquired by the Pennsylvania Railroad System in 1871. With the merging of the NJR & T into the Pennsylvania, it made the Exchange Place facilities the busiest terminal on the Jersey shore of the North River.

A tenth ferryboat, the *New Jersey* (18785), the second vessel to be so named, was added to the fleet in 1873, but was not placed in service until the spring of 1874. *New Jersey* was, by far, the largest vessel ever built for the Exchange Place ferry. She showed the concept of the Pennsylvania Railroad's "think big, do big." Her overall length was 227 ft., breadth overall 65.6 ft. and depth of 12.8 ft. Her hull was made of yellow pine and oak. Cobanks & Theall's New York Iron Works built the 800 hp vertical beam engine of 50 in. × 144 in. stroke, which

had a Stevenson valve gear, with steam being supplied at 30 lbs. psi by a 33 ft.- × 33 ft.- × 10¼-ft. diameter drop-flue boiler.

The Lehigh Valley Railroad started using Exchange Place and its ferry facilities on June 28, 1875, with four trains running in each direction between Jersey City and Easton, PA.

During the twelve-month period ending December 31, 1875, Exchange Place terminal and the ferries handled 8,714,434 passengers.

In 1879, the famous Scottish author Robert Louis Stevenson made a trip across the United States. He described a Paulus Hook ferry crossing in the chapter entitled *"Notes by the Way to Council Bluffs"* in his 1892 book *Across the Plains or the Amateur Immigrant.* He was not favorably impressed.

Monday. — It was, if I remember rightly, five o'clock when we were all signalled to be present at the Ferry Depot of the railroad. An emigrant ship had arrived at New York on the Saturday night, another on the Sunday morning, our own on Sunday afternoon, a fourth early on Monday; and as

Pennsylvania Railroad Ferry Terminal and Bridge across West Street, Manhattan at corner of Cortlandt Street circa 1880.

there is no emigrant train on Sunday, a great part of the passengers from these four ships was concentrated on the train by which I was to travel. There was a Babel of bewildered men, women, and children. The wretched little booking-office, and the baggage-room, which was not much larger, were crowded thick with emigrants, and were heavy and rank with the atmosphere of dripping clothes. Open carts full of bedding stood by the half-hour in the rain. The officials loaded each other with recriminations. A bearded, mildewed little man, whom I take to have been an emigrant agent, was all over the place, his mouth full of brimstone, blustering and interfering. It was plain that the whole system, if system there was, had utterly broken down under the strain of so many passengers.

My own ticket was given me at once, and an oldish man, who preserved his head in the midst of this turmoil, got my baggage registered, and counselled me to stay quietly where I was till he should give me the word to move. I had taken along with me a small valise, a knapsack, which I carried on my shoulders, and in the bag of my railway rug the whole of Bancroft's *History of the United States,* in six fat volumes. It was as much as I could carry with convenience even for short distances, but it ensured me plenty of clothing, and the valise was at that moment, and often after, useful for a stool. I am sure I sat for an hour in the baggage-room, and wretched enough it was; yet, when at last the word was passed to me, and I picked up my bundles and got under way, it was only to exchange discomfort for downright misery and danger.

I followed the porters into a long shed reaching downhill from West Street to the river. It was dark, the wind blew clean through it from end to end; and here I found a great block of passengers and baggage, hundreds of one and tons of the other. I feel I shall have a difficulty to make myself believed; and certainly the scene must have been exceptional,

for it was too dangerous for daily repetition. It was a tight jam; there was no fair way through the mingled mass of brute and living obstruction. Into the upper skirts of the crowd, porters, infuriated by hurry and overwork, clove their way with shouts. I may say that we stood like sheep, and that the porters charged among us like so many maddened sheep-dogs; and I believe these men were no longer answerable for their acts. It mattered not what they were carrying, they drove straight into the press, and when they could get no farther, blindly discharged their barrowful. With my own hand, for instance, I saved the life of a child as it sat upon its mother's knee, she sitting on a box; and since I heard of no accident, I must suppose that there were many similar interpositions in the course of the evening. It will give some idea of the state of mind to which we were reduced if I tell you that neither the porter nor the mother of the child paid the least attention to my act. It was not till some time after that I understood what I had done myself, for to ward off heavy boxes seemed at the moment a natural incident of human life. Cold, wet, clamour, dead opposition to progress, such as one encounters in an evil dream, had utterly daunted the spirits. We had accepted this purgatory as a child accepts the conditions of the world. For my part, I shivered a little, and my back ached wearily; but I believe I had neither a hope nor a fear, and all the activities of my nature had become tributary to one massive sensation of discomfort.

At length, and after how long an interval I hesitate to guess, the crowd began to move, heavily straining through itself. About the same time some lamps were lighted, and threw a sudden flare over the shed. We were being filtered out into the river boat for Jersey City. You may imagine how slowly this filtering proceeded, through the dense, choking crush, every one overladen with packages or children, and yet under the necessity of fishing out his ticket by the way;

but it ended at length for me, and I found myself on deck, under a flimsy awning, and with a trifle of elbow-room to stretch and breathe in. This was on the starboard; for the bulk of the emigrants stuck hopelessly on the port side, by which we had entered. In vain the seamen shouted to them to move on, and threatened them with shipwreck. These poor people were under a spell of stupor, and did not stir a foot. It rained as heavily as ever, but the wind now came in sudden claps and capfuls, not without danger to a boat so badly ballasted as ours; and we crept over the river in the darkness, trailing one paddle in the water like a wounded duck, and passed ever and again by huge, illuminated steamers running many knots, and heralding their approach by strains of music. The contrast between these pleasure embarkations and our own grim vessel, with her list to port and her freight of wet and silent emigrants, was of that glaring description which we count too obvious for the purposes of art.

The landing at Jersey City was done in a stampede. I had a fixed sense of calamity, and, to judge by conduct, the same persuasion was common to us all. A panic selfishness, like that produced by fear, presided over the disorder of our landing. People pushed, and elbowed and ran, their families following how they could. Children fell, and were picked up, to be rewarded by a blow. One child, who had lost her parents, screamed steadily and with increasing shrillness, as though verging towards a fit; an official kept her by him, but no one else seemed so much as to remark her distress; and I am ashamed to say that I ran among the rest. I was so weary that I had twice to make a halt and set down my bundles in the hundred yards or so between the pier and the railway station, so that I was quite wet by the time that I got under cover. There was no waiting-room, no refreshment-room; the cars were locked; and for at least another hour, or so it seemed, we had to camp upon the draughty, gas-lit platform. I sat on my valise, too crushed to observe my neighbours; but as they were all cold, and wet, and weary, and driven stupidly crazy by the mismanagement to which we had been subjected, I believe they can have been no happier than myself. I bought half a dozen oranges from a boy, for oranges and nuts were the only refection to be had. As only two of them had even a pretence of juice, I threw the other four under the cars, and beheld, as in a dream, grown people and children groping on the track after my leavings. (God knows they would get little comfort from these balls of yellow fibre. But the touch completes the misery of the picture.)

You will tell me, perhaps, that people are jostled, driven, and condemned to wait in the cold and rain, to get upon an excursion train or to see a new piece in a theatre; and that these discomforts are constantly, if not always cheerfully supported. I cannot deny it; but whether it was because the trial lasted so long, or because we were here whole families together, carrying all their worldly goods and bent upon a serious end, I know only that I have never seen fellow creatures so stricken down, nor suffered, in my own person, such complete paralysis of mind. The whole business was a nightmare while it lasted, and is still a nightmare to remember. If the railway company cared — but then it does not, and I should address the winds. The officials, who are to blame for this unnecessary suffering, are without doubt humane men and subscribe to public charities; but when all hands are piped, they may find their duty lay some other way. Kindness is the first of virtues; and capacity in a man's own business the greatest kindness in his reach.)

At last we were admitted into the cars, utterly dejected, and far from dry. For my own part, I got out a clothes-brush, and brushed my trousers as hard as I could, till I had dried them and warmed my blood into the bargain; but no one else, except my next neighbour, to whom I lent the brush, appeared to take the least precaution. As they were, they composed themselves to sleep. I had seen the lights of Philadelphia, and been twice ordered to change carriages and twice countermanded, before I allowed myself to follow their example. (pp. 100–104) Across the Plains, Reprinted by Charles Scribner & Sons's, New York 1925.

In 1879, a smaller boat, the *Princeton* (150187), was delivered by Devine Burtis, her 525-hp vertical-beam 46-in. × 132-in. engine provided the power to propel this 888-ton, 206-ft. vessel.

The Pennsylvania Railroad decided to establish an uptown ferry route and, on January 9, 1880, the Exchange Place-to-West 34th Street route was started. The 215-ton *Mechanic,* built in Camden, NJ in 1856, was purchased and brought to the North River for this service.

During the year 1880, the ferryboats made 167,973 trips between Jersey City and New York. The year 1881 saw another Delaware River ferryboat, the 598-ton *Camden* (5,602), built at Camden in 1865, bought from the Camden & Philadelphia Ferry Co., and brought to the North River and placed on the 34th Street route.

The Pennsylvania Railroad was operating its vessels for a longer period than did NJR & T before retiring them. In 1882, the 37-year-old *Hudson* was scrapped and two new iron-hulled, single-decked boats, the *Baltimore* (3207) and the *Chicago* (126102), were built by Harlan & Hollingsworth of Wilmington, DE. These vessels were 206 ft. overall length, 65.5 ft. breadth over guards and drew 12.6 ft. of depth; their 46-in. × 132-in. vertical-beam engine developed 625 hp.

Since 1880, the Pennsylvania Railroad had been operating three ferry routes from Exchange Place: the Cortlandt Street line, the Branch Ferry to Desbrosses Street, and the uptown line to West 34th Street. By 1886, ferry routes were crisscrossing the river in several directions. This traffic, plus oceanliners, coastal and river steamers, and tugboats with barges, made for very heavy traffic in one concentrated area between the Battery and 34th Street. Accidents were bound to happen. The line to Desbrosses Street was more prone to accidents than either the Cortlandt Street or 34th Street lines. The route from Cortlandt Street to Exchange Place was almost a straight line and it normally would cross only up- and downriver traffic, as it crossed above the Communipaw Avenue-Liberty Street line and below both the Hobo-

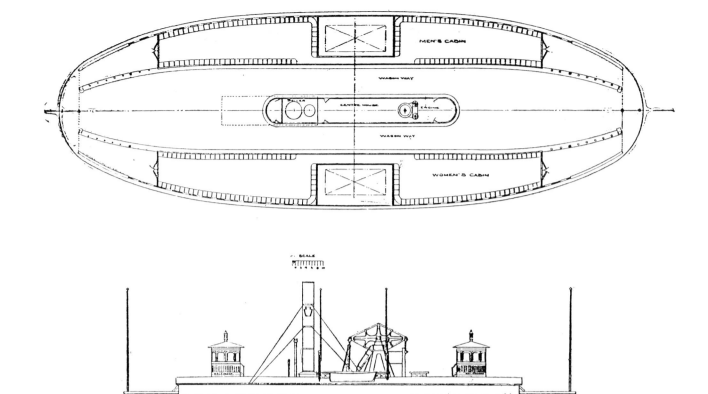

Ferryboat *Baltimore*, Jersey City ferry built 1882 reconstructed and double-decked 1890–91.

ken-Barclay Street line and the Chambers Street-Pavonia Avenue line. Whereas the 34th Street line boats had sufficient room to get at right angles to both the Barclay Street and Chambers Street boats before crossing them, thus making for a very distinct rule-of-the-road situation, the Desbrosses Street line crossed both of these other railroad company lines on a diagonal, at times causing very confusing situations. Such a situation took place on March 19, 1886, between the Pennsylvania Railroad *Baltimore*, Erie's *Delaware*, and Hoboken Ferry's *Lackawanna*. Newspaper accounts report that *Baltimore* had left Desbrosses Street for Jersey City, heading downriver on a crossing angle; the *Lackawanna* had left Barclay Street for Hoboken, and the *Delaware* had left Chambers Street for Jersey City, both heading upriver, at a crossing angle. The *Delaware* was ahead of the *Lackawanna*. The pilot of the *Delaware* signaled the *Baltimore* that it should pass starboard to starboard (right side to right side), which *Baltimore* acknowledged. The *Lackawanna* sounded the same signal. The *Baltimore's* pilot stated that he was frustrated by the *Lackawanna's* pilot who jammed his helm astarboard and exposed his port side to the *Baltimore*. *Baltimore* struck the *Lackawanna* on the port side, about 20 feet forward of the wheelhouse (paddle housing). *Baltimore's* bow cut through the

guardrail and cabin, almost reaching the hull of the *Lackawanna*.

Baltimore seemed to be a hard-luck boat that year, for again on September 15, 1886, she struck the steamboat *Catskill*, off Desbrosses Street. Once again, contradicting signals seemed to be the cause of the accident.

New Brunswick was not immune to trouble either, in 1886. On Saturday, August 21, she left Jersey City at 7:45 A.M. for Desbrosses Street. Upon arriving at the lower slip, she did not back properly and rebounded off the bridge. As deckhand Patrick McNulty was standing at the gates, the force of the collision threw three horses attached to their wagons off balance and, as they lurched forward, sweeping McNulty overboard with them, all were drowned.

New Jersey, having been fitted with electric lights in 1884, was once again taken into the yard and steam steering gears were installed, in 1887, as they were on five other boats.

During 1886, the boats of the three ferry routes carried 15,546,275 passengers and 1,173,873 teams on 161,267 trips.

On April 17, 1889, fire was discovered in the ferryboat *New Brunswick's* engineroom as she was leaving the slip and she burned to the water's edge. No one was

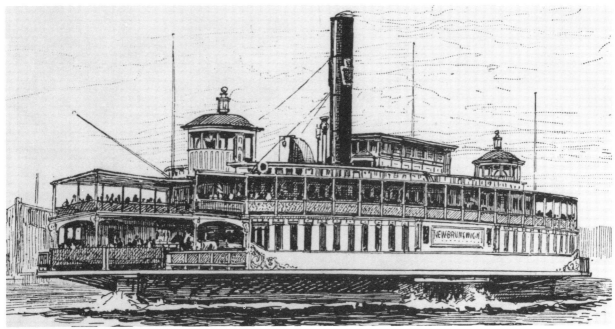

An artist sketch of the Pennsylvania Railroads side wheel ferryboat *New Brunswick* after her rebuilding in 1889.

PRR *New Brunswick* after her remodeling in 1891 when the second deck was added. She was completely destroyed by fire on December 28, 1896. — Courtesy of John A. Breynaert

hurt, but *New Brunswick* sank in the North River. She was raised a month later on May 18 by Jonas Baxter, towed to the flats near Bull's Ferry, Weehawken, and pumped out. Between September 28, 1889, and February 17, 1890, *New Brunswick* was completely rebuilt. She was fitted with steam steering gears, and a new upper deck was added to accommodate two hundred additional passengers. *New Brunswick* became an experimental vessel: If her new saloon cabin proved successful, the Pennsylvania Railroad intended placing upper cabins on other boats.

By March 8, 1890, *New Brunswick* was double-decked to service the new elevated terminal at Exchange Place and the new upper walkway across West Street at Cortlandt Street, Manhattan. In downtown Jersey City, from the west side of Brunswick Street to Exchange Place terminal, the road was elevated to get the tracks off the streets. From Brunswick Street west, to Waldo Avenue east of Journal Square, the tracks were on an elevated fill.

Upon arrival at Exchange Place, passengers were duly impressed by the railroad's new modernized terminal, which replaced the antiquated terminal and ferryhouse built in 1856. Travelers to New York emerged from their coaches in a twelve-track, canopied train shed, then passed through the new station and a large concourse to the harborside ferry slips. Train passengers boarded the boats from the upper-deck passage directly to the saloon cabins of the remodeled *New Brunswick*.

June 1891 saw the *New Brunswick* back in the yard, where her saloon cabin was shortened by 40 feet, her pilothouses placed on the upper deck, and her lower cabin hoods extended.

The Pennsylvania Railroad had undertaken a massive modernization program with the building of new terminals in Jersey City and Cortlandt Street, N.Y. and most of their boats were also modernized during this period, except the *D. S. Gregory* which was disposed of.

During 1890, the *Chicago* was double-decked and overhauled with a new heating and ventilating system, and electric lights.

Chicago and *Baltimore* were the last sidewheel ferryboats built for the Pennsylvania Railroad, except for the small sidewheel boats built for the Brooklyn-Fulton Street Annex run. In 1890, Jackson & Sharp of Wilmington, DE built the 501-ton, 150.11-ft. *Annex 4*. This small sidewheeler was powered by a 40-in. × 108-in. vertical-beam engine which developed 425 hp.

Cincinnati (126803) was the name chosen for the Pennsylvania's next vessel, a different type of vessel that S. L. Moore & Sons Shipyard, of Elizabethport, NJ would launch on April 28, 1891. *Cincinnati* was of average overall length of 206-ft. and her breadth was 65 ft. (comparable to the other boats), but she had 15.6-ft. depth of hold, steel-hulled, with a gross tonnage of 1,255 and double decked with upper-deck loading and unloading capabilities. But she had no paddlewheels, for she was the railroad's first screw-propeller boat and she was powered by two steeple compound engines, 18 in. × 36 in. × 26 in., which developed 1,016 hp to drive her two 8.9-ft. diameter propellers, which had a 13.6-ft. pitch.

That was not all: She was equipped with Williamson steam steering gears, mechanical telegraph, speed and direction indicators, and mahogany staircases in the center of her cabins. Below decks, she had five compartments with transverse bulkheads and two longitudinal bulkheads extending between the collision bulkheads on either side.

The year 1891 also saw the second *Annex* boat, the sidewheel *Annex 5* (106860), delivered by Jackson & Sharp of Wilmington, DE. She was six gross ton heavier than *Annex 4*, but within several inches in size of her and the same horsepower.

The second double-deck Pennsylvania screwboat to take her place in the fleet was the *Washington* (81386) of 1892. *Washington* was a sister to *Cincinnati*, but was built by the Delaware River Iron Works of Chester, PA.

The 34th Street ferryline operated only until 1897. Both the *Camden* and *Mechanic* were sold before 1890.

In 1895, Jackson & Sharp delivered a third Annex boat, *Annex* (107187), a sister to *Annex 4 & 5*, for the Brooklyn run.

The new single-deck *Camden* was built for the Camden & Philadelphia Ferry Co., in 1896.

A new type of ferryboat was needed for the new West

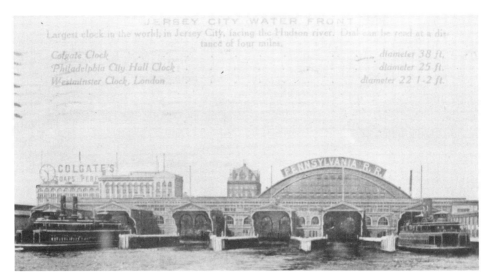

Pennsylvania Railroad's largest Exchange Place Terminal in Jersey City seen from the river. From an old post card. Colgate's large clock was the time piece for ferryboat captains. When Captain Tom Hogan was steering the night boat on the Erie he used this clock when on the New York side and the Home Life Building time signals when on the Jersey City side. — James Lee Collection

Entrance to Pennsylvania Railroad Ferry, Jersey City, New Jersey 1907. The ferry terminal and train terminal including the elevation of the railroad tracks over Railroad Avenue, Jersey City were built in 1890. Photo is from an old Jersey City business directory.

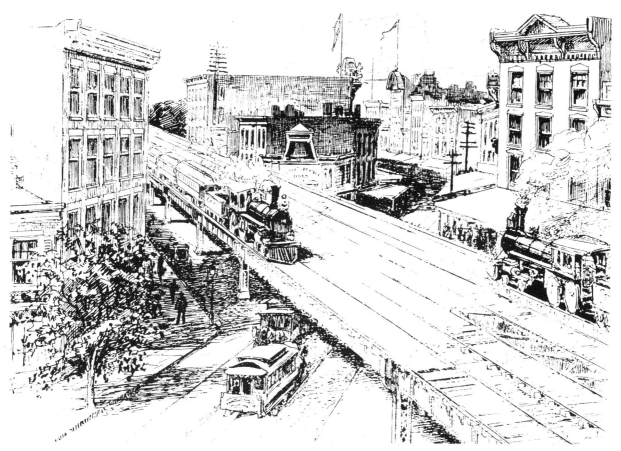

Railroad elevation across Newark and Railroad Avenues in Jersey City leading to Pennsylvania Exchange Place Terminal.

Newark Avenue in downtown Jersey City at Henderson Street where the overhead elevated tracks of the Pennsylvania Railroad run down Railroad Avenue to Exchange Place Terminal, in October 1947.

Twenty-third Street route which was to be opened in 1897. In 1896, Charles Hillman of Philadelphia, PA delivered the *St. Louis* (116755) a double-decked, twin-screw ferryboat of 1,273 gross tons. She was steel hulled, with overall dimensions of 206 ft. in length, 65 ft. over breadth of guards, powered by two triple-expansion engines 20 in. × 30 in. × 30 in. × 24 in., which delivered 1,800 hp to her 7.10-ft. diameter propellers. Steam was supplied by four watertube boilers with a working steam pressure of 200 psi.

William Cramp & Sons' Philadelphia shipyard delivered a sister vessel, the *Pittsburg* (150,741) in October 1896. *Pittsburg's* name was later changed to *Pittsburgh*.

With the addition of these two boats, the Pennsylvania fleet consisted of seventeen ferryboats, the oldest being the sidewheel *John S. Darcy,* dating back to 1857. Also in 1896, *New Jersey* was rebuilt and a second deck added. Tragedy was once again to strike the *New Brunswick* for the second time in nine years. On December 28, 1896, she was completely destroyed by fire, thus bringing an end to the first experimental double-decked boat on the Pennsylvania Railroad, climaxing a very short career of only twenty-three years.

Charles Hillman was again contracted to build the third twin-screw vessel for the Pennsylvania and, on December 4, 1897, the second *New Brunswick* was launched, less than a month short of the first anniversary of her namesake's disasterous fire.

Twenty-third Street was opened with *St. Louis* and *Pittsburgh* in 1897 and, when *New Brunswick* was com-

pleted, she too was added to that run. By December 1897, the ferries were carrying annually 21,324,540 passengers and 1,300, 167 teams, making 187,035 trips and employing an average of 314 men.

With a fleet of seventeen boats, all fairly new or rebuilt, the railroad saw no need for additional boat construction until 1899 when the Delaware River Iron Shipbuilding & Engine Works, of Chester, PA delivered the last of the twinscrew boats, the 1,273-ton *Philadelphia* (150806).

The rebuilt sidewheel *Chicago* was involved in a collision and sank on October 31, 1899, thus reducing the fleet to seventeen ferryboats. The loss of the seventeen-year-old *Chicago,* which had been rebuilt with a second deck in 1890, was substantial to the company.

At the turn of the century, the Pennsylvania was operating four ferry routes and Jersey City had become the major railhead of the Eastern United States. Even though the Pennsylvania Railroad operated some of the plushest trains in the country, its eastern terminal was still one mile away from the financial heart of America, Wall Street. Under normal conditions, the railroad would have built a bridge across that one mile. That idea was actually considered in 1884 when the company planned to build a high-level bridge over the North River, but the War Department turned it down. Again, in 1890, the Pennsylvania encouraged the eminent engineer, Gustave Lindenthal, to come up with a plan to cross the river. Lindenthal devised a plan for a three-deck bridge, to carry fourteen tracks and roadways

THE RAILROAD FERRIES OF THE HUDSON

Like other Pennsylvania Railroad ferryboats the *Washington* of 1892 had her lower cabins removed and was sent to other ferry routes. Here *Washington* is operating on the New Castle Ferry from New Castle, Delaware to Pennsville, New Jersey in April 1941. — Library of Congress photograph

Pennsylvania Railroad ferryboat *Annex #3* which operated between Exchange Place, Jersey City and Fulton Street, Brooklyn for many years. — Courtesy of The Railroad Museum of Pennsylvania

Pennsylvania Railroad's *Philadelphia* appears to just have had a new paint job and an annual overhaul in this photograph. She was the last twin-screw boat built for the company and a product of Delaware River Iron Shipbuilding of Chester, Pennsylvania in 1899. — Courtesy of The Mariners' Museum, Newport News, Virginia

Ferryboat *Chicago II* as she was originally built for the Pennsylvania Railroad. The Pennsylvania boats were Tuscan Red with gold lettering. They carried a red designation light which can be seen on the staff over the forward pilothouse. — Courtesy of The Mariners' Museum, Newport News, Virginia

Pennsylvania Railroad's *Newark II* launched June 28, 1902, the last boat built for that company's ferry service in New York Harbor, is shown heading for Exchange Place with a full load of vehicles. One of the *St. Louis* class twin-stackers can be seen over her stern. — Courtesy of The Mariners' Museum, Newport News, Virginia

across the river at 59th Street, including an act of Congress to permit the construction. The big drawback was the fact that the 3,000-ft. arch bridge would cost $100 million to construct, which sum the Pennsylvania could not swing alone. It went to the other railroads on the west side of the river, but when they too refused to put up that kind of money, the plan was discarded. The Pennsylvania had no alternative but to continue ferry operations. With this in mind, they turned to Burlee Shipbuilding and Drydock Co. of Port Richmond, NY, which, in 1901, delivered the double-decked, single-screw, second *Chicago* (127509), a 1,344-ton vessel powered by a triple-expansion engine whose dimensions were 22 in. × 32 in. × 32 in. × 24 in. and which developed 700 hp, with two watertube boilers of 225 lbs. psi.

On November 9, 1901, *Newark I* was sold and renamed *America*. The following year, on June 28, 1902, the second *Newark* (130994) was launched at T. S. Marvel's Yard in Newburgh, NY. *Newark* was a sister to the *Chicago,* but she had several minor differences: she was only 1,308 tons, 26 tons lighter and her engine developed 750 hp, 50 more than *Chicago's*. With the arrival of *Newark* and *Chicago,* the 39-year-old *New York* was scrapped, followed in 1903 by the scrapping of the 46-year-old *John S. Darcy.*

Newark of 1902 was the last steamboat built for the Paulus Hook Ferry, writing *finis* to steam vessels built for that ferry, started by Robert Fulton in 1812 when he introduced the centerwheel *Jersey* to the line.

For years to come, the Pennsylvania Railroad would operate train and boat service from Exchange Place, Jersey City with its remaining fleet of screwboats and aging sidewheelers.

Commodore Vanderbilt's New York Central System would continue to be the only railroad with direct access to New York City from the western part of the United States. This fact frustrated the mighty Pennsylvania Railroad Co.'s board of directors—something had to be done. Back in the mid-1870s, a man by the name of D. C. Haskins envisioned a tunnel under the Hudson River from Jersey City to Washington Square, Manhattan. Haskins managed to find capital for his project, but the time was not right for the mighty Hudson's bed to be broached and, on July 21, 1880, she fought back and reclaimed her bed, taking twenty men to a watery grave. Haskins failed financially in 1882. The tunnel lay dormant for the next eighteen years. Finally, in 1900, came a man who would unknowingly, though not in his lifetime, cause the demise of the North River ferries. This man, William Gibbs McAdoo, a struggling young lawyer, raised sufficient capital to complete the remaining 2,000 feet of Haskins' first tunnel in 1902. A second tunnel was commenced and, on February 25, 1908, the Hudson & Manhattan Railroad commenced operation from Hoboken to 19th Street, New York. In 1909, service was opened to downtown New York, including a station at Exchange Place, Jersey City.

In 1902, Alexander Johnston Cassatt, president of the Pennsylvania Railroad, after noting McAdoo's enthusiasm, decided that it was time for the Pennsy to make its move and head for the heart of New York City. Property was acquired and a two-track-high line fill was constructed from east of Newark across the Jersey meadows in Hudson County to Bergen Hill on the west side of North Bergen, NJ. Twin tunnels were bored under the hill and the Hudson River to 33rd Street and 8th Avenue, New York, where a massive new terminal was built. Three more tunnels were driven under the East River to Long Island City, where a large yard complex was built. The new Penn Station in New York was opened in 1910. The opening of Penn Station brought the discontinuance of the Fulton Street Annex to Brooklyn on November 29, 1910, followed the next day by the West 23rd Street service being halted.

Even with the rerouting of a large share of the Pennsylvania trains to New York City, the Exchange Place terminal still retained a great deal of local service, including the plush, shore executive trains of the New York & Long Branch Railroad and the trains of the Lehigh Valley Railroad. With the discontinuance of two ferry routes, the Pennsylvania had no need for their aging ferry fleet. *New Jersey II* was dismantled, at Brooklyn, in May 1912, followed by *Hudson City,* also in 1912. All the *Annex* boats were disposed of, as were *Princeton, Baltimore,* and *Jersey City,* by 1917.

The Erie-controlled New York, Susquehanna & Western Railroad train operation was transferred to the Erie's Pavonia Avenue terminal on December 1, 1911.

The Pennsylvania refused to renew the Lehigh Valley's lease and trackage rights so, in 1913, the Valley transferred its trains to the Central Railroad of New Jersey's Communipaw Terminal and started using the Liberty Street and Twenty-third Street ferries of that line.

Exchange Place still retained prominence, however, since it was the focal point of a large part of Jersey City's financial district which was located at Exchange Place and along Montgomery Street, to Henderson Street, a few blocks to the west, City Hall stands within walking distance of the ferry. Public Service operated a large fleet of trolley routes to its large Exchange Place terminal across the street from the station and next to the ferry. Colgate's large soap and cosmetics factory lay just south of Exchange Place.

The Pennsylvania Railroad's ferry was still a busy operation and the eight remaining propeller boats continued to ply the North River. Europe was in the middle of the Great War and harbor traffic and business were booming, but it was only a matter of time before the United States was drawn into the war. With this nation at war, the United States Government assumed control of the railroads on December 28, 1917. All railroads in the

Newark and *Philadelphia* depart from the Pennsylvania Railroad's Exchange Place Terminal, Jersey City for one of the terminals in Manhattan. The *Philadelphia* is a twin screw vessel and had four boilers, while the *Newark* was a single screw vessel with two boilers. Both of these vessels had their lower cabins removed in order to carry more vehicles, finishing out their years on other Pennsylvania routes in Maryland and Delaware. – Courtesy of The Mariners' Museum, Newport News, Virginia

Pennsylvania Railroad ferryboat *Chicago II* entering Cortlandt Street slip after her conversion to a four gangway vehicle carrier. *Chicago* was taken off Cortlandt Street and sent to the Delaware Bay area, she was replaced by *New Brunswick*. – Courtesy of The Mariners' Museum, Newport News, Virgnia

country came under the jurisdiction of the U.S. Railroad Administration. On September 15, 1918, six local trains of the Lehigh Valley were transferred back to Exchange Place Terminal and the Valley's through trains to Penn Station in New York. After the war, when the railroads were returned to private control in 1920, the Lehigh Valley locals continued to operate from the Jersey City terminal until the late 1930s when, because of declining traffic, the remaining daily local was operated to the Valley's Johnston Avenue, Jersey City facility, a short walk from the Jersey Central ferry.

Desbrosses Street was discontinued on January 21, 1930, bringing to an end the sixty-eight-year tenure of the Branch Ferry. This now left only the original Paulus Hook ferry operation.

The posture of the ferry line started to change from that of a passenger carrier to that of a vehicle carrier.

For a short time around 1935, the Pennsylvania oper-

ated a vehicle ferry to Atlantic Avenue, Brooklyn from Jersey City.

As the depression of the 'thirties wore on, the ferry traffic continued to decline. Slowly, the eight remaining screwboats started to disappear. April 1941 found the *Washington* on the Delaware & New Jersey ferry line out of New Castle, DE.

Since the Penn ferries were now primarily vehicle-carrying ferries, the lower cabins were removed to make way for two more gangways, making them four-gangway boats. Passengers were still carried in the upper cabin. The addition of the third and fourth gangways doubled the vehicle-carrying capacity of the boats.

After WW II, the Cortlandt Street route was down to one boat, the *Newark*, with the *Chicago* in reserve, tied up at Jersey City. *Philadelphia* and *New Brunswick* were operating on the Love Point Baltimore, MD ferry line, while *Washington*, *St. Louis*, and *Pittsburgh* were

THE RAILROAD FERRIES OF THE HUDSON

operating on the Delaware & New Jersey ferry line from New Castle, DE to Pennsville, NJ.

In 1941, the Pennsylvania razed the 1890 station and canopied train shed at Jersey City, leaving only the large concourse at the ferry terminal. Fewer and fewer trains operated into Jersey City. But Jersey City still wanted ferry service and Mayor Frank Hague, long a political power in the state, would see that the Pennsy kept it. For several years, the Pennsy had been attempting to discontinue ferry service, having its train passengers use the Hudson & Manhattan Tubes, which it now owned stock in, as it would provide additional revenue to the ailing H & M. Each time the Pennsy would try this, Frank Hague's city hall would say that "if the ferry stopped, the Railroad Avenue elevation would be torn down also." So the boat plied on, making her sixteen round trips daily, from 9 A.M. to 5 P.M., six days a week. There was no Sunday service.

Frank Hague stepped down as mayor of Jersey City, putting his nephew Frank H. Eggers in as mayor. This action infuriated the people of Jersey City. Hague continued to retain the title of County Democratic Leader. In the municipal elections of May 1949, Frank H. Eggers was defeated in his bid for reelection by a former Hague lieutenant, John V. Kenny. Between May and December, the *Chicago* and *Newark* were towed to the Delaware River and the *New Brunswick* returned to replace them on the Cortlandt Street route. Service on the line became unpredictable as the familiar sign "No Boat Service Today" began to appear more and more frequently. *New Brunsiwck* started to make fewer and fewer trips across the Hudson. Between July 1, 1949, when Kenny took office as mayor, and the end of the year, the wheels in Philadelphia corporate headquarters moved fast. The ICC was petitioned to abandon the serv-

ice, with little or no opposition from the powers-to-be in Jersey City, and the abandonment petition was granted as of December 31, 1949, bringing the final curtain down on one hundred and eighty-nine years of service from Paulus Hook to Cortlandt Street, which was started by famous Jersey City resident Cornelius Van Voorst and had its first steamboat placed in service by another famous Jersey City resident, Robert Fulton.

No longer would the tuscan red-and-gold-lettered boats, named for famous American cities, cross the North River. The only place that one would see the famous Pennsylvania keystone logo would be on its many tugboats which plied the harbor. But that, too, was to disappear in less than two decades, to be replaced by the ill-fated "PC," the new logo on the shortlived merger of the mighty Pennsylvania Railroad and its chief rival, Old Commodore Vanderbilt's New York Central System, in 1968. Eight short years later, all the famous railroad names, whose vessels used to ply the famous North River, would disappear from the river forever, as the government-owned Consolidated Rail Corporation (Conrail) became the sole railroad into New York, continuing no marine operations whatsoever.

The remainder of the terminal was demolished in the 1960s, after all train service was transferred to either Newark's Penn Station or New York, and the Hudson & Manhattan Railroad became P.A.T.H., a subsidiary of the Port Authority of New York and New Jersey.

In 1986, the only trace of the Pennsylvania ferry service that can be found is part of the rack and some piles in the river at the foot of Exchange Place; they, too, will be removed in the not-too-distant future, as a developer is even now building an office complex on the site of the slips. In 1987 plans have just been announced for a new third Penn Station in New York.

Both *Newark* and *New Brunswick* have had their lower cabins removed as they are seen here at Cortlandt Street. *Newark*'s captain just finished backing her engines as she approaches the bridge and *New Brunswick* is loading. The Pennsylvania Railroad ran many New Jersey shore trains and local commuter trains from Exchange Place, Jersey City for many years after the opening of Pennsylvania Station, New York, in 1910. — Courtesy of The Mariners' Museum, Newport News, Virginia

THE JOHN G. MCCULLOUGH:

A Pencil Sketch by Mr. Samuel Ward Stanton

As I sat looking through a book of pencil sketches by the late Samuel Ward Stanton, a television news commentator announced that a joint United States and French venture group from Wood's Hole Oceanographic Institute had located the wreck of the ill-fated liner *Titanic* which was lost after striking an iceberg in the early morning hours of April 15, 1912.

Mr. Stanton was one of the 1,513 persons who lost their lives in this disaster. With his death, the New York Harbor area lost one of its most talented marine artists.

I felt this volume would have been incomplete without one of Mr. Stanton's sketches. I have chosen his sketch of the Erie Railroad's *John G. McCullough*. Even though the *McCullough* (which went through two name changes — first to *Chautauqua* in 1906, when she was rebuilt with new engines and a second deck added; and second, to *Rutherford* in 1935) was gone before I started to work for the Erie in 1947, I heard many stories about the "Chickie."

There is one interesting thing about Mr. Stanton's sketch: the "Diamond" with the letter "E" in the center of the stack. All the photographs that I have seen of early Erie boats and railroad engines indicate it was not used. The word *ERIE* was on only the engine tenders, while the boats all had four horizontal white bands around the stack, each one containing one black letter which spelled "ERIE," vertically.

In fact, when you stood on the hurricane deck of the *Arlington, Jamestown,* or *Tuxedo,* traces of the four bands were still visible.

The Erie "Diamond," to my knowledge, did not become the company symbol, on engines or boats at least, until long after Mr. Stanton's death. The Erie diamond first appeared on the engine tenders of the new S-1 class 2-8-4 Berkshire engines in late 1927 and on the *Erie Magazine* cover of the January 1928 issue, under the Erie presidency of Mr. John J. Bernet.

RAYMOND J. BAXTER

CHAPTER 8

PAVONIA FERRY COMPANY OF THE ERIE RAILROAD COMPANY

The Erie Railroad Co. was originally chartered as the New York & Erie Railroad Co. on April 24, 1832, in the state of New York, to build a railroad entirely within New York State. Because of this restriction, the eastern terminus of the New York & Erie became Piermont, NY as it was the town nearest to New York City within New York State on the west side of the Hudson River.

The first ground for the railroad was broken at Deposit, NY at sunrise on November 7, 1835. April 1838 saw ground broken in Piermont and Dunkirk, respectively. The new railroad had difficulty in completing the line as directed in its charter. It became necessary, because of geographical obstructions on the north side of the Delaware River, to ask that the restriction be removed. Once this was granted, the line crossed into Pennsylvania just north of Port Jervis, NY, returning to New York State just south of Narrowsburg. The removal of this restriction by the New York State Legislature was to play a key part in the saga of the Pavonia Ferry.

Finally, after a rocky start, including bankruptcy, the New York & Erie Railroad was completed from Piermont, formerly Tappan Landing, NY, on the west bank of the Hudson River to Dunkirk, NY on Lake Erie. New York City was reached by steamer down the Hudson River to the company's terminal at the Duane Street Pier.

From the mid-1840's trains operated from intermediate points to Piermont and connected with steam boats of other lines running to New York City. The Erie's own service was regularized in 1851.

The inaugural trip of the new railroad was held on May 14 and 15, 1851. Some very influential personalities were roused from their beds at 5:00 A.M. on May 14 for a 6:00 A.M. departure of the steamer *Iron Witch,* which

had been purchased by the company in 1847 and renamed *Erie. Erie* departed the Duane Street Pier and made the trip to Piermont in about an hour and a half.

Among the distinguished guests who walked the decks of the *Erie* that May morning over 130 years ago were President of the United States Millard Fillmore and his Cabinet, incuding Secretary of the Navy W. C. Graham, and Postmaster General W. K. Hall, as well as ex-Governor William L. Marcy, Senator Stephen A. Douglas of Illinois, William H. Seward, and Hamilton Fish. Upon arrival at Piermont, the dignitaries boarded two special trains for their trip over the Erie Railroad.

Thus began the Erie Ferry service, but not the Pavonia Ferry Co. The first vessel to operate on the Erie, as said previously, was the *Iron Witch,* built in 1846 and acquired by the New York & Erie and renamed *Erie.* She ran for many years on the Piermont route. Lytles' List shows her abandoned in 1862. Yet, like many witches, she was not completely dead and a part of her would yet come to life.

Piermont, and the long ride to New York City, became distasteful to the passengers and, when two small railroads in Northern New Jersey commenced operation in October 1848 (prior to completion of the Erie through to Dunkirk), many travelers would disembark Erie trains at Suffern and use the faster new all-rail route. This route consisted of the Paterson & Ramapo Railroad and the Paterson & Hudson River Railroad. At this point the Erie saw that it must get the charter restriction removed and acquire its own all-rail line. Rather than build an entirely new line, on September 9, 1852, they leased the Paterson & Ramapo and Paterson & Hudson River through the Union Railroad. This line had previously been incorpo-

Erie ex *Iron Witch* arrives at Castle Garden (Battery), New York to pick-up President Millard Filmore and other dignitaries for the trip to Piermont, New York and their trip across New York State on the new Erie Railroad, May 1851. From an old print.

Birds-eye view of Jersey City, New York Ferries, and Pennsylvania Railroad Station. — James Ransom Collection

Exchange Place, Jersey City looking towards the river. The New Jersey Railroad and Transportation Co. terminal is on the right and the Paterson & Hudson River Depot to the left. — From a wood cut in Appleton's Rail Road and Steam Boat Companion, 1848

rated to take-over the one critical mile of Paterson & Ramapo line between the New Jersey-New York State Line and the Erie depot at Suffern. The Union Railroad, in turn, leased the Paterson & Ramapo and Paterson & Hudson River. The Erie had a third rail laid on all three lines — the Union Railroad, the Paterson & Ramapo, and the Paterson & Hudson River. From that time on, both broad (6 ft.) standard gauge and (4 ft. 8½ in.) gauge trains could use the same track between Jersey City and Suffern. The third rail reached Paterson by October 1852, and all the way to Jersey City by November 1853. Prior to this, the Paterson & Hudson River trains had utilized the New Jersey Railroad & Transportation Co.'s terminal at Exchange Place in Jersey City and Cortlandt St. ferry terminal in Manhattan. With the coming of the Erie Railroad's through trains, it was felt that a separate facility was required, and the Paterson & Hudson River built one at the foot of Newark Street, just north of the NJR & T's terminal.

Actually, the Paterson company had anticipated the Erie's moves and completed the new terminal in 1851 and established its own ferry to Duane Street — which was also the starting point for the Erie's steamer-ferry to Piermont! When all the leases were completed, the Erie found itself with a ready-made ferry to its already established Manhattan terminal. This line operated until 1861 when the Pavonia Ferry to Chambers Street commenced operations.

In 1855, Erie President Homer Ramsdell quietly purchased 212 acres of land and water frontage a half-mile into the Hudson River between Jersey City and Hoboken. Erie then formed the Long Dock Co. which was incorporated by the New Jersey Legislature. The Long Dock Co. was empowered to improve the property south of the center line of Pavonia Ferry in the Fourth Ward of Jersey City, to purchase other lands, and to establish a ferry.

On June 1, 1856, the Long Dock Co. commenced driving an 8,000-ft. tunnel through the lower Palisades. This tunnel was to connect the tracks of the Paterson & Hudson River Railroad on the west side of the Palisades and terminals of the Long Dock Co. on the east side on the west bank of the river. The Long Dock Co. was the actual entity of the New York & Erie Railway which created the Pavonia Ferry Co. The original charter for the Pavonia Ferry had been granted by King George II in 1733, but had lain dormant for 128 years until brought to reality by the Erie Railway Co. in 1861. The New York & Erie went into receivership in 1859 and was reorganized as the Erie Railway Co. in 1861 by Samuel and Nathaniel Marsh.

On May 1, 1861, the Chambers Street line was officially inaugurated, to run from Pavonia Avenue, Jersey City to the foot of Chambers Street, Manhattan.

The centennial issue of the *Erie Magazine* in May 1951 and *Men of Erie* (Hungerford, 1946) both state that the Pavonia Ferry was started with three secondhand boats from Brooklyn service: the *Niagara*, the *Onalaska*, and the *Onala*. Exhausting research has found both the *Onalaska* and *Niagara*, but not the existence of the *Onala*. Either this vessel was never registered or, in fact, only two ferryboats were transferred and the third was really the steamer *New Haven*. This second theory can be documented as follows: *Niagara*, built in 1849 by Perrine, Patterson & Stack, in Williamsburg, NY for the Williamsburg Ferry Co., was conveyed to the Brooklyn Ferry Co. on May 26, 1859, and conveyed again on October 9, 1861, to the New York & Erie Railroad Co. The

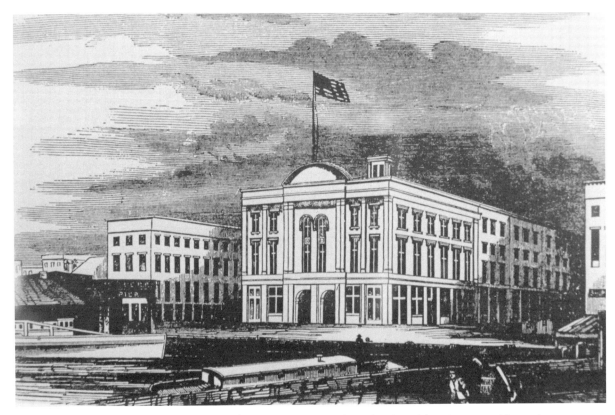

Erie's Duane Street Depot, New York City, 1851 as seen from the river side. – From an old wood cut

Onalaska, built in 1849, also by Perrine, Patterson & Stack for the Williamsburg Ferry Co., was conveyed on April 30, 1859, with the *Oneota* to the Brooklyn Ferry Co. On October 9, 1861, she was enrolled by Nathaniel Marsh, then secretary of the New York & Erie Railroad Co.

On December 28, 1861, both these vessels, along with the *New Haven,* were conveyed by the New York & Lake Erie Railway Co. to the Erie Railway Co.

The *New Haven* came under the ownership of the New York & Lake Erie Railway on December 1, 1847. In 1849, *New Haven* was towing barges to Piermont while steamer *Erie* carried passengers. Another account states that, in 1852, Erie Railroad steamers *New Haven* and *Erie* were used as Jersey City ferryboats, probably running between the Paterson & Hudson River terminals at Newark Ave., Jersey City and Duane St. On December 28, 1861, they were conveyed, along with *Niagara* and *Onalaska,* by Nathaniel Marsh, receiver for New York & Erie Railway, to the Erie Railway Co.

Another very interesting fact is found in an unpublished document on file in the Smithsonian Institute, Washington, DC. Entitled *Floating Equipment,* it concerns the Pennsylvania Railroad Co.'s marine operations. "The ferryboat *Philadelphia,* after April 15, and the *Hudson,* after May 1, 1861, were run under charter to the New York & Erie Railroad Company's Terminal" (p. 10).

This indicates that the Pavonia Ferry Co. operated four boats on its line. In the beginning, they were all chartered: *Onalaska* and *Niagara* from the Brooklyn Ferry Co. (until purchased in October 1861), and *Philadelphia* and *Hudson* for an undetermined period.

The *New York Tribune* of April 14, 1862, stated "The Erie's New Ferryboat *Pavonia* has just taken her place on the line. A trial trip was held on April 12, 1862. Afterward she commenced operation in regular service".

Cornelius Vanderbilt, who made a tremendous fortune in shipping, came to the Erie's financial aid by endorsing $400,000 of Erie paper and taking a mortgage on the road itself and its rolling stock. Following the "Commodore's" lead was another prominent New York City financier who was also involved in steamboating – Daniel Drew, founder of the People's Steamboat Line. Drew took a $980,000 mortgage on all remaining assets of the company.

In October 1857, all work stopped on the Bergen Tunnel as Erie's new president, Charles Moran, refused to pay the contractors. For a year and a half, nothing was done on the tunnel. In August 1859, Moran's salary was cut radically and, about a week later, he resigned from the Erie. Samuel Marsh was elected president and his nephew Nathaniel Marsh was appointed receiver by the courts.

Nathaniel became the president of the newly organized Erie Railway Co. in April 1861. The Civil War, like

Pier 20 and the Chambers Street Ferryhouse around 1910. The buildings looked the same in 1947, but the street was vastly changed with the building of the old West Side Highway. The trolleys were replaced with buses and a hot dog stand stood just about where those barricades near the trolley stand. Many a quick hot dog and orange drink were purchased by commuters and deckhands alike. — Railroadians of America

East River ferry slips and ferryboat *Alaska* taken from the Brooklyn Bridge in 1885. *Alaska* was similar to the first boats operated on the Pavonia Ferry in 1861.

most wars, gave the railroad a temporary shot in the arm. Once again, the figure of Dan Drew appeared in the Erie's path. In order to purchase new rolling stock for increased business, the Erie Railway sold its steamboats on Lake Erie to the Erie Railway Steamboat Co., which was owned by Drew. Under Marsh's guidance, the Erie prospered. Buffalo replaced Dunkirk as the main Lake Erie terminal, then Rochester was added, and finally, the Atlantic Great Western, running west from Salamanca, NY, became an Erie partner, thus creating a direct route from Jersey City to Cleveland, OH and St. Louis, MO. On July 18, 1864, however, diaster struck the Erie with the sudden death of Nathaniel Marsh, throwing the Erie into complete turmoil. Samuel Marsh once again became president pro-tem. After a battle of the board-room, Robert H. Berdell became president. Berdell was a longtime associate of Commodore Vanderbilt, who had grandiose intentions of merging the Erie with the New York & Harlem and Hudson River Railroad properties and with the New York Central.

Dan Drew, like a bad penny, turned up again, only this time, on the Erie board of directors, where he had been since 1854. Drew always seemed to come up with money when the Erie needed it, and, in three years, he became the company treasurer. By 1867, Drew had picked up two more memorable names in the dark pages of Erie History, Jim Fisk and Jay Gould.

Gould had ambitions of a transcontinental system and for this, he would keep pressing. He foresaw Erie as part of a greater system.

By 1868, the Erie was badly wrecked with all the good of Nathaniel Marsh's years gone. Drew had manipulated one of the biggest stock frauds of the time—all at the expense of the Erie. The great Commodore Vanderbilt was also involved in it. Drew had outfoxed him. Vanderbilt became obsessed with breaking Drew, even if it meant losing the money invested in the Erie. His idea of merging the Erie into the New York Central was forgotten, and all his energies were directed against the Erie. The Commodore was successful in breaking Drew, leaving him embittered and bankrupt.

Jim Fisk was the playboy of the Erie and wasted a great deal of the company's money on non-railroad fancy frills like the Grand Opera House on Manhattan's Twenty-third Street, which became the Erie's general offices for several years. Many lavish parties were held there, using Erie money and tying up company equipment. Jim met his just deserts on the short end of a lovers' triangle on January 6, 1872, when he was shot by Edward Stokes, the lover of Josie Mansfield, Fisk's mistress.

With Drew and Fisk out of the picture, Gould was left sitting in the president's chair, with complete control of the Erie. In 1868, Gould assumed command of a totally rundown system and undertook a major rebuilding job

Grand Opera House, 23rd Street and 8th Avenue in 1868 from a Rockwood picture.

Jay Gould

on the Erie. He was obsessed with creating a transcontinental system. But there were others in the field who were also looking westward, and they began to fear Gould. Commodore Vanderbilt had now become an enemy, rather than a friend, of the Erie. Others looking in the same direction as Gould were J. Edgar Thomson and John W. Garrett, representing the Pennsylvania and Baltimore & Ohio Railroads.

The next four years were stormy ones for the Erie. Its system was being rebuilt, but its advancement toward Chicago was halted by the successful countermeasures of Vanderbilt, Thomson, and Garrett. Once it became apparent that the Erie would not reach Chicago under the administration of Jay Gould, a rupture was caused by board member James McHenry, the controlling partner of the Atlantic Great Western Railway. With the internal strife among the Erie's directors, the company suffered. It became more and more apparent that the only solution was to get control from Gould. After many boardroom battles, a new board of directors was elected whose task it became to remove Jay Gould once and for all from the Erie. This was finally accomplished on March 12, 1872, when Gould resigned as president; three months later, he also resigned from the board of directors, forever giving up his hold on the Erie. Thus ended the reign of Erie's

blackest manipulators. But the Erie's problems were not at an end. In 1872, the Erie was completely changed over into a standard-gauge railroad, which increased its mobility and ability to interchange cars directly, as well as to handle high and wide loads, a considerable asset in later years.

Even with Black Friday and the Depression of 1873, the Erie paid a dividend on its common stock, something that it would not do for the next sixty-nine years.

Gould's dream of westward expansion was achieved in 1880 when the Erie entered Chicago, which thus became the Erie's most westerly terminus. By 1885, it had an all-Pullman train departing Jersey City at 6:00 P.M. for the west with sections to Chicago, Cleveland, Cincinnati, and St. Louis.

The original terminal in Jersey City, built in 1861, became too congested for the vast new passenger service.

Other, shorter, railroads then coming under Erie control needed terminal space in Jersey City. Therefore, the Erie started construction of its second Jersey City terminal, just north of the original one. Opened in 1886, this terminal was to serve the Erie Railroad for the next seventy-two years. The first Jersey City terminal was itself a marvel for its time. It boasted every possible facility, including an interpreter who spoke thirteen languages, as well as public stenographers, barbers, fine restaurants, and much elaborate woodwork. The second terminal was just as lavish as the first, and prodigious rush-hour traffic poured through it: In 1946, during the evening rush hour between 5:05 P.M. and 6:05 P.M., 30 trains departed and 2 arrived; 28 sets of equipment were backed into the station, and during one 41-minute period, 24 trains left Jersey City. During this era, Erie traffic was handled with a 99% on-time performance—absolute, to the minute—a skill which modern American railroads seem to have lost. Each day, this total traffic was handled by 61 trains, 6 gas-electric cars, 55 locomotives, and 255 coaches each with an 84-seat capacity. Trains ranged in length from 2 to 9 cars, and carried between 50 and 800 passengers each![1]

Apparently the Erie had a few good years, but they were not to last, for, in May 1893, the New York, Lake Erie & Western Railway Co., successor to the Erie Railway Co., went into bankruptcy. President John King and John G. McCullough were appointed coreceivers. On November 13, 1895, the Erie Railroad Co. was reorganized as a New York State corporation. Two of the companies absorbed under the new railroad were the Long Dock Co. and the Pavonia Ferry Co. After King's and McCullough's reorganization in 1895, the company

[1]In 1947, when I started with the Erie, on-time performance was demanded. The Erie had a reputation of being a freight railroad of the highest caliber. Its commuter passenger service was handled with the same pride and requirements for high standards as its freight service.

retained the same corporate structure until November 1960, when it absorbed the Delaware, Lackawanna & Western Railroad Co. and the name was changed to the Erie Lackawanna Railroad Co. In 1966, to allow for the merger of the Norfolk & Western and the Nickel Plate Railroads, the ICC ordered the Erie Lackawanna to be included as a subsidiary company. The Dereco Co. was thus formed and the Erie Lackawanna Railroad Co. became the Erie Lackawanna Railway, a subsidiary. In 1972, Dereco allowed the Erie Lackawanna to enter receivership; this time, it did not come out of it. On April 1, 1976, the Erie Lackawanna became part of the government-subsidized Consolidated Rail Corporation. It has since been chopped up and sections abandoned . . . thus ending the story of the Erie Railroad Company.

Pavonia Ferry, on the other hand, the Erie's maritime arm, was to have a somewhat happier history. Chartered in 1773, though dormant until 1861, it ran a rather good service until its closing in 1958. Erie Ferry service itself actually dated farther back—to 1847 when it purchased the *New Haven* and *Erie ex Iron Witch*.

By 1863, both *Erie ex Iron Witch* and *New Haven* were gone. But, as I mentioned earlier, the *Witch* was not totally dead. The main line between Suffern and Piermont was downgraded to a branch line. The *Traveler's Official Railway Guide* of June 1870 shows train service out of Piermont on the Piermont Branch. The guide's *River and Sound Steamboat* section, however, shows no listing of any vessels stopping at Piermont any longer. (Table 100)

Niagara and *Onalaska* were now owned by the Pavonia Ferry Co. *Philadelphia* was sold by its owner to the United States Quartermaster Department on April 17, 1863. *Hudson,* on the other hand, could have remained in Pavonia Ferry service at least until a replacement boat was built.

What of Erie's first boats? The *Pavonia* was built at Red Hook, in Brooklyn, NY by Devine Burtis. Her dimensions and specifications were:

Length Overall   205   ft.   Registered length   193.6 ft.
Breadth Overall   62   ft.   Registered breath   34   ft.
Depth   13.3 ft.   Gross Tons   831 40/95
Hull and superstructure wooden

Engine—Vertical beam with a 48-in. cylinder and 132-in. stroke. And, yes, the *Witch* had come back, for *Pavonia's* engine came from *Erie ex Iron Witch*. *Pavonia* had two return-flue boilers, 24-ft. long by 9-ft. diameter. Her paddlewheels were 22-ft. diameter and had a 9-ft. face.

In the pages of the *New York Tribune* of April 9, 1862 appeared the following review:

NEW FERRY-BOAT *Pavonia*

This boat, built for the Pavonia Ferry, to New Jersey, has just taken her place on the line. She is built of the best white oak, and is firmly braced from stem to stern. Her dimensions are: length of keel 190 feet; length over all 201 feet, breadth of beam 24 feet 4 inches [sic]; width overall 62 feet 8 inches. The boat is furnished with an engine of 48¾ in cylinder and 11 foot stroke, and two return-flue boilers, 24 feet long and 9 feet in diameter. The wheels are 22 feet with 9 feet face. She is supplied with four water tanks 18 feet long and 4 feet in diameter.

The boat is intended to carry forty teams. The cabins are spacious, are finished with black walnut and white ash, and lighted with gas. A new improvement in the shape of the gas signal lights is carried on the pilothouse. The *Pavonia* was built at Red Hook by Devine Burtis, and the engines were furnished by Fulton Iron Company of New York. On the trial trip, a few days ago, the boat accomplished 12 miles an hour with 8 pounds of steam.

And from the November 16, 1882—*Nautical Gazette*— "Cobanks & Theall, NY Iron Works, rebuilding 48 in. × 132 in. engine for Erie Ferry *Pavonia*. Engine: vertical beam, originally used in steamboat *Erie ex Iron Witch*."

During her career, the *Pavonia* was not immune to accidents; on July 8, 1871 (inspector's report), the *Pavonia* was run down and sunk by the *Oceanic* of the White Star Line. January 3, 1873, she was in a collision with the Pennsylvania Railroad ferryboat *D. S. Gregory*. In September 1878, she collided with the *James W. Baldwin*. On December 10, 1886, the barge *Alpha*, being towed by the tug *Valiant,* collided with *Pavonia*. On February 1, 1887, it was reported that the fog had been very troublesome and that the ferryboats *Pavonia* and *Lackawanna* had collided that Friday.

But by far the most serious accident involving the *Pavonia* happened on December 16, 1887, as she made the 4:50 P.M. trip from Chambers Street to Jersey City. Her captain was Alonzo Decker. *Pavonia* had left the north slip and was proceeding across the river bucking a strong ebb (outgoing) tide and northwest wind. Captain Decker reported that he saw the iron steamer *Breakwater* coming upriver off Barclay Street and about 400 feet in the river. *Breakwater* gave him one whistle (indicating that the ferry should cross in front of the steamer), which signal Captain Decker acknowledged. He rang a "jingle" for the engineer to "hook up" the engine (full speed). He stated that his wheel was "hard-a-port"[2] and fastened by the bracket. Apparently, the strong tide and wind, pushing downward, caused the *Pavonia* to slow to almost a complete stop and maybe even drift downstream, for the *Breakwater* caught the *Pavonia* just aft of the wheelhouse on the port side, ripping a large hole in the men's

[2]For many years, steamboats had a direct steering linkage. When you turned the wheel to port (left), the rudder would turn to starboard (right), causing the vessel to go to the starboard. So, if a captain wanted the vessel to go to starboard, he would turn the wheel to port. These vessels were all hand steered in those days. It took the Steamboat Inspection Service many years to change the steering system so that when you turned the wheel to port, the vessel *went* to port.

cabin. At the time of the accident, *Pavonia* was carrying between 600 and 700 passengers. Amazingly, there were only three or four injuries. Of these, only one was hospitalized, at St. Francis Hospital, Jersey City.

On March 14, 1889, the *Pavonia* and the Hoboken Ferry Co. *Montclair* collided. Then, the following November 29, she struck the tug *Etta Moon* off Chambers Street.

On November 19, 1902, the *Pavonia* was renamed the *Rutherford* and she ran until 1911 when she was scrapped. She ran for the company for fifty years.

In 1865, on May 2, the yard of J. Siminson of Greenpoint, NY launched the second Erie-built boat, the *Susquehanna.* This boat was larger than *Pavonia,* measuring 212 ft. × 64 ft. beam, 14-ft. depth and 921 gross tons. Her power plant was a 650-hp vertical-beam engine.

Like *Pavonia,* the *Susquehanna* was not immune to accidents. She collided with the canal boat *Victor* in tow of the tug *May Clinton* off Chambers Street slip on October 2, 1898.

In 1868, the *Delaware* became the third boat built for the Erie to join the fleet. Unfortunately, the Erie did not enjoy an increase in its fleet for, on the night of January 26, 1868, the recently refitted *Niagara* burned at the pier in Jersey City. The *Niagara* was a spare boat and had not been used in several months, but her loss was estimated at about $25,000. It was reported that the fire was of an incendiary nature. Never rebuilt, she was eventually scrapped.

On November 7, 1868, the John Englis and Son shipyard at Greenpoint, Brooklyn, NY launched the *Jay Gould,* which was somewhat smaller than *Pavonia* or *Susquehanna.* She was only 663 tons and 170 ft. in

length. *Jay Gould* had the distinction of being the inaugural vessel that officially opened the Twenty-third Street Ferry, leaving Pavonia Avenue, Jersey City at 10:00 A.M. on May 5, 1869 with an official party aboard. She cruised up the East River to Grand Street, up the North River to Weehawken, then landed her party of guests at Twenty-third Street where a gala luncheon was served.

Surely, during the reign of Jay Gould as president of the Erie, this vessel was queen of the fleet. But even queens have accidents for, on August 16, 1882, she collided with the steamer *Albany,* without injuries. Then again, on January 7, 1888, *Gould* collided with *D. R. Martin,* badly damaging the former's joiner work.

Even the flamboyant Jim Fisk had a vessel named after him. Charles Sneeden & Co., based on the East River at 12th Street, Manhattan launched the 745-ton, 550-hp *James Fisk* on April 12, 1869. *Fisk* was powered by a 42-in. × 120-in. vertical-beam engine. The namesake vessel of a man as flamboyant as Jim Fisk naturally could not pick on just any old barge or tug; *Fisk* collided with the sailing yacht *Josephine* on October 15, 1873, causing the death of one of the yacht's passengers. There is a good chance that the captain of the *Fisk* was not held responsible, however, as the yacht was not displaying any lights and the accident happened at night.

Until 1873, all Erie boats were built locally, mainly on the East River. On May 1, 1873, a totally new type vessel was launched for the Erie Railroad. Her name, very appropriately, was *Erie* and she was the first iron-hulled vessel on the North River. Her builder was Delaware River Iron Steamboat and Engine Works of Chester, PA. John Roach & Sons delivered this 981-ton vessel, powered by a 46-in. × 132-in. vertical-beam engine, on July

New York, Lake Erie & Western Railway's ferryboat *Jay Gould* launched November 7, 1868, was the vessel chosen to run the inaugural trip of the new West 23rd Street service opened on May 5, 1869. She was rebuilt and renamed *Chautauqua* in 1894. — Courtesy of The Mariners' Museum, Newport News, Virginia

A boat from Jersey City has just arrived in the upper slip at 23rd Street and the passengers are waiting surface transportation in this 1910 Bailey glass plate taken for the Erie Railroad Company. — Railroadians of America

24, 1873. *Erie* became the third such vessel in New York Harbor, the other two being the *Fulton* and *Farragut,* built in 1871, and owned by the Union Ferry Co. on the East River. There may have been some type of relationship between the Pavonia Ferry and Union Ferry Co., as Union boats were known to have replaced Erie boats on routes when the latter were laid up for repairs. Both *Osprey* and *Mineola,* for example, were Union boats recorded replacing *Susquehanna* and *Pavonia.*

December 31, 1873, saw the last of the original Brooklyn Ferry Co. boats, the *Onalaska,* taken off the roster. She was reduced to a barge and her papers surrendered to the steamboat inspectors.

In 1879, the *James Fisk* was renamed *Passaic I*. She became the first Erie boat to be named after a town on the Erie line.[3]

The last sidewheel vessel built for the Erie was the *John King,* named after the president of the company at that time. *John King* was also built with an iron hull and came from the yard of William Cramp and Son, Philadelphia, PA. Her gross tonnage was 1,057, the heaviest of any Erie boat to date, and the first one to go over 1,000 tons. The *King's* vertical-beam engine was 50 in. × 120 in. and 700 hp; steam was supplied by one return-tube boiler with a pressure of 40 lbs.

Erie once again went to Philadelphia for a boat in 1891 — this time, to Neafie & Leavy's Yard, which pro-

duced the second propeller-driven ferryboat for New York Harbor, and the first with a compound engine. Her engine had two cylinders — a low-pressure of 50-in. diameter, a high pressure of 26 in., and a 30-in. stroke which developed 800 hp. She was named the *John G. McCullough,* after one of the court-appointed receivers of the Erie Railway. *McCullough,* like the Hoboken Ferry Co.'s *Bergen,* the first propeller boat of modern times, was single deck. The main difference between the two was that the engine used in the *Bergen* was a triple-expansion engine, meaning that it had an intermediate-pressure cylinder between the low- and high-pressure cylinders. *McCullough* was a big boat. Her overall length was 215 ft. with a registered length of 200.6 ft. Her beam over guards was 62 ft. with a 38-ft. beam of hull, and a depth 16 ft. Her gross tonnage was 1,309.67 with a net of 1,007.88. The propellers were 8 ft. 6 in. in diameter and connected by a continuous shaft to the engine. Like the *Bergen,* her rudders were completely below the water, directly behind the propeller; and, as the propeller turned, the water was forced past the rudder, which, when turned, forced a drag on the water and forced the vessel in the direction of the drag. *McCullough* had two Scotch boilers which produced 100 lbs. of steam. She was the first vessel on the Erie to have high-pressure boilers.

Sometime in 1894, the Erie started the practice of naming its vessels after cities and towns along the line. As previously mentioned, the *Fisk* was renamed *Passaic* and the *Jay Gould* was renamed *Chautauqua I*. In 1899, *John King* was renamed *Paterson*. Several years went by before any more changes took place and, in 1902, the *Erie* became the *Ridgewood* and the *Pavonia,* the

---

[3]Pavonia was a section of Jersey City's Fourth Ward where the Erie terminal was located. Susquehanna is a county in Pennsylvania and a river in that state. Delaware is a county in New York and a river comprising the boundary of New York and Pennsylvania, alongside of which, the Erie tracks run.

Rutherford I. On August 27, the *Delaware* appeared on the river as the *Sterlington*.

Just after the turn of the century, Erie announced that it was building three new double-deck propeller ferryboats. These boats were to be identical, but all three were contracted out to different shipyards. Although it was reported that the first vessel would be the *Tuxedo*, the first one actually launched was the *Arlington* of 1,446 gross tons, on November 21, 1903 at the Burlee Dry Dock Co., Port Richmond, Staten Island, NY. *Arlington's* trial trip was made on March 15, 1904, and she then joined the fleet.

Just about two weeks after *Arlington* slid down the ways, her sister, the *Tuxedo*, of 1,483 gross tons, was launched on December 5,1903, at Harlan & Hollingsworth's yard in Wilmington, DE. *Tuxedo's* trial trip was held on February 25, 1904, about two weeks earlier than *Arlington's*. So, essentially, these two boats were the same age. *Arlington's* papers show her built in 1903, and *Tuxedo* in 1904. Apparently both *Arlington* and *Tuxedo* went into service at approximately the same time. *Arlington* was a day boat on Chambers Street and *Tuxedo*, a 23rd Street boat.

The contract for the third boat had been let out to Lewis Nixon's Crescent Shipyard of Elizabethport, NJ, but the yard failed and the boat's building was delayed almost a year. On October 29, 1904, Harlan & Hollingsworth launched the *Goshen* of 1,459 gross tons. Like her sister, the *Tuxedo*, the *Goshen* was delivered in February of the following year. Arriving at the Erie on February 2, 1905, *Goshen* was considered built in 1905 according to her records.

The three sisters were designed by J. W. Millard of New York. The overall length of these vessels was 224 ft., breadth over guards of 64 ft., and a depth of 16.4 ft., powered by two 18-in. × 38-in. × 28-in. compound en-

gines of 1,200 hp with steam supplied by two Scotch boilers of 150 psi. Each vessel had five watertight bulkheads, so built that doors could never be left open by mistake.

The most novel feature of all was the method of seating the passengers. Instead of having the seats around the sides of the cabin, they were placed side by side, three deep, so that six persons sitting facing each other could look out on the water.

Access to the upper deck was via two stairways in the women's cabin. Stairways were omitted in the men's cabin in order to exclude smoke and tobacco odors from the upper deck. There were two stairways at each end of the upper deck, on the men's cabin side, which descended directly to the quarterdecks. The interiors of two of the boats were finished in quartered oak and the third, in mahogany.

With three new boats added to the fleet, all of them double deckers, the company took the single-deck *John G. McCullough* out of service and undertook her complete rebuilding. Her single-compound engine was doubled up to make her double compound, like the three new boats, increasing her hp to 1,500. A second deck was added, increasing her tonnage to 1,327 gross. Lastly, the *McCullough* left the yard in 1906 as the *Chautauqua II*. She was the second boat to be so named, the first being the *Jay Gould* in 1894.[4]

Erie's newest sidewheeler, the *Paterson*, was involved in a disasterous collision on the night of December 29, 1906, with the tug *Joshua Lovitt*, causing the *Paterson* to sink.

---

[4]The first *Chautauqua* ex *Jay Gould* having been sold to the Billingsfort Philadelphia Ferry Co. which registered her in Camden, N.J. on June 8, 1905. She was scrapped on March 31, 1912.

Erie Railroad ferryboat *Passaic* ex *James Fiske* built in 1869 and renamed in 1879 on the West 23rd Street run. Hoboken Ferry, 14th Street, Hoboken dock visible in background. — Courtesy of The Mariners' Museum, Newport News, Virginia

Erie *Paterson* ex *John King* built in 1886 and renamed in 1899 the *Paterson* was sunk in a collision with the tug *Joshua Lovitt* in 1906. To our knowledge she was the only Erie ferryboat to ever have sunk in the 97 years history of the Erie Ferry service. — Courtesy of The Mariners' Museum, Newport News, Virginia

Ferryboat *Arlington* leaving the Erie's old Pavonia Avenue, Jersey City Terminal for Chambers Street, New York, with a few *Susquehanna* passengers in the final days of service while the *Jamestown* lays dead in the lower slip, no longer serviceable. The date is August 28, 1958. — Dan Biernacki Collection

Although not condoned by management, ferryboat racing was a common practice between captains of the various lines. *Ridgewood* appears to be running hooked-up trying to get the edge on a Pennsylvania Railroad *St. Louis* class propeller boat. *Ridgewood* is ex *Erie*. — Courtesy of The Mariners' Museum, Newport News, Virginia

Ferryboat *Tuxedo* is carrying an evening rush hour load of commuters the nice summery day of August 27, 1945. — Dan Biernacki Collection

Goshen running under a slow bell as she makes for the middle slip in Jersey City. — Dan Biernacki Collection

J.E. Bailey, Erie Railroad photographer, snapped the ferryboat *Chautauqua* around 1910. *Chautauqua* ex *John G. McCullough*, was the second propeller boat in New York Harbor, following *Bergen*. She was double-decked in 1906. In 1936 her name was changed to *Rutherford*, and she was sold to the Navy in 1943, where her number was YFB 48. She was scrapped in 1946. — Railroadians of America

Interior of ferryboat *Chautauqua*, taken by Erie photographer J.E. Bailey, of Meadville, Pennsylvania around 1910. — Railroadians of America

An account was found in the *New York Times* June 6, 1907, headed "Tugboat Captain Suspended. Held Responsible for Sinking of the Ferryboat *Paterson*."

The article went on to detail the *Paterson's* fate:

After months of trials Supervising Captain Ira Harris of the Local Board of Steamboat Inspectors decided yesterday the question of who was at fault in the collision between the Commercial Towboat Company's tug, *Joshua Lovitt*, and the Erie ferryboat *Paterson*, by exonerating Capt. George S. Funston of the *Paterson*, and suspending Capt. Charles E. Baker for sixty days.

On Dec. 29 the *Paterson* was sunk with the loss of one life, by the barge *Flora*, which was in tow of the *Joshua Lovitt*. Charges were preferred against Capt. Baker on two counts. The first was that he carried three lights on his mast, which indicated that he had a vessel in tow at least 600 feet astern, and second that he violated the pilot rules because the *Paterson* was on his starboard bow and therefore had the right of way.

Capt. Funston was also tried. The charge against him was based upon the allegation of Capt. Baker that instead of crossing the river, he was bringing the *Paterson* upstream.

Capt. Baker admitted the first charge and was found guilty on the second.

In 1907, the Erie had four double-deck propeller ferryboats plying the North River. And, on September 26, 1907, their fifth, the *Jamestown*, was launched at Burlee Dry Dock Co., Port Richmond, NY. *Jamestown* joined the Erie fleet on December 21, 1907, making her maiden voyage. *Jimmy*, slightly larger than the three sisters of the *Arlington* class, measured in at 225 ft. overall length and 1,538 gross tons, almost 100 tons heavier than *Arlington*. Yet, like *Arlington*, the *Jamestown* was only 1,200 hp and had a boiler pressure of 150 psi. But *Jimmy* had one problem — port (left) list — which, for some reason, was never corrected. This list caused problems when a deckhand didn't watch his vehicle loading, as a heavy truck on that side caused the list to increase; if it got too severe, it was so difficult to steer that you put out cabin windows as you entered the slip and passed the end clumps.[5]

_____

[5] I remember when I first started working and I was assigned to work the *Jamestown* days. I put one truck on the port gangway and the *Jimmy's* list must have increased by what I thought was 25° and I never did get it upright. The *Jamestown* went across the river like a sailboat on a strong tack. The Captain was Ernie Rodgers and he called me up to the pilothouse and bawled the hell out of me. That afternoon, Tom Hogan explained to me why I had to be very careful loading the boats and always favor the port side when loading. (RJB)

Erie's ferryboat *Jamestown* had to wait for Dalzell tugs to push the AP 74 out of her way before she could enter the Jersey City slips on August 27, 1945 just a few weeks after the end of World War II. – Dan Biernacki Collection

January 30, 1908, saw the original *Delaware's* name changed for the second time, from *Sterlington* to *Suffern*.

February 1908 was a very interesting month for Hudson County, NJ and the City of New York as they were connected by the first, direct rail link. The Hudson & Manhattan Railroad made its first trip from 19th Street, New York City to Hoboken, New Jersey on February 25. Within a year, the H & M, or "Tubes" as they became known, had opened its lines to 33rd Street, NY and downtown New York, where the Hudson Terminal Buildings were located at 30 and 50 Church Street, and to Exchange Place, Jersey City. The station which would affect the Erie Ferry was called "Erie" or "Pavonia." This station was on a section of track parallel with the river. It was served by trains which ran to and from Hoboken and Hudson Terminal (Church Street, NY). The uptown service was from Exchange Place, and later Grove Street and Journal Square, to and from 33rd Street Terminal located near Sixth Avenue, NY. So the Erie Station had service to both uptown (midtown) and downtown, New York. One must realize one thing: Though ferry passage was free for persons holding railroad tickets, in 1908, it cost a nickel to ride the Tubes in each direction. A nickel may not sound like much money, but in those days, people were only making a dollar or so for a whole day's work. So the nickel was a big price to pay.

May 27,1910, the *Passaic I* ex *Fisk* was sold and by September 1910, she was in service on the Brooklyn & Manhattan Ferry and renamed the *Broadway*.

Susquehanna, in 1906, had her gangways removed and made into a passenger only boat. Apparently this did not prove practical, as she was reported tied up and out of service at the Weehawken Coal Docks in 1908. After that *Susquehanna* was rebuilt as a regular ferry once again and on January 12, 1912, she appeared on the river sporting the name *Arden*.

The Erie sidewheel boats were getting old, and with the loss of the *Paterson*, the newest of the sidewheelers was the *Ridgewood* ex *Erie*, built in 1873. The company decided to purchase two West Shore Ferry Co. boats which had been out of service since 1911. So, on February 16, 1916, the West Shore *Oswego* and *Newburgh* became the property of the Erie's Pavonia Ferry Co. renamed *Oswego, Passaic*.

Staten Island Shipbuilding Co. at Mariner's Harbor, NY, launched the *Youngstown* on October 26, 1922. The *Youngstown* was built on the same plan as the *Jamestown*, but slightly modified in the engine room. *Youngstown* had a surface condenser, 1,600 hp double-compound engines and was 15 tons heavier, than the *Jamestown*, weighing in at 1,553 gross tons.

Youngstown became the workhorse for the Erie in later years. She was the night boat, running seventeen hours a day and all weekend from 5:00 P.M. Friday right through to 9:45 A.M. the following Monday. She was also the day relief boat when another boat had to be tied up for a small repair job.

With the adding of the *Youngstown* to the fleet, the Erie had eleven ferryboats at year's end. The oldest was the 57-year-old *Arden* ex *Susquehanna*. During the next two years, *Arden* was scrapped and *Newburgh* was sold to the Staten Island Steamboat Co. on March 24, 1924,

Ferryboat *Suffern* ex *Sterlington* ex *Delaware* built in 1868 she was the third boat built new for the Erie. – Courtesy of The Mariners' Museum, Newport News, Virginia

Ferryboat *Passaic II* leaving Pavonia Avenue, with a new Erie diesel tug in the background. This is the second *Passaic,* she was purchased in 1916 from the West Shore and scrapped in June 1935. She was the last sidewheel ferryboat on the Erie. Note difference in pilothouses. I was told that when the *Arden* was scrapped a pilothouse from her was removed and put on the *Passaic*. – Dan Biernacki Collection (RJB)

Ferryboat *Youngstown* leaves Jersey City with 9:18 A.M. rush hour trip, normally her last trip for the night boat crew. But this morning she will make a special trip to 42nd Street Terminal of the West Shore Ferry with a special group. The two men just outside of the pilothouse will remove the sheer pole in order for her to use the West Shore slip at 42nd Street.

to later be renamed the *Governor Albert G. Richie* of the Claiborne & Annapolis Ferry Co. On May 26, 1926, she was reengined with a Baldwin-Lima-Hamilton diesel. Next of the Erie sidewheel boats to be disposed of was the *Suffern* ex *Delaware* built in 1868. She had been rebuilt in 1912, but her hull was wood and apparently she was due for another rebuilding; the Company felt that she was due for retirement, so the 58-year-old boat was scrapped in 1926.

The year 1927 brought a new competitor to the ferry business. In 1908, the Tubes started to attract passengers and now, just four city blocks away, at 12th and Henderson Streets, was the new Holland Tunnel, which was capable of taking both vehicles and passengers away from the railroad ferry business. With the opening of the tunnel, motor buses could go directly between New York and New Jersey with passengers who would have otherwised used the trains and ferries.

By July 1929, the last Erie-built sidewheeler, the *Ridgewood* ex *Erie*, had been removed from the roster leaving only the second hand *Passaic II* ex *Oswego* of the West Shore as the sole sidewheeler and single-deck boat operating out of Pavonia Avenue.[6]

---

[6]In the photos of *Passaic II*, you can plainly see two different-shaped pilothouses. I was told by Tom Hogan that a pilothouse from the *Arden* had been put on the *Passaic II*. *Arden* had been rebuilt in 1912 after the *Jamestown* was built and if you look at the New York-end pilothouse of the *Passaic II*, you will note a distinct similarity to the *Jamestown's* pilothouses. It should be noted that most of the railroads had excellent marine yards in which most of the major rebuilding was done. They also paid their carpenters, boilermakers, and other craftsmen a fairly good wage. (RJB)

This left the Erie with seven boats to operate two ferry routes. For the next five years, the Erie maintained a four-boat rush-hour schedule on Chambers Street and a two-boat schedule on 23rd Street. The *Passaic II*, now 52 years old — her days were numbered. Even though the nation was in a serious depression, the Erie knew that it must consider a replacement for the *Passaic II*. Once again, Erie management went back to the very successful Delaware River shipbuilders for a boat. In Chester, PA was the Sun Shipbuilding and Drydock Company, where, on June 10, 1935, the keel was laid for the last Erie ferryboat to be built; also, the last ferryboat to be built, from the keel up, for any New York Harbor railroad ferry operation. Between June 1935 and March 1936, the *Meadville* began to take shape. Finally, on March 7, 1936, Mrs. Adeline Kiebort, wife of the Meadville, PA mayor, broke a bottle of champagne across the bow and the *Meadville* slid down the ways into the Delaware River. She was by far the largest vessel ever built for the Erie, with a tonnage of 1,599 gross and 1,074 net. Her overall length was 234 ft., breadth over guards of 64.3 ft., and a depth of 17.9 ft. *Meadville* was capable of seating 1,100 passengers, with gangway space provided for thirty cars and trucks.

Meadville was different from the other boats in many ways. Her hull was of a totally different design than any other Erie boat. It was a "spoon" hull with barely any keel at all. The *Meadville* worked diametrically opposite the other boats, too, in that she approached the slip against the tide rather than on the tide. When the older boats would be going upriver and coming down across the pin at the end of Dock 4 on the ebb tide, the *Meadville* would be coming upriver, and just about the time she

THE RAILROAD FERRIES OF THE HUDSON

Meadville on the ways at the Sun Shipbuilding and Drydock Company, Chester, Pennsylvania. Taken a few days before her launching on March 7, 1936. — Courtesy of The Sun Company, Inc.

Even after crossing the river the excellent steaming *Meadville*'s safety valves release as she enters the ice bound upper slip at Chambers Street. — Dan Biernacki Collection

was almost abreast of the slip, the captain would swing the stern against the tide and work into the slip. She handled the same as a tugboat and float, but had a quicker responding engine—a Skinner-Unaflow Marine engine.

The Unaflow consisted of five 25-in. high-pressure cylinders and a 24-in. stroke supplying 1,750 hp at 135 rpms. The engine was powered by two Babcock & Wilcox watertube boilers, each supplying 13,500 lbs. of steam per hour at 175 lbs. pressure.[7] Her forced-draft boilers were coal fired with anthracite, which was mixed two parts buckwheat and one part pea. The gangways of the *Meadville* were also somewhat different in that the steering columns, which normally ran directly from the pilothouse down to the steering engine compartments, were removed, as the *Meadville* did not have ropes or cables from the steering engine to the hand wheel in the pilothouse as did the other boats. She had a series of rods, cogs, and gears connected to the handwheel and steering engine. Because of these, there was no need for the columns, as the rods could be run up through the centerhouse. The removal of the column on the Jersey end allowed the coal trucks to back right to the coal

hatch and hence the deckhands could get three cars in the extra space.

Another advantage was that her handwheel was not engaged and thus not spinning around as the captain turned the steam steering wheel. This removed the danger of someone getting hit with the spokes of that big wheel. If it became necessary to engage it, the captain or wheelsman could do so in a matter of seconds by lining the wheel up with the sprocket, engaging the clutch, then releasing the tension on the steam gear. Her boat gates did not go up and down like the other boats; rather, they slid across the deck on casters. This type of gate never got broken by passing trucks. It was said that the *Meadville* could stop on a dime and give you nine cents' change!

A good engineer could go from full ahead to full astern without using the throttle lever, just by moving the eccentric levers in the opposite direction, but the trick was that both levers had to pass each other at just the right spot so that the stops lined up.

On March 18, 1936, a trial trip of the *Meadville* was run on the Delaware River, at which time a speed of 16 mph was attained.

On March 23, 1936, she arrived at the Erie Railroad Co. in Jersey City in tow of *Susan A. Moran*. The tow from Chester, PA to Jersey City, NJ took thirty hours.

---

[7]*Meadville*'s boiler pressure had been increased to 200 lbs. pressure by 1947.

Erie ferryboat *Rutherford II* ex *Chautauqua II* ex *John G. McCullough* heading up river toward West 23rd Street, New York. *Rutherford* was sold to the Navy in May 1943 and became YFB 48 and operated out of Pensacola, Florida until the end of World War II. — Courtesy of The Mariners' Museum, Newport News, Virginia

Because of her operating differences, *Meadville* caused a lot of damage when she first was put in service on Chambers Street.[8] The men who first worked on her attributed a lot of the damage to the fact that the captains were handling her like conventional ferryboats.[9]

With the *Meadville* on the roster, the Erie now had eight boats; so, on June 30, 1936 the *Passaic II*, Erie's last sidewheeler, was scrapped.

In 1936, the Erie decided to change the name of the *Chautauqua II* to *Rutherford II*. So the *John G. McCullough* was now the second Erie boat to have that name and the second one to have had her name changed more than once.

With the addition of *Meadville* and the scrapping of *Passaic*, the Erie still operated the four boats on Chambers Street and two on 23rd Street. As Chambers Street was still the main New York terminal, the bigger boats were used there. *Meadville, Youngstown, Jamestown,* and *Arlington* were the main Chambers Street boats

while *Tuxedo* and *Goshen* ran 23rd Street, leaving the *Rutherford* as a spare boat alternating with *Goshen* on 23rd Street.[10]

This operation continued until July 5, 1942, when the Erie discontinued its 23rd Street route. *Rutherford, Tuxedo,* and *Goshen* then became spare boats. Even though *Arlington* was older than both *Tuxedo* and *Goshen*, she had always been a day boat, operating only about ten hours a day, so she stayed in regular service. *Rutherford* was now 51 years old, *Tuxedo*, 38, and *Goshen*, 37.

During WW II, the U.S. Government wanted to expand the shipyards on the Hoboken/Weehawken city line. The Erie marine yard and Weehawken freight yard ran north from the Hoboken city line next to the shipyard, so Erie had to build a new marine yard.

Around September 1939, the Erie grain elevator located at Pier 1, Jersey City, just south of Pavonia Avenue, caught fire and, along with Dock 2, was totally destroyed. This location was decided upon for the new ma-

---

[8]*Meadville* remained a Chambers Street boat because of her length and the short racks at 23rd Street. (They did try her at 23rd Street, where one captain hit the bridge, causing a considerable amount of damage.)

[9]One of her captains who was working the afternoon job when I started in 1947 was Frankie Windknuckel. He was one of the most happy-go-lucky persons I have ever met. They say that Frankie had a friend who worked on the city ferries at Whitehall who, one day, was riding in the pilothouse with Frankie. Noticing the problem that Frankie had in making the slip, he suggested that *he* try to land against the tide or swing the boat, like they did on the city boats. Frankie let him take the boat to New York and make a swing landing. It made the difference and, after that, Frankie started to swing the *Meadville*. The word got around and all the other captains who steered her started to do the same thing. Some of the Erie captains re-

fused to steer the *Meadville,* Ernie and Steve Rodgers were two whom I knew of.

[10]It is not clear from what I was told whether *Goshen* or *Rutherford* was in regular service on 23rd Street along with *Tuxedo*. I do know that Captain John Stein, Sr. ran into a ship's anchor chain in the fog, ripping open the women's cabin of the *Rutherford*. The same day, Captain G. Wolfer, brother of William Wolfer, had an accident with the *Jamestown,* badly damaging the men's cabin. John told me that he put the *Rutherford* in the upper slip in Jersey City. Wolfer, coming in the middle slip with the *Jimmy*, yelled over to him, "Hey Steinie, you're going to have to run for me — I just ripped open the men's cabin." John's reply was, "I can't, I just left the women's cabin wrapped around an anchor chain in mid-river!" Even though the company renamed *Chautauqua* the *Rutherford*, she always was the "Chickie" to the men who worked on her.

The Jersey City team entrance to the Erie Railroad Ferry. The 23rd Street fare collector is in the booth to the left of the sign and the Chambers Street booth is to the right. Both fare booths had been removed by 1947 and one fare booth placed in the center of the entrance. — Railroadians of America

rine yard. The actual shop buildings were on a concrete pier, about 450 ft. × 200 ft., running from the South Yard bulkhead east toward the river. From this, a dock about 300 ft. × 30 ft. was built into the canal. Two ferryboats could be tied up there, one on each side. Since each boat had to be inspected annually, there was almost always a boat on the north side of the pier. The south side was used for general repairs of car floats, barges, and the like.[11]

---

[11]The marine yard is the only part of the Erie marine operation still in Jersey City in 1985. True, there are still some of the tugs on the river, under different owners, but the marine yard is still in the same place and operating as a marine repair facility. The estate of the Erie-Lackawanna Railway Co. sold the property to the Tug and Barge Drydock Co. of the McAllister Bros. Towing Co. It has recently been sold to the Jersey City Redevelopment Agency because of a total waterfront area redevelopment. I might add that McAllister did not want to sell. Jersey City's McCann administration also forced the Rodermond Dry Dock Co. at the foot of Henderson Street to sell and move to Brooklyn, NY. Rodermond had been serving the marine industry at that location on the Morris Canal Basin for over a hundred years.

On May 8, 1943, the *Goshen* and *Rutherford* were sold to the U.S. Navy for use in Pensacola, FL Naval Air Station. *Goshen* became the *YFB 47* and *Rutherford* became the *YFB 48*. It was rumored that the Erie wanted to keep the *Goshen* and sell the *Tuxedo*, but the Navy refused to accept the *Tuxedo*, so the *Goshen* went south to Florida with the *Rutherford*. Both vessels were sold and scrapped after the war.

The remaining five boats comprised the Erie fleet for the remainder of WW II — right through the end of the Korean Conflict.

At the beginning of WW II, the Erie Terminal was fifty-five years old and a wooden firetrap. The City of Jersey City had indicated that it should be replaced. The war prevented this. After the war, in 1946, the city renewed its demand for the replacement of the station. For the next five years, the Erie and the Jersey City fathers fought back and forth on a new structure. Erie wanted to move the location of the new station to the juncture of the terminal tower and the Hudson Tube entrance and abandon the ferry operations. The city indicated that they would fight the abandonment of the ferry, so no terms could be reached. Several sets of plans were submitted

An Erie Railroad patrolman and a couple of commuters stand around the ferry terminal of the Erie Station at Pavonia Avenue in this Bailey shot. There was little difference between this scene of around 1910 and 1954 when the author patrolled this terminal on the afternoon shift. The windows were closed in and a modern look was given by installing smaller oval windows. The Union News Company bar was located in this part of the terminal. — Railroadians of America

Pavonia Avenue looking towards downtown Jersey City. Dock 2 is to the left; it burned down in a spectacular fire in 1939. Track 1 of the station is to the right. The Henderson Trolley was replaced by Public Service bus route #27, which was discontinued in the early 1950's. But the cobble stone street remained long after the station was torn down in the 1960's. — Railroadians of America

One of the Erie's new *Arlington* class propeller driven ferryboats leaving Pavonia Avenue for Chambers Street. Just above the boat is the Erie's large grain elevator, which burned down along with Dock 2, which was alongside the ferry slips around 1939. Up until the fire the lower slip and that nice long rack was the regular night boat slip. The long rack helped many a captain in foul weather to make a safe landing. — Railroadians of America

but all were rejected by the city, for one reason or another.

Then came the Korean Conflict and the Erie once again used the war as an excuse for not being able to get materials. After the ceasefire and the end of the conflict, Jersey City, which now had a new administration in power, condemned the sixty-nine-year-old structure. Now, Erie had to do something, so they resubmitted their original plan to move the location of the new station to the Hudson Tube entrance and abandon the ferry operation. Once again, the city rejected the plan to abandon the ferry and made radical alterations to the terminal plans which would have increased the cost prohibitively. The Erie figured there was no way they could come to terms with Jersey City. So what did they do? In March 1953, Jim Buesing, the chief engineer, instructed all the engineers that the boats had to make better time, so "Start running them." Everybody knew something was amiss, but no one could put a finger on it. One day, Captain John Stein, Jr. was ordered to take the *Meadville* to the Hoboken/Lackawanna terminal and try her in the ferry slips there.

Finally, with the seasonal change of the timetable in the fall, it all came together. The night boat was abolished and the late-afternoon boat was to work until the last mainline train boat trip, and then tie up. She became the overtime boat rather than the night boat. The night boat was rebid as an early-morning boat, which came out just before the arrival of the first trains. This saved the

company one crew and left the relief crew working only four days a week. A short time later, a three-boat schedule was adopted. The *Tuxedo's* certification papers were allowed to run out and the company applied for an extension, which was granted. At year's end of 1954, the *Tuxedo* was retired from service and sold for scrap in 1955. In late 1955 and early 1956, the Erie and the Delaware, Lackawanna & Western Railroad reached an agreement on track consolidation in upstate New York between Binghamton and Corning where the two main lines are but feet apart. Talk of this nature was to spell doom for the Jersey City terminal.

The Erie ran with four boats during the year 1956. But things were happening along the line. A consolidation agreement was reached between the Erie and the Lackawanna where the Erie Jersey City passenger operation would be moved to the Lackawanna terminal in Hoboken. Hoboken would be operated by the Lackawanna as a consolidated terminal and the ferry operation would remain a Lackawanna operation. A new track connection was built in the meadows between the Erie mainline and the Lackawanna-Boonton Line. The second connection for the Erie-Greenwood Lake trains was made at the west end of the West End interlocking plant and an addition was put on West End Tower to handle the additional switches and turnouts, plus the old Erie-Bergen interlocking plant.

With the completion of the track connections, phase one was ready to be implemented. The first phase of the

Ferryboat *Meadville* is in the middle slip at Pavonia Avenue Terminal and a tug prepares to tie up to a carfloat on a busy day on the Erie Railroad.

Aerial view, taken around 1945, of Erie's Pavonia Avenue, Jersey City waterfront property. The two ferryboats are tied up in the marine yard.

Pavonia slips August 25, 1958, just a few months before abandonment.

With an early evening group of commuters on her bow the *Jamestown*'s captain has just stopped the boat after the first back of the engines—Dan Biernacki Collection

Middle ferry slip gates at Erie's Jersey City Pavonia Terminal are open awaiting passengers for the boats one mile trip to New York City.

The main ticket counter of the old Erie Pavonia Avenue Terminal in Jersey City.

The evening rush hour at Erie Pavonia Avenue Terminal, is just about to start The three ferry slips are just slightly to the right of the terminal. The "Erie" sign is on Dock 4.

Diesel engines are just starting to appear on Erie property in this 1950 photograph of their Pavonia Avenue complex. The terminal lies in right rear center and the ferry slips slightly to the right of the towers. The upper slip was in front of the North tower, while the middle and lower slips were directly at the end of Pavonia Avenue, which ran between the engine yard and the mid-Hudson warehouse.

The American flag is well displayed in this 1910 Bailey photograph of Chambers Street as the *Goshen* reverses her engines entering the upper slip. — Railroadians of America

Chambers Street slips — Erie's only electrically operated can be seen in this cold winter scene.

The last men to work the Erie Ferry pose for Erie photographer Jack Dimond in August 1958: in the pilot-house; Captain William Wolfer (hand on telegraph), and Wheelsman Joe Yacono; sitting on the hurricane deck; unknown fireman; Fred Petri, Engineer; unknown fireman; John Di Nuto, Deckhand; Ross Esposito, Deckhand; and Steven Perricane, Bridgeman. — Dan Biernacki Collection

World War II was only over about three weeks as the *Arlington* enters the slips at Chambers Street in Auguust 1945. — Dan Biernacki Collection

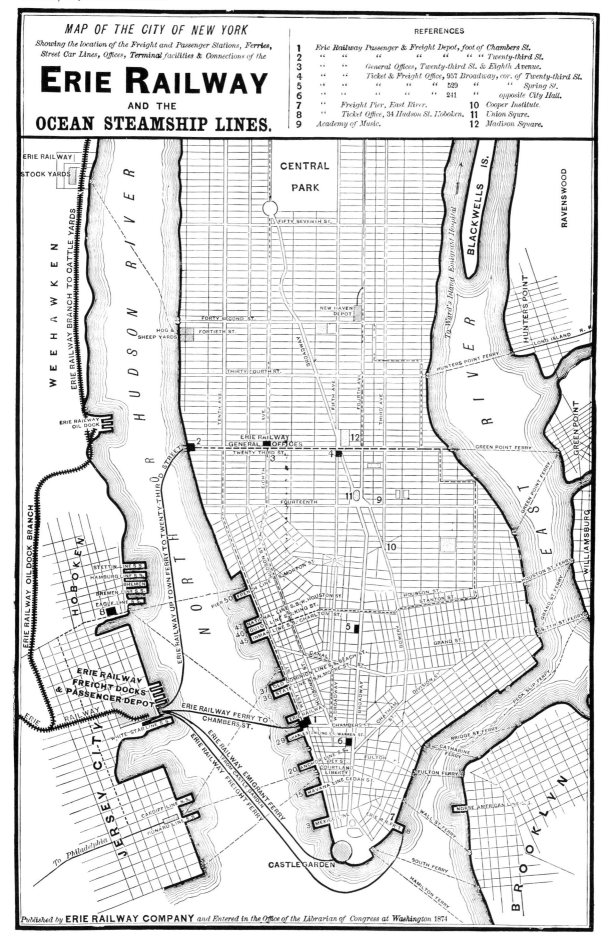

MAP OF THE CITY OF NEW YORK

Showing the location of the Freight and Passenger Stations, Ferries,
Street Car Lines, Offices, Terminal facilities & Connections of the

ERIE RAILWAY
AND THE
OCEAN STEAMSHIP LINES.

REFERENCES

1	Erie Railway Passenger & Freight Depot, foot of Chambers St.
2	" " " " " " Twenty-third St.
3	" " General Offices, Twenty-third St. & Eighth Avenue.
4	" " Ticket & Freight Office, 957 Broadway, cor. of Twenty-third St.
5	" " " " " 529 " " Spring St.
6	" " " " " 241 " opposite City Hall.
7	" Freight Pier, East River.
8	" Ticket Office, 34 Hudson St. Hoboken.
9	Academy of Music.
10	Cooper Institute.
11	Union Squre.
12	Madison Square.

Published by **ERIE RAILWAY COMPANY** *and Entered in the Office of the Librarian of Congress at* Washington *1874*

THE LAND OF
Suburban Homes
ON THE LINES
OF THE
ERIE **RAILROAD SYSTEM**
ADJACENT TO NEW YORK

ACCURATELY COMPILED FROM LATEST U. S. GEOLOGICAL SURVEY MAPS

Scale of Miles.

One Inch = 1¾ Miles.

consolidation began on the morning of October 13, 1956, for all Erie through-line passenger trains, those going beyond Port Jervis, NY, and non-rush-hour trains. The first train to enter Hoboken was Train #6, "The Lake Cities."

Meadville was taken out of service for good; now came the reason for Captain Stein's trip to Hoboken. She was towed to Bethlehem Shipyard in Hoboken where two prefabricated 15-ft false bows were added to make up for her wider beam and different bow/bridge configuration. These bows increased her gross tonnage by 18 tons to 1,617.

On February 20, 1957, *Meadville,* renamed *Maplewood* and, repainted in Lackawanna brown livery, left the Jersey City marine yard for the last time and was officially transferred to the Delaware, Lackawanna & Western Railroad's Hoboken ferry.

Phase II of the consolidation came on March 25, 1957, when all rush-hour trains, except the Northern Branch and the New York, Susquehanna & Western trains, started operating in and out of Hoboken.

Youngstown, like *Meadville,* was taken out of service and had her bows extended, painted brown, renamed the *Chatham,* and transferred to the Lackawanna.

The Pavonia Ferry was now reduced to a two-boat fleet—*Jamestown* and *Arlington.* Ferry service had been reduced to one boat, the *Jamestown,* which no longer carried trucks, and only made a few train trips a day: six for Northern trains and about twenty for the Susquehanna, and some of those were combined. In other words, one boat trip could have Northern and Susquehanna passengers on the same trip.

The Erie applied to the ICC to abandon the ferry operation. A long court battle commenced between the various commuter groups, the City of Jersey City, and the State of New Jersey Public Utilities Commission, all teamed up against the railroad. However, in the end, the railroad won out when a federal court upheld the ICC's approval to abandon. The court ordered that the Northern Branch trains must be operated to Hoboken by the end of the year and that the Susquehanna had until February 1959 to move its trains.

By the time the court battle was over, the *Jamestown* was laid up and the *Arlington* was running. The main generator of the *Jamestown* had exploded and the company laid her up, rather than fix it.

At 6:20 P.M., December 12, 1958, the 55-year-old *Arlington,* with Captain William Wolfer, a thirty-seven-and-a-half year veteran at the helm, left Chambers Street, for Jersey City. Thus, at about 6:30 P.M. with the final three-whistle salute, the final bells rung down to the

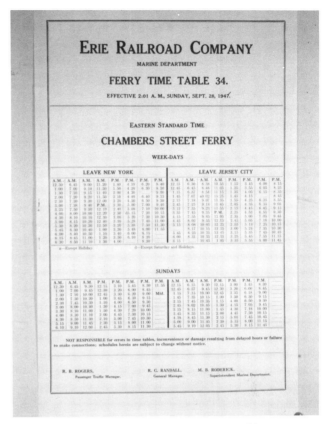

Erie Railroad Company Ferry Time Table.

engine room, the final three cowbells rung, to indicate finished with engines and the boat, *Arlington* ended ninety-seven-and-a-half years of continuous operation of the Pavonia Ferry Co. It also brought to an end over 107 years of continuous Hudson River passenger service of the Erie Railroad Company.[12]

[12]The wheelsman on this trip was my close friend and mentor, Captain Tom Hogan, who less than two years before had been the Erie skipper who turned the *Meadville* over to Captain Tom Devaney of the Lackawanna, making the trip from the Jersey City marine yard to Hoboken with Devaney. Also in the pilothouse was M. B. Roderick, superintendent of the Erie marine department and Jess Baker, the port captain. I had asked Baker for permission to make the trip in the pilothouse, but he refused, saying, "There are too many up there now." It's no wonder, though, because I didn't like him nor he, me. But I was not to be deprived of my final trip on the *Arlington,* the boat that I broke in on almost twelve years earlier, in some place that was not just a place for regular passengers. I had to get somewhere with the crew. So I went down in the engine room where I rode over with another friend, Fred Petri, the chief engineer. Fred was the chief engineer of the *Tuxedo* when I first started working on the boats back in 1947. (RJB)

Susquehanna of 1865 poses just off the pins of the slip at the 1st Erie Railroad Station in Jersey City. *Susquehanna* was later renamed *Arden* after rebuilding in 1912. She was scrapped in 1924. First Erie Pavonia Avenue terminal is visible in the background. Note radial paddlewheel. – Courtesy of the Mariners' Museum, Newport News, Virginia

CHAPTER 9

HOBOKEN FERRY COMPANY OF THE DELAWARE, LACKAWANNA & WESTERN RAILROAD COMPANY

The early history of the Hoboken Steam Ferryboat Co., as it was first named when incorporated by Colonel John Stevens on November 3, 1821, is tied closely to Robert Fulton's Paulus Hook Ferry Co. of Jersey City.

Jensen's Communipaw Ferry, of 1661, was the first-known commercial ferry route on the North River, but it has had nowhere near the impact on ferryboat history and technology as either the Paulus Hook or Hoboken Ferry companies.

Robert Fulton is commonly known as the father of modern steamboating, yet he really was not the inventor of the steamboat; rather, it was he who successfully applied the ideas of several other men into one unit capable of performing the necessary task.

Shortly before the turn of the nineteenth century, there were some important experiments underway by Colonel John Stevens, who has been referred to as the father of the American railway. Many experiments had been conducted in both America and Europe with hand-powered, propeller-driven boats. As early as 1799, Colonel Stevens conducted experiments with a steam screw propeller. In 1802, he built a 25 ft. long, flat-bottomed boat with a 5-ft. beam, which was powered by a small rotary engine, with a multitubular boiler. In the summer of 1802, he launched this boat, named *Little Juliana* for his daughter, in the Hudson at Hoboken and ran it occasionally until the following winter. She attained a speed of 4 miles per hour.

Messrs Nicholas Roosevelt and Robert R. Livingston became involved with the colonel and, in 1803, they decided to replace the rotary engine with a noncondensing reciprocating engine and a multitubular boiler. During

the trials on the Hudson River, the boiler gave way, adding another year to the experiment. Colonel Stevens converted the *Little Juliana* to a twin-screw boat in 1804, which was described in many writings over the years as having a cylinder 4½ inches in diameter and 9-in. stroke: the beam was omitted; the boiler 2 feet long, 15 in. wide, 12 in. high, consisted of eighty-one tubes, each 1 in. in diameter; the boat was 25 ft. long, and 5 ft. wide. This was tried May 1804, and had a velocity of four miles an hour. After having made repeated trials with her, his son undertook to cross from Hoboken to New York, when, unfortunately, as the boat nearly reached the wharf, the steam pipe gave way, having been put on with soft solder. This boiler being damaged, the next one was constructed with the tubes placed vertically. The engine was kept going for a fortnight or three weeks, the boat making excursions up and down the Hudson River. For a short distance, it is said, the boat would go at a rate no less than seven or eight miles an hour.

Hoboken is truly the birthplace of the steam ferry. However, long before the practical introduction of the steamboats, the Elysian Fields in Hoboken were a popular pleasure resort for New Yorkers, who came hither in all kinds of small boats for a day's outing. The first charter for a regular ferry operation was granted to Hermanus Talman in 1774. The ferry was then known as the Horsimus Ferry, after a small creek in the south end of Hoboken, which was then virtually an island. This early row-and-sail operation was given importance by the establishment of a stage line to New Bridge, near Hackensack, by Andrew Van Buskirk in 1775. It was on

February 21, 1775, that the first ferry operation was begun between New York City and Hoboken. Sometimes it took nearly a half-day to make the trip.

During the Revolutionary War, there was no regular ferry service operating as the British Army took control and would allow no one to leave or enter the City of New York without permission. However, Van Buskirk was a notorious Loyalist during the war and this line ran through an area more or less under British control.

On October 8, 1784, the ferries again started and this time the second type of ferryboat was introduced: the two-masted canal boat, which, with the aid of sails, often made the trip in less than one hour. These vessels were commonly known as periaugers.

For the period from 1789 to 1791, Colonel John Stevens purchased the ferry rights. He owned considerable real estate in Hoboken, which included a vast amount of waterfront property. In 1799, the franchise was in the hands of one Joseph Smith, who operated a periauger. In 1802, the Bergen Turnpike was extended from Bulls Ferry to the Hoboken Ferry and, in 1808, the ferry was leased to David Goodwin. However, in 1810, John Stevens regained control in his own name. On May 21, 1811, he obtained a patent signed by President James Monroe for his engine which consisted of one cylinder firmly bolted to the keelsons of a boat and connected by shafts to paddle wheels.

This was one of the "firsts" on the Hoboken Ferry. On September 10, 1811, the first steam ferryboat, Stevens' *Juliana*, was placed in service on the Vesey Street Ferry, making sixteen trips and carrying an average of one hundred persons per trip. Robert Livingston had secured from the New York State Legislature the exclusive rights to all steamboat operations on the waters of New York State and he was now associated with Robert Fulton in the operation of the *North River Steamboat of Clermont*. In March 1811, simultaneous leases were issued to Robert Fulton and the Associates of the Jersey Company for a steam ferry service from Cortlandt Street, NY to Jersey City, and to John Stevens for ferry service from Barclay Street, NY to Hoboken. Stevens' vessel was in operation before Fulton's *Jersey*, which did not commence operating until 1812.

It now became a matter of competition between these rival leases represented by Fulton on the one side and Stevens on the other, who should first bring a steam ferryboat into actual operation. In this Mr. Stevens was successful; and in the early part of October 1811, invited the city authorities and several leading citizens on the first regular steam ferryboat which plied in any part of the world. The voyage to Hoboken was successfully accomplished, and a formal entry of the fact was made in the city records of New York on the eleventh of October, 1811.

The *Juliana* operated on the Vesey Street, and later on the Spring Street, routes until 1812. Robert Livingston exercised his claim to exclusive steamboat privileges within the navigable waters of the State of New York. Colonel Stevens withdrew the *Juliana* from the route on July 12, 1812, and she was sent through Long Island Sound to the Connecticut River where she operated for the remainder of 1812. *Juliana* was not to be outdone even in the Connecticut River. With the War of 1812 still

First steamboat with screw propeller, built by John Stevens, 1804.

Horse ferryboat on Hudson River, 1813.

underway, British naval squadrons were roaming the East Coast; on one occasion when *Juliana* was near the mouth of the river, she was chased by vessels of a British squadron, but they were no match for the young lady from Hoboken, as she outran them.

Actual operation of the line was conducted by David Goodwin. Having removed the *Juliana* from the line, Stevens replaced her with teamboats and the *Juliana* was dismantled in Connecticut, in 1813. There is one thing that Livingston's monopoly could not take away from Colonel John Stevens—the fact that he, not Livingston or Fulton, operated the first steam ferryboat in the world, so ensuring his and his *Juliana's* place in history.

Horseboats continued operating on the Hoboken ferries until May 1821 when all the Stevens/Livingston controversies were settled.

In 1814, the line reverted to the use of periaugers and Moses Rodgers' horseboats. These were double boats connected by the deck beams, with a single paddlewheel between them. Six horses walking in a circle turned a vertical shaft geared by mitre wheels to the waterwheel shaft. This continued for only a relatively short time. By May 1821, Fulton's Associates of Jersey Co. and Stevens worked out a licensing arrangement which allowed the Hoboken line to return to steam operation.

It might be interesting to note that the *North River Steamboat of Clermont* used a Boulton & Watts bell-crank mine engine adapted for boat use. The engine turned a large geared wheel which, in turn, turned the paddle wheels, whereas the Stevens engine was a cross-head engine, where the vertical piston motion operated a shaft that turned the paddle wheels. It was found that

the Stevens engine was superior to the Boulton & Watts engine for steamboat operation and the Associates of the Jersey Co. adopted the Stevens engine for their boats. Colonel John Stevens became interested in railroads and his son Robert Stevens undertook an interest in the ferries. Fulton's death in 1815 now left the Associates as the ones to deal with. The most famous case in the United States Supreme Court on the Livingston/Fulton Monopoly was Gibbons v. Ogden (9 Wheat 1,6 L.Ed. 23) argued in 1824, which struck down the New York State monopoly grant as contradicting the U.S. Constitution, thus allowing anyone to operate a steamboat. Yet, three years before this famous decision, Mr. Stevens was once again operating steamboats on the Hoboken Ferry and the Paulus Hook boats were running with an engine of the Stevens design.

The Hoboken ferry operated with some measure of success during the eight-year period when it was using horseboats.

Reflecting on his early experiments building a steam ferry vessel for the Hoboken-to-New York route in 1804, Colonel Stevens wrote on this matter in January 1812:

In 1804 I had two cylinders cast at Mr. McQueen's furnace, each sixteen inches in diameter. These were bored at a boring machine put up for the purpose at Hoboken. One of these I determined to put on a boat to ply as a ferryboat, and had newly concluded a contract with a ship-carpenter for building a boat eighty feet long and twelve feet wide. But considering his terms extravagant I broke with him. The engine when finished was put on board of one of the ferryboats, but owing principally to the defect of the boiler and furnace she did not answer my expectations. The two cylinders were afterward put on board of the *Phoenix;* and after taking her round by sea into the Delaware, were removed, and the present engine put on board.

The ferry operated the route from the foot of Newark Street, Hoboken to Vesey Street from May 1, 1775 until May 3, 1817, except for a period of interruption during the American Revolution. On March 29, 1813, the second line was started to Spring Street, Manhattan. On May 3, 1817, the Vesey Street terminal was shifted to Murray Street and finally to Barclay Street on August 14, 1819.

Colonel John Stevens's son, Robert L. Stevens, became the principal figure in the operation of the Hoboken Steam Ferryboat Company as the colonel became more and more obsessed with his ideas of a steampowered railroad in America.

Around this time, Robert Stevens developed the "working" beam (later called the skeleton walking beam) engine, in which the radius of half the length of the working beam is slightly greater than the length of the stroke. This engine became the most widely used engine on ferryboats for the next fifty-odd years.

Robert Stevens also formed the general plan of steam ferryboats and bridges which were used for the next 150 years, with only minor changes.

Francis B. Stevens wrote in a letter dated December 27, 1897, on the subject of Fulton's boats and Robert Stevens' plan:

> I remember seeing the two boats crossing the Hudson from my earliest childhood until I was about thirteen years of age. They were painted yellow and were very unsightly, and had a speed of less than three miles an hour. These two double ferryboats, and the log-raft slips were used on the Jersey City ferry for about fifteen years and up to the year 1827 or '28. The boilers of one of them exploded about the year 1822, with fatal results, just as the boat was leaving the Jersey City slip.

> After the success of the *Clermont*, Fulton had built a machine shop at Paulus Hook (then a village of less one hundred inhabitants), now Jersey City, and there during seven years, until his death in 1815, he made the engines for the boats he then successfully built, and by which he firmly established steam navigation. These engines were strict copies of the engines he imported from England, with the exception that the crosshead was substituted for the bell crank; and that the boilers were different. When twelve or thirteen years old, I frequently saw his steamboats *Firefly*, *Lady Richmond*, and *Olive Branch*.

> In the year 1821, Robert L. Stevens formed the general plan of the steam ferryboat of the present day; together with that of the ferry slips and bridges, and at that date adopted it on the Hoboken ferry, and then planned the details and built the large ferryboats *Hoboken* and *Pioneer*. Previous to this date the wheel-guards or paddle-boxes on all steamboats extended only a short distance beyond the wheels, as in the ocean paddle-wheel steamers of the present day; but, in the

two boats named, the overhanging deck was carried to the ends of the hull, where it formed a broad passageway for extrance and exit, and at the same time completely protected the water-wheels. The engine was placed in the centre of the hull, and on each side of it a double carriage-way was provided.

> The spring rack that he then applied to guide the boat into the slip, and to yield when struck by the wearing piece of the overhanging deck, was the same in every detail as the spring racks of all the ferries of the harbor at the present day. He also substituted the lever or beam-engine – now in general use – for the crosshead engine, then in general use on all steamboats.

> Immediately afterwards he built the ferryboat *Union* at Philadelphia, together with the spring-rack slip.

Robert and the colonel put the steam ferryboat *Hoboken I* into operation on May 11, 1822. The *Hoboken I* was 98 ft. long, 200 tons' burden, and operated at 9 mph.

In September 1823 the 115-ft. 143-ton *Pioneer* was placed on the Spring Street route, thus bringing steam to the second route. A trial route to Hulbert Street was operated from August 24, 1822, until discontinued on October 27 of the same year. On January 6, 1823, a third route was started to Canal Street and the third steam ferryboat, the smaller *Fairy Queen*, was added to the fleet in 1825.

Fairy Queen was followed by the largest boat built to date, the *Newark* (18288), of 1828 which was 162 tons. The year 1834 saw Stevens launch the 211-ton *Bergen* (2313). With the addition of *Bergen* to the fleet, the Christopher Street line was opened for business on July 1, 1836. July 1 also saw the discontinuance of both the Spring Street and Canal Street routes. *Hoboken I* was scrapped in 1836, also. The company was now concentrating its five boats on two ferry routes: Christopher Street directly across the river from Newark Street, Hoboken, and Barclay Street/downtown.

The year 1846 saw the Hoboken Ferry Co. decide to name its new vessels after important personalities in the steamboat transportation field, with the launching of the *John Fitch* (13164). *John Fitch* was named after the American inventor who pioneered U.S. steamboat transportation by operating a serviceable steamboat before Robert Fulton. The same year, the *James Rumsey I* joined the fleet. The *Rumsey I* was named after the man who launched the second successful steamboat, in the Potomac River, in 1787.

In 1851, the Stevenses chose to honor the man whose engine Robert Fulton used in his *Clermont*, and the large 372-ton *James Watts* was launched. The name of the small *Fairy Queen* was also changed during 1851 to *Phoenix*.

Chancellor Livingston (4863), named after an old friend of Colonel Stevens who was a prominent New

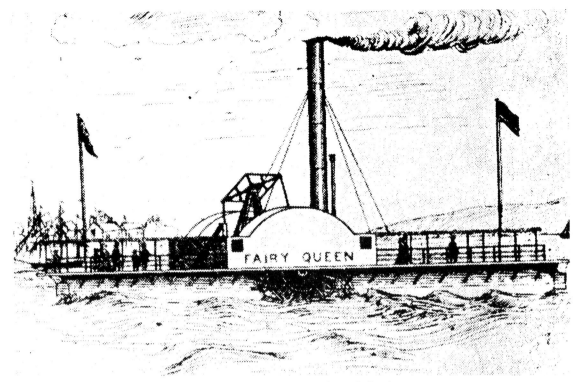

The *Fairy Queen*, 1827. — Adams Collection

York State figure, was launched in 1853, her tonnage, 457. November 4, 1853 was a tragic day for the Stevenses and the Hoboken Ferry Co.; the seven-year-old *James Rumsey I* caught fire and was totally destroyed. A year later, in 1854, the Hoboken Ferry Co. returned to the practice of naming vessels after cities, with the addition to the fleet of the small 360-ton *Paterson* (19907).

At the beginning of the Civil War, the Hoboken Ferry Co. was operating two lines with nine boats, but the old *Pioneer* was scrapped before the end of 1860. *Phoenix ex Fairy Queen*, which had been out of service since 1855, was also scrapped.

Pioneer's replacement appeared in 1861 as the *Hoboken II. Hoboken II* was not to remain in the fleet for long, as she was requisitioned by the War Department and sent south where she served in General Burnside's expedition and was lost early in 1862. With the loss of *Hoboken II*, the company very quickly launched yet a third *Hoboken*, (11468), in 1863. *Hoboken III* was larger than her predecessor by 21 tons, weighing in at 551 gross.

With the completion of the New York & Erie's mile-long tunnel under Bergen Hill in 1861, Mr. E. A. Stevens purchased perpetual operating rights for Morris & Essex Railroad trains to use the tunnel, for the sum of $116,550. November 14, 1862 saw Morris & Essex using its new terminal at the foot of Newark Street, Hoboken, which adjoined the terminal of the Hoboken Ferry on the south side. This new service brought new traffic to the ferry and also affected the Paulus Hook ferry by taking some traffic away.

The next vessel to be added to the fleet was the *Morristown*, in 1864. An old engraving in the New York Public Library clearly shows an interesting thing about these early boats; they had cabins on both sides and the team gangway was exposed to the weather. A second vessel, the *John Stewart*, was also added to the roster in 1864. Once again, the Stevens reverted to naming vessels after people. Three years later, a second *James Rumsey* (13828), was launched. *Rumsey II* was the last vessel to be named for a person, and *Weehawken* (26900) slid down the ways in 1868.

January 15, 1868 saw the opening of the second Hoboken railroad terminal of the Morris & Essex Railroad. This new terminal was larger than the one it replaced and had a walkway from it to the ferry terminal, to keep passengers out of the weather. This new terminal also served both the standard gauge (4 ft. 8½ in.) Morris & Essex Railroad and the broad gauge (6 ft.) Delaware, Lackawanna & Western Railroad, which would bring passengers from as far away as northeastern Pennsylvania and the southern tier of New York State. The first broad-gauge train ran between Washington, NJ and Hoboken on September 12, 1870, but because it was a freight train it did not operate to the new terminal. It took almost three years before passenger service commenced to Hoboken on August 16, 1873, when the first interstate passenger train arrived at Hoboken. This train also brought the first sleeping car to the terminal, along with passengers from Scranton, PA, as well as from Binghamton, Syracuse, and Oswego in New York State.

On August 1, 1870, the Stevens were to lose a second

vessel to fire, caused by a gas explosion: the *James Watts* of 1853 was destroyed.

The Stevens family, having interests in both the Hoboken Ferry Co. and the Morris & Essex Railroad Co., foresaw increased revenue for their boats and, in 1871, *Hackensack* was added to the fleet, to replace the *James Watts.*

A major fire destroyed the Morris & Essex terminal in June 1873 and a temporary structure was built, along with a new ferryboat, the *Secaucus.* Another vessel, the aging *Newark,* was removed from the roster and scrapped. The following year, 1874, *Paterson,* a 20-year-old boat, was scrapped.

Age apparently was not a factor in determining whether or not to keep a boat, as one year, we see a 20-year-old boat scrapped and the next year, the 41-year-old *Bergen.*

Hoboken ferry's last wooden-hull boat, the *Moonachie,* was placed in service in 1877.

The DL & W Railroad had problems with using the Erie's Bergen Tunnel, so the company decided to construct its own tunnel. Work commenced in 1873 and the tunnel was completed on May 12, 1877.

John Fitch was scrapped in 1878, followed two years later by the *Hoboken III,* of 1863.

A new era was taking shape on the Hoboken ferry when the *Lackawanna I* was launched in 1881. Iron replaced wood as the material used in hull construction, at a cost of $76,000. The same year, the fourth vessel to bear the name *Hoboken* was built at Newburgh, NY. As iron replaced wood in hull construction, Stevens turned to outside companies to build its boats. Prior to *Hoboken II* and *Lackawanna I,* all boats had been built in Hoboken.

Hoboken II dimensions were:

Registered length	200 ft.
Registered breadth	35.5 ft.
Gross tonnage	831
Net tonnage	654

Newburgh, NY was also the location where *Paunpeck* was launched in 1882.

The Delaware, Lackawanna & Western Railroad was now the operator of the Hoboken terminal after it leased the Morris & Essex Railroad around 1868. The railroad continued to expand during the late ninetenth century and, in 1885, the fourth Hoboken Terminal was opened. This new terminal had eight tracks covered by three train sheds. To coincide with the opening of the new terminal, two new ferryboats were placed in service, *Hopatcong I* and *Musconetcong.*

As the Lackawanna was expandings its lines in New York and Pennsylvania, the Hoboken Ferry Co. expanded on the North River, with the opening of the 14th Street/Hoboken-to-14th Street/New York route on May 1, 1886. Two new boats were added to the fleet in that year, *Orange* and *Montclair.* These vessels were sisters, built in Newburgh; they were both considered large vessels, with dimensions of:

Registered length	218.5 ft.
Registered breadth	35.4 ft.
Depth	13.8 ft.
Gross tonnage	1096
Net tonnage	901
Horsepower	600
Engine 1 cyl. vertical beam	46 in. × 120 in.
Boiler-return tube	1
Working pressure	45 lbs

These vessels were also the last sidewheel vessels constructed for the Hoboken Ferry Co. Also, 1886 saw the *Chancellor Livingston* taken out of service and scrapped.

Another new era was about to unfold and the Hoboken Ferry Co., along with the Stevens family, were shortly going to write an entire new chapter in ferryboat history and technology.

As noted in earlier chapters, the single-engine, walking-beam engine and the simple low-pressure boil-

Orange, sister of *Montclair* follows an unknown sidewheeler up river towards Hoboken. Note the difference in the saloon cabins of *Orange* and her sister *Montclair. Orange* still had low pilothouse and smaller salon, while *Montclair* had been rebuilt with raised pilothouses and extended aprons for upper deck unloading. — The Railroad Museum of Pennsylvania

Lackawanna Railroad's ferryboat *Montclair*, one of the last sidewheel ferryboats to operate on a North River Railroad ferry route, approaching the Company's Hoboken Terminal, prior to her being taken out of service in 1944. Note *Leviathan*, in background.

ers had reached a maximum of 1,000 horsepower at 50 lbs. pressure. Even though the sidewheel vessels were considered highly efficient vessels for their time, they did have certain disadvantages, and limited horsepower was one. In order to build larger boats which were capable of increased speeds and load-carrying capacity, changes were necessary. Another problem of sidewheelers was their lack of ability to maneuver in ice. Harbor ice created a problem when it built up in the slips, making it impossible for the boats to reach the bridge even when running the engine at full-speed. Oldtime captains relate that the companies would assign tugboats to each ferry terminal to push the boats to the bridge in heavy ice. Tugs would even go in the slips to break it up after a ferryboat left. Ice also would break the buckets, reducing the vessels' power.

Colonel Edwin A. Stevens, president of the Hoboken Ferry Co., wrote in *Cassier's Magazine* Vol. VI, No. 34 in August 1894 a very interesting article relating to the ferryboat of the time:

The New York ferryboat engine remained practically unchanged until within the past few years. It was what is known as the American beam engine, with Stevens or Sickle valve gear, single cylinder, and jet condenser. The only auxiliaries were a fire and bilge pump. The wheels were radial and, until lately, mostly built of wood. The boiler pressure long stood at 30 pounds, but in the later boats rose as

high as 45 and even 50 pounds. The whole arrangement was simple, easy of access, and gave good results both as regards economy and in performing the duties expected of it. (p. 279)

Minor changes were made to the boats over the years to improve the efficiency of operation and riding comfort of the passengers. Some of these improvements were: iron replaced wood for hull construction, stepped or half bucket, and iron wheel frames; cabin decorations were more modernly styled; hard woods were introduced in the decor; compressed Pintsch gas and electric lights replaced oil lamps; steam heat replaced wood or coal stoves; and steam steering gears were added.

A new technology was tried on sidewheel ferryboats with the construction of the Staten Island ferryboats *Erastus Wiman* and *Robert Garrett,* both built in 1888, in Baltimore, MD. They were equipped with an inclined compound engine, but they were still sidewheel vessels equipped with the new feathering wheels.

Weehawken was taken out of service and sold to New York & Cottage Point Ferry Co. in 1887.

Early in the 1850s, the Stevenses planned, and actually contracted with Hoag & Delamater, for a screw ferryboat. For some reason, the vessel was not constructed. With the testing and ultimate success of the gunboat boiler in *HMS Iris,* high-pressure boilers became a reality. New engine designs could be tried. Compounding

Originally built as a single deck boat the Lackawanna Railroad's *Bergen* was the first propeller ferryboat built for the North River. Her second deck was added in 1906. — Courtesy of The Mariners' Museum, Newport News, Virginia

was done with sidewheel engines on the two Staten Island boats. What was to come next?

Way back in 1799, Colonel John Stevens had operated a successful propeller-driven vessel, (1802). Colonel Edwin A. Stevens, working with Captain C. W. Woolsey, Superintendent of the Hoboken Ferry Co., had on the drawing board the design of a totally different double-end ferryboat. This boat subsequently became the first propeller-driven ferryboat in New York Harbor. Another "first" for the Hoboken Ferry Co. There were other propeller-driven ferry vessels in other parts of the world. In 1867, Mr. Livingston Brady of New York patented a system of screw propulsion for ferryboats. Two vessels were built for use on the Mississippi River, but were not successful on account of the action of the quick water against the levees.

Bergen (3418) was launched in 1888 at T. S. Marvel & Co.'s yard in Newburgh, NY. Her hull and superstructure were designed by Captain Woolsey and Edwin Stevens, while her engine was designed by J. Shields Wilson and built by C. L. Delamater. *Bergen* was a single-decked vessel and had the following dimensions:

Registered length	200.4 ft.
Registered breadth	37 ft.
Depth	16.6 ft.
Gross tonnage	1120
Net tonnage	746
Housepower	800
Engine	18½ in. × 27 in. × 42 in. × 42 in.
Boilers	2
Boiler location	below deck
Boiler working pressure	175 lbs. PSI

This vessel was so highly successful that, within the short span of four years, there were a half-dozen propeller boats on the North River. By 1892, the Hoboken Ferry had three running, the Pennsylvania had two, and the Erie Railroad had one.

The principle of the screw ferryboats of New York on the North River is a rigid shaft extending from bow to stern, with a propeller on each end. There were various types of engines connected inline of the shaft. *Bergen* used a three-cylinder, triple-expansion engine. Other boats used a compound engine, a double-compound engine (two compound engines coupled back to back, which was the most popular), or a quadruple-expansion engine. One propeller pulls ahead as the other propeller pushes her forward. The action is reversed to stop the vessel.

Mr. Edwin Stevens comments in the article regarding the *Bergen* that

You want, first of all, stopping power, after that some other qualities, such as handiness in steering, quickness in starting, and ice fighting qualities, but above all, and again, stopping power. The man who pays the bill will add economy in first cost and operation. These are the data of the designer. Every one will be perfectly content if the boat can make twelve or thirteen knots on her trial trip and hold the same number of statute miles at full speed on her route. The engineer must have an engine that he can repair quickly and cheaply, and that will do the backing when called on, and not stick on centres or churn up the water uselessly. The hull must be well shaped, so that it will steer quickly and will not sink at the bow when loaded by the head. It must be good for ice work, with easy lines and, above all, must be staunch and strong and as nearly unsinkable as skill and money can make it. (p. 285)

Further on, he says, "After a careful study of all the pros and cons it seemed clear that, if it's possible to keep the vessel and the shaft in line, a single shaft with one engine and a screw at each end would be best suited to the conditions" (p. 287).

Bergen surpassed all expectations of both management and the designers, and she was the model of things to come.

It has been said that people waited in long lines to ride the new boat expecting her to turn in circles because of the "odd" propeller arrangement.

James Rumsey II was sold to the New York & Cottage Point Ferry Co. in 1889. They did not have her long when she was sunk on February 20, 1891.

The March 28, 1891 *New York Times* ran an article, "Fine Types of Ferryboats—New York Takes the Lead in Displacing The Old Paddle Wheel":

In these days of long strides in marine architecture the meek and lowly New York ferryboat gets its full share of the pace. Nowhere on the globe are types of these light-draught carriers in such abundance and in such remarkably efficient design as one finds along the North River slips from Barclay Street south to the slip of the Staten Island boats. The first thing that arrests the attention of the ferryboat observer is the gradual passing away of the paddle wheel and the substitution therefore of the screw propeller at bow and stern. This improvement has been a long time coming, but now it is here to stay.

The first propeller boat used for ferry purposes was constructed in 1800 [sic] by John Stevens of this city, and it ran between Hoboken and Barclay Street, the nephews of the designer acting as pilot and engineer. The engines of this vessel are now in the Stevens Institute at Hoboken. In 1867 two screw propeller ferry boats of 900 tons each were built by Edwin L. Brady. They were used at the mouth of the Mississippi, but the washing away of the levees caused by the "quick water" from the screws was of so serious a nature that they were abandoned. Through all these years, however, improvements in the propeller system were going on until in 1889, Marvel & Co. of Newburgh, N.Y. launched the *Bergen* for the Hoboken Ferry Company. This vessel was of so nice a design that an experiment was undertaken to determine her relative economy as compared with the best type of paddle-wheel ferryboats having the common style of overhead beam engine, jet condenser, and drop return flue boilers. The *Orange* designed by F. B. Stevens in 1887, was selected as the *Bergen's* rival. The terms of the race provided for a run from this city to Newburgh and back, 120 miles, without stopping. The relative sizes and weights of the two boats are best seen from the following table:

Artist's sketch of the *Bergen's* cabin interior.

	Bergen	Orange
Built	1889	1887
Hull	Steel	Steel
Engines	Triple expansion	Low pressure
Length in feet	200	217
Beam	32.16	32
Overguards	62	62
Space for passengers**	4,330	3,791
Number of seats	296	254
Space available for teams**	3,448	3,940
Cost	$125,000	$100,000

**Square feet

The results of this trial, briefly told, were that the *Bergen* maintained a speed very slightly in excess of that of the *Orange*, but with less steam pressure; her consumption of coal was more economical, and her engines were subjected to less strain. It is said that when the *Orange* exerts 810 horsepower and makes full speed distance between Hoboken and Barclay Street in seven minutes she travels at the rate of fourteen miles an hour. The *Bergen* claims, however, to be able to maintain a speed slightly better than this, with a horsepower considerably less than her rival. These things having been proved repeatedly by practical tests, it cannot be wondered at that the propeller boat has become "all the rage."

One of the first of these boats to get in the water after the *Bergen's* success had been proved was the *John G. McCullough*, built by Neafie & Levy of Philadelphia for the New York, Lake Erie & Western Railroad Company in this city. Everybody who crosses the river is familiar with this fine craft and with the ruddy face of old Capt. Sam Martin which beams from the pilothouse. The *McCullough* is of steel, and is, perhaps, the largest ferryboat in the harbor. The fine paddle-wheel Staten Island boats and the *Central* and *Communipaw* of the Central Railroad of New Jersey are two feet longer than the *McCullough*, but her beam measurements and carrying capacity are greater than theirs. The *McCullough* is 215 feet long, 38 feet beam, 62 feet overguards, and 16 feet deep. She runs between Pavonia

Highly decorative interior of the single deck ferryboat *Bergen*. When the second deck was added some benches were removed from the inboard side to make way for the center staircases in each cabin. — Courtesy of The Mariners' Museum, Newport News, Virginia

Avenue, in Jersey City, and Chambers Street, on this side. Her cost was $140,000.

The *McCullough's* machinery, which may be taken as a type of the working portions of the ferryboats of the future, is entirely below deck. It consists of a compound surface condensing engine, with a high-pressure cylinder 26 inches in diameter and a low pressure 50 inches. The stroke is 30 inches. The propeller at each end of the boat is 8 feet 6 inches in diameter, and the engines are capable of turning them through 120 revolutions per minute. There are two scotch boilers 12 feet in diameter and 11 feet long, with a working pressure of 100 pounds to the square inch.

Of course, there are not enough of these boats now in the water to displace the old paddle-wheelers, but their number and strength are increasing day by day. The Pennsylvania Railroad Company is having one built at the Cresent Yards, in Elizabethport, N.J., that will be a beauty. It will be built of iron and called the *Cincinnati.* Its engines will be of the double-compound type, each propeller having separate machinery. Its length will be 216 feet; beam, 46 feet; overguards 65; depth 17. A companion to the *Cincinnati,* to be called the *St. Louis.* Each of these boats will cost $135,000. The Hoboken Ferry Company is also having two more screw ferryboats built at Newburgh, each 217 feet long.

The Brooklyn & Manhattan Ferry Company acquired the *Hoboken IV* from the company in 1888. *John Stewart* was disposed of in 1890.

Mary Stevens, the young daughter of John Stevens, vice president of the Hoboken Ferry Co., christened the *Bremen,* (3,523) at T. S. Marvel's Yard on May 12, 1891. *Bremen* was the second screwboat and the first double decker on the company roster. The ferry company, by this time, was part of a larger Stevens' enterprise, the Hoboken Land and Improvement Co. The *Bremen* slid down the ways with no problem. The hull was towed to Hoboken where her machinery was installed and the superstructure completed. Among the long list of dignitaries who attended the launching were Andrew and William H. Fletcher of Hoboken, whose engines were famous within the maritime industry. The dignitaries were transported to Newburgh by a special five-car train of the West Shore Railroad Company.

Like *Bergen, Bremen* was somewhat experimental and tests continued on both vessels. Mr. Edwin Stevens recounts in *Cassier's Article:*

A screw at each end would give fair handiness, good protection and backing power, and it seemed probable, as it has since been proved by experience, that the head of the boat would not fall off materially when the engine was reversed. The system, however, as a method of driving a vessel is not efficient, as the increased friction on the fore body, due to the race of the forward screw, causes a considerable increase in resistance. This has been proved by careful experiment as related by Prof. J. E. Denton in a paper on the *Bergen,* read before the American Society of Mechanical Engineers in 1890, and by running one boat—the *Bre-*

men —in actual service, with only one screw. I may add that the economy found did not warrant the increased risk of navigation and the delay necessary in making landings. (p. 287)

The *Bremen* was larger than the *Bergen* in both length and tonnage. She also had a different engine and a second deck, as the following comparison table shows:

	Bergen	*Bremen*
Built_____	1888	1891
Hull_____	Steel	Steel
Decks_____	1	2
Tonnage: Gross.	1120	1252
Net__	746	822
Registered length_____	200.4 ft.	219 ft.
Registered breadth_____	37 ft.	40.2 ft.
Breadth overguards__	62 ft.	62 ft.
Engine_____	Triple Expansion	Double Compound
Size_____	18½ in. × 27 in. × 42 in. × 24 in.	20 in. × 36 in. × 28 in.
Horsepower___	800	1000
Boilers: Type__	Gunboat	Gunboat
Working pressure	175	125

July 9, 1891, was the day that the third screwboat, the *Hamburg,* (96148) was to be launched at Marvel's yard, in Newburgh. A large group of spectators had gathered at the ways waiting the moment. Finally the signal was given to cut away the last block and the *Hamburg* started to slide toward the Hudson River and her first taste of water. Suddenly there was a crash as the ways spread apart, permitting the boat to drop to the earth. A portion of the hull had reached the water, but the majority rested on dry land. The hull was not damaged, but her day of glory was denied the *Hamburg,* the third propeller boat of the famous Stevens fleet. *Hamburg* was to have been christened by Miss Dod of New York. It is reported that this type of accident had not happened at Marvel's yard since 1871. This accident, so soon in her career, was not to mar *Hamburg's* years on the river.

Hamburg was a sister to *Bremen* and both vessels would spend many years on the North River carrying their charges back and forth across it.

Orange, of race fame against the *Bergen,* finished out the year 1891 for the Hoboken Ferry Co. with an accident on December 30. *Orange* had left Barclay Street at 1:40 P.M. for Hoboken. Shortly before 2 o'clock, when about one-third of the way across the river, the tugboat, *New York Central No. 3,* was noticed heading for the New York side. Captain Myers, of the *Orange,* blew two whistles at the tugboat, indicating his intention; the tug-

Ferryboat *Bremen* approaches the well maintained slips of the Hoboken Ferry Co. Lackawanna Terminal, Newark Street, Hoboken. — The Railroad Museum of Pennsylvania

boat's Captain Hulesner, responded with one whistle. Immediately the *Orange's* engines were stopped and reversed, but it was too late to avoid a collison. *No. 3* was struck amidships on the port side by the stem of the *Orange*. The *Orange* and *No. 3* were locked together by impact of the collision. *No. 3's* crew was taken aboard the ferryboat. One member of the tug's crew, fireman C. Ostran, fell overboard and had to be pulled from the water. Both vessels were carried downriver by the strong ebbtide. When it was ascertained that all the tug's crew was safely aboard the ferryboat, Captain Myers backed off the stricken vessel and the *No. 3* sank in the channel, 700 feet off Barclay Street.

As 1892 began, the Hoboken Ferry Co. was operating three lines with thirteen boats, the oldest of which was the *Morristown* of 1864. Of the thirteen, three were the new screw boats and ten were sidewheelers. Eight boats were ten years old or under; of the remaining five, three were under 20 years of age; and of the other two, *Hackensack* was 21 years, and *Morristown* was 28 years. The year 1892 marked the Stevens' great white fleet of the Hoboken Ferry Co. as one of the best and most modern in New York Harbor.

The Stevenses did find some problems with their new screwboats. The principal troubles were that screw ferryboats, in common with all propeller vessels, are apt to steer more easily to one side than the other, depending on the pitch of the screw, and that, when the engine is stopped and the vessel is forging ahead by its momentum, or is forereaching, it does not respond to the rudder. The first of these troubles ought not to cause difficulty in a well-designed vessel; the second was the main fault of the *Bergen*. To secure a better result, when forereaching, in the boats that followed the *Bergen* on the Hoboken Ferries, the cutout at the ends was increased from 11 ft. to 16 ft., the rudders were widened fore and aft, and the pitch of the screws was increased from 9 ft. to 11 ft.

In 1892, the sidewheel ferryboat *Secaucus* had a second deck placed upon her. She was the only wooden-hulled single-decked sidewheeler to be so converted.

In April 1893, the *Netherlands* (130644) became the next product of T.S. Marvel's yard at Newburgh. *Netherlands* was different than the previous Stevens' boats. Her length was shorter than *Bergen* by almost 10 ft., but she grossed 9 more tons. She had a double-compound engine smaller than either *Hamburg* or *Bremen*. She truly was a one-of-a-kind vessel.

Netherlands as originally built with a three-bladed propeller rather than the traditional four-bladed one, to reduce the forereaching problem. Mr. Edwin Stevens noted that this was the only area where a sidewheel ferryboat surpassed the screw ferryboat.

Netherlands was the last vessel to be built by Marvel

Hoboken Ferry Co. ferryboat *Netherlands*, photo taken from the deck of the *Orange*. Official D.L. & W. railroad photograph dated March 17, 1916. — Jack Emerick Collection

It appears that the *Ithaca*'s propeller has run into a lot of river driftwood and needs to be replaced. Photo taken March 19, 1914. — The Railroad Museum of Pennsylvania

for the Hoboken Ferry Co. and also the last vessel built for the Stevens' interest in the Hoboken Ferry Co.

To secure good steering, the screw of a ferryboat is set a little away from the hull and her rudder is quite a distance from the screw. The midships section is a decided "V," and the shape of the longitudual sections, water, bow, buttock, and diagonal lines are carefully modeled to give screw and rudder a full supply of unbroken water.

The construction of the *Netherlands* completed all new vessel programs of the Hoboken Ferry Co. until after the turn of the century.

The New York & Cottage Point Ferry Co. once again approached the Stevenses for a boat and thus acquired the 22-year-old *Hackensack* in 1893.

For the next five years, the Stevens' ferry continued to operate its service with the remaining twelve boats without additions or deletions. In 1898, the 34-year-old *Morristown,* one of three wooden-hulled vessels left in the fleet, had reached an age when she would cost the company a large sum of money to repair. So she was taken out of service and scrapped.

The coming of the twentieth century found the Hoboken Ferry strongly associated with the Lackawanna Railroad, yet the ferry maintained a separate terminal in Hoboken.

In 1902, the Lackawanna Railroad acquired a slip at West 23rd Street, New York. The following April (1903), the Lackawanna Railroad bought stock ownership of the Hoboken Ferry Co. and assumed operation at a cost of $3,300,000.

On November 1, 1904, the 14th Street/New York operation was transferred to West 23rd Street and the 14th Street terminal was abandoned. After that, the uptown route from Newark Street and the 14th Street/Hoboken both operated to 23rd Street.

Lackawanna Railroad's West 23rd Street ferry terminal in midtown New York City. – The Railroad Musem of Pennsylvania

On December 29, 1904, the Delaware, Lackawanna & Western Railroad formally leased the Hoboken Ferry Co.

With the entry of the Lackawanna into the operation of the Hoboken Ferry Co., plans were made for the construction of five new ferryboats. The Newport News (VA) Shipbuilding and Drydock Co. was awarded the contract to build the boats. They were to be double-deck boats with a spoon hull design, which is excellent for ice breaking, and counter deck spray and wash. The dimensions of these boats are:

Registered length	187 ft.
Registered breadth	43.4 ft.
Breadth overguards	62 ft.
Depth	16.5 ft.
Hull	Steel
Tonnage: Gross	1462
Net	676
Engine:	Double compound
Size	18 in. × 36 in. × 28 in.
Horsepower	1400
Boilers	2 Scotch single end
Working Pressure	150 lbs. psi

The first of these vessels to be delivered was the *Scranton* (201628) in 1904, followed by *Binghamton* (201734), *Elmira* (201684), and *Scandinavia* (201816) in 1905. The last one of the Barclay class boats, as they became known, to be delivered was the *Ithaca* (203492) in 1906.

Around the turn of the century, the DL & W management decided that a much larger passenger facility was needed at Hoboken – one that was not prone to fire. New plans for a consolidated train and ferry terminal were drawn up. While plans for the fourth terminal's demolition were being made in the summer of 1905, they were unexpectedly cancelled by a massive fire which started aboard the ferryboat *Hopatcong I* tied up in the slip on August 7. This spectacular fire destroyed both the ferry terminal and the railroad terminal. It was reported that the fire was so hot that it melted the terminal's copper facade which then dripped into the street. Fortunately, the only loss to the ferry company was the one boat and the terminal.

Seven months later, on March 25, 1906, construction commenced on the fifth terminal at Hoboken. *Hopatcong I* was burned to the water line and converted to a coal barge.

1905 was not a good year for the Hoboken Ferry Co., as it finished out the year with the loss of both its Hoboken terminal and the *Hopatcong I.* To make matters worse, its West 23rd Street terminal was badly damaged by fire on December 20.

In 1906 that second deck was removed from Secaucus and placed upon the single deck *Bergen.* With the addition of the second deck to *Bergen,* it meant that all

The Lackawanna's *Binghamton* is one of the few ferryboats still in existence today. She has been placed on the National Historic Register and is tied up at Edgewater, New Jersey, where she is a restaurant. — Adams Collection

Horse and wagons enter the old Hoboken ferry slips of the Hoboken Ferry Co. at Newark Street. This terminal was destroyed by fire in 1905. — The Railroad Museum of Pennsylvania

An official Lackawanna Railroad aerial photograph of their Hoboken/Jersey City facilities. Five of the largest fleet of D. L. & W. ferryboats are laid up in slips #1, #3, #4, #5, and #6. Although you cannot notice it in this photograph, slips #1 and #2 face down river, #3 and #4 slightly more towards across river to Christopher Street and slips #5 and #6 up river towards 23rd Street. Directly to the north of the terminal is the Public Service Street Railway Terminal and their elevated trolley line along Observer Highway and on up to Jersey

THE RAILROAD FERRIES OF THE HUDSON

the screwboats were now double-deck boats. *Orange* and *Montclair* were also double-decked during this modernization period.

After nine months of rebuilding, the West 23rd Street Terminal was completed on September 26, 1906.

Construction of the new Hoboken Terminal was completed early in 1907. Robert Murchison designed the terminal building and ferry dock and Lincoln Bush, the train shed and concourse. The new complex was formally opened to the public at 6:00 A.M. on February 20, 1907, and is still in operation as a railroad terminal today.

In the year 1907, two double-deck ferryboats, named the *Woodbury*, (1905) and the *Callahan* (1906), both products of Harlan & Hollingsworth, were bought from the Norfolk & Washington Ferry Co. The *Woodbury* was renamed the *Lackawanna II* and the *Callahan* became the *Hopatcong II*. After some modification, these vessels were placed in service on the Newark St./23rd Street route, where they remained until being sold years later. Both of these vessels were lengthened by twenty feet in 1926.

With the addition of these two boats, the 30-year-old *Moonachie*, one of the last remaining wooden-hulled sidewheelers, was sold. Also sold was the steel-hulled sidewheeler *Lackawanna I*, built in 1881, and the first

such steel-hulled vessel built for the Hoboken Ferry Co. Oddly enough, she was sold to the Norfolk & Washington Ferry Co., the same company from which DL & W had purchased the *Woodbury* and *Callahan*.

The year 1909 was a monumental year on the Hudson River, as it was the hundreth anniversary of the successful operation of Robert Fulton's 1809 *North River Steamboat of Clermont*. During September and October, the Hudson-Fulton celebration was held. To commemorate this memorable date, on October 1, 1909, a race was held between the ferryboats *Ithaca* and *Lackawanna*. The race was run over the same course that the *Orange* and *Bergen* had run back in 1891: a 120-mile round trip to Newburgh.

Both vessels were 1,400 hp, but that was their only similarity. *Ithaca* had a double-compound engine and a gross weight of 1,462, whereas *Lackawanna's* engine was a triple expansion and her weight was only 1,079. The results were as follows:

	Ithaca	Lackawanna
Northbound trip	3 hrs 30 mins	3 hrs 30 mins
Southbound trip	3 hrs 35 mins	3 hrs 55 mins

The ferries continued to operate with a measure of financial success for the next several years. In 1907, they

The interior of the Bush train shed of the Lackawanna Railroad's Hoboken Terminal. Neon sign points to the large ramp to the upper deck waiting room of the terminal for the ferryboats. — Jack Emerick Collection

---

The Christmas tree in the upstairs dining room of the former Lackawanna Railroad's Terminal in Hoboken, New Jersey. This room later became the General Managers offices of the Erie Railroad Co. and then the Erie Lackawanna Railroad. It is presently the superintendents office of New Jersey Transit.

Public Service Trolley elevation that climbed from Hoboken's Lackawanna Terminal to the top of the Palisades in Jersey City. This elevation was built in the 1880's and was torn down in 1949. These cars added a great number of travelers to the Hoboken Ferries from the Hudson County area.

carried 39,880,572 passengers on four routes for a total of 125,000 per day.

The year 1907 was the last one of operation prior to the opening of the Hudson & Manhattan Railroad in 1908. By 1911, ridership on the ferries was down by just under three million per year.

With the entry of the United States into WW I in 1917, the City of Hoboken became the major port of embarkation for troops to Europe. The ferries played a part in this operation. Public outcry regarding certain vessels being named after cities in Germany caused the company to rename the *Bremen*, the *Maplewood I* and the *Hamburg*, the *Chatham I* in 1918. During the war, the Lackawanna Railroad was operating sixteen ferryboats on four routes.

In 1920, the last wooden-hulled sidewheeler, *Secaucus*, was sold to the Carteret Ferry Co., which operated her until 1935 when she burned at Bay Ridge in Brooklyn. Fire once again took a toll on the Hoboken Ferry Co. when the 29-year old *Chatham I* ex *Hamburg* caught fire and was badly damaged. *Chatham I* was totally rebuilt that year.

Both the *Paunpeck* and *Musconetcong* became excess with the completion in 1922 of two new single-deck screwboats built by the John W. Sullivan Shipyard in Elizabethport, NJ. These two large, 1,900 hp boats, the *Buffalo* and *Hoboken V,* were built specifically for the 14th Street/ Hoboken-to-West 23rd Street/ Manhattan run.

In 1923, there were still four sidewheel ferryboats in operation on the company's roster. Over the years, when requested, the Hoboken Ferry Co. would charter boats out to various upriver ferry operations. One of these companies was the Westchester Ferry Co., which operated the Alpine, NJ-to-Yonkers, NY ferry. In 1923, the *Paunpeck,* the oldest sidewheeler, a product of 1882, was sold to the Westchester Ferry Co. Westchester operated her until she was scrapped in 1939. Along with *Paunpeck,* Westchester Ferry Co. also bought the *Musconetcong,* built in 1885, and renamed her the *F. R. Pierson. Musconetcong* ran on the Alpine ferry for twenty-three years until she was scrapped in 1946. With the sale of these two boats, that left only two sidewheel ferryboats in the Lackawanna's fleet—the *Orange* and the *Montclair.*

With *Hoboken V* and *Buffalo* on the uptown route, *Lackawanna II* and *Hopatcong II* were left to run from Newark Street to 23rd Street, and the 1905 Barclay Street boats to run the downtown route with the 1890 class boats for Christopher Street.

November 1927 saw the Hoboken Ferry Co. confronted with the same problem that the Erie's Pavonia Ferry had—the opening of the Holland Tunnel taking some traffic from the ferry lines. In 1930, some two years after the opening of the tunnel, passenger traffic had decreased by some 12 million annually. This directly affected the Christopher Street line and, in 1928, the company discontinued night and Sunday service on the line. This now made Christopher Street basically a commuter-only line. Vehicle traffic from the 14th Street, Hoboken route was still good and, early in 1928, the terminal was rebuilt.

Even with the decrease in traffic in 1930 the boats were making 810 daily crossings.

In 1935, the name of the *Netherlands* was changed to *Oswego* and the *Scandinavia,* to *Pocono,* completing the naming of all the company boats after cities or places on the lines of the Delaware, Lackawanna & Western Railroad. By 1935, passenger traffic had decreased another ten million persons and, by this time, the nation was in the deep Depression. The year 1937 saw the second tunnel under the Hudson River completed when the Lincoln Tunnel was opened for business just north of the Hoboken/Weehawken boundary line. One thing that tunnels did not permit was a vehicle carrying inflammable cargo. This type of cargo had to be carried all the way up to the George Washington Bridge at Fort Lee, NJ and travel all the way back down on the New York side. In

Lackawanna II ex *Woodbury* tied up in #3 slip in Hoboken in 1945, just three years before she was sold. — Jack Emerick Collection

Vehicle gangway of *Lackawanna II* ex *Woodbury* looking toward the Jersey end, note wooden snow pusher between anchor and trash can. Deckhands used these to push any excess coal which might have been dumped on the deck. — Jack Emerick Collection

Ithaca loaded with home bound commuters and vehicles, backs to kill her headway, in an almost perfect landing in this Official Lackawanna Railroad photograph. This is one of the 8 × 10 negatives loaned to Mr. Baxter, by Mr. George Eastland, former Public Relations Director for the Erie Lackwanna Railroad Co.

Ferryboat *Chatham I,* ex *Hamburg* heads across river as the *Netherlands,* seen just off her bow, is coming down from uptown and *Bergen* is heading up river. — The Mariners' Museum, Newport News, Virginia

---

THE RAILROAD FERRIES OF THE HUDSON

Hoboken Ferry Company's ferryboat *Buffalo* heads for Hoboken from Christopher Street, New York. — Dan Biernacki Collection

April 1939, the Lackawanna Railroad established a tariff for inflammable cargo and the ferries began handling these shipments between Hoboken and Christopher Street. The boat would carry no passengers and a red flag was displayed on the vessel's flagpole; the trips thus became known as the "red trips."

When December 7, 1941, saw America's entry into WW II, problems started to arise on the ferries. Shipbuilding was also a business in Hoboken: Bethlehem Steel had a big yard in the vicinity of 14th Street, and Tiejen & Lang had a yard on the Weehawken/Hoboken boundary line. With the war, Tiejen & Lang needed more room for its operation, so the government bought the property where the uptown ferry terminal was located and the southern portion of the Erie's Weehawken yard for the shipyard. On April 26, 1942, the last 14th Street, Hoboken to West 23rd Street trips were made. *Hoboken V* and *Buffalo* were brought down and placed on the Christopher Street run. *Montclair* and *Orange*, the last two remaining sidewheels, were taken out of service and held in reserve. Harry J. Smith, a longtime clerk with the Hoboken Ferry Co., in his book *Romance of the Hoboken Ferry*, indicates that these boats operated only until 1942. *Orange* was taken out of service first, leaving *Montclair* as the last operating sidewheeler on the North River. Both vessels were sold to Maritime Salvage Co. in 1944. *Orange* was scrapped in 1946, followed by *Montclair* in 1947, but their scrapping did not bring to an end sidewheel-powered vessels on the river,

as there were several sidewheel steamers operating on the river after 1947.

After WW II ended, a whole new traffic mode started to develop in the New York metropolitan area — buses!

The Lackawanna was the last ferry company to have an operation to and from West 23rd Street. The company filed to abandon the route with the Interstate Commerce Commission (ICC). Commuter groups filed counteractions to stop the abandonment in the various courts of the State of New York and in Federal District Court. After a long, hard fight, the ICC approval was confirmed and the 23rd Street line was discontinued on December 31, 1946. While this fight was going on, fire once again showed no mercy to the Hoboken Ferry Co. The best of the Barclay boats, the *Ithaca*, was on drydock in the company yard at Brighton in August when she caught fire and was totally destroyed and scrapped. Another vessel to leave the company roster in 1946 was the second screwboat to be built for the company, the *Maplewood* ex *Bremen*. She was sold to Tampa-New Orleans Tampico Air Lines and towed down south.

The year 1947 saw the company operating two lines with eleven boats. *Lackawanna II* and *Hopatcong II*, the two secondhand boats purchased back in 1907 for the Newark Street to 23rd Street route, were in reserve and tied up on the north side of the terminal.

In 1948, *Lackawanna II* was sold to the Delaware River Ferry Co. The following year, *Hopatcong II* was sold for scrap. In 1949, the company roster consisted of

THE RAILROAD FERRIES OF THE HUDSON

With a fresh coat of paint *Pocono* looks almost like a new boat in this Lackawanna Railroad Co. photograph. – The Railroad Museum of Pennsylvania

the three remaining pre-1900 boats: *Bergen, Chatham* ex *Hamburg,* and *Oswego* ex *Netherlands;* the four remaining Barclay boats, *Binghamton, Elmira, Pocono* ex *Scandinavia,* and *Scranton;* and the two newest single-deck boats, *Hoboken V* and *Buffalo.*

Service was good on the two lines; three boats were operating days and evenings on the Christopher Street line – *Hoboken, Buffalo,* and *Oswego,* with *Bergen* as a spare. Barclay Street was operating four boats – *Binghamton, Elimira, Pocono,* and *Scranton.* Service was decreased in the evening to two boats, and one all-night boat. *Chatham* was the Barclay Street spare boat. There were times when one would see *Oswego* or *Bergen* running on Barclay Street, but I never recall seeing the two fast, single-deck *Hoboken V* or *Buffalo* running downtown.

Chatham was taken out of service in 1949 and the company operated with one spare boat, the *Bergen.* It was rumored thast the *Chatham* would be converted to a diesel. Why the *Chatham?* The *Bergen* was 61 years old and had been reboilered three times during her career. She had no major superstructure rebuilding. *Oswego* was 56 years old and, like *Bergen,* had no superstructure rebuilding; *Chatham,* however, had been totally rebuilt in 1920 after a fire . . .so she was the most realistic choice for diesel conversion.

The Brighton Marine Yard, which was owned jointly by the Lackawanna and the Lehigh Valley Railroad, was going to do the conversion.

There were several areas in which the conversion of the *Chatham* from steam to diesel was shortcut. For some reason, chief of which could have been money, a complete replacement was not done.

As previously mentioned, *Chatham's* boilers were not removed but rather, stripped and welded closed so they could be used as fuel tanks. New tanks should have been installed.

Her old steering gears were stripped of their steam engines and an electric motor attached. Here again, the steering gears should have been completely removed

Christopher Street terminal of the Hoboken Ferry Co. and a little four wheel city trolley await the arrival of a Hoboken boat. – The Railroad Museum of Pennsylvania

Ithaca rests on drydock for some necessary repairs – the year is 1914. – The Railroad Museum of Pennsylvania

and new ones installed. Tugboats use a hydraulic unit which give an even, continuous flow of the rudder. The unit on the *Lackawanna III,* as the *Chatham* was re-named, was an electric contact unit. There were so many contacts to the right and left of midships. Each contact moved the rudder a specific number of degrees either way. The bad thing about this was there was no way that you could place the wheel in between con-tacts. So there were times when you just did not get that little bit extra rudder that you needed.

The Lackawanna Railroad attempted to save wher-ever possible.

By far the biggest problem the *Lackawanna III* had was the fact that she was slightly lower on the old boiler-room end. This proved to be a serious problem in that, when traveling with a load of passengers and this end forward, she tended to take a great deal of water over the bow. This caused many a commuter to travel home with soggy shoes and socks and sometimes much worse. The only possibly attributable cause was that when she was converted, the placement of the new power plant could not be lined up exactly midships. As a result, when the boiler/fuel tanks were filled, she displaced more water on one end. Had the boilers been removed and proper tanks installed, they could have been placed differently. Whatever the cause of the problem, she was taken back

to the yard and scuppers were placed under her bow overhangs. These proved to be of little value. The simplest solution was to turn the boat. So every day, the *Lackawanna III* was turned twice. The afternoon crew would turn her on its first trip downtown, so that the high end was heading toward Hoboken. The night crew was ordered to turn her sometime during the night so that the high end was facing New York. The afternoon crew would pull out of No. 6 bridge about 4:40 P.M., heading up river, rather than the normal route downriver. The captain remained in the Hoboken-end pilothouse and backed the boat out. The wheelsman went to the New York end and steered the boat from that end. When she was out far enough in the river, the captain would stop the boat; the wheelsman centered the steering wheel, then rang for the deckhand to drop the rudder pin, and she was on her way downtown. Off Hoboken was the easiest place to turn her, as the river was a little wider there and did not interfere with traffic.

Once the bugs were ironed out, the *Lackawanna III* ran continuously from 1950 until November 22, 1967, when she made one of the last trips of the Hoboken/Barclay Street, New York service, bringing to a close ap-proximately 297 years of continuous commercial ferri-age across the North River.

The *Lackawanna* ex *Chatham* ex *Hamburg* was

brought from Brighton Marine Yard in 1950 by Shore Supervisor Captain Thomas Devaney. On this trip, as he brought her into number two slip in Hoboken, there was a power failure and she struck the bridge, ripping up dock planks. *Lackawanna* was taken back to Brighton and repairs were made.

Lackawanna replaced the *Scranton* as the night boat on the Barclay Street run and the *Scranton* became the Barclay spare boat.

During 1953, the Christopher Street line lost the third boat and within six months a second boat was discontinued, making the service a one-boat line with half-hour service. *Bergen,* now a spare boat, was scrapped, leaving *Oswego* as a spare boat.

The Christopher Street line ran as a one-boat line for several years and, for a short time during this period, the night boat was switched from Barclay Street to Christopher Street. This did not meet with customer approval, evidenced by a decline in vehicle traffic, as most of the night-boat customers were people going from New Jersey to the produce markets in lower Manhattan. Manhattan's lower west side was a very interesting place. During the daytime, it was busy with blue-collar workers and white-collar financial people. After the evening rush hour of commuters, there was a little lull and then, like

Lackawanna ex *Chatham* ex *Hamburg* approaching the bridge at Hoboken on a dreary day, January 3, 1964, when the author snapped her.

magic, the entire area changed to a busy marketplace. Commission merchants opened their doors to stack their produce neatly on the broad sidewalks and in the buildings. Tugboats ran carfloat after carfloat across the river to the many produce piers; by midnight, the whole west side of lower Manhattan from just below Canal Street to Vesey Street was one giant marketplace.

Once again, the railroad would put the commuters to a test, when it applied to the ICC for permission to discontinue the last boat on Christopher Street. In reality it was no test: The company obtained permission and the Christopher Street route became another victim of economy.

On March 31, 1955, the large single-deck *Buffalo,* a 1922 product of Sullivan's yard, made the last trip on the 118-year-old line. The *Buffalo's* master was Captain William L. Schopf, son of a former Lackawanna marine department superintendent.

Another noted figure on the last trip of the *Buffalo* was Mr. A. Schaller, of East Orange, NJ, a veteran commuter, who had made 28,000 crossings. During 1955, all the boats were kept, but things were happening. The Erie Railroad and the Delaware, Lackawanna & Western Railroad were considering certain consolidations of services, of which the ferry operation was one. The Erie Terminal at Jersey City had been condemned by the City of Jersey City, yet The Erie and the City could not reach any agreement on a new terminal.

Oswego ex *Netherlands* was the first to be scrapped in 1956, while *Hoboken* and *Buffalo* were in reserve down at Brighton. Consolidation plans had been formalized and the Erie was coming to Hoboken. In October 1956, Erie non-rush-hour trains started operating in and out of Hoboken. Within six months, the rush-hour trains would also operate into Hoboken. Barclay Street, then operating a four-boat schedule, planned for a fifth boat to be placed in service once the Erie rush-hour trains started using Hoboken.

The Erie was to sell two of its boats, the *Meadville* and the *Youngstown,* to the Lackawanna. The die was cast. *Hoboken V* and *Buffalo* were only single-deck boats, too small for this operation, so in 1957 they were scrapped.

On February 20, 1957, the *Meadville,* now modified to fit the Lackawanna slips and painted in the traditional Lackawanna brown color scheme (replacing the white color scheme of the Stevens' era), was transferred from the Erie to the DL & W.

She left the Erie Marine Yard at Jersey City with a load of officials from both railroads aboard. The Erie captain was Tom Hogan, and Tom Devaney was the captain for the Lackawanna. Hogan handed over the steering to Devaney and the *Meadville* sailed from the Erie Marine Yard for the last time, as the Lackawanna's *Maplewood.* Several months later, the *Youngstown* would take her place in Hoboken as the Lackawanna Railroad's *Chatham.*

Hoboken Ferry Co. (D. L. & W.) Barclay Street terminal just after the arrival of a boat from Hoboken. — The Railroad Museum of Pennsylvania

On March 25, 1956, the Erie rush-hour trains commenced using the Lackawanna Terminal in Hoboken, and consolidation was complete.

The Delaware, Lackawanna & Western Railroad and the Erie Railroad continued to operate as separate entities out of Hoboken for about the next four years. During this period, the Lackawanna's president and chief executive officer, Perry Shoemaker, and Erie's chairman of the board, Paul Johnston, continued to talk about a total merger of the two roads. After the stockholders of the two companies approved the merger and a stock purchase option was worked out, the proposed merger agreement was sent to the ICC for final approval.

It came, and the Delaware, Lackawanna & Western Railroad was absorbed by the Erie Railroad Co., the company name officially changed to the Erie Lackawanna Railroad Co.

The final roster of the ferryboats of the Delaware, Lackawanna & Western Railroad read: *Binghamton, Elmira, Lackawanna III, Maplewood II, Pocono,* and *Scranton.*

The five-boat schedule was carried over to the new company. Unfortunately, the *Chatham II* never enjoyed reownership by her former owner, as she was involved in a collision off the old Erie Chambers Street slips on the morning of August 29, 1960. At about 9:12 A.M. on that foggy Monday morning, Captain Roy Wanvig left Hoboken with about two hundred passengers aboard.

He was moving at a moderate rate of speed as the fog started to lift. He observed the coastal steamer *Seatrain Georgia* coming upstream toward her berth in Edgewater. Apparently, Wanvig misjudged her speed and distance as he headed across her bow toward the Barclay Street slips. Just off Chambers Street, the *Seatrain Georgia* struck the *Chatham* on the starboard side aft of midships, ripping a large hole in the men's cabin, through the overhang, and into the hull, breaking some plates and causing her to take on water in the fireroom. *Chatham* was helped to the Chambers Street slips of the Erie and her passengers were discharged. She was then towed to Barclay Street where she laid in the south slip, kept afloat by a New York City fireboat's pumps until temporary repairs could be made. *Chatham* was towed to Hoboken where she laid in No. 6 bridge for a short time; she was then finally taken to Brighton Marine Yard and the decision made to scrap her in 1963. *Youngstown,* built at Mariner's Harbor in Staten Island, was also scrapped there by Witte Marine.

Some interesting notes about the Erie boats that were taken in by the Lackawanna line: The Lackawanna boats had an overguard breadth of 62 ft., while the Erie boats' overguard breadth was 64 ft. This extra two feet kept the Erie boats some twelve feet from the bridge. In addition, the bows of the Erie boats had a larger radius and would not fit the Lackawanna bridges. They also had a higher freeboard at main deck and upper-deck landing hoods.

The Erie Railroad Marine yard forces wave goodbye as the *Maplewood* ex *Meadville* leaves for the last time. — Dan Biernack Collection

Maplewood ex *Meadville* is escorted to her new home in Hoboken by the Lackawanna tug *Newton* and Erie tug *Akron*. The date is February 20, 1957. Official Erie Railroad photograph. — Dan Biernacki Collection

Ferryboat *Chatham II* ex Erie *Youngstown* arrives at Lackawanna Terminal, Hoboken for the first time in June 7, 1957.

Lackawanna Railroad Terminal, Hoboken, New Jersey ferry slips as seen from an incoming ferryboat, single deck *Buffalo* is in slip. Print from an old Lackawanna Co. magazinne.

A New York City Fire Chief stands in the gaping hole on the starboard side of the *Chatham* surveying the damage, caused when she collided with *Seatrain Georgia* on August 29, 1960. — Jack Dimond Photograph

After some consideration, it was decided to modify each end of these boats to fit Lackawanna bridges and slips. This included building a 15-ft. extension on each end of the boat so as to match the bridges with a bow radius similar to the Lackawanna boats and modifying freeboard measurements to provide proper upper- and lower-deck levels.

The added weight of the new ends add 4 inches submersion to each boat.

The ends were prefabricated in the shipyards and then welded to the hulls, with care taken to have main-deck channels extend onto the old hulls for strength.

Chatham ex *Youngstown* and *Maplewood* ex *Meadville* were both much heavier than any of the Lackawanna boats, and when they were operated on the Erie, they required two firemen. The Lackawanna boats operated with one fireman, with an extra fireman to go from boat to boat to help the regular fireman clean fires. This did not work on *Chatham* or *Maplewood,* and the complaint that these boats were bad steamers was commonly heard by the Lackawanna engineers. The engineer on the *Maplewood,* Freddy Kobb, had the firedoors on the boilers changed and a second telegraph indicator installed in the fireroom so the fireman would know that the boat was moving. To anyone who had worked on the *Meadville,* this was foolishness. I worked on the Lackawanna for a short time in 1958 and I managed to get down in the engine room once or twice. I remember going across on her and standing at the engine-room gangway hatch listening to the sound that the engine made when backing and I knew that Kobb did not know how to handle that engine. It seemed to me that the boat no longer had the snap she had when Sam Burns was her engineer on the Erie. I made that comment to Mr. Carmen DiJoia, former superintendent of the Erie Marine Department, one day, and he told me, "Ray, they refused our help when we wanted to send an engineer and captain up there to teach them how to handle her." As a result, the *Meadville* sadly had a bad name on the Lackawanna.

CHAPTER 10

NEW YORK CENTRAL SYSTEM

~~~~~~

WEEHAWKEN & WEST SHORE FERRIES

The first informal ferries were operated between Weehawken and Manhattan by Samuel Bayard in 1700. In 1742, he and Francis Kouwenhoven petitioned the governor and council of New York "for a ferry to Weehawk." These early boats were sail- and rowboats. This pioneer route was abandoned in 1834, owing to diversion of patronage to the new Hoboken steam ferry.

On March 25, 1852, the state of New Jersey granted a ferry charter to a group of nine men, including Judge Francis Price and Dudley S. Gregory, the first mayor of Jersey City. These men, on the same day, chartered the Ramapo and Weehawken Plank Road Co., to build a toll road between the said places. Ferry service commenced on New Year's Day, 1859, between Slough's Meadow in Weehawken and West 42nd Street, Manhattan. It was a miserable, rainy day, according to early newspaper accounts. The first two vessels were purchased second-hand from the Union Ferry Co. of Brooklyn. Named *Abbie* and *Lydia,* they were sidewheel beam double-enders. Federal law precluded changing their names to *Hackensack* and *Weehawken,* as originally planned. The company never enjoyed any prosperity and was discontinued in 1872. *Lydia* was abandoned (Lytle's List) in 1872 and *Abbie* was sold to the Albany & Bath Ferry Co. where she operated on the North Ferry until abandoned in 1884 (Lytle's List).

The next group interested in a ferry operation from Weehawken was the New Jersey Midland Railroad, (NJMR) predecessor of the New York, Susquehanna & Western Railroad, which secured about forty acres of land in Weehawken, with 1,100 feet of waterfront on the Hudson River, including the ferryboats and franchise of the Weehawken Ferry Co., for all freight and general passenger business. New Jersey Midland purchased this land and franchise in 1871, but it is not known if it immediately started to operate the ferry or not. There seems to have been a lapse of several months to a year, until new boats were placed in service.

In 1873, New Jersey Midland bought the *Roslyn,* built in 1860 for the Union Ferry Co. of Brooklyn. She was a 462-gross-ton, wooden-hulled, double-end beam sidewheeler. The next vessel to be placed in service was the *Midland,* ordered from Lawrence & Foulkes of Greenpoint, NY in 1872 and placed in service in 1873. Midland was also a double-end beam sidewheeler. New Jersey Midland was transferred by lease to the New York & Oswego Midland on June 17, 1872, and the first advertised timetable calling the road the "New York Midland" was published.

On January 1, 1873, the Montclair branch of the New Jersey Midland was operating to Jersey City, where it connected at Marion Junction (Newark Avenue) with the New Jersey Railroad and Transportation Co. (NJRR), predecessor of the Pennsylvania Railroad Co., and used NJRR tracks for 2½ miles to Exchange Place terminal, where it used the Cortlandt or Desbrosses Street ferries to Manhattan. On August 18, 1873, through service was advertised between Jersey City and Oswego via the NJRR connection. Midland still was not using its own terminal facilities which had been acquired at Weehawken.

Like both the Erie and Delaware, Lackawanna & Western railroads before it, the New York & Oswego Midland (NY&OM) wanted its own terminal facilities on the Hudson River. On March 9, 1873, the name of the Weehawken Ferry Co. was changed to Midland Terminal and Ferry Co. The permanent lease of the New Jersey Midland was consummated on September 4, 1873. On September 19, 1873, less than a month after the lease was concluded, a receiver was appointed to operate the New York & Oswego Midland. Mr. Abram S. Hewitt, of Passaic, New Jersey, was designated by the court for this position.

On November 17, 1873, the New Jersey Midland assumed complete possession of its lines from the New York & Oswego Midland, thus freeing itself from the domination of the New York road. However, New York & Oswego Midland retained ownership of the Midland Terminal & Ferry Co. Even though New Jersey Midland was no longer controlled by the New York & Oswego Midland, the trains of the latter continued to use the New Jersey line to get to Manhattan.

The New Jersey Palisades formed a natural obstacle which had to be overcome by every railroad operating north of approximately present-day Journal Square, Jersey City. This meant that either a large, deep cut or a tunnel had to be dug before a through connection could be accomplished. Prior to the bankruptcy of 1873, this project had not been started and there was no way that it could be started during bankruptcy proceedings. So, apparently, the Midland Terminal and Ferry was operated only as an independent ferry operation during this period.

The days of this bankrupt Oswego Midland were numbered and the line, which had been for sale for some two years, was finally purchased on November 14, 1879, by a syndicate represented by Conrad N. Jordan of the Third National Bank of New York. It was said that this syndicate had ties to Mr. George Pullman, who was interested in building a new line—the New York West Shore & Buffalo—to compete with the New York Central & Hudson River line of Commodore Vanderbilt (Vanderbilt had used Pullman's competitor, Wagner's sleeping cars, on his line).

The name the syndicate chose for the Oswego Midland was the New York, Ontario & Western Railway Co. (NYO&W), which was incorporated on January 21, 1880. The new owners of the railroad had a couple of possible choices by which to enter New York City: continue the route over the New Jersey Midland, (which they did for a time), transferring at Middletown, NY to the tracks of the Erie Railroad and using their terminal at Pavonia Avenue, Jersey City (which they did not want to do); or build a new branch of their own. They chose the latter course.

The charter of the Jersey City & Albany Railroad was acquired through the Midland Terminal & Ferry Co. With the bankruptcy of the Oswego Midland, three separate railroads—the New Jersey Midland, the New York, Ontario & Western Railroad, and the New York, West Shore & Buffalo Railroad (NYWS&B), were all seeking appropriate terminals. Apparently, in the beginning, the Ontario & Western and the West Shore had very close ties and the two companies formed the North River Construction Co. to complete both terminal facilities at Weehawken and railroad lines from Cornwall, NY to Weehawken, NJ.

Once the line was completed to New Durham (North Bergen), NJ, the West Shore and Ontario & Western trains transferred to the New Jersey Midland there. So, the Jersey City & Albany Railroad became the major route for New York Ontario & Western trains east of Middletown, NY.

The Midland Terminal & Ferry Co. was reorganized in 1883 as the Open Cut & General Storehouse Co., but promptly again renamed the West Shore & Ontario Terminal Co. Both NYWS&B railroad and the NYO&W railway were coguarantors of a $10 million mortgage from

Albany I built in 1883 for the New York, Ontario & Western Railway *Albany* was traded to the West Shore for a new locomotive. She was one of four sister boats built for the New York, Ontario & Western Railway all of which were traded for locomotives. She was sold to the Carteret Ferry Co. in 1917. — Courtesy of The Mariners' Museum, Newport News, Virginia

West Shore ferryboat *Oswego* built in 1883 which was sold to the Pavonia Ferry Co. (Erie Railroad) in 1916 and renamed *Passaic* in 1917.

the Central Trust Co. of New York. The Weehawken Tunnel, to run under the Palisades to North Bergen, on the west side, was started in 1883 and a large new terminal was built on the west bank of the Hudson River at Weehawken. Ferry service from the new terminal to West 42nd Street commenced on January 1, 1884. On Sunday, June 21, 1885, a second route, known as the West Shore Ferry, was started downtown to Jay Street. This line operated to Jay Street until 1892 and was removed to Franklin Street in 1893. The downtown terminal was changed again in 1909 to Desbrosses Street, where it operated out of the Pennsylvania Railroad terminal until 1930 when it was again moved to the Pennsylvania Terminal at Cortlandt Street.

The Slough's Meadow-to-42nd Street ferry line continued to operate until 1902, when its terminal was moved to West New York, NJ from whence it operated until its abandonment twenty years later in 1922.

When the West Shore & Ontario terminal company started operation on January 1, 1884, it had seven boats which served the Slough's Meadow and Weehawken terminal lines: the *Roslyn,* which was acquired in 1872; the *Midland,* built for the NY&OM in 1872; and four new boats which had been ordered by the NYO&WR in 1883—the *Albany, Kingston, Newburgh,* and *Oswego.*

Like most vessels of their time, they were decorated in the most elegant decor and had iron hulls. Their dimensions were: overall length, 205 ft., width overguards, 65 ft., and a depth of hull of 13.3 ft., with gross tonnage of 1,056 and a net tonnage of 824 powered by a 50-in. × 120-in. vertical-beam engine of 800 hp which drove the paddlewheels. The last boat of the 1884 fleet was the *Chester W. Chapin,* a sidewheel vessel built in 1875 for the Boston & Albany Railroad by J&J McCauseland of

Kingston, NY and purchased by Midland Terminal in 1881.

In 1885, after a disasterous rate war, the New York, West Shore & Buffalo Railroad was acquired by the New York Central System and reincorporated at the West Shore Railroad Co. The West Shore & Ontario Terminal Co. became part of the New York Central System. The New York, Ontario & Western Railway Co. retained the Middletown-to-Cornwall branch and was given trackage and terminal rights from Cornwall, NY to Weehawken. The New York Central System acquired the West Shore for a much different reason than any other of its previous acquisitions—to control competition, rather than to expand or to acquire better terminal facilities. This is a consideration which one must take into account when looking at the overall picture of New York Central service at a later date.

In 1888, *Roslyn* was converted to a derrick and was no longer registered. Nine years later, in 1897, the Central did a very peculiar thing—it ordered the single-deck sidewheel *Buffalo* from Harlan & Hollingsworth of Wilmington, DE. To that point, the trend had been towards the far-superior screwboats ever since the Hoboken Ferry Co.'s experimental *Bergen,* launched in 1888, had proven so successful. (*Buffalo,* incidentally, was the last sidewheel vertical-beam vessel built for a North River railroad ferry company or service.)

In 1900, the West Shore did a complete reversal in ordering T. S. Marvel of Newburgh, NY to build the *West Point,* the Central's first propeller, double-end, double-deck ferryboat. T. S. Marvel was the yard that had built the Hoboken Ferry Company's *Bergen, Hamburg,* and *Netherlands,* all screwboats, and the latter two, double decked.

Harlan & Hollingsworth of Wilmington, Delaware produced the last side wheel ferryboat, the *Buffalo* for the New York Central System in 1897. In 1925 the Central sold the boat to the Chesapeake Ferry Co. and she was renamed *Chesapeake*. — Courtesy of The Mariners' Museum, Newport News, Virginia

West Point was the first "new era" propeller ferryboat of the New York Central System, and the first of a series of boats to be built by T.S. Marvel of Newburgh, New York. Marvel built six of these boats between 1900 and 1914. *West Point* was sold to the Norfolk Ferry Co. in 1941. — Courtesy of John L. Lochhead

Chester W. Chapin, which had served the line for only twenty years, was sold to the Staten Island Railway in 1901. The West Shore, like most other railroads, had painted its boats white for many years. In 1902, they were painted pea green – actually more of an olive drab.

The following year, the double-decked screwboat *Syracuse* was delivered by T. S. Marvel. *Syracuse* was 1,344 gross tons with dimensions of 194 ft. × 40 ft. × 17 ft. registered measurements. She was of a design unique to the Central boats, except for the *Albany.* These boats were designed by the famous marine architect, J. W. Millard. Millard designed these vessels with the upper, or saloon, cabin between the pilothouses. Access to the pilothouses was gained through a locked door at the end of the cabin. This afforded the captain and wheelsman the protection of a covered area while walking from one pilothouse to the other. That same year, 1903, also saw the *Midland* leave New York Harbor, having been sold to the Thames Ferry Co. Two years were to pass before a sister of the *Syracuse* was delivered by T. S. Marvel, as the 1,338-ton *Rochester* took her place on the line in 1905. The year was 1910 when another of upper New York State's famous names was to appear on the side of a Central ferryboat: Once again, T.S. Marvel delivered this vessel – the 182-ft. × 40-ft. × 16-ft., 1,351-ton *Utica.* The year 1911 saw two of the four NYO&W side-wheelers, *Newburgh* and *Oswego,* taken out of service.

But, a year later, on June 1, 1912, the 1,600-hp 183.7-ft. × 40-ft. × 16.6-ft. 1,250-ton *Niagara* slid down the ways at Marvel's yard in Newburgh. *Niagara* was powered by a W. & A. Fletcher & Co. double-compound engine 19 in. × 38 in. × 28 in. with steam supplied by two single-end Scotch boilers. Her joiner work was done by John Englis under Contract No. 115 and, on August 27, 1912, she made her trial trip and was conveyed by W. & A. Fletcher & Co. to the New York Central & Hudson River Railroad Co. the next day.

The West Shore saw two new additions to its fleet arrive in 1914, when the 1,400-ton *Catskill* was delivered by T. S. Marvel and the 1,402-ton *Weehawken* was built by Harlan & Hollingsworth of Wilmington, DE., breaking a thirteen year tradition of T. S. Marvel shipbuilding monoply with the Central. These vessel's registered measurements were 188 ft. × 39 ft. × 16 ft. The *Catskill* was last vessel that Marvel would build for the West Shore Ferry.

In 1916, the Erie's Pavonia Ferry Co. purchased the *Newburgh* and *Oswego,* which had been out of service for several years. Both of these vessels were to run for many years to come. The *Newburgh* was sold in 1924 by the Erie and later renamed the *Governor Albert Ritchie* of the Clairbourne & Annapolis Ferry and, still later, converted to a diesel, while the *Oswego* was renamed the *Passaic* and ran until scrapped on June 30, 1936.

In 1917, Harlan & Hollingsworth of Wilmington, DE delivered the 1,391-ton *Stony Point,* whose registered dimensions were 197 ft. × 39 ft. × 16 ft. The *Stony Point* was really the last boat built in the traditional New York Central style. With the arrival of *Stony Point,* the two remaining NYO&W boats, *Albany* and *Kingston,* were taken out of service, placed for sale, and purchased by the Carteret Ferry Co. for service elsewhere in the New York Harbor area, namely, Carteret, NJ to Staten Island, NY across the Arthur Kill on the "New Blazing Star" route.

In 1922, the Central abandoned the West New York

Catskill was the extra boat on the New York Central service for many years, taking the place of one of her sisters in for repairs. – Courtesy of The Mariners' Museum, Newport News, Virginia

Weehawken built by Harlan & Hollingsworth in 1914 was the first boat to be built by Harlan & Hollingsworth for the Central in over 17 years. — Courtesy of The Mariners' Museum, Newport News, Virginia

ferry to 42nd Street, as it served only vehicle and foot passenger traffic, not the railroad.

The *Buffalo,* the last sidewheel, vertical-beam boat, which was only twenty-eight years old, was taken out of service and sold to the Chesapeake Ferry Co. in 1925, thus bringing to a close a vessel design known to the Weehawken ferry for over sixty-six years.

That same year, a total maverick was to appear on the West Shore. If this boat had been painted green and white, she would have been a double for the Erie Railroad's *Youngstown.* The *Albany* was her name and she was delivered by the same builder who built the *Youngstown,* Staten Island Shipbuilding & Drydock Co., of Mariner's Harbor, NY. The *Albany,* was the second boat to bear this name, and her dimensions were 203 ft. × 45 ft. × 16 ft. registered measurements. As a point of comparison, the *Youngstown's* registered measurements were 206 ft. × 44.1 ft. × 17.4 ft. The *Albany* was powered by the last double-compound engine built by W. & A. Fletcher & Co. of Hoboken, and bore builder's No. 303.

She was 1,389 gross tons, 164 tons lighter than the *Youngstown. Albany* was the last vessel built for the New York Central Railroad and the next-to-last vessel to be built from the keel up for any North River Railroad Ferry service.

Traffic grew on the New York Central's West Shore division and the NYO&WR, for, in 1927, the traffic reported carried by the ferry that year was twenty-seven million passengers. This increase in traffic volume was not to continue, for the nation was only a few short years away from the infamous stock market crash of 1929 and the Great Depression which followed. These two calamities had an effect upon the ferry operation, along with the Port of New York Authority's opening of the Holland Tunnel on November 13, 1927, followed a few years later in 1931 by the opening of the George Washington Bridge. Ferry passenger and vehicle traffic were declining steadily.

In 1937, with the opening of the Lincoln Tunnel between Weehawken, near the Hoboken City line, and

Stony Point was the last "low pilothouse" boat built for the Central and she also was the only other boat built by Harlan & Hollingsworth in the post 1900 fleet. *Stony Point* had the sad task of making the final trip from Cortlandt Street on March 24, 1959 ending that service. — Courtesy of The Mariners' Museum, Newport News, Virginia

Albany II was the odd-ball of the Central fleet. Built by the Staten Island Ship Building Co. at Mariner's Harbor, New York. She was the largest of their boats. I used to jokingly call her the "*Youngstown's* sister," because she so closely resembled that Erie boat, which also came from Staten Island Ship Building. — Courtesy of The Mariners' Musuem, Newport News, Virginia

The New York Central ferryboat *Niagara* steams toward Weehawken with her first evening rush trip. Author took this photo in the summer of 1950 from the hurricane deck of the Erie ferryboat *Jamestown*.

New York City at 39th Street, the West Shore Ferry to Cortlandt Street was reduced to rush-hour, weekday-only service, and remained that way for years to come.

As traffic declined, so did the need to maintain a large fleet of boats; so, in 1941, the forty-one-year-old *West Point* was sold to the Norfolk Ferry Co. When I went to work on the Erie in 1947, the West Shore was a fairly cheap, but circuitous route for me to travel home to Tenafly. When I first started work, I had to use public transportation (a car was still somewhat of a luxury even in 1947). To get from Tenafly to downtown Jersey City, except during the rush hour when the Erie ran three trains to Pavonia Ave., it was easier to go to New York City via the George Washington Bridge buses and then take the subway downtown to Chambers Street and walk across Chambers Street to the ferry. The entire trip took about an hour and fifteen minutes. The trip on the Jersey side meant changing buses and waiting on cold street corners. The West Shore route was a good route to go home by, as I could use the Cortlandt Street boats which ran back to Weehawken after the last rush trip downtown. The boat made a midmorning train connection for a train to either Dumont or Bergenfield, where I could catch the Public Service #54 or #166 for Tenafly. On a nice day, the trip was exceptionally beautiful and interesting. For a young man interested in the harbor and the possibility of getting a pilot's license, I could use the knowledge gained by traveling the river from Cortlandt Street to Weehawken. There are several courses that a student studying for his first class pilot's license had to know when he took the test for the territory he wished to travel, and the West Shore boats to Cortlandt Street covered two of them: Battery to 23rd Street and 23rd Street to Day's Point.

During these trips, I became friendly with Captain William Smith of the *Niagara,* Captain Al Lozier of the *Albany,* and a deckhand on the *Albany,* Tom Lyons. Willie Smith invited me into the *Niagara's* pilothouse on

many of the trips up the river and later, in the *Albanys'* pilothouse, after Lozier bid the *Niagara* on a schedule change. I guess they say, "If you've seen one pilothouse, you've seen them all," but, T'ain't so, my boy!

There were several differences between Erie and New York Central pilothouses: First and foremost, all the Erie boats had their pilothouses on the upper, or hurricane, deck and you had to go outside to get from one to the other; second, the Erie boats had their telegraphs on the right side, whereas the NYC boats' were on the left side; third, the shere poles on the Erie boats were long and the NYC boats', very short and at a sharper angle; Erie boats had two whistle cords running across the ceiling of the pilothouse and down to loops mounted on the windowsills, while the NYC's had a whistle handle mounted on the wall just ahead of the telegraph and attached to a cable which ran under the pilothouse floor and then to the whistle. The large hand steering wheel on the Erie boats turned each time you turned the smaller, steam-powered steering wheel (except on the *Meadville,* and on all the Central boats, which all had a clutch which disengaged the wheel and only the drum turned). The Erie boats had an engine-direction indicator which was attached to the engine crankshaft by a long series of shafts coming from below decks; these were attached to an arrow which turned in a round clocklike dial on the wall of the pilothouse, below the window on the left side. As the boat went ahead, the arrow turned in the same direction and, when the engine was reversed, the arrow went backwards. The engine-direction indicators on the West Shore boats were operated either by vacuum or by air and they had two pistons, one in a transparent tube for ahead, and the other transparent tube for astern. As the engine propelled the boat forward, the ahead piston would pop up and down; and when the engines were reversed, the astern piston would pop up and down. To me, when I first went up in the pilothouse of the *Niagara,* the continuous pop-pop-

pop of the piston was a little monotonous, but I guess you got used to it.

After Willie was on the *Albany,* I started using the West Shore less and less. Willie was a friendly man and it was always a pleasure to ride up the river with him to Weehawken. It was a general habit of boatmen on the river to offer a passing salute of a long, low-sounding whistle signal, followed by a short toot, to a fellow boatman on a passing boat's first or last trip. Willie Smith and Tom Hogan, my very close friends on the Erie, used to do this for many years on Willie's first trip downtown in the afternoon. He would miss the *Niagara* on her last trip upriver, as she left Cortlandt Street around 5:06 P.M. while he was only leaving Jersey City at 5:05 P.M., so they were on different sides of the river. Later on, when Tom was to bid the *Meadville,* Al Lozier was then steering the *Niagara.* But Willie and Tom continued to salute each other after they found out which boat the other was on. It seemed funny to see the *Albany* pass the *Meadville* and then hear a salute from the *Albany.* I often wondered what the passengers thought about this sudden change of heart between two boat captains who used to fight tooth and nail to get the best position in the river over the other fellow.

One day, I asked the engineer of the *Niagara* if I might ride upriver with him in the engineroom. For years, the New York Central boats had been oil fired, as the NY Central had no coal interest like the Erie, DL&W, CNJ, and Pennsy (thus had no incentive to continue to burn coal over oil). The boats were all fired by this heavy, black oil known as bunker "C," which was pumped aboard from a large three- or four-inch hose which hung at the end of the ferry bridges in Weehawken. On the north side of the terminal, there was an oil barge tied up to the dock and the oil was pumped from it to the boats through the dock hoses. I do not recall how frequently the boats were fueled.

The engineroom crew, or below-decks crew, consisted of an engineer, who was in direct charge, an oiler who assisted the engineer in the engineroom, and a fireman who tended the two single-end scotch boilers. The engineer was a licensed officer. He had to have a license covering the horsepower or greater for which the vessel was rated. An engineer licensed up to only 1,000 horsepower could not legally run a steamboat whose horsepower rating was 1,600.

The engineer normally handled the engine and the oiler tended the various pieces of machinery necessary

July 1939, Cortlandt and Liberty Street ferry terminals in lower Manhattan as seen from the river. Pennsylvania Railroad ferryboat *New Brunswick* is in the upper slip, while the New York Central's *Niagara* is in the lower slip of Cortlandt Street and the Central Railroad of New Jersey's *Bound Brook* is in the lower slip of Liberty Street. — Library of Congress Photograph

West Street and ferry and steamship piers circa 1900. West Shore Cortlandt Street Terminal in foreground. – Smith's New York Harbor Guide

for the running of the vessel. He would check the condition of such things as the air pump, condenser, and generators – oiling and greasing moving parts where needed.

The fireman on West Shore boats could have been more rightly called a boiler tender, for all he did was handle the lighting and cleaning of the oil burners. When the boat was in the slip, the two outside burners were shut down and only the center burners were lit. Once the boat got underway, the outside burners were lit. The *Niagara* had two boilers and each boiler had three fireboxes. The two outside fireboxes were high up and the inside firebox was lower. If a burner became clogged or dirty on a trip, the fireman would change it while the boat was in the slip. He would put a clean burner in and then clean the one he just took out.

Like wheelsmen, oilers were not licensed but, from their ranks, came future engineers. So, while working as an oiler, prospective engineers received their training. Both the engineroom and fireroom of the *Niagara* were exceptionally clean, bright, and really cheerful places to work.

The regular downtown boats were the *Niagara* and *Albany*, with *Stony Point*, *Weehawken*, *Rochester*, and *Utica* all making a trip or two downtown. The *Syracuse* was the 42nd Street night boat and the *Catskill* was the extra boat. It seems strange that one of the newest boats was an extra boat. From what Willie Smith told me, she was fast and thus a good boat to replace one of the regular downtown boats, as she could keep the time sched-

ule. In 1947, the Central had eight boats and each boat had to be inspected annually. So *Catskill* did not spend much time out of service. Each boat was only laid up for inspection about six weeks.

On July 25, 1952, tragedy struck the West Shore as the fast and very excellent-handling *Catskill*, the third newest vessel in its fleet was on dry dock at Rodermond's Shipyard, at the foot of Henderson Street, Jersey City, caught fire and was totally destroyed to the guards. She lay tied up to the open dock at Rodermond's for several months where I photographed her one gray day in December, 1952, as I recalled that evening many years before when the *Jamestown* and *Catskill* had come so close to kissing each other on the North River. *Catskill* was finally towed to the Central's West New York marine yard, where she lay for several years – never to be rebuilt, but scrapped in 1955.

River traffic was declining for the railroads, as not only were more and more passengers going to the new air-conditioned fleet of local buses, but also highways had improved and the Port of New York Authority had opened the third tube of the Lincoln Tunnel in 1954. Also, as more and more freight was being lost to trucks barge and lighterage freight revenue started to decline. The New York Harbor railroads had a problem: money. Cuts in operational costs had to be made and it became more apparent each passing day that they were going to come from the services which least benefitted the railroads.

In 1957, while the Erie Railroad was attempting to get

the Pavonia Ferry abandoned, the New York Central petitioned the ICC to abandon the West Shore and Weehawken ferries. The Central stated that, in 1927, their boats carried 27,000,000 passengers, which declined to 12,401,645 in 1938, and only 783,631 in 1957. Just as on the Erie, local commuter groups started to spring up along the West Shore line to oppose ferry-service cuts.

But the die was cast. The federal government was not much interested in continued operation of railroads and the services they provided. This became evident when, over the objections of New York State's legislature and many outspoken upstate New Yorkers, the NYO&WR was ordered to cease operation in March 29, 1957. The commuters groups fought on. They voiced their objections, as they became increasingly aware of the fact that if the ferries went, their commuter trains would be of little value, as commuters would be stranded in a no man's land—the Weehawken flats—with a mile of water between them and their destination, Manhattan. Finally, after lengthy hearings and strongly contested legal battles, the Vanderbilt philosophy of "the public be damned," prevailed. U.S. Supreme Court Justice William Brennen signed the issuance ordered on March 23, 1959, so placing another nail in the coffin which eventually would contain all the remains of the New York Harbor railroad ferryboat industry.

An immediate press release from the New York Central management followed, stating that all ferry service would terminate at the end of the business day on March 24, 1959.

The West Shore Railroad commuter service did not long survive the end of the ferry service, and the last train ran on December 10, 1959.

With the discontinuance of ferry service, ridership fell dramatically, as the Weehawken Terminal was not adequately accessible from New York City by bus connections. In order to eliminate the ferry service the New York Central had to get an amendment to the Transportation Act of 1958, sponsored by Senator Smathers of Florida, and drawn up by Robert Minor of the ICC, who subsequently became Vice President for Law of the New York Central.

At 6:00 P.M., March 24, 1959, *Stony Point* eased from under the bridge toggles at Cortlandt Street, gliding past the lower clump of the Lackawanna Railroad's Pier 13 and headed up the river for Weehawken, some twenty minutes away. Within a half-hour, *Stony Point* would bring to an end a ferry service started seventy-three years and nine months before by the bankrupt New York, West Shore and Buffalo Railroad. *Stony Point* was the last Millard-style boat built for the Central some forty-two years earlier, in 1917.

Commuters leave New York Central ferryboat *Albany* at Cortlandt Street, near the end of service in 1959.—AGA Photograph

All that remains of the New York Central ferryboat *Catskill* after she was destroyed by fire while at Rodermond's Yard, Jersey City in July, 1952. This photo was taken by the author in December 1952, shortly after returning to work for the Erie.

It looks like a "full house" with all slips full at Weehawken, New Jersey, with *Utica, Catskill, Albany* and *Stony Point* holding down the southern most slips, in this pre 1952 photograph. — Courtesy of The Mariners' Museum, Newport News, Virginia

The three Cortlandt Street slips of the Pennsylvania Railroad as seen from a departing New York Central boat, the Central leased a slip from the Pennsylvania for its downtown operation. — AGA Photograph

The 42nd Street ferry was discontinued early on the morning of Wednesday, March 25, 1959. At 12:45 A.M., *Uticas'* gates were closed for the last time at 42nd Street and her wheelsman peered out of the inboard pilot-house window, watching the 42nd Street terminal fade into the darkness.

Shortly thereafter, at 1:10 A.M., *Weehawken* departed her slip in Weehawken, making the last eastbound trip to 42nd Street and, upon her return to Weehawken, she officially and very quietly brought to an end a ferry service begun at the turn of the eighteenth century with a rowboat and a strong oarsman.

A friend of mine, Erie Railroad Wheelsman Joe Glennon, who for years worked the night boat *Youngstown,* spent about one week on the Lackawanna Hoboken Ferry after the close of the Pavonia ferry's main operation in 1956. I was working in the Lackawanna Police Department by then; as I met Joe on the dock one day, he said, "This place is not for me. I got a job on the West Shore. I think I'll be steering the night boat." Joe did, becoming the captain of the 42nd Street night boat, *Syracuse.* After closing the Central ferry, Joe found himself working on the Electric Ferries between Brooklyn and Staten Island, commonly known as the 69th Street

New York Central *Weehawken* prepares to depart for 42nd Street. Photo taken from Cortlandt Street Boat. — AGA Photograph

Several years after ferry and rail service were discontinued on the West Shore Division of the New York Central, the Weehawken Terminal burnt down and all that remained of the once beautiful wooden structure are the train sheds. Barges are now tied up where the ferry slips once were. Now even the yards are gone in 1986.

ferry. He remained there and closed that line after the Verrazano Bridge was opened. He then took one of those boats up north somewhere and operated it until another bridge was completed. Returning to New York, Joe once again found himself working on a railroad ferry route—this time the Jersey Central Lines Liberty Street

route, where he steered one of the two Electric Ferryboats which the CNJ had leased. Again, Joe closed another ferry route. He later became a councilman in the Town of Weehawken.

What became of the seven remaining ferryboats after the Central abandoned its service? These boats were all

A derelict *Weehawken* of the New York Central System lays in the mud at Black Tom, Jersey City opposite the Lehigh Valley Railroad's grain elevator in 1966. Today both the *Weehawken* and the grain elevator are gone. The Black Tom area is now part of Liberty State Park and the New York Central and Lehigh Valley Railroads are part of Conrail. — RJB Photograph

in good shape. Surely, someday, someone will want them for a ferry service somewhere.

Albany — the *Youngstown's* double — sold to Mowbray Tug and Barge Co. — scrapped down behind the Statue of Liberty in Black Tom, Jersey City.

Niagara — sold to PSE&G, where she served as a floating office and machine shop at Seawaren, NJ — later towed to Jersey City where she was a floating machine shop at the Marion generating station. She was finally cut up and scrapped at that location in the late '70s or early 1980s.

Weehawken — sold to Mowbray Tug and Barge and also towed down behind the Statue of Liberty at Black Tom where she sank in the mud and laid derelict for many years — finally broken up during Liberty Park cleanup in the late 1970s.

Utica — sold to Mowbray Tug and Barge, who later sold her to a group that was going to take her to Florida, but only made it as far as Wildwood, NJ. While entering the channel, her stack struck a bridge and was knocked off. *Utica* spent her remaining years tied up just below

Rio Grande Avenue in Wildwood, serving as a dance boat, PAL Teen Center, and a bait shop, finally being dismantled and scrapped in the mid '70s.

Stony Point — sold to Mowbray and sent to Florida where she was used as a shrimp-packing plant and later sank.

Rochester — was purchased by Mowbray and scrapped (I believe also in the Black Tom area of Jersey City). She had never been repaired after losing her pilothouse in a 1958 mini-cyclone while crossing on the 42nd Street-to-Weehawken route.

Syracuse — like her sister, *Rochester,* purchased by Mowbray and scrapped in Jersey City.

In 1959, while I was working for the Jersey City Police Department, sometimes I would get down to the Black Tom area. There I saw these beautiful boats lying in the mud flats and remembered the many interesting days I had spent on the North River as a ferryboat deckhand . . . a life which was pleasanter and much cleaner than the fastpaced diesel world of modern-day boats.

CHAPTER 11

UPTOWN FERRIES

≈≈≈

PUBLIC SERVICE AND ELECTRIC FERRIES

About a mile below the George Washington Bridge, at the foot of the Palisades south of Fort Lee, and where the present-day River Road, Hudson Terrace, and the Henry Hudson Drive come together, there is a location that has been known by various names throughout the years. A trading post and sloop landing was established here in 1658 by Etienne Burdette, a Huguenot merchant. For many years, he operated sloops to various points and a row and sailferry to Carmansville on Manhattan Island, near about 152nd Street. Burdette's lies at the foot of a natural clove from the top of the Palisades near Fort Lee, and was well-suited for a colonial-period ferry and landing. A stage line ran from here to Hackensack, by way of Leonia. In later years the location became known as Tillie Tudlem or Tilly Toodlum and, still later, as Pleasant Valley and Fort Lee Park.

The large Octagon House Hotel and Fort Lee Park Hotel were also located here and, in the nineteenth century, this became an important landing for local steamboats. The Fort Lee & New York Steamboat Co. was formed in 1832 and ran to 22nd Street, Spring Street, and Canal Street in Manhattan, making way-landings in New Jersey at Edgewater, Bull's Ferry, Guttenberg, and Weehawken. Ships on this line included the *Edwin*, *Thomas E. Hulse*, *Fort Lee*, *Pleasant Valley*, and *Shady Side*. Also, between May 23, 1880 and 1896, a double-ended steam ferry operated from here to 129th Street Manhattan.

THE PUBLIC SERVICE FERRY COMPANY

In modern times, the principal line to upper Manhattan was the Edgewater ferry to 125th Street, sometimes known as the Public Service Ferry. This line was started in 1894. In 1900, it was acquired by the then newly organized New Jersey & Hudson River Railway & Ferry Co., which operated an extensive network of electric railways in New Jersey. The line had good connections with the Broadway IRT subway near its Manhattan terminal. Also, Day Line and Night Line steamers stopped at an immediately adjacent pier, and the Iron Steamboat Co. had a pier at 129th Street and operated service downbay and to Coney Island until 1932, making this a popular excursion route. There was also a crosstown trolley car on 125th Street, connecting with the New York Central and New Haven Railroad Stations.

In 1911, the ferry and electric railways were taken over by the Public Service Railways, a division of Public Service Electric & Gas Company, which also operated a ferry line from Bayonne, NJ to Staten Island. In 1938, the last trolley rolled out of Edgewater Terminal, over the switchback route up the cliffs, and Public Service put on buses in substitution. Public Service soon lost interest in the ferry and began running most of its buses directly across the George Washington Bridge, or through the Lincoln and Holland tunnels, to Manhattan. In 1943, PS sold the ferry line, which was now primarily a vehicular traffic route, to the Electric Ferry Co., which operated the line until December 16th, 1950. During this period, an automobile ferry toll of 25¢ was still an attractive bargain, compared to a 50¢ bridge or tunnel toll, and long lines were still usual. Only with the gradual loss of value of the dollar, coupled with ever-rising labor costs, did the economic margin disappear and the ferries become uneconomic. When rising costs made a 35¢ fare necessary, the differential was no longer attractive and traffic fell off tremendously, making it unfeasible to continue operations.

Shortly after ferry services ended, the Port of New

York Authority increased bridge and tunnel tolls to 75¢ and later to $1.00. Since that time, Edgewater has become a true "backwater." However, recent major apartment house developments in the area have created persistent calls for resumption of at least foot-passenger ferry service to Manhattan, as the George Washington Bridge and the Lincoln tunnels represent long detours and frequent traffic jams.

The majority of boats operated by the 125th Street Ferry was purchased secondhand from other ferry companies. The predecessor of Public Service acquired the *Leonia,* an 1893 product of Harlan & Hollingsworth in Wilmington, DE from the Central Railroad of New Jersey. *Leonia,* ex *Easton,* was built expressly for the Royal Blue ferry route which operated from 1896 to 1905 from Communipaw Avenue, Jersey City to Whitehall Street, Manhattan. When this service was abandoned in 1905, the *Easton* was tried on the newly opened 23th Street route, but was found to lack sufficient boiler pressure for a sustained long run; consequently, the New Jersey & Hudson River Railway & Ferry Co. bought her for its shorter 125th Street route. *Leonia* had an overall length of 158 ft., overall breadth of 45 ft. and drew 14.4 ft. of water. She was a steel-hulled, single-decked, propeller, double-ended ferryboat with a single compound engine of 16 in. × 30 in. × 22 in. which developed 500 hp. She had one return-tube boiler which supplied 125 lbs. steam pressure and was coal fired. As mentioned earlier, Public Service acquired the ferry route from Bayonne, NJ to Staten Island, NY. This ferry was the Port Richmond & Bergen Point Ferry Co., one of whose boats was the 1896 sidewheeler *Englewood,* built by Jackson & Sharp of Wilmington, DE as the *City of Englewood.* She

had a registered length of 135 ft., registered breadth of 31.8 ft., and drew 12 feet of water. Her oak- and yellow-pine hull was fastened with copper and iron. A single-cylinder, vertical-beam engine provided her with 420 hp, with steam supplied by one boiler at 60 lbs. psi; like *Leonia,* she was coal fired. This single-decked vessel was 347 gross tons with a net tonnage of 218. It was reported in later years that this vessel worked on the Dyckman Street-to-Manhattan line—very possible, as the Bergen Point Ferry was sold in 1937 to the Sunrise Ferry Co. which used small diesel boats.

Another secondhand vessel to be used by Public Service, whose ferry company was known as Riverside & Fort Lee Ferry, was the *Paterson,* a single-decked propeller vessel of 579 gross tons whose original name was the *Governor Russell* and was built in Boston, MA in 1898. Like the *Englewood,* the *Paterson* had a wooden hull, but she had a double-compound engine, whose dimensions were 14 in. × 28 in. × 24 in. which developed 700 hp with steam being supplied at 125 lbs. psi by two gunboat boilers. As Public Service was preparing to sell its ferry route in 1942, *Paterson,* being the oldest of its fleet, had already been scrapped.

The company, like many other ferry companies at the turn of the century, decided that it should have a new ferryboat, and so Harlan & Hollingsworth was contracted to produce the company's first new vessel: the 687-gross-ton *Edgewater* was delivered by H&H in 1902. She was a steel-hulled boat with a compound 850 hp engine whose dimensions were 22 in. × 30 in. × 24 in. with two single-end boilers developing 140 lbs. The registered length of this vessel was 146.6 ft., registered breadth of 39.9 ft., and a depth of 15.5 ft.

Public Services ferryboat *Leonia* ex CNJ *Easton* built in 1893 by Harlan & Hollingsworth of Wilmington, Delaware.

Jackson and Sharp of Wilmington, Delaware built the Public Service ferryboat *Englewood* in 1896. This little sidewheeler ran for many years on Public Service routes in New York Harbor. The Evening Journal Directory of Jersey City, New Jersey for 1900 lists her as the *City of Englewood*, length of 135 feet and 484 tons. — Courtesy of John L. Lochhead

The Public Service ferryboat *Paterson* ex *Governor Russell* operating between Edgewater, New Jersey and 125th Street Manhattan. — Courtesy of The Mariners' Museum, Newport News, Virginia

Public Service ferryboat *Tenafly* ex *Babylon* of the Long Island Rail Road before the second deck was added. Harlan & Hollingsworth built her and her sister the *Hackensack* ex *Hempstead* in 1906. — Courtesy of Mariners' Museum, Newport News, Virginia

Two more secondhand boats were purchased from the Long Island Rail Road — the *Hempstead* and *Babylon*. These also were single-decked boats. The *Hempstead* was renamed *Hackensack* and the *Babylon*, the *Tenafly*. Both of these boats later had a saloon cabin added, between their pilothouses, and were to be the largest of the Public Service ferryboats. These boats were sisters, having been built in 1906 by Harlan & Hollingsworth of Wilmington, DE. Their gross tonnage was 1,310 and a net tonnage of 890, their registered length was 185.5 ft., registered breadth of 45.1 ft., and a depth of 16.5 ft. Their 1,600 hp double-compound engines measured 18 in. × 38 in. × 28 in. with steam supplied at 200 lbs. by two watertube boilers. Both of these vessels were scrapped in 1946.

In 1915, the last new Public Service boat, the 923-gross-ton *Fort Lee*, was launched at Wilmington, DE in the yard of Harlan & Hollingsworth. It was a nice, sunny June day, as Miss Ellen McCarter, daughter of Thomas N. McCarter, Public Service's chairman, christened the vessel. Although smaller, *Fort Lee* was a powerful vessel with a 1,000-hp compound engine with cylinders measuring 17 in. × 34 in. × 26 in. and she had two single-end boilers with a steam pressure of 150 lbs. psi. When Public Service sold the ferry route to the Electric Ferry Co. in 1943, *Fort Lee* was sold to the Norfolk County Ferries.

The last addition to the Fort Lee Ferry Co. fleet was in May 1938 when the company purchased the *Philadelphia* from the Reading Co. The *Philadelphia* was built by Bethlehem Steel Ship Building Co.'s Harlan Plant and was launched on May 1, 1926. She had a registered length of 189.5 ft. her breadth was 36.2 ft. and a depth of 14.5 ft. Her overall dimensions 200 ft. × 55.6 ft. × 14.5 ft. Her 1200 horsepower was developed by a double compound engine whose high pressure cylinder measured 17 in. in diameter and her low pressure cylinder 34 in. with a 24 in. stroke. The two gunboat boilers supplied steam of 167 psi.

Of course, like many purchases of second-hand vessels, there must be a middle man and this transaction was no different, with the Northern Metal Co. of Philadelphia purchasing the vessel on May 31, 1938 and immediately selling it to the Fort Lee Ferry Co. on the same day.

On June 30, 1938 the Fort Lee Ferry Co. renamed the *Philadelphia* the *Thomas N. McCarter*, in honor of its parent company's chairman of the board. This was a deviation from its normal practice of naming or renaming boats after cities and towns served by the Public Service Street Railway Co. Naming boats after cities and towns along its lines was the practice of most of the major railroads of the area. Another railroad which on occasion deviated from this normal practice was the New York Central System. It numbered all of its tugboats, yet there was no tug #1. In place of number 1, the boat was named the *Chauncey M. Depew*, for one of the most famous chairmen of that company. In retrospect, Thomas N. McCarter was the dominant person and factor behind the growth of Public Service into the largest conglomerate in the State of New Jersey, so why not do as the Central had done?

After the Public Service divested itself of the ferry service in 1943, the *Thomas N. McCarter* was sold to the Norfolk Ferry Co.; it in, turn, renamed the old *Philadelphia* once again and she became the *Newport News*.

It is interesting to note and sometimes difficult to research the history of a boat because of the number of times its names are changed and the various ports that these so-called inland water vessels are found in. Just

Public Service ferryboat *Tenafly* after she had the second deck added on her. *Tenafly* was the ex *Babylon* of the Long Island Rail Road. She and her sister *Hackensack* were the largest in the Public Service fleet.

Fort Lee built for the Fort Lee & Riverside Ferry Co. in 1915 at Wilmington, Delaware by Harlan & Hollingsworth. She was christened in June, 1915 by Miss Ellen McCarter, daughter of Thomas McCarter, President of Public Service Electric & Gas Co., the parent company. She was sold to Norfolk County, Virginia Ferries. — Courtesy of John L. Lochhead

look at the *McCarter:* She was built in 1926 for the Reading Co. by Bethlehem Steel's Harlan Plant (which I believe was in Wilmington, DE), then taken to Philadelphia where she ran on the Reading's ferry service; then to Edgewater, NJ in the North River, and finally wound up in Norfolk, VA. In each place, she sailed under a different name.

The southern ferry companies were a great source of revenue to the North River ferry companies as a disposal source for excess boats. Several New York Central boats went south to Norfolk and the Lackawanna Railroad also sold boats to Norfolk ferry companies. Most of the Pennsylvania boats sailed their final days in the Baltimore area on the Love Point ferry or in the Delaware Bay on the Delaware and New Jersey Ferry Co. Two Erie boats, the *Goshen* and the *Rutherford,* were bought by the Navy and used at Pensicola, FL.

Tugboats from the railroads fell under the same type of travels and dispositions.

Because of the sale of the Public Service Street Railway ferry route at 125th Street to the Electric Ferry Co., whose ensuing tenure of operations lasted for the next seven years, its boats will be briefly discussed.

THE ELECTRIC FERRY COMPANY

Prior to assuming the operation of the 125th Street ferry route from Public Service, the Electric Ferry Co. was operating the Undercliff ferry. This route ran from Baldwin Avenue, Weehawken, NJ to the west 23rd Street terminal in Manhattan. Until the opening of the Lincoln Tunnel, this line was considered an overflow route for the Hoboken Ferry Co.'s 14th Street-to-23rd Street line and the New York Central's 42nd Street-to-Weehawken line. On July 31, 1943, the Electric Ferry Co. discontinued its Undercliff ferry and all boats were used in the operation of the 125th Street line.

During WW II, some of the harbor ferryboats were acquired by the U.S. Navy for operation within the various naval districts. Two of these were the Electric Ferry's *Hudson* and *Gotham,* with *Hudson*—turned over on April 4, 1942 and renamed the *Gould Island* (YFB 31)—assigned to the First Naval District. On December 19, 1942, *Gotham* was acquired, renamed *Asquith,* and given the designation YFB 42. *Gotham* was also assigned to the First Naval District. Both of these vessels were subsequently returned to Electric Ferry at the end of the war.

The Electric Ferry Co. ran chiefly vehicle routes, and its boats were designed for vehicle traffic. Like the Pennsylvania boats of later years, the Electric ferries all had four gangways and no passenger facilities on the main deck; passengers were carried in a small upper deck. In 1943, when the Electric Ferry acquired the 125th Street line, it had the *E. G. Diefenbach, Hamilton,* and *Palisades.*

All the Electric Ferry's boats were of the same basic design, even though they were built by several different builders. *Diefenbach* and *Hamilton* were both products of the Levingston Shipbuilding Corp. of Orange, TX and built in 1940. The *Hudson* was a 1941 delivery from General Shipbuilding & Engine Works, East Boston, MA. Another 1941 delivery was the *Gotham,* which came from a Long Island shipyard, the Jakobson Yard of Oyster Bay, NY. General Shipbuilding was again called upon in 1942 to build the *Palisades.* With *Gotham* and

The *Newport News* was a real bouncer! She was built for the Reading Company as the *Philadelphia,* for their Delaware River service. Sold in 1938 to Public Service she was renamed the *Thomas N. McCarter,* and used on the 125th Street ferry. Public Service sold her, after they discontinued operating the ferry service, to the Chesapeake Ferry Co. who renamed her the *Newport News.*—Courtesy of The Mariners' Museum, Newport News, Virginia

Former electric ferry *The Tides*, while operating on charter to the Central Railroad of New Jersey in 1966.

Hudson in the service of their country, the 125th Street Ferry was operated with three boats until the end of WW II when, in 1946, local builders were again called on and Jakobson delivered the *The Narrows*. The following year, Jakobson's yard launched the *The Tides*. This completed the construction of boats for the Electric Ferries.

In a little more than four years, Electric Ferry would see its traffic decline and would file for abandonment; service would be abandoned as of December 16, 1950. The boats were laid up and chartered out to whoever needed them. By 1954, the boats would all be running on the 69th Street, Brooklyn-to-Staten Island Ferry, where they would carry many millions of vehicles and passengers across the Narrows.

For many years, the State of New York and the City of New York wanted a bridge across the Narrows, but the United States Navy, through the War Department, kept refusing to allow its construction. The Navy claimed that it was vital to national defense to maintain a clear channel to the Brooklyn Navy Yard. Finally, political pressure and a reduced need for the navy yard came to pass and

the Verrazano-Narrows Bridge was built, but the navy yard was abandoned. With the completion of the bridge, there was no longer a need for the ferry and it, too, was abandoned. The boats were disposed of as follows: The 1940 *Diefenbach* and *Hamilton* were sold, the former to Nicaragua and renamed *Fonseca,* the latter to Costa Rica and renamed *Nicoyano.* The *Hudson, Gotham,* and *Palisades* (the last had been renamed the *St. George* during its time on 69th Street) were sold to the Delaware River Port Authority for service on the Chester, PA-to-Bridgeport, NJ ferry and renamed *Chester, Delaware,* and *Bridgeport,* respectively. The two newest boats, *The Tides* and *The Narrows,* ran under charter to the Central Railroad of New Jersey until its ferry was abandoned on April 25, 1967; then, they, too, were sold in 1968 to the United States Coast Guard for the Governor's Island Ferry. The *The Narrows* was stripped of its machinery, to provide parts for the *The Tides,* and her hull was sold to become a restaurant in Rhode Island. *The Tides* is still in service today.

CHAPTER 12

ERIE LACKAWANNA RAILROAD

The Erie Lackawanna Railroad Co. had its beginning as the result of the absorbing of the Delaware, Lackawanna & Western Railroad into the Erie Railroad. I had always understood that the Erie and the Lackawanna had merged to form a new company. Much to my surprise, this was not true. Research of the Certificate of Incorporation of the Erie Lackawanna Railway Co., dated March 1, 1968, confirms this fact:

Whereas, Old EL is a corporation duly organized and existing under the laws of New York, having been incorporated on November 14, 1895, under the name of Erie Railroad Company, and has an authorized capital stock of 5,685,238 shares, consisting at December 31, 1967, of (1) 140,238 shares of 5% Series A Preferred Stock of the par value of $100 per share, of which 125,120 shares are issued and outstanding, (2) 545,000 shares of 5% Series B Preferred Stock of the par value of $100 per share, of which 510 shares are issued and outstanding, and (3) 5,000,000 shares of Common Stock without par value, of which 4,701,380 shares (including certificates of beneficial interest for such shares and rights to exchange certificates for shares of The Delaware, Lackawanna & Western Railroad Company for Old EL Common Stock certificates) are issued and outstanding; all of which outstanding shares (other than such rights to exchange) are entitled to vote, the shares of each class and series being entitled to vote as a class with respect to certain matters. (p. 6)

Officially, the Erie Lackawanna Railroad Co. came into existence on October 17, 1960, when the name of the Erie Railroad Co. was changed and the Delaware, Lackawanna & Western Railroad ceased to exist.

For years after the consolidation, you were either an Erie or Lackawanna employee. This did cause some problems and it had to be overcome in other departments; not in the ferry division, however, as in the 1956 consolidated operation agreement, there were no seniority guarantees for Erie Railroad ferryboat personnel.

Each Erie man who went to the Lackawanna under the 1956 consolidated passenger terminal agreement went as a new man. The Lackawanna tried to keep some of the Erie licensed personnel, but they managed to attract only one or two.

The merger of the two companies had its grass roots early in 1954, as mentioned in Chapter 8 on the Erie Ferry Service. The Erie had determined right after WW II that it needed a new station at Pavonia Avenue, Jersey City. After many plans had been submitted to the Jersey City Planning Board without agreement reached, Erie Railroad President Paul W. Johnson met with Lackawanna President Perry M. Shoemaker and a consolidation agreement was reached. Here, we are concerned with the New York terminal area agreement with respect to its operation, mainly, but there were other areas where adjoining trackage was connected, as well as freight house and passenger station consolidations.

Erie non-rush-hour trains started using the new connections in western Jersey City and ran into Hoboken's Lackawanna Terminal on October 13, 1956 — four years and four days to the day of the actual merger of the two roads.

Rush-hour trains, except the Northern Branch and the New York Susquehanna & Western Railroad trains, commenced operating to Hoboken on March 27, 1957. Northern Branch trains were not transferred to Hoboken until December 15, 1958, after a long court battle between the railroad and the Northern Valley Commuters Association. Several months later, the last Susquehanna train departed Jersey City and its trains were terminated at Susquehanna Transfer, North Bergen, NJ.

To those people working on either road in the New York terminal area, it became apparent that a total merger was only a matter of time. By the time the so-called merger was completed in 1960, all the little bugs had been removed from the passenger operation.

Erie has been placed over the original Lackawanna sign on the river side of the Lackawanna Terminal in Hoboken in this 1964 photo taken by the author. The boats are from (l-r): *Binghamton,* in slip #1; *Maplewood,* in slip #4; *Pocono,* in slip #5; and *Elmira,* in slip #6. — RJB Photograph

The Erie Lackawanna started its ferry operation with the former Lackawanna ferryboats *Binghamton, Elmira, Pocono, Scranton,* and *Lackawanna;* also included in the fleet was the ex-Erie ferryboat *Meadville,* which was acquired under the passenger consolidation in 1956 and renamed *Maplewood.*

Three boats—the *Binghamton, Maplewood,* and *Pocono*—were operated Monday through Friday as dayboats covering both the morning and evening rush hours. The *Elmira* was a two-crew boat, with each crew working eight hours, operating from shortly after 5 A.M. to 9 P.M. Monday through Friday. The diesel *Lackawanna* covered the rush hours, but in reverse. She started shortly before 5 P.M. Monday through Friday, changing crews just after midnight with the second crew running her until after the morning rush when she would then tie up for the day. The *Lackawanna* also became the workhorse for the Erie Lackawanna as she had for the former DL & W, running the entire weekend without a break. She would start around 4:40 P.M. Friday afternoon and run right on through until 9:15 A.M. Monday morning.

This schedule was retained for many years until it became apparent that the boats were old and the cost of maintaining them was skyrocketing. The pending merger of the Nickel Plate Road and Wabash Railroad into the Norfolk & Western system was giving management a great deal of concern as the NKP interchanged a great

deal of freight at Buffalo. Furthermore, the New York Central and Pennsylvania Railroads were also attempting to merge, and this, again, was a matter to be reckoned with.

The Barclay, or *Scranton,* class boats were all about 60 years old and their boilers, at least 30 years old. The *Lackawanna's* hull was almost 75 years old and her diesel

February 1967, *Maplewood* laid up in Mowbray's Yard, Morris Canal Basin, Jersey City, either to be scrapped or sold. She laid in Jersey City for about 10 years until towed to South Jersey. — Peter Klapper Photograph

engine was 15 years old. The *Maplewood,* by far the newest boat in the fleet at 29, having been built in 1936, was larger than the other boats and thus more costly to operate. On average, the ferry operation was becoming an out-of pocket loss just like the commuter passenger operations. The commuter equipment was no better, with respect to age and maintenance cost. The multiple unit electric equipment was over 30 years old, the former Erie suburban cars average age was 35½ years, and the Boonton Branch cars of the former Lackawanna were over 50 years old. The State of New Jersey had just started to consider the possibility of state grants and loans for new commuter equipment.

The pending New York Central–Pennsylvania merger was also to include the New Haven Railroad with whom the EL interchanged a large volume of New England freight at Maybrook, NY and things did not look good. Erie Lackawanna management filed a petition with the Interstate Commerce Commission for protection from these pending mergers. In the meantime, schedule cutbacks on the ferry service were put into effect to reduce the losses. Service on the night boat was abolished and, one by one, the dayboats were taken off, cutting the service back even further.

Around June of 1967, it became apparent that the EL and the Delaware & Hudson Railway would become part of the Norfolk & Western system in some manner or form. Norfolk & Western management did not like the deficit-ridden ferry operation, which by now was down to two boats—the *Elmira* and *Lackawanna*—both of which ran only from just before the start of the morning rush hour until just about 6 P.M. at night.

It became apparent that the State of New Jersey was not going to permit the Erie Lackawanna a complete and total passenger-operation abandonment, such as the ICC had granted the New York Central in 1959 on the West Shore. The EL had an "out" in the form of the Port Authority-owned PATH. (the former Hudson & Manhattan Railroad Co. which the Port Authority acquired in 1962). Port Authority money had rebuilt the H&M and new air-conditioned cars had been put in service. The free ferry ride had been replaced with a 25¢ ferry fare, since the EL now sold tickets only to Hoboken and no longer to New York. This meant that for a nickel more, a commuter could now ride to downtown or midtown Manhattan in an air-conditioned train. The day of the much beloved, but old and tired, ferryboat was rapidly coming to an end. The *Elmira* and *Lackawanna* were now the only two ferryboats of a mighty fleet of well over one hundred boats which had once plied the North River for the five major railroads with New Jersey terminals remaining in operation. The Central Railroad of New Jersey abandoned its last ferry operation on April 25, 1967, when the Aldene Plan went into effect. Finally,

Lackawanna III ex *Chatham* ex *Hamburg* approaching the slip in Hoboken. Quartermaster has left the pilothouse to go down on the main deck and drop the rudder pin after the trip is completed. *Lackawanna III* was one of the last boats to run on the Barclay Street line for the Erie Lackawanna Railroad in 1967. — RJB Photograph

The 60 year old *Elmira* still manages to step right along in this 1965 photo taken by the author from the upper deck of an outbound boat at Hoboken. Little did I know at the time that she would be the boat making the final trip of the Hoboken Ferry and the last ferryboat to operate on the North River.

on November 22, 1967 the end came at 5:50 P.M. when the *Elmira* eased out of the slip at Barclay Street, New York and headed for Hoboken for the last time.

The Elmira's crew was an all-around Erie Lackawanna crew. Captain Cornelius Steevels was a veteran pilot of the former Delaware, Lackawanna & Western Railroad; Engineer Paul Randall was a veteran engineer of the Erie Railroad's Pavonia Ferry. They were just part of the teamwork that finally prevailed on the Erie Lackawanna after the bias of the two roads was finally overcome.

The Elmira's last sailing from Barclay Street was not only the end of a company's service to a community or state, but also the end of an era. When the *Elmira* touched the bridge in Hoboken and Captain Steevels rang the "stop engine" bells down to Engineer Randall, who closed the throttle of the Elmira's tiring, 62-year-old double-compound engine, bringing the *Elmira* to her final rest in the slip, it signalled the end of a ferriage service across the North River that had begun over a century before the signing of the Declaration of Independence and thus was older than this mighty nation.

Today, the New Jersey Legislature has ordered the Port Authority of New York and New Jersey to study the viability of reestablishing ferry service across the North River from Hoboken, New Jersey to downtown Manhattan.

Gone are the high-pitched whistles of the Jersey Central and Pennsylvania Railroad steamboats, along with the beautifully deep whistles of the Erie, Lackawanna, and New York Central boats, as are the melodious whistles of the large Hudson River Day Line sidewheelers which gracefully carried their merrymaking and happy people up the mighty Hudson River for a day's outing at Indian Point, West Point, Poughkeepsie, and Albany.

Today, in 1986, there are just a few diesel tugboats with their tinny horns, which are used very rarely now, plying up and down the North River. About the only sounds of yesteryear are on a foggy morning when one hears either the big foghorn of Governor's Island sounding its warning to the few mariners who might venture too close, or the fog bell at the Battery.

The river traffic of yesterday has long since died away, yet the mighty Hudson rises and falls every day as its waters make their way seaward, and later the seawaters invade the river with their salty brine.

Occasionally, I return to the Pavonia Avenue area of Jersey City and, looking around at the large parking lot that has replaced the old Erie Terminal, I sadly remember the days of my youth and the beautiful green and white Erie ferryboats that once plied back and forth in days of steam and a much slower and calmer life.

CHAPTER 13

WEATHER AND THE ELEMENTS: THEIR EFFECT ON DAILY OPERATIONS

~~~~~~

Ferryboats, just like trains and other modes of public transportation, operate on a fixed schedule. In the case of railroad ferryboats, their schedule was very closely tied to train connections. The only exception to this was during the morning and evening rush hours. Most railroad timetables had a notation indicating that trains would not wait for their ferry connection on the New Jersey side during certain evening hours and a similar notation that ferries would not wait for train connections during certain morning rush hours. Nevertheless, every attempt was made to ensure the normal, harmonious passage of the traveler. If this flow was disrupted in any way, it caused problems.

The chief cause of disruptions was the weather. In the 1940s and 1950s, ferries ran regardless of the weather. Such new instruments as radar and other such navigational aids were not standard equipment during those years.

SNOW, FOG & RISING WATERS

The February 1948 issue of the Erie *Railroad Magazine* carried an article on winter railroading by then-president Robert Woodruff, titled "*E*ver *R*eady *I*n *E*mergency —A Slogan That Once More Proved True." Even though this article basically told how the Erie train service came through in the spectacular snowstorm of December 26, 1947, which dumped 25.8 inches of snow on the New York area, it tells of how hard Erie Railroad employees worked to get their commuters home.

T'was the night after Christmas and—*what a night!* The snow began falling in the New York area at about 3 A.M. on the 26th and ended shortly after 3 A.M. on the

27th; in that 24 hours, there was a record snowfall of 25.8 inches, the greatest ever recorded in this area, surpassing by approximately six inches the much-talked-about blizzard of '88.

By 6 P.M. on the day after Christmas, it was estimated that between five and six thousand people were in the old station's waiting room and other areas. Ferry service was curtailed and passengers were held at Chambers Street until there was room for them in Jersey City. The station restaurant and snack bars ran out of food. Both the Jersey City and Chambers Street stations were wall-to-wall people. But everyone got home. The Erie did its job once again. It has been said that the Erie was a freight railroad and did not care about passengers. To some, this may have been true, but those of us who worked on the passenger side of the Erie definitely cared about our passengers.

On Saturday, December 27, 1947, all extra hands were put to work cleaning up the mountain of snow that had fallen the day before. All extra deckhands were put to work shoveling snow. The boats were loaded with snow. The *Arlington* tied up in Jersey City while it was still snowing, so she was loaded with snow and had to be completely cleaned. Even the other boats that were still running had a lot of snow on them. By Monday morning, the ferry terminal and boats were clean and it was business as usual.

Snow was just one of the elements that affected the daily operation of the ferries. Snow was a problem during only one season—winter. The biggest year-round problems that hampered our daily operations were fog and rising water.

Fog is caused by the air being either warmer or colder than the earth and water surface. So, fall and spring are

"A Beleaguered City" was the title of this March 15, 1888, newspaper drawing, depicts how the city became completely immobilized by the famous blizzard. The blizzard of 1947 had almost the same effect upon the railroads. The only reason that the Erie ferries were stopped was that there was no more room in the Jersey City station for the amount of passengers waiting for trains.

excellent seasons for fog, because weather is so prone to change. Then the other element that caused us problems on the Erie was rising water. A good Northeaster could cause the tide to be extra high, as well as the moon tides. The moon does affect the tides and there are certain times when the tides run three to six feet above normal in the North River.

I was working on the *Meadville* one day, when the tide started to rise; it continued to a point that if it rose just another few inches, we were going to be ordered to lay in the river until it receded.

During these tidal stages, the company had large platforms which the maintainance men would string out from the station to the ferry bridges. This greatly hampered the normal operation of the service, as you could not load trucks and the people had to file off the boats almost single-file. The old Erie station was the only one I knew of that had this problem. The Lackawanna's Hoboken terminal and the Jersey Central Station at Johnston Avenue, Jersey City were both newer. I know that the Lackawanna had a seawall around it to ward off these tides, and I believe that the CNJ did, also. Pennsylvania Station at Exchange Place, Jersey City, was also higher so that the people could enter and exit the boats from the upper deck.

During all of these various weather situations, all of

THE RAILROAD FERRIES OF THE HUDSON

Snow is still visible on the *Youngstown*'s decks as she moves through the ice of the Jersey City slips. — Dan Biernacki Collection

Ferryboat *Youngstown*'s safety valve releases as her boilers reach 160 lbs psi while waiting for the incoming boat at Chambers Street in a winter day many years ago. — Dan Biernacki Collection

the railroad ferryboats ran. Tying up was not an accepted practice. During all the years I worked for the Erie and, later, the Lackawanna Railroad-marine departments, I knew of no serious accidents between the various ferry lines. To be sure, there were minor accidents where one boat struck another and pushed in a quarter deck or two.

The most significant accidents that I remember caused by weather were between ships and ferries, or ferries striking bridges.

THE GENERAL SLOCUM STORY & MARINE SAFETY

It's never a nice thing to speak of tragedies; unfortunately, it sometimes takes a tragedy to make human beings realize the necessity for change. When one speaks of the *General Slocum,* it brings to mind one of the worst tragedies to befall New York Harbor.

General Slocum was tied up to the 3rd Street, East River pier, awaiting the parishioners attending St. Mark's Lutheran Church on East 6th Street, on the Lower East Side of Manhattan. The date was Wednesday, June 15, 1904. The recently inspected and certified *Slocums'* wooden hull and superstructure shone brightly in their fresh coats of white paint, as did her interior of dark woods, which had been freshly varnished. With flags and banners flying in the gentle breeze of the river, she was truly a splendid sight, with her two thwartship smokestacks rising high above her three decks and "Gen'l Slocum" painted in large, gold letters on her large paddleboxes. Reverend Haas had chartered her for the day, from the Knickerbocker Steamboat Co. of Staten Island, to transport the members of his congregation to Locust Grove on Long Island for their annual Church picnic.

Rev. Haas's congregation was made up of predominantly German immigrants, who had settled on the lower East Side of New York. A steady stream of brightly dressed women and children poured onto the vessel. The mothers had taken much care to prepare picnic hampers of roast chicken, all kinds of *wurst,* pickles, dark bread, homemake cakes, and *strudel.*

The strains of the vessel's band, playing, "A Mighty Fortress Is Our God," echoed out over the water and pier as mothers, older brothers, and sisters carefully guided the younger children up the long gangplank.

Finally, at 9:15 A.M. the *Slocum's* master, Captain William van Shaick, gave the order to cast off. The large sidwheeler's lines were slipped as the bells were pulled, commanding her engineer to engage her mighty, single-cylinder beam engine. With steam hissing through its cylinder, the *Slocum* slowly moved into the East River. Turning her large steering wheel, the helmsman brought the sharp bow of the vessel around until headed upriver.

Quickly, the *General's* large engine had her striding the East River at 12 knots with her human cargo, which largely consisted of happy women and children. Since it was a weekday, the majority of the male members of the congregation were working. These men had little fear for their loved ones, as the *Slocum* was a proven and safe vessel: She had 2,350 life preservers, 6 metal lifeboats, and 4 life rafts; her fire equipment consisted of 2 hand firepumps, 200 feet of hose, 90 firebuckets, 3 water barrels, 4 watertanks, and 10 axes.

Mothers danced with each other, as their children played, while others watched the operation of the massive engine which was propelling the vessel rapidly toward the picnic ground and a day of fun and games at Locust Grove. They had passed through the treacherous *Hell Gate,* with its swift currents and riptides. The vessel was opposite 130th Street in the Bronx, as one of the young engine-watchers sauntered away from watching the massive piston's steady movement, toward a locker where he thought he had seen wisps of smoke. He informed a crewman of his suspicions. The crewman cautioned him not to cry out an alarm. As the crewman opened the locker, dull orange flames leaped out,

Pages from the original Safety Rules given to author (RJB) when hired on the Eries Railroad, March 1947.

ERIE RAILROAD COMPANY

SAFETY RULES

Marine Department Employees

The Rules herein set forth govern all Marine Department employees of the Erie Railroad Company. They take effect August 1, 1940, superseding all previous rules and instructions inconsistent therewith.

P. W. JOHNSTON,
General Manager.

Approved:

H. D. BARBER,
Vice-President.

(l) Jumping from boat to dock or dock to boat, or from boat while it is moving.

104. Covers and hatches must be properly fastened.

105. Steam, gasoline or hand hoists must not be used to lift loads in excess of marked capacity of hoist or derrick.

106. Chains or other gear must not be overloaded when hoisting freight.

107. Chains used for lifting must not be patched with bolts or patent links.

108. While working around machinery, clothing should be buttoned closely. Loose, baggy or torn clothing, gloves, flowing neckties, rings or chains must not be worn.

109. Ladders and scaffolding not in safe condition must not be used.

110. Before using ladders employees must know they are in good condition and properly secured. When using ladders, the sides must be grasped instead of rungs.

111. Every employee shall report to his foreman, or superior officer, any defect in the guarding of or the absence of guards on any machine or appliance required by law to be guarded and must not use nor operate such machine or appliance unless properly guarded. Guards must not be removed except for purposes of repair and then only by express consent of the supervisor.

4

It is the duty of every employee to report any defect or unsafe condition in the ways, works, plant, tools, machinery or appliances to his employer before using same or at any time when any such defect or unsafe condition or failure to guard shall come to his notice. Such duty to report is hereby made a condition of such employee's employment.

112. If in doubt about the safe performance of work, employee must ask his foreman or superior officer for instructions.

113. The necessity for care must be kept in mind at all times as the rules contained herein may not cover all practices essential to safety.

FERRY DEPARTMENT EMPLOYEES

114. Gates must be kept closed, gate chains hooked up and chocks in place on ferry boats except on end where boat is made fast to bridge.

115. Gangplanks must be inspected daily. Defective gangplanks must not be used.

116. Ticket collectors on driveways and deckhands must be careful to avoid being struck by vehicles.

117. Hauling-in-windlass must be pulled to release the ratchet dog.

118. Employees must not:
(a) Put arm through wheel to take pawl off.
(b) Use feet on hand wheel to take pawl off.

5

(c) Throw pawl on wheel when wheel is turning.
(d) Leave lines lying on deck.
(e) Hang cloths, lines or inflammable material on steam pipes or close to smokestack.
(f) Close a boiler without first making careful inspection to make sure no person is in it.
(g) Allow passengers or unauthorized employees to stand on outer end of bridge before boat is made fast to bridge.
(h) Allow passengers or unauthorized employees to stand outside of gates before boat is made fast to bridge.
(i) Allow passengers to smoke in or around automobiles on deck or driveway of boat.
(j) Wash the outside of windows except when boat is fast to bridge or dock.
(k) Wash windows from rack without notifying captain of their presence.

119. Employees must not permit persons or vehicles to board boat after starting signal has been given.

120. Ferry house doors and bridge gates, after being closed, must not again be opened until boat has left dock.

6

121. Employees must warn passengers to keep out of driveway while vehicles are going on or off boats.

122. Employees must see that pike pole, ladder and life-ring are in position and condition for immediate use.

123. When fog chains are used, stop lights at each end of boat must be lighted.

124. Safety ropes must be put up on hurricane deck during stormy weather or when deck is covered with snow or ice.

125. Vehicles loaded with hay, straw or other inflammable material must be covered by tarpaulin and carried on stern of boat.

126. Employees must promptly remove loose ice and keep ice on bow and quarter deck covered with sand.

127. Employees must keep cabins clean and ends of boat swept clear of water.

128. Employees must see that gangplanks are properly secured.

129. Lockers and storage space for clothes must be cleaned daily and kept free from combustible material.

TUGS, BARGES AND STEAM LIGHTER EMPLOYEES

130. Care must be used to avoid injury from:
(a) Ropes slipping, rending or parting under strain.

7

swirling higher and higher, as they were fed by the river breezes. The locker contained barrels of hay, used to store the ship's lamps, oily rags, paints, old rope, tarpaulins, and scraps of lumber. As the flames leaped higher, they ignited the inflammable paint and varnish with which the vessel had been so recently refurbished.

Captain Van Shaick was notified of the situation. He immediately sounded, on the ship's whistle, the required fire signal, to get assistance from the surrounding harbor craft. Hearing the fire signal, the cook in the galley exited it in a mad dash, knocking over a can of kerosene in his hasty retreat. As the kerosene reached the hot stove, it ignited and exploded. By this time, the fire was burning aft, fanned rapidly by the gentle breeze of the river and the forward motion of the vessel.

Meanwhile, Captain van Shaick was attempting to find a place to beach the vessel. If he turned toward the Bronx shore, the fire could ignite the coal and lumberyards along the shore, but if he made for the opposite shore, she would hang up on the rocks and there would be no chance for escape from the fire. His only choice was a sandy beach on North Brothers Island.

Onward steamed the *General*, as fire consumed more and more of her wooden superstructures. Terrified women and children were now jumping overboard in their attempts to escape the flames. Life preservers could not be pulled from the overhead racks, as the support slats were wired together, rather than loosely nailed, as required. Those life preservers which were accessible were so badly decomposed that they disintegrated upon being handled.

Over one thousand people perished on the *General Slocum* that tragic Wednesday morning of June 15, 1904. The unidentified dead were buried in a mass grave in the Lutheran Cemetery, Queens Village, New York. This disaster ranks with that of the *Titanic* and *Lusitania* in life-consuming maritime disasters.

Captain van Shaick, who was in his seventies, was found guilty of negligence and sentenced to ten years in prison, later to be pardoned by presidential order.

One might ask, what does the steamer *General Slocum* have to do with ferryboats of the North River?

My answer must be, "A lot." It was mentioned earlier that *Slocum* had been recently inspected. The inspector who inspected the *Slocum* for the steamboat inspection service was a hull inspector named Lundberg. He was the true culprit of this tragedy, and he knew it, for he hid his guilt behind the Fifth Amendment.

The tragedy of the *General Slocum*, that June day in 1904, made travel by ship, whether it be harborcraft or oceanliner, safer for everyone. In 1905, a maritime safety conference was held to improve and strengthen inspection procedures and rules, with results that have borne fruit ever since. Vessels are no longer inspected by one man, but by a team. Hull plates are drilled and measured while the vessel is in dry dock. Boilers are hydrostatically tested, fire equipment is inspected and tested. Life-saving equipment is stress-tested. A life preserver must support a required amount of weight, for a specified period of time, before it is passed, and only then is it stamped "Approved" and dated. Preservers must be accessible, with their locations clearly marked and instructions placed throughout the vessel. I have seen an inspector open a life-preserver box, pick one up, look at the date, then take it by the shoulder straps and pull as hard as he could; if it ripped, it had to be replaced.

Crews are trained in fire-fighting procedures and boat drills. The vessel's master must fill out a monthly equipment certification, stating that all equipment has been tested and is operating properly.

So, the *General Slocum's* tragedy has had a bearing on every mariner who has plied the waters since that day. Modern marine safety is the real monument to the women and children who lost their lives that tragic June 15, 1904.

New Jersey Police Officers Journal — Vol. 5 No. 4, Robt. T. Egan, Winter/Spring 1981 — P.O. Box 6637 — Jersey City, N.J. 07306.

Reference for their article came from — New York Public Library, South Street Seaport Library, The New York Historical Society, the Slocum Memorial Committee, the Bronx Frontier.

CHAPTER 14

A NOTE ON PRESENT-DAY NORTH RIVER FERRY POTENTIAL

The rebirth of the Jersey City and Hoboken waterfronts, plus New York City's new construction along the west-side of lower Manhattan, has given political leaders, in both states, just cause to be concerned with future transriver transportation problems.

New Jersey's Governor Thomas Kean and members of the New Jersey legislature, addressing the problem of increasing numbers of New Jersey residents commuting to Manhattan, have come to realize that, by 1990, the Port Authority Trans-Hudson PATH trains will be grossly inadequate to carry the projected increase in passenger load. PATH is currently operating at capacity, with its present facilities, and something must be done. All the New Jersey station platforms must be lengthened to accommodate longer trains. Tight curves in the Hudson River tunnels prohibit the use of longer cars, therefore, more cars must be purchased.

PATH and New Jersey had considered a third tube for the Holland Tunnel as a desired alternative to solve the problem; but, is even more congestion on lower Manhattan's streets the answer?

Governor Kean has expressed concern about construction time and costs for both a new tube for the Holland Tunnel and PATH's platform-lengthening programs. Kean recommended looking into the use of new ferry crossings. The legislatures of New York and New Jersey have allocated appropriations for the Port Authority to study the ferry-service potential.

SEABUS – A PATH PLAN

A group of PATH advisors traveled to Vancouver, British Columbia, to observe the operation of "Sea Bus," a cata-maran type of vessel used there to transport commuters across Burrard Inlet, from North Vancouver, a city of 60,000, to Vancouver, a city of 500,000, over a route distance of 1.75 nautical miles.

The *Vancouver Sea Bus* is a twin-hulled, double-ended, single-deck, superstructure vessel, with a capacity of 400 passengers. Constructed of lightweight metals, her overall length is 112 ft., overall breadth 39 ft., and a full-load draft of 10 ft. The vessel is totally enclosed and has twelve doors which are 5 ft. 6 in. wide and operated automatically by crew members. She is diesel powered and her exhaust system is between the hulls, rather than overhead.

The shore facilities are of a floating-stage type, which rises and falls with the tide, built in the shape of an "E."

As we read an article entitled, "The Sea Bus Story," by John N. Case, in *Marine Technology Magazine,* we came to realize that the Sea Bus is no more than a modern-day version of Robert Fulton's first ferryboat, the center-wheel *Jersey,* built in 1812. *Sea Bus's* shore facility is a technical improvement over Fulton's floating-log shore facility for the *Jersey* and her two sister vessels, *York* and *Nassau.*

Fulton's system would shortly become obsolete once Colonel John Stevens had developed the far superior single-hulled vessel with a new vertical rack and floating bridge. Within a few years, people refused to ride on the "ole ice catchers," forcing Fulton's successors to build two new single-hulled vessels.

Sea Bus's inflated costs are not really realistic, considering the limited passenger capacity of the vessel. Hi-tech problems could ruin a cost-saving concept placed before the public by Governor Kean.

A conventional type of ferryboat, based on the highly

---

successful Stevens' design, could carry upwards of 2,500 persons per trip. It could also use the planned rehabilitated Hoboken Terminal, with a cost factor much lower than the proposed Sea Bus facility.

In 1985, developers of the former New York Central waterfront property in Weehawken, NJ started a launch type of passenger-only ferry service between Weehawken and West 42nd Street, New York.

Upriver, Blount Marine Corp. of Warren, RI demonstrated a hi-tech vessel between Nyack and Tarrytown, NY. This fast, passenger-only vessel can carry 149 paying passengers.

Ferries may once again prove to be a reasonably low-cost method of moving the masses across the mighty Hudson River.

Have we, indeed, come full circle in less than a quarter of a century after the sixty-two-year-old *Elmira* steamed from Manhattan's Barclay Street on her final trip that November evening in 1967?

PART II

THE STORIES OF A DECKHAND

⥦⥦⥦

REMINISCENCES OF A FERRY MAN

In every person's life there are certain times, occasions, people and things that become etched in one's mind for time everlasting. March 1947 was the beginning of one such occasion for this author. World War II had ended and many veterans returned to the work force. The economy was in a middle period with the war over and the Korean Conflict not yet a reality.

Armed with my latest record of achievement, a Tenafly (New Jersey) High School diploma, I decided it was time to put some kind of a handle on what I was going to do to obtain what every young high school grad needed badly — money.

My grandfather had spent many years on the Lackawanna Railroad as a freight conductor and I remembered my mother telling me stories of how "Pop," as he was affectionately known by everyone in the small Pennsylvania town where he lived, would slip her money each time he saw her. So, to a young man like me, the railroad sounded like a moneymaker.

At the time, I was palling around with a fellow by the name of Rudy, who had a 1939 Pontiac sedan. Gas was only 20¢ a gallon in those days. So, early one morning, Rudy and I headed for Jersey City to see what the Erie Railroad had to offer us. We found a parking space along Pavonia Avenue and headed for the Erie Terminal. After looking around for a while, we told someone that we were looking for jobs. Rudy thought he would like to work on the tugs. I agreed that tugs would not be a bad place to work. The fellow that we spoke with turned out to be Claude Turse, the day ferrymaster, known as "Toots" to everyone at the terminal. Toots took us upstairs to the Marine Department Office, between the middle and upper ferry slips. He introduced us to old Harry "Buck" Weaver, the Port Captain. When we told

him that we wanted jobs on the tugs, Buck looked at us and said, "You guys ain't big enough to work on the tugs, besides there's no openings right now." We looked at him: Rudy was over 6 ft. and I was 5 ft. 8½ in. Buck quickly followed with, "How about deckhand on the ferries?" Rudy looked at him and just as quickly replied "No, not for me." I said, "I guess I can try it for a while."

Buck told me to go over to the employment office to fill out an application, then down to the doctor's office for a physical. After I finished, I returned to his office and he quickly turned me over to Toots. Not wanting to be a ferryboat deckhand, Rudy left and returned to Tenafly.

Toots explained that the job was a "shape job." Because of the nature of railroad work, most operating jobs were this type. Basically, a shape job covers extra work and crew assignments when a crew member is off duty. When the company had to put an extra boat on a particular run or assignment, they would need additional crew, so they hired "extramen" as they were commonly known, to handle those assignments. Extramen covered vacations, sickness, and personal days when the regular crew men were off. When a regular crewman had to be off for some reason, he was required by contract to notify the ferrymaster's office within a prescribed time before going on duty. For this reason, the extramen "shaped" at the ferrymaster's office at 6:45 A.M. and again at 1:00 P.M. Monday through Saturday. Then, each night at 9:00 P.M., they were to call the office for night work. On Sunday, if need arose, the ferrymaster would call them to give assignments. The Erie never did maintain a large extra list, so one's chances of working were not that bad. Of course, in the summer, when the weather was nice, the regulars worked and the extras had the vacations. In the winter, however, certain regular men took the really bad-weather days off, thus giving more work to the extramen.

The advent of the 40-hour week provided me with a stay assignment as the senior deckhand on the *Meadville,* an assignment that I held several years. There is no doubt in my mind that given a choice, I would have stayed on the boats until I reached retirement age, but this was not to be. The declining financial situation of the major eastern railroads, of which the Erie was one, started to surface early in 1954. Changes in hours of operation, number of boats operated, and other factors started to take shape. By April 1954, I was back on the extra list, so I transferred to the Erie Railroad Police Department. I had hopes that a police job would be more secure, but it wasn't. For the next four and one-half years I worked for almost every railroad on the Hudson County waterfront, missing only the Pennsylvania and New York Central.

On December 12, 1958, the old *Arlington* labored across the North River for the last time. Her skipper was William J. Wolfer, the very same captain who was skipper of the *Meadville* back in 1949 when I held my first stay deck job. Her wheelsman was Tom Hogan, the captain who taught me to steer a ferryboat and became like a father to me. As the careers of the *Arlington* and *Jamestown* were about to end, I was about to embark on a new one: on December 16, 1958, I was sworn in as a probationary patrolman for the city of Jersey City. I came to learn, early on, that civil service was the course followed by many former railroad men. My extra partner on the *Meadville,* Fred Wesels, became a New York City fireman. I ran into Fred several years later at a pier fire in the Lackawanna yards; he was working on a fireboat. Bob Wester, my partner when the *Meadville* hit the bridge in 1949, became a Paterson fireman.

Finally, after retiring from the Jersey City Police Department, I look back upon my entire working life and find that the years on the boats were the most enjoyable and satisfying. RAYMOND J. BAXTER

1. THE ERIE WORKWEEK

In March 1947, I started to work as a deckhand for the Erie Railroad marine department on the Chambers Street ferry.

Claude Turse, "Toots" as we called him, put me on the *Arlington* with Al Fulton and Joe Marino to break in. I do not remember the first day that I worked a full day on deck.

In 1947, the Erie had five ferryboats. Four were used in regular service and the fifth kept as a spare boat. They were the *Meadville, Youngstown, Jamestown, Arlington,* and *Tuxedo.* A couple of the boats had nicknames. For example: the *Meadville* was the *Mudville;* the *Jamestown* was the *Jimmy;* and the *Tuxedo* was called just plain *Tux.* There were no split shifts or tour watches on the Erie, as several of the other railroad ferries had. The

Lackawanna had split watches well into the mid-1950s. On the Erie, you started and you worked a full shift and you got paid for all the hours that you worked.

The boat crew assignments, starting at 12:01 A.M. with crew #1, called the night boat, were as follows:

1) *Youngstown* – 12:45 A.M. to 8:45 A.M. with overtime as required (usually one hour Monday to Friday).
2) *Meadville* – 5:15 A.M. to 1:15 P.M. (Monday to Saturday); 6:30 A.M. to 2:30 P.M. (Sunday)
3) *Jamestown* – 6:45 A.M. to 3:00 P.M. (Monday to Saturday)[a]
4) *Arlington* – 7:30 A.M. to 3:30 P.M. (Monday to Saturday)[a,b] (with overtime as required – usually two hours daily).
5) *Meadville* – 1:15 A.M. to 9:15 P.M. (Monday to Saturday); 2:30 P.M. to 10:30 P.M. (Sunday)
6) *Jamestown* – 3:00 P.M. to 11:00 P.M. (Monday to Saturday)[a]
7) *Youngstown* – 4:30 P.M. to 12:45 A.M. (Sunday through Saturday)
8) *Relief Crew* – Worked the days off of the *Meadville* A.M., *Meadville* P.M., *Youngstown* A.M., and *Youngstown* P.M. crews.

[a]*Arlington* and *Jamestown* were tied up on Sunday.
[b]*Arlington* worked 8:45 A.M. to 4:45 P.M. on Saturday.

Here is the breakdown of Erie boats operating in 1947.

Monday to Friday

One boat from midnight to 5:45 A.M.
Two boats from 5:45 A.M. to 6:45 A.M.
Three boats from 6:45 A.M. to 7:45 A.M.
Four boats from 7:45 A.M. to 9:25 A.M.
Three boats all day from 9:25 A.M. to 4:45 P.M.
Four boats from 4:45 P.M. to 5:30 P.M.
Three boats from 5:30 P.M. to 8:55 P.M.
Two boats from 9:00 P.M. to 10:45 P.M.
One boat from 10:45 P.M. to midnight

Saturday

One boat from midnight to 5:45 A.M.
Two boats from 5:45 A.M. to 7:05 A.M.
Three boats from 7:05 A.M. to 9:00 P.M.
Two boats from 9:00 P.M. to 10:45 P.M.
One boat 10:45 P.M. to midnight

Sunday

One boat from midnight to 6:30 A.M.
Two boats from 6:30 A.M. to 10:00 P.M.
One boat from 10:00 P.M. to midnight

July 1956 about six months before the *Meadville* and *Youngstown* are sold to the Lackawanna Railroad *Youngstown* approaches Jersey City as *Meadville* heads for Chambers Street. — Dan Biernacki Collection

After the marine department went on a forty-hour week, the company operated the above schedule for a short time; then it was amended with the following time changes:

Saturday

One boat from 12:00 A.M. midnight to 6:30 A.M.
Two boats from 6:30 A.M. to 10:00 P.M.
One boat from 10:00 P.M. to midnight

On Sunday, one boat covered the entire twenty-four-hour period. There were no changes Monday through Friday.

The Erie relief crew schedule was as follows:

Sunday	— *Youngstown*	8:45 A.M. to 4:45 P.M.
Monday	— *Meadville*	5:15 A.M. to 1:15 P.M.
Tuesday	— *Meadville*	1:15 P.M. to 9:15 P.M.
Wednesday	— *Youngstown*	4:30 P.M. to 12:45 A.M.
Thursday	— Day off	
Friday	— *Youngstown*	12:45 A.M. to 9:45 A.M.
Saturday	— *Arlington*	8:45 A.M. to 4:45 P.M.

With institution of the forty-hour week, a second relief crew became necessary, with the following schedule:

Relief Crew #1 was a five-day job:

Sunday	— *Youngstown*	8:45 A.M. to 4:45 P.M.
Monday	— *Meadville*	5:15 A.M. to 1:15 P.M.
Tuesday	— *Meadville*	1:15 P.M. to 9:15 P.M.
Wednesday	— *Meadville*	1:15 P.M. to 9:15 P.M.
Thursday	— Day off	
Friday	— Day off	
Saturday	— *Youngstown*	8:45 A.M. to 4:45 P.M.

Relief Crew #2 was a four-day job:

Sunday	— *Youngstown*	12:45 A.M. to 8:45 P.M.
Monday	— *Youngstown*	12:45 A.M. to 9:45 P.M.
Tuesday	— *Day off*	
Wednesday	— *Youngstown*	4:30 P.M. to 12:45 A.M.
Thursday	— *Youngstown*	4:30 P.M. to 12:45 A.M.
Friday	— Day off	
Saturday	— Day off	

The fifth day could be filled from the extra board. The two boats that worked seven days were the *Youngstown* and the *Meadville*. The *Arlington* and the *Jamestown* were both off Saturdays and Sundays.

Later, changes were made in the scheduling by running only two boats on Saturday and one boat on Sunday, and tying up Sunday mornings between 2:30 A.M. and 6:30 A.M. The company managed to abolish one relief crew and worked the weekend crews overtime, filling the open crew from the extra list.

The *Youngstown's* afternoon crew used to come out at 4:45 P.M. and work until 2:00 A.M.

The forty-hour week caused several other problems, especially with the coal gang. It only worked Mondays to Fridays and had Saturdays and Sundays off, just like the marine yard. So, late Friday afternoon, the *Meadville* and the *Youngstown* would get one or two extra loads of coal. The deckhands had to have this pushed down the coal hole and the grate on the hole closed before the rush hour. Many a night we were still pushing the coal down as the boats were going in the slip to make the first rush trips. We had a big wooden pusher that we used. Like most of the tools used on the boats, they were made in the marine yard, and I will discuss these later.

A couple of mornings, both the *Youngstown* and *Meadville* ran out of coal and the firemen started to complain about the volume of ashes that were all over the fireroom deck because the ash bunkers were full. So the Erie management made some further changes. *Youngstown* ran Saturday on the night boat and then tied up in the morning. Either *Jamestown* or *Arlington* ran Saturday all day until 2:30 A.M. on Sunday morning. Whichever boat ran on Saturday, the other ran on Sunday. In this way, the coal lasted and the ashes were not all over the fireroom deck before the coal gang could come on board and pull ashes. The last running boat got the first load of coal on Monday mornings.

2. COFFEE TIME

There was very little or no cooking done on the Erie boats, but most of the crews all had their own coffee pots—the skipper and wheelsman, the deckhands, and the engineroom crew. We carried our water from the dock in gallon jugs, but we all made our own coffee. Most of us used condensed milk because it did not need as much refrigeration as regular milk. Besides, in this way, we did not need to carry milk and sugar—only milk.

All the boats had a wooden icebox on them, both in the engineroom and on the hurricane deck, which is what the top deck of a ferryboat is called. These iceboxes were wooden boxes lined with sheet metal and a tight-fitting lid. The wheelsman got the ice for the upper-deck and the oiler, for the below-deck crew. They would go over to the ice dock by track #12 at the Jersey City terminal. There was an alley that ran from the ferryhouse and the mail platform, along the north side of the station, to track #12. This alley way was used by the mail and express handler to pull the loaded mail trucks (a four-wheeled truck about 6 ft. long and 30 in. wide, pulled by little tractors in groups of three or four) from the mail and express dock at the northeast side of the station to the mail and express cars on track #12, where all, or at least most, of the through-line trains came in.* They got their ice, tied a rope around it and pulled it back to the boat, and then took it to their respective iceboxes.

I think that the smell of fresh brewing coffee was just

*The trains operating west of Port Jervis.

as much a part of the Erie ferryboats as the diamonds on their stacks. More than one traveler got a cup of coffee from the deckhands on an Erie ferryboat. In fact, there were truckdrivers who came over night after night, around the same time, and they would bring the buns or rolls to go with the coffee. I never drank a cup of coffee until I went to work on the Erie. I had my pail, coffee pot, and electric stove, which I used to keep in my locker on the dock. Whatever job I worked, I took this gear with me if that crew did not make its own coffee. I still have that coffee pot and use it when I go camping.

We worked a six-day week and the men on the extra list shaped twice a day and called once. As an "extra," your day started at 6:45 A.M. in the Jersey City ferrymaster's office. At 6:45 on the nose, the night ferrymaster, Eddie Bednarski, would give out the jobs for the morning crews, if there were any. If there were no jobs, you went home, or wherever, and came back at 1:00 P.M., with the hope that there would be a job on one of the afternoon boats. If not, then you went home and called back at 9:00 P.M. in case someone might have taken the night off on one of the night jobs. There was many a day I made both shapes and called, only to find out that there was nothing. And then there were the days we all dreaded: You made two shapes and called, only to be told, "Come in on the night boat at 12:45 A.M." In my case, that meant that I was up from 4:30 A.M. in the morning and I would not see a bed until about 11:00 A.M. the following morning!

The extra list was a "rotating list," which meant that when your name was on the top, you were the first man out and you stayed there until you either worked a job or refused a job. Then your name went to the bottom of the list and you worked your way up to the top again. There was no seniority on this extra list—only when it came to bidding for regular jobs. As long as Distrct #50 United Mine Workers (UMW) had the contract, this was the way the list worked. Later, when the Transport Workers Union became the bargaining agent, it was changed to a strict seniority type list. This meant that the senior man was always top extra, and so on down the list; but they cut the list and there were fewer extra men. I was lucky and was the third extra under this system, and when the railroads went to forty hours, I was able to hold a steady job on the *Meadville* days, with Sundays and Mondays off.

After your ninety-day probation period was up, you had to join the union. District #50 UMW was the bargaining agent in 1947 when I started for the Erie.

Captain Tom Hogan was the president and Fred Koleberg, a tugboat captain, was the vice president. They used to meet in Bednarko's Tavern Hall at the corner of Henderson Street and Pavonia Avenue in Jersey City. These two men were the power behind the organization. Some years later, the TWU became the bargaining agent for the deck and unlicensed engineroom personnel. The captains went into Local #1 Masters, Mates & Pilots Association, and the engineers into the Marine Engineers Union. The reason stated at the time was that each craft would gain more in bargaining with the companies if they all banded together by crafts. I personally felt that the TWU was far less effective a labor organization than District #50. In 1954, and later, my feelings were to prove correct, as discussed in a later chapter. District #50, during its tenure on the Erie, got the men one of the best and strongest contracts in the railroad marine industry. Even though it was an independent union, it was much stronger than the TWU local with which it merged.

Both Tom Hogan and Freddy Koleberg were fighters for their men. They had an excellent relationship with Mr. Charles Blackton, the superintendent of the marine department, and with Harry "Buck" Weaver, the port captain. After Blackton retired, Marcy B. Roderick, the former master mechanic of the marine yard, became the superintendent. About the same time that Blackton retired, "Buck" Weaver did likewise, and he was succeeded by Captain Jess Baker, skipper of the *Youngstown* afternoons. Everyone said that the reason Roderick made Baker the port captain was because he did not like the way Baker steered a ferryboat. There were others who had different ideas.

With the appointment of these two men, Tommy and Freddy both had their work cut out. Roderick would roam around at all hours of the day and night trying to catch people off base. Baker was just as bad, but not as smart as Roderick.

3. MY PROBLEM WITH "RODERICK & BAKER" ON THE JERSEY CITY BRIDGE

I remember one day I was working with John DiNuto on the Jersey City day bridge job. Claude "Toots" Turse weas the ferrymaster. Your assignment was to open the gates when the boat arrived in your slip, lower the bridge onto the boat's deck, then tie the boat to the bridge with a big steel hook attacked to a one-inch rope which was attached to a winch and big wheel. Once the boat was secured to the bridge, you then directed the vehicle traffic off and on the boat. When the boat was loaded, and the ferrymaster ordered the boat out, you rang a large gong to alert the captain and crew and then closed the gates. You remained by the gates until the boat left, then went to stand or sit, whichever your preference, near the entrance to the ferryhouse at the end of the sidewalk on Pavonia Avenue. The purpose of this was so that you could see that ferry passengers paid their fare when entering from the street. Little did it matter, because most of the people said that they were going into the railroad station, and then, when the boat came

in, they walked onto the boat hidden by the crowd getting off the train. But anyway, that was the job.

This day, I was told by my photographer friend, Jack Dimond, on his way to his shop in the station, that some pictures of mine were ready and I should come and get them. So, after the rush hour was over, I asked John to watch out for me and I walked up the alleyway on the south side of the station to Jack's shop. I was in there just a minute waiting for Jack to finish with a customer, when in walked Roderick. We exchanged hellos, I picked up my pictures and left, and returned to the "nickel box" as the little shanty was known. I saw Roderick come across the dock and go upstairs to the office. A few minutes later, Baker came down from the office and went into the ferrymaster's office. The next thing I knew, both Baker and "Toots" were on their way over to the "nickel box" where I was standing. Baker started to bawl the living daylights out of me for leaving my post and all that stuff. You would have thought that I was on sentry duty in the service and that I was about to be courtmartialed. He kept on going, to the point where he said that he was going to give me thirty days' suspension. That's where the amusement stopped, and the thing got serious. He could yell at me all he wanted, but he was not going to cost me money; not without a fight, at any rate.

Before he could realize the full impact of what he had done, I told "Toots" that I wanted Tommy Hogan's telephone number, that "no one gives me any time off without union representation." Baker kept on yelling and I told him that I wanted either an official hearing or to be left alone. Well, that did not go over too big and he said, "If you leave this dock once more, you're on suspension." Needless to say, I stayed extremely close to the bridge and the "nickel box" for the remainder of my tour. But at about three o'clock, Tom Hogan came across the dock to sign in at the ferrymaster's office before going on the *Jamestown*. I yelled across the dock for him to come over, and when he said for me to come into the office with him, I told him that I could not. With this, he knew something was wrong and when he came over, I told him of the day's events. He said, "You stay here; I'll be right back." He went across the dock and talked to "Toots" for a minute or two and then up the stairs he went to the office. Just as Baker was able to watch me from his desk in the office, I was able to see what was going on in the office. There was Tom Hogan, shaking his fist at Baker and yelling at him. A short time later, Roderick came out of his office and the three of them went into the back office where I could not see what was happening. A little later, Tom came back downstairs and over to me and said, "You won't have any more trouble with him, but just keep your nose clean." I didn't have much more trouble with Baker, because a couple of months later, I caught "Toots" in a timeslip situation where he put a junior man to work when I could have collected a day's pay for it. When he told me that he had made the mistake and that I was entitled to a day's pay, I said only, "Anyone can make a mistake, even you. That's one that you owe me, okay?" And that was the way that it was left. "Toots" made that day's pay up in many other ways, later on.

4. EVEN THE PRESIDENT OF THE UNION GETS CAUGHT ONCE IN A WHILE

When the president of the union local had a problem, he went to his hearing with another union representative. Tom Hogan was steering the *Jamestown* afternoons and his wheelsman was John Stein, Sr., more commonly known as "Ole Man Stein," because his son, John, Jr., also worked on the Erie as captain of the relief crew. Most of the captains used to let the old man off in New York on his last trip, because after 11:00 P.M., his subway connections to get home became worse, and just that fifteen or twenty minutes he saved meant an hour's travel sometimes. This night, no one spotted Roderick come aboard the boat. The bridgeman closed gates and signalled the boat to go. Tommy stayed in the aft pilothouse, backed the boat from the bridge, and walked to the outboard end. "Ole Man Stein" and the bridgeman stood at the head of the bridge to make sure that no one ran down the gangway in an attempt to make the boat. When Tommy got in the outboard pilothouse, he threw

Captain Tom Hogan with hat, and Deckhand Bill Heaney chat near the tie-up wheel of the middle bridge.

over the engine-direction indicator and started for Jersey City. He had just blown the slip whistle when the pilothouse door opened and in walked Roderick.

Mr. Roderick sat down in the wheelsman's chair, saying, "Where's your wheelsman, Captain?" Tom had no choice but to say that he had let him off at Chambers Street. "Then you're running shorthanded, right?" "I guess I am," was Tommy's reply. There was nothing more about it that night, but Tom knew that he was in trouble.

Roderick brought Tom up on charges for running shorthanded in violation of Coast Guard regulations. A hearing was held in Roderick's office. As superintendent, he could be the whole thing—complainant, judge, and jury. Roderick had made his decision before the hearing that Tom would have to be suspended for a few days. Since Tom was the president of the union local, he took Freddy Koleberg, his hardnosed vice president, to represent him. Freddy had made his decision also, and that was that Tom was *not* going to lose a minute's pay. At the hearing, Roderick presided as the hearing officer. Jess Baker was the port captain, and Jim Finley, the chief clerk, was the recorder. Freddy Koleberg and another union official, whose name I have forgotten, and Tom Hogan made up the group that filled Roderick's office. The marine department and passenger traffic manager's offices were between the middle and upper slips, with the main portion overlooking the dock, and the superintendent's and manager's private offices looked out over the river. The station was built in the late 1880s and it had big windows in most of the offices. Roderick's was no exception and he kept the blinds up so that he could see what was going on out in the river. Anyone in a ferryboat pilothouse could look over the top of the rack and into the windows and see what was going on. All I know is that the hearing lasted a long time and the arguments got pretty hot at times. We were all interested to see what was going to happen to Tom, as every captain ran shorthanded at one time or another. I found out that afternoon on the *Jamestown*, since I used to ride with Tommy until my train left at 5:00 P.M. I was privy to the conversation that went on between Tom and several union men that afternoon. It seems that, since Roderick was an official of the company, and he rode in the pilothouse with the captain, he had the authority to represent or act in the capacity of the wheelsman, so the union contended that Roderick had been, in effect, "Ole Man Stein's" relief—because he rode with Tom Hogan in the pilothouse. Roderick would not accept this and stated that Hogan must be given some time off, since he violated the rules of the Coast Guard. Koleberg's opinion was that Hogan had a full crew and he did not violate the rule. There the argument stood on dead center for quite some time. Finally, Fred Koleberg said that Roderick must either make a decision or let Tom go back to work with all charges dismissed. Roderick said that he was going to give Tommy a couple of days off. Then Freddy hit him with his trump card: "If Tom Hogan loses one day because of this, then so will everyone else," and he started to reach for the phone, saying, "You are going to have a strike on your hands, Roderick." Roderick said, "Wait a minute. Okay. No time off, but no more running shorthanded by anyone." Both Freddy and Roderick knew that when the general offices in Cleveland found the reason for the strike and that freight and passengers would get only as far as Jersey City, someone's head would roll, and I guess we can all figure whose head. As long as I can remember, that's the closest that the Erie ever came to a strike in the years that I worked for them.

5. MY FIRST STEADY JOB WAS A GOOD ONE

When the railroads went to a forty-hour week, I bid on a steady job and was awarded the *Meadville,* known as the "Early Boat." This job worked Tuesdays to Fridays, 5:15 A.M. to 1:15 P.M., and Saturdays, from 6:30 A.M. to 2:30 P.M. with Sundays and Mondays off. I had to either bid or lose my seniority to a junior man, whatever job he was awarded that I failed to bid on. So when a group of bids went up on the board, you bid them all, placing a choice by number behind your name. You were awarded the one of your choice on which you were senior. I came out as senior deckhand on the *Meadville* "days" and, as such, I had my choice of "ends." By this I mean that the work was divided by the end of the boat that you preferred. If you took the Jersey end, you would drop the rudder pin, hook the boat up to the bridge in Jersey City, and take up the slack on the bridge on the Jersey side. You would throw the boat gates and take down the vehicle chain on the New York side. The New York-end deckhand would collect all the vehicle tickets on both ends, hook up the boat in New York, take up the bridge slack in New York, and pull the rudder pins, throw the boat gates, and take down the vehicle chain on the Jersey side.

Most of the senior men took the Jersey end, because they did not want to handle the tickets. I chose the Jersey

Deckhands Bob Wester (left) and Bill Heaney (right) stand by the gates of the *Meadville* talking, awaiting her arrival at Jersey City Terminal's middle slip.

end, but it had its disadvantages on the *Meadville* since, as she was the longest boat on the Erie, you had further to walk. When I first started on this job, I had no car and I lived in Tenafly, NJ, along the Northern Branch of the Erie. There were only three trains each way a day on this line, the first arriving in Jersey City at 7:12 A.M., about two hours too late. The bus service from Tenafly did not help either, as the first bus and subway connection did not get me to Chambers Street until about 6:15 A.M. As a result, I used to take the last bus out of Tenafly at about 1:00 A.M., go to New York City via the George Washington Bridge to 178th St., then take the 8th Avenue Subway to Church and Chambers Streets, walk to the Chambers Street ferryhouse at West Street, and then sleep on the boat for a couple of hours. It made for a long day, but I was young. Later on, I bought my first car, a 1935 Ford Tudor for $300. I felt like a rich man—my own car and a steady job! I held this job on the *Meadville* until I went into the service in November 1950.

Note:
The Erie ferryboats were what are known as double-enders and had propellers and rudders on both ends. The propellers were connected by a continuous shaft to the engines in the center of the vessel. When the vessel was going forward, the rear propeller was pushing and the front propeller was pulling. In order to steer the boats in both directions without turning around, they had two rudders, each independent of the other. Each pilothouse had two steering wheels; one was steam powered and the other, an auxiliary, hand-powered wheel. The steam wheel is the one that was always used. This wheel was connected to a steering engine in the forward hold of the vessel and cables ran from the engine, along the upper sides of the hull, to the rudder quadrants at either end. The quadrants were connected to the rudder posts, and the rudder posts, in turn, to the rudders. This is the basic principle for the steering apparatus of all ships. The difference for ferryboats is in the principle by which the forward-facing rudder is locked into place when not being used. In order for a double-end ferryboat to steer properly, it is necessary to lock the rudder facing forward. The Erie, West Shore, Jersey Central, and Penn boats all had a pin which went through the deck and fit in a hole in the center-forward section of the rudder quadrant. The Lackawanna boats had a long tapered pin which ran from the deck through the hull and fit directly into the top of the rudder itself. On the Lackawanna, this pin and its housing were located outside the gates. On the other lines, the pins were inside the gates, above the quadrants. The Lackawanna pins were about 17 ft. long; all you had to do was lift the pin up about 6 to 8 in., turn it a half-turn, and drop it back in slots on the side of the pin housing or sleeve, as there were two ears sticking out on the sides of the pin. This system applied only on the Lackawanna. On the other lines, the much shorter rudder pins (about 30 inches) were pulled directly out of the quadrant and placed in a socket on one of the support columns for the upper deck, except on the Jersey Central, where the pin was stored in another hole in the deck behind the rudder quadrant when not in use.

6. THE FASTEST RAILROAD FERRY ON THE NORTH RIVER

The average running time on the Erie's Chambers Street-to-Pavonia Avenue ferry route was about nine minutes. *Meadville* and *Youngstown* could make it in seven minutes, while *Arlington, Jamestown,* and the *Tuxedo* took closer to ten.

The *Meadvilles'* last trip out of Jersey City was at 8:55 P.M., followed by tie up in the lower slip at Chambers Street, Manhattan. The crew always tried for an early "let go," knowing that, if they could get out of Jersey City one or two minutes ahead of schedule, they could catch the 9 o'clock boat out of Chambers Street. This boat would be waiting in the other slip at Chambers Street and the skipper would wait for the boys off the *Meadville*. An early let go was okay, provided you had a full load of cars, there were no cars or trucks in the street, or your trip was not a train connection. Ours was not.

This particular night, Gus Matasak, the afternoon ferrymaster, held us right to the second, claiming that he was waiting for a late train. I yelled up to Tommy Hogan, the skipper, that I wanted to make the 9 o'clock boat back to Jersey as I had a date. He said, "You better talk to Johnnie, [John Byrwa, the engineer]; he's running the boat." By the time we were let go and the first bells rang to the engineroom, it was 8:56 P.M. I could see my date going right out the window, but I would not give up. I went down to the engineroom and said to John, "Hey, let's get moving—I gotta make the 9 o'clock boat—I have a date."

"Okay, let's open her up and see just what this girl will do," was John's answer. The *Meadville* had an rpm indicator coming off the shaft just below the throttles. Slowly, it started to climb from the normal 120 once John got the links fine tuned, and Tom straightened out the rudder. The rpm indicator maxed at 160, showing us that the *Meadvilles'* engine really put out when needed. We touched the lower bridge at Chambers Street at 9:00 P.M. The *Youngstown* was still loading cars and trucks. We had crossed the Hudson in four minutes, bridge to bridge!

When the whole *Meadville* deck crew came walking off the *Youngstown* in Jersey City at about 9:10 P.M. we yelled, "Good night, Gus!" He took one look at us in sheer amazement and almost swallowed his brass whistle which he used to dispatch the boats. From that night on, Gus always let us go at least two minutes ahead of time on our last trip.

I saw Joe Yacono, the skipper of the *Youngstown*, a couple of nights later and he told me that he heard our slip whistle as we left Jersey City, and the next thing he knew we were coming into the Chambers Street slip. "Whadya do, *fly* over?" he asked. I told him what had happened and he admitted he knew she was a fast boat,

With an evening rush hour load of commuters the *Meadville* enters the slack area of Dock 4 under a slow bell in the early 1950's. In the background just over the forward pilothouse can be seen a Lackawanna boat entering Barclay Street, a West Shore boat heading for Cortlandt Street and a Jersey Central ferryboat plying between Jersey City and Libery Street. While several tugs are handling carfloats and a United Fruit Company "Great White Fleet" vessel is being helped by a tug. – Dan Biernacki Collection

but never thought that he would make a trip in four minutes.

7. VEHICLE TICKET SELLER

All extra deckhands worked both the deck and bridge jobs. The marine department also supplied the men for the vehicle gates. Their job was to sell the tickets to the vehicles that used the ferries. Even though the men were from the marine department, the job was considered a clerk's job and came under the jurisdiction of the clerks' union. So, there was a special roster for gatemen. Claude Turse needed an extra gate ticket seller, and I was asked, as an extra deckhand, if I wanted to break in as one. I said that it was okay by me and, besides, I was thus assured of at least one night's work a week, since the night Jersey City ticket seller was an extra ferrymaster, and he covered the night ferrymaster's job on Saturday night. I stayed on this list for several years and became one of the main gate relief ticket sellers in both Jersey City and Chambers Street. The job in Chambers Street had an additional responsibility. You also had to dispatch the boats and, in the daytime and part of the afternoon, you had two machines, one in each slip, be-

cause of the way the terminal was built with the passenger waiting room in the middle between the two vehicle passageways between West Street and the landing bridges. Jersey City only had one vehicle gate ticket booth, which was at the end of Pavonia Avenue, at the beginning of the ferry dock. For all of the extra work and responsibility of handling money, the rate of pay was only 10¢ more per hour than for a deckhand. I believe this was the chief reason why so few men worked the gate jobs. I was still an extra ticket seller after I bid the job on the *Meadville,* so when someone took off, I would get called to handle that job and this made work for an extra deckhand off the list.

Having worked in the family store was an asset, as I was able to make and count change fairly fast. Because I would set up change of a dollar on the side of the ticket machine, I could get a boat loaded and out in a matter of minutes. The captains used to like my working Chambers Street because I tried to keep the boats on time. This gave them a chance to get out of the slip before the incoming boat caught them. Sometimes this was hard to do, with a boat getting in the slip with only two or three minutes to unload and then load. In 1947, a car could cross on the ferries for 26¢ and a tractor-trailer for about $1.00.

One Sunday afternoon, I was working the day gate job in Chambers Street and it was one of those warm, beautiful sunny days which were ideal for a nice ferry ride across the river and then out to suburban New Jersey. In order to get the boat loaded, you would look out in the street and punch out the prices of the vehicles that you could see. I had done this as the boat was unloading and I started to load the dock up to the bridgeman's shanty. This way he could start the ongoing traffic as soon as the last vehicle cleared the bridge apron. The boat was about three-quarters loaded when this guy came back and said that he had given me a $5 bill. I told him that he gave me only a dollar, and that I did not have any $5 bill in my machine. I refused to give him the four dollars and said that I would check out my cashdrawer and, if I was over, I'd call ahead by phone to the other side and they would pay him. I checked out my machine and it balanced right to the penny. The next thing I knew, the bridgeman was calling me to tell him that I had a phone call from the ferrymaster, Gus Matasak, in Jersey City. He told me that I better send over $4 because he just paid some guy who claimed that I gypped him. I told Matasak that I had refused to pay the guy, and that I had just finished balancing the machine, and that I came right out to the penny. "I don't care about that," said Matasak. "We paid him and you send over the $4." It cost me four bucks to learn a bitter lesson, but the next time I saw Matasak, I told him in no uncertain terms that, if he ever pays someone before checking with me again, I was not going to send over the money, and that he would have to bring me up on charges and he had better be right.

As I stated earlier, the gateman at Chambers Street dispatched the boats. This really was not our job, but the Chambers Street stationmaster apparently dumped it on the gatemen somewhere over the years. This one evening, I was working the afternoon gate job for Red Devlin and, as was my practice, I walked into the station to check my watch just before the rush hour. Jimmy Ramaggli, the regular lower bridgeman, was off and I had an extra man in his place. Everything went fine until the 5:28 P.M. *Youngstown* trip. I did not have any trucks or cars to load because, since we did not carry vehicles during the morning and evening rush hours, I would stay down by the bridgeman and help him close the passenger doors. I looked at my watch and it was 5:28 P.M. so we closed the doors. There was a little more than the usual banging on the door by the commuters who wanted to make the boat, but out she went. That is far from the end of this story.

Apparently my watch had gained two minutes and, as a result, a lot of very angry Erie commuters missed their supper that night. That boat was the connection for trains #67 to Port Jervis, #127 to Waldwick, #319 Newark Branch train to Waldwick, #527 Greenwood Lake Line train to Midvale, #129 Bergen County Line

train to Ramsey, #133 Bergen County line train to Wald-wick, #619 New Jersey & New York Railroad train to Woodbine, NY, and #1103 Northern Branch train to Nyack, NY. Train #67 was the last train to Port Jervis until #5 left at 8:15 P.M. Believe me, I really caused a furor all the way out to headquarters in Cleveland. When I started to get complaints from the commuters, I went out to the ticket office and rechecked my watch. Tom Whelan, the station ticket clerk, came to my aid. He turned out to be the delegate for the Clerks' Union, and he had all the answers for the extremely mad commuters who were out for my blood. He told them that the company should have provided us with clocks and that it was not our jobs, but that of an official, to dispatch the boats. The next night, both the Chambers Street stationmaster Oscar Krech, and assistant stationmaster, Ed Doan, were out to dispatch the boats for me. For years after that, the assistant stationmaster used to kid me about how I made more work for him. He was not mad, because he knew in his own mind how many years he beat the system and got an early break going home.

I had at least one very serious run in with the U.S. Mail while selling tickets at night in Chambers Street.

One night, while working the 11:00 P.M. to 7:00 A.M. trick for Tommy Sullivan, I had sold the 11:30 P.M. boat and closed the gates, and, as was the practice for all through-line train-connecting boats, went into the ticket office to see if there were any last-minute passengers for those trains. A through-line train was any going west of Port Jervis—99 miles from Jersey City. Having no last minute passengers, I ordered the boat out. Before the *Youngstown* had reached the end of the slip, I heard a "Beep-beep" outside of the teamway gates. From the sound, I knew it was one of the old "White" mail trucks, and the next thing I heard was a voice yelling, "Where's the boat, man?" My reply was, "If you look real hard and fast you will see her stern passing the end of the pier." His next words were "I'm supposed to be on that boat . . .I got Registered Mail and it's a train connection." There wasn't much that could be done about that at this point, so I said, "I guess you'll be the first one on the next boat at 12 midnight," and I went about my work. The next thing I knew, the driver came to the gate and said that his dispatcher wanted to talk to me. I went into the station and he pointed to one of the pay-phone booths. I picked up the phone and right after I told this guy who I was, he started to read me the riot act—all this stuff about mail priority and that they were supposed to be put on the boats before all other traffic. I did not even get a chance to find out whom I was talking to. I got a little mad about this time and decided that it was my turn to speak and I gave out a real loud . . ."Now, you just hold on Buster, who the hell do you think you are talking to, one of your mail-handling flunkies? Now I want to have *my* say!" And I told him that his driver never got the ferry until two minutes after the boat was due to leave and they should give him more time to get here. Once things cooled down between the mail dispatcher and me, and we put things together, he apologized for jumping all over me and said that he must file a report and suggested that I do likewise, since the incident would be turned over to the postal inspectors.

Little did I know at the time, that train #7 had to wait a half an hour for that mail truck. Ed Bednarski, the night ferrymaster, called and wanted to know why the mail truck was not on the boat. When I told him what had happened, he also told me to get something to the office by morning.

A couple of months later, two postal inspectors came to the Jersey gate where I was working an afternoon job and checked my story. After I told them what had happened, they said that it all checked out. The driver was at fault. I asked them what happened and they told me a real tale: Registered mail drivers were armed in those days and they were ordered not to leave their vehicle for any reason. This driver would leave Church Street Station, the Federal Building, at 90 Church Street, which was about a five-minute walk from the ferry, go to a bar on Chambers Street, leaving the truck parked outside, go in and have a couple of drinks with the barmaid, then get in his truck, drive to the hot dog stand in front of the Ferry Terminal, get his hot dog and orange drink, and then get on the boat. The regular gate ticket seller would hold the boat for him. That boat would leave as much as five minutes late from Chambers Street.

This particular mail driver caused more than one problem on our boats. In fact, one night, they could not find him and his truck was the first vehicle on the boat and, in order for the other trucks to get off the boat, they had to back all the way to the stern and then come off from the other gangway. The boat went back to Jersey City with only a half a load, one damned good list, and one very mad captain. It turned out that the driver was up in the upper cabin, which was closed at night, asleep. The final outcome was that he was taken off the ferry runs and given a pick-up run along the East Side of Manhattan. I believe he was later fired.

8. FRUIT PIERS

The North River of the '40s and '50s was a busy river. The piers, all the way from the Battery to midtown New York on the east side of the river, and from below the Statue of Liberty to Edgewater on the west side, were occupied by railroads, and transatlantic and coastal steamship companies. In addition to this, you had the river traffic, generated on the Brooklyn and Long Island City waterfronts, which ran to and from the various railroad companies in New Jersey. A great deal of business was floated between the Erie Railroad at Jersey City and the Long Island Rail Road yards in Long Island City. Nor-

mally, the Erie had at least six car floats a day to Long Island City—two on each tour—days, evenings, and nights. Besides this regular freight traffic to the various other railroads via float interchange, the Erie and Penn were very heavy carriers of fruit and produce. It was said that at one time the Erie handled 98% of all the Western fruit shipped East. The Penn, on the oither hand, had the lion's share of the Southern fruit. The B&O, CNJ, Reading combination handled some, as did both the DL&W and the Lehigh Valley, but none of these handled the volume of the Erie and the Penn. Early in the afternoon, both the Erie and Penn started to float fruit across the river to their Manhattan piers. Erie used #20 and #21 while Penn used #27, #28, and #29. B&O, Reading, and CNJ used B&O pier #22.

The New York Fruit Auction House was at Harrison and West Streets. Fruit and produce had to be on the docks and set up for display at midnight, and the auction was held in the early hours of the morning.

This caused many problems for the Erie ferryboats. The ferry slips were on the south side of Pier #20 in New York, and on the south side of Dock #4 in Jersey City. The float bridges were on the north side of Dock #4, and the float tie-up racks were on the end of Pier #9, Jersey City, and just south of the ferry slips at old Dock # 2. You now had the ferryboats running between Jersey City and Chambers Street and the tugboats, with car floats of fruit, running from the float bridges north of the ferry slips in Jersey City running to the piers just north of the ferry slips in New York City. Then, when a loaded float was taken out of the float bridge, you had another float being taken from either Dock #2 up across the ferry slips to the float bridge, or one from Pier #9, with the tug dropping down across the ferry slips to put the float in the bridge. Plus, you had both the tug and ferry having to take the tide into account so as not to have an accident. This was the problem created by our brothers on the Erie tugboats. Then, finally, you had the Penn boats which had to move their floats across all the ferry routes to get their floats to Piers #27, #28, and #29, as the Penn's Jersey Terminal ran from Exchange Place, Jersey City, to the canal of the New Jersey stock yard and Erie marine yard just south of Dock #2.

This mad dash of float movement usually started sometime after 2 P.M. We got to know when the fruit was running heavy because the tug *Akron* was an extra tug on which they would put an extra crew from around 2 P.M. to 10 P.M. Since the *Akron* was in the marine yard and her fires were fresh, she would not have any ashes to blow out and she would be ready for a float within a half-hour.

Many a night you would be coming over to Jersey with a swinging load of commuters, only to find a tugboat with a float laying across the ferry slip.

The Erie boats were ordered not to interfere with the ferryboats entering and leaving a ferry slip. Many a night you would see Roderick looking out his office window, watching the evening rush-hour operation. In those days, the ferryboats were not radio equipped, so we could communicate to the tugs only by whistle signals. After the Erie started to get the new diesel boats and the older steamboats were scrapped, the radios from these boats were put on the ferryboats. But right up to the time that the Erie abandoned the ferry service, the ferry-master had to call the tug dispatcher by phone to relay a message to one of his ferryboats.

9. FOG AND FOG SIGNALS

All of the heavy river-traffic problems were compounded when you were hit with a nice pea-soup fog. Back then, the ferryboats ran in fog, just as in clear weather, but a lot slower and, in most cases, with a lot more people, because trips would be doubled up or combined. To the deckhands, it looked like people wanted to live dangerously and take their chances with the fog. The real truth, apparently, was that you had the same people riding with a few taking the Hudson Tubes, but you spent more time in the slip loading and you would get people off the following boat's trip.

Over the years, you got to know the whistle sounds of the various boats simply because you heard them so many times a day. I could tell each Erie boat by its whistle. All of the Erie boats had nice, deep-sounding whistles, but each boat had a different pitch. The West Shore and Lackawanna boats also had deep-sounding whistles, whereas the Penn boats and Jersey Central boats all had high-pitched, shrill-sounding whistles. This also was true for the tugboats.

In the fog, the deckhands had to stand bow watches, both deckhands on each end. Sometimes, when the fog was extra thick, the captain would have one deckhand on the bow and the second one stand on the saloon cabin deck. This way, you had one watching person just a few feet above the water level, a second one about fifteen feet higher, and the captain and wheelsman on the top deck in the pilothouse. The Lackawanna always had one deckhand on the main deck and the second one outside of the pilothouse on the top deck. The Erie had two very good fog signals for its ferryboats. On the south end of Pier #20/New York was a very loud siren, and on the south end of Dock #4/Jersey City was a loud air whistle or horn. This made it nice for our boats, but the bad part of it was that all the other boats used to home in on our fog signals. The West Shore boats coming down from Weehawken would come down along the Jersey shore and they knew that if they kept our horn to starboard and forward they were okay. All they had to watch out for were the Lackawanna boats coming out of

Hoboken for Christopher and Barclay Streets. Once they came abreast of our horn, they would head to port and start to cross the river with our siren forward of them. This meant that you could have an Erie boat coming from New York to Jersey City and a West Shore boat coming from Weehawken to Cortlandt Street, Manhattan on the same collision course. Believe it or not, in all the years that I worked with the Erie and was associated with the river, I knew of no accidents between the West Shore and Erie boats on this course, but there were many near misses. The Lackawanna boats used to do the same thing as the West Shore boats, and there were several accidents between Erie and Lackawanna boats. The Lackawanna operated on a ten-minute headway between Barclay Street and Hoboken, just as the Erie did between Chambers Street and Jersey City. Consequently, you had an Erie and a Lackawanna boat both leaving New York on the hour, at ten past, at twenty past, on the half-hour, twenty to, and ten to, the hour. Also, both companies' boats were leaving Jersey City and Hoboken, respectively, at five after the hour and five to the hour. So, with this many boats, you were bound to have problems. Most of the accidents were one boat striking the other boat in the stern and ripping up a quarter deck or two. As I said before, we got to know the sound of our boats' whistles. In the fog, a vessel must sound the prescribed fog signal as set down in the *Pilot Rules For Inland Waters* of the United States Coast Guard. The U.S. Coast Guard has jurisdiction over the operation of vessels and the placing of buoys within and around U.S. waters. The United States Army Corps of Engineers has the responsiblity of dredging and maintaining the waters of the United States. Article #16 of the Coast Guard rules, determining speed in fog, basically states that, in fog, vessels will go at a moderate speed, so as to be able to stop when impending danger is ascertained and thus avoid the risk of collision. The rules also determine and spell out the specific signal that a vessel will sound and how often it shall sound that signal in fog. A ferryboat is considered a light vessel, or a vessel without a tow, and as such, she shall sound at intervals of one minute on prolonged blast of the whistle or fog horn (a blast of four-to-six-seconds' duration). This fog signal has a twofold purpose: (1) it alerts any vessel in the immediate vicinity of your location, and (2) the sound of the whistle rebounds off solid objects, such as other boats and docks. By counting the number of seconds that it takes your whistle signal to return, you can determine how far you are from an object.

10. FOG STORIES

Tom Hogan was the captain who taught me to steer a ferryboat, but, because of the responsibility involved,

Tom would not let me handle the boat in the fog—not because I would have been steering without a license, but simply because all captains, even those who had licensed wheelsmen, steered their own boats in the fog. It was dangerous and the captain was the person who had to answer to the Coast Guard.

This one evening in particular, Tom was making the 5:20 P.M. out of New York with a swinging load of passengers, and I was working on deck with Walter Swan. We let the boat go and went right up to the Jersey bow. We got to the bow just about the same time that the *Jimmy* was reaching the mouth of the slip and starting to round the clump heading upriver. As Walter and I looked upriver, all we could see was the New York Central ferryboat *Catskill,* baking a heap (going maximum full-speed astern) and blowing backing whistles (three short blasts of her whistle). About that time, we heard a jingle bell being rung down to the *Jamestown's* engine-room, and we felt her start to vibrate as she started to increase speed. She also started to turn faster. We could see the *Catskill* starting to turn out towards the middle of the river. As a result of the fast thinking of two experienced captains, William Smith on the *Catskill,* and Tom Hogan on the *Jamestown,* a near collision was turned into a safe move and the *Jamestown* passed safely up inside between the *Catskill* and the docks.

About the oddest fog story that I heard was one that happened off the Erie Chambers Street slips between three ferryboats—two Erie and one Lackawanna. Again, my friend Hogan was involved. This one was told to me by Tom, and again he was making the 5:20 P.M. trip out of New York. The *Youngstown* was already in the lower slip with the *Meadville* on the way to New York, and the *Arlington* was just about in Jersey City. When he was let go, Tom had to get out of the upper slip to make way for the *Meadville.* He gave a bridge toot of the whistle (a real short blast to alert the other boats that he was moving) as the *Meadville* started to move closer to the slip. As a result, the *Jamestown* was heading upriver and the *Meadville* was coming upriver swinging into a position to open up the slip. Just about that time, the DL&W boat *Lackawanna* was seen passing in front of the slip, making her way to Barclay Street. Her captain spots the *Meadville* and he goes back in a heap. Unfortunately, the diesel-powered *Lackawanna* did not respond as fast as the DL&W steamboats, and he bounced off the *Meadville* and, while still backing, struck the *Jamestown,* which was now behind him, a glancing blow. Fortunately for all concerned, there was no damage and all three boats went on their way. Several years later, I went to work for the DL&W marine department; I worked on the *Lackawanna* with that very same captain, who added an interesting finish to this rather odd story. It was his first night steering on the Lackawanna Railroad. Boy, what a way to start your steering career!

11. ACCIDENTS

A. A Day To Remember

I was working a vacation "hold down" on the relief crew. (A hold down is a fill-in job for a specific period of time, such as a vacation.) The day was Tuesday, July 19, 1949. On Tuesday the relief crew worked the *Meadville* afternoon shift—1:15 P.M. to 9:15 P.M.

John Stein, the regular captain of the crew, was also off this particular day, so Walter Huess, an extra captain, was steering in Stein's place.

Our first trip was the 1:15 P.M. trip out of Jersey City, which was routine. We had made the 1:30 P.M. trip out of New York and discharged our trucks and passengers. We picked up our load of vehicles and passengers departing Jersey City on schedule at 1:45 P.M. After casting off the boat, Bob Webster and I closed the gates, set the wheel chocks, put up the safety chain across the gangway, and watched the boat depart the slip. Once out of the slip, we went into the deckhands' room in the gangway on the Jersey end.

We heard Walter blow a whistle signal, the bells go down to the engineroom, and the boat slowed down. I looked out the door toward the New York end and saw a Lehigh Valley tug and float crossing our bow. I told Bob, "We got time, he just slowed down for a tug." A little while later, we heard more bells rung to the engineroom, followed by a "jingle bell" and the alarm being sounded on the main whistle. I looked out the compartment door and was surprised to see that we were in the South Slip at Chambers Street, Manhattan. I yelled to Bobby, "My God, we're in the slip!" Both of us ran forward and, jumping over the safety chain, I landed on the deck just as the *Meadville* struck the bridge.

When the dust cleared, the *Meadville* had pushed the bridge off its cradle and the bridge approach was in shambles. Willie Grace, the bridgeman, was nowhere to be found. (We found out later that, when he heard the first alarm whistle sound, he took off across West Street and kept right on going home as it was his last boat to work.) She would have done more damage except that her bow wedged between the dock piles on the lower side and the concrete oil bunker on the upper side between the slips.

We had a load of old, chain-driven Bulldog Mack trucks on board, which did not move an inch upon impact, but a couple of cars rear-ended the trucks in front of them, causing some damage.

After it was ascertained that the boat was still operational, we backed out of the lower slip into the upper slip and unloaded our vehicles and passengers. The injured were mostly in the station complex. The station floor was buckled so badly it looked like a roller coaster. The Union News stand canopy was down on top of the front of the stand. The two women news employees, Edith Hughes and Helen Naporski, were both hurt, as was Mamie Solomon, the ladies' room attendant. They say that Mamie rolled all the way across the station floor from the newsstand to the ladies room.

After the Jersey City ferrymaster was notified, the port captain and chief engineer came over to New York to see what had happened. With us in the north slip and the south slip out of service, the entire ferry operation was suspended, so we were ordered to run light to the Jersey City marine yard. We let go and started to get the dock tie-up lines laid out on the deck and put the heaving lines on them. Once in the marine yard, the boat became a beehive of activity. The master mechanic, chief machinist, riggers, carpenters, and laborers all came aboard to inspect the damage.

Walter Huess called Bob Webster and me up to the pilothouse and asked for a report on the damage on deck. All we had was the damage to the vehicles. Walter then started to make out his report for the superintendent. One very interesting thing happened while we were in the marine yard. A New York City Police launch came alongside. Shortly, a man came walking across the hurricane deck and right into the pilothouse. Walter looked at him and said, "Who are you?" his reply was, "Captain, I am a New York City Harbor Police lieutenant and you have left the scene of an accident." Upon that, Walter looked him in the eye and said, "I do not come under New York City, but the Coast Guard jurisdiction and I am telling you right now to get off my vessel or I will have you put off." A few words were exchanged and then the cop left and returned to his launch.

After the yard forces and the engineers examined the boat and deemed her serviceable, we went back on our run for the evening rush hour.

The south slip was out of service for about three weeks and the *Meadville* was tied up in the lower slip in Jersey City rather than in New York. The *Arlington*, which normally tied up in the lower slip in Jersey City, was tied up in the marine yard. The reason for this was that the company did not want a boat going into the marine yard at night.

B.   What Happened?

I had mentioned that Walter Huess slowed the *Meadville* down to allow a tug and float to pass across our bow. He let the *Meadville* run into the slip on a slow bell. Normally, the next signal to the engineroom should have been a stop bell,, to stop all engines. I might add that, in 1949, the Erie boats all had an annunciator and not a true engineroom telegraph. No signals were repeated back to the pilothouse by the engineer. Here is where Walter Huess deviated from normal procedure, by ringing from slow ahead to full astern. In the

engineroom, Oiler Bob Slays was handling the engine for Engineer Percy Harris. Apparently, the deviation from normal procedure confused Bob and he thought he had reversed the engines. The *Meadville's* engine was enclosed and you could not see the cranks turning as with a regular compound engine. So, Bob opened the throttle. Walter's second mistake was a normal one: Thinking the boat was not backing, he pulled the "jingle bell" which, when used with the annunciator, means "full speed in which ever direction the indicator is pointing – ahead or astern." Bob, in turn, opened the throttle all the way, turning loose the full 1,700 hp of the *Meadville's* engine. Had Walter looked up at the engine direction indicator which was located directly over his head and just above the windows, he would have noticed the error of the vessel's engine and could have rung the cow bell for "dead stop," then rung "full astern" and a jingle. With the *Meadville's* speed and power, she might have stopped just before striking the bridge.

The Coast Guard steamboat inspectors conducted a hearing. Percy Harris was deemed responsible and his license suspended for a period of time – I think for thirty days. Walter Huess was exonerated. We all thought that Walter also should have been given some suspension because he deviated from normal procedure. But then again, the engineer's responsiblity is to answer whatever bells are rung to the engine room.

Percy Harris accepted his responsibility, but rather than return as an engineer, he voluntarily set himself back to oiler and never ran another Erie boat. Percy died several years later. Walter Huess, Bob Wester, and Bob Slays all remained on the ferries after I left in 1954. The *Meadville* was sold to the Lackawanna Railroad in 1957 and renamed the *Maplewood,* until retired in 1965 and sold.

12.   HERBIE DROPS THE PIN

The Erie boats had a shoeshine concession that was run by a little Italian by the name of Rocco. Rocco used to hire young boys to work the boats, shining shoes. There was this one little character by the name of Herbie, and Herbie was forever getting into trouble of one kind or another. I was decking the *Jamestown* day boat and Ernie Rogers was the skipper. Herbie came on the boat to shine shoes. Everything was okay for a few trips and then it happened: Ernie was shaping up for the slip in Jersey City when all of a sudden we hear him ring the fire gong. I ran to the bow and looked up. Ernie yelled down, "Pull the pin!" I reached down and pulled the forward rudder near my feet. "Not that one," Ernie said, "the other one!" I ran to the stern and, sure enough, the rudder pin was dropped in the quadrant. I tried to pull it but it was jammed. I yelled, "On the wheel!" and after a second it came up. I asked some of the people standing around the stern if they saw anyone mess around with the pin. One of the truckdrivers said, "Yeah, the little colored boy with the shoe box." I went forward and tied the boat up to the bridge and then down came Captain Ernie Rogers with a big head of steam and all hell broke loose. He wanted to know what was going on as he almost got his arm broken when the steering wheel kicked back.*

I told him what I had been told by the truckdriver, and off the boat he went. The next thing we saw was the trio of Captain Rogers, "Toots" the ferrymaster, and Rocco, coming up the bridge. In about thirty seconds, off the boat comes Herbie with Rocco holding him by the nape of the neck. Herbie did not work for several weeks, and he never did work on Ernie Rogers' boat again.

13. FIRE! FIRE!

One thing that we were always afraid of on the docks was fire. Most of the piers in lower Manhattan were made of wood and corrugated metal. All of the piles and underpinnings were made of creosoted lumber, and creosote burns. I was working the night bridge at Chambers Street from 11:00 P.M. to 7:00 A.M. and with only one boat running, the trips were a half-hour apart. So, I would spend a lot of time in the ticket office with the ticket clerk. I guess it was sometime after 3:00 A.M. when I was in the ticket office waiting for the 3:25 A.M. boat. Eddie Wall was the clerk and we both smelled this odd smell. We looked at a vent in the wall and saw black smoke coming from it. We jumped up and ran out of the office – me, toward the north slip and Eddie, to the front of the building. When I got to the outer waiting room between the slips, I saw that the north slip was on fire. I yelled to Eddie, "Back here!" and I reached up and pulled the fire alarm. By the time Eddie got back to me, I had the firehose reeled out and I told him to turn on the water. It didn't do much good as the hose was only one length and reached only to the door, so all I could do was wet down the corner and try to keep the fire from going up the wall. Eddie called Jersey City to tell them not to send the boat over, but she had already left. As I said before, we got to know our boats by their whistles, and I heard the *Youngstown's* whistle blowing the fire call (two long and three short). Captain Brodhead kept it up and before long, there were at least two tugboats in the slip spraying water from the pilothouse deck nozzles on the fire between the bridge and slip wall. A couple of Erie tugboats were in the south slip taking the *Tuxedo* out of it so that she would not catch on fire. The New York City Fire De-

partment was on the scene and all I had to do was watch the action. A New York City fireman came down the dock and on the bridge, yelling to one of the tugboats, "Get that thing out of the way! They're coming in here with the fireboat!" I guess the deckhand did not like his boat being called a "thing," for the next thing I saw was rusty river water washing down a fireman. Anyway, in came the pride of the New York City Fire Department's marine fleet – The Firefighter – nice and shiny with her red-and-white paint scheme with gold lettering on a black background. Her main deck gun had a 4-in. tip on it and when she sprayed a column of water it looked like a solid stream about a foot wide. The pier was burning from underneath and there was no ferry service for several hours. Both slips were back in operation by the morning rush hour and the only thing that the commuters saw was some charred wood and missing clapboards. The *Tuxedo* was towed by the tugboats, one from Erie and the other, from one of the other railroads, to our marine yard where she was tied up until her crew brought her out at 5:15 A.M.

Both Eddie Wall and I were commended by the company for our fast action, which avoided a major catastrophe for the company. While there was nothing in writing, it was good to have your bosses go out of their way to come and thank you and tell you that they had forwarded to the general offices in Cleveland their comments about what you did.

14. A LOT OF SPEED AND A LOT OF DAMAGE DONE

During her time on the Erie roster, the *Meadville* did a lot of damage. They say she was a good boat for speed, one of the fastest on the river. She could also make a fool out of unsuspecting captains. She was a boat that you had to master and keep a wary eye on. Al Wilson told me that he worked on her during her trial runs in the North River, just after she was brought up from Sun Shipbuilding in Chester, PA, on the Delaware River. She was the only boat, because of her Uniflow engine, which could go from full ahead to full astern and get an almost immediate response from the engine. She could stop in three-quarters of her length, which meant that, since she was 234 ft. long and her gross tonnage was 1,599, you were stopping almost 1,600 tons in 175½ ft. Yet she hit almost every bridge in the Erie System. The *Meadville* was a fast boat and, as such, she would have been ideal for 23rd Street. I was told by an oldtimer that the *Meadville* didn't do too well running up there, because of the short racks and her length. In fact, the Erie kept the big boats downtown mostly. The *Jamestown, Youngstown,* and *Meadville* were regular downtown (Chambers Street) boats, along with the smaller *Arlington.* The *Goshen* and *Tuxedo* ran uptown. Of course, that did not mean that you

---

*When someone drops the pin, it locks the rudder and when you turn the steam-powered steering gear, steam builds up in the steering-engine cylinders, with the result that when sufficient pressure builds up and has no place to go, it takes the line of least resistance and pushes the steering wheel back abruptly.

Erie Railroad Chief of Police Charles Stern examines damage to the middle ferry bridge approach at Jersey City.

Claude Turse Day Ferrymaster, (back to camera) walks towards Erie Railroad Police Chief Charles Stern and Bridgeman John Di Nuto who are surveying the damage to the middle slip bridge approach at Jersey City.

would never see one of these boats making a trip on the other line. There was also the possibility that a boat would have a split run: so many trips downtown and so many trips uptown. I know that, on the New York Central, its downtown boats were the *Niagara, Albany,* and *Stony Point,* yet these boats also ran on 42nd Street. During the time that I was on the river, I saw every one of the New York Central boats run downtown at one time or another. Even the Lackawanna Railroad ran the slower and much older *Bergen* and *Oswego* to Barclay Street once in a while to replace one of the "Four Sisters" or "Barclay" boats as they were commonly known, meaning the *Binghamton, Elmira, Pocono,* and *Scranton.* The fifth one of these boats was the *Ithaca,* which burned at the Brighton marine yard while in drydock in 1946.

They tell about one captain who ran the *Meadville* in the slip at 23rd Street and never rang a bell to go back (full speed astern). When the engineer saw the clump at the end of the rack through the escape hatch in the hull, he backed the boat, but much too late, the *Meadville* sent the 23rd Street bridge up the street and almost tore the New York end pilothouse completely off. The pilothouse roof was just about even with the roof of the ferry slip. This story was verified many years later by a Lackawanna Railroad ferry captain who, at the time, was awaiting the departure of his boat to Hoboken. Personally, I would say that you can not blame the boat if the skipper is not able to handle her.

15. BEFRIENDED BY ONE OF THE FINEST MEN I HAVE EVER HAD THE PLEASURE OF KNOWING

I became very friendly with Tommy Hogan and it was Tom who taught me how to steer a ferryboat. I always kept saying "Hey, Tommy, when are you going to let me steer?"

I was working a two-week hold down on the 1:00 P.M. to 9:00 P.M. Chambers Street bridge. The *Tuxedo* was running in place of the *Jamestown,* which was in the yard for her annual inspection. After 9:00 P.M., the boats went from ten-minute headway to a fifteen-minute headway and only one slip was used on each side of the river—usually, the middle slip in Jersey City and the upper slip in Chambers Street. The last boat that I worked was the *Meadville* as she tied up in the lower slip at Chambers Street. I would make the 9:15 P.M. trip to Jersey City and always go up in the pilothouse to ride with Tom. This night, when "Ole Man Stein" rang the all-clear signal and threw over the engine indicator, Tom said to me, "Well, go ahead and take her out." Without a second glance, I jumped up, threw the beckett, (wheel lock and running light switch) off the king spoke, turned the wheel to port to pull the boat away from the rack, and

pushed down the annunciator to full ahead.* About halfway out of the slip, I blew the slip whistle. Once the boat was away from the rack, I started to turn the wheel to starboard so that the boat would be heading upriver as we passed the clump at the end of Pier #20. The Jersey City slips were further upriver than the Chambers Street slips. In fact, they were about opposite Piers #27 and #28 North River, New York. Since the *Tuxedo* was a conventional "boat," I automatically headed upriver regardless of the tide.

When the tide is coming in or at "flood stage," as it is known, you head upriver, but at a lesser angle so that you approach the Jersey City slips from the under side, or downriver, side. During slack water,** you could approach the slips from almost head on. Tom stood directly behind the steering wheel, watching the sheer pole.† Tom would say, "Ease her up, don't let her come around too fast," or "Use less wheel," or other

---

*The Erie boats were not equipped with engineroom telegraphs until after the *Meadville's* accident in Chambers Street, previously mentioned. At that time, the Coast Guard inspectors ordered all ferryboats to be equipped with an engineroom/pilothouse repeat telegraph system.

The difference between an annunciator and telegraph is that an annunciator only indicates the engine order from the pilothouse to the engineroom. The engineer has no way to repeat the command back to the pilothouse, whereas the telegraph has the ability to return the command from the engineroom back to the pilothouse.

One added feature of a telegraph is the "cross signal" alarm. Every time the telegraph handle goes past the "stop indicator," an alarm bell sounded in the engineroom. This alarm would not stop until the engine was reversed or the telegraph handle was brought back to a speed indication on the side of original setting (i.e., if you were running at full speed ahead and you pulled the telegraph lever up to slow astern you passed the "stop" position and the alarm would ring. If you did not go back to any ahead position, the alarm would continue to ring until the engineer started to back the vessel at a slow astern speed).

Some captains had the habit of sweeping the telegraph to make sure that the engineer would hear his signals. This was okay with the annunciator, but with the telegraph, he would ring the alarm at least twice between engine-speed changes. Men like Tom Hogan, who had extra-good engineers like Fritz Kompers, did not find it necessary to sweep the telegraph. Fritz stood by the throttle from the time the first bell was rung until Tom pulled the cow bell. Thank God, he was so good, because one night he saved me from hitting the bridge in Jersey City. Tom and I used to kid each other that "the *Jamestown* was the only pilothouse-controlled steamboat on the river.

**Slack water is the time between the changing from one stage of the tide to the other, i.e., from ebb to flood. In the North River, slack tide lasts for about twenty minutes off of Chambers Street, New York and Pavonia Avenue, Jersey City. Slack water along the docks is at a different time than slack in the middle of the river, whereas the East River has a very short, or almost no, slack-water stage.

†The sheer pole is the long pole in the front of the pilothouse that looks like a flagpole. The sheer pole is used as a pointer to steer by. On a tug or a vessel with a pointed bow, the bow stem is used as a guide. In fact, I have seen tugs with a pole that fits into the stem.

Captain Tom Hogan, right and Wheelsman Joe Glennon, left outside the pilothouse of the Erie ferryboat *Meadville*, 1950.

me his little pointers and we got closer and closer and still closer, but no "Okay, Son, I'll take her." All he kept doing was telling me just what to do. I started to get a little scared as I thought to myself, "When is he going to take this boat? . . . Boy, we're getting awful close to the dock and boy, it sure looks big. . . . I hope he knows what he is doing, because I don't." But Tom just kept saying, "Bring her around a little more, that's good, not too much wheel, okay, slow your boat down, bring her around, now keep her between the clumps, okay, stop your boat." Then, just as the bow of the *Tuxedo* came abreast of the clumps at the end of the rack, Tom said, "Go Back [full stern] . . . That's good, you don't want to kill all her way . . . Give her the next back just about halfway in the slip to kill some more of the way." When we were just about up to the bridge, Tom said, "Give her a quick back . . . Slow ahead . . . Half ahead . . . Okay, when she's all tied up, stop your boat and ring the cow bell." After I did that, Tom said, "Well, that's it. You just took your first ferryboat across the river."

That was my first night behind the wheel of a ferryboat. As I recall, when I first finished I kind of thought, "This is not for me." But the more I thought about it, the more I liked it and later, as we crossed the river going back to New York, Tom said to me, "Well what do you think, was it interesting?" I said I liked it and thanks very much. Then he told me that the reason he would not let me bring the boat over the first night was that he wanted me to get the feel of her and that the tide was not right in Jersey City. He waited for a night when he knew that the tide would be slack just off of the slip and that since the middle slip was so wide I could fall in it without much trouble. Some time later, I found out that no matter how big the middle slip is there are times when it's never big enough.

quiet little orders. About halfway across the river, Tom would say, "Okay, Son, I'll take her from here." Believe me, was I disappointed! Each night, that "Okay, Son, I'll take her" came later and later. Till about the fifth night, It happened: I left Chambers Street and Tom was giving

Ferryboat *Tuxedo* heads for Chambers Street during a wintery February 1, 1948. A D. L. & W. Railroad Barclay Street boat is just astern of her. – Dan Biernacki Collection

THE STORIES OF A DECKHAND

16. OH! TO STEER A FERRYBOAT

After this, I became a regular fixture in the pilothouse of the *Jamestown* afternoons with Captain Tom Hogan. Every chance I got, I would go up and steer a trip or two. I was up fairly high on the extra list and I would get a lot of day work, either on the boats or the bridges, and when I did, I would take the train home in the evening, since it was free transportation as against paying for the bus.

This would give me eight trips that I could steer and, most times, once I started, I would keep right on steering and go home on the late Northern Branch train which left Jersey City at 6:35 P.M.

Tom was a very jovial person and he was always kidding around with someone. The engineer on the *Jamestown* afternoons was an old Dutchman by the name of Fritz Kompers. Fritz took his job seriously and was one of the best engineers on the Erie. He was smart and knew how to make the tide work for us. In order to do this, Fritz had to know the conditions of the wind and the tide. So, every day, he would whistle up the speaking tube to Tom and ask, "What's the wind and tide?" Tom would put on his best German accent and say, "Das vind iest ebb und de tide ist norteast," and we would all laugh. But old Fritz loved it and he liked Tom very much. They were a good working team.

17. DIFFERENCES BETWEEN BOATS

Over the course of years I worked for the Erie, I steered all five boats, and they all handled somewhat differently. Each and every boat had its own peculiar trait that made it seem almost human. Although the same in build and appearance, they were all different in reactions. Some of the traits that I remember are:

Youngstown: by far the best handling of the conventional boats; she was an excellent backing boat; she had a surface condenser, which meant that it required water only once a tour; she was easy on all of the crew, from the captain right on down to the fireman. She was a heavy and true boat. Because of her excellence, she was the night boat and served as relief boat in the daytime. If there was some kind of a small job that had to be done on one of the other boats, the *Youngstown* would run in that boat's place and the deck crew, oiler, and firemen from the other boat would change to the *Youngstown.* The engineer, however, would always stay with his assigned boat on the day tour.

Jamestown had a port list (downtown), with the result that all the weight had to be placed on the starboard (uptown) gangway; she had a jet condenser which required that water be taken aboard every trip on the Jersey side, and a steaming problem which required that she have a special mix of coal. As I mentioned previously, the *Jamestown* was only 1,200 hp and about a

hundred tons heavier than the *Arlington;* became of this, she was slower than the other boats. Like *Youngstown,* though, she was a steady and true boat. I remember one evening at slack tide, I left Jersey City and did not touch the steering wheel until about two-thirds of the way across the river. The pitch of the propeller turned the boat just enough so that she headed slightly downriver. I was told that the test of a true boat was when the right-hand pitch of the propeller turned her slightly to the right. So, by that standard, the *Jamestown* was "true."

Arlington, was a good handling boat, was the lightest of all the Erie boats (as of 1947); thus she had a tendency to slide with the tide (a sideward action in strong tides); a good backing boat but no bypass (in bypassing the throttle, admits live steam directly to the cylinders mainly used to give the engine a extra kick when needed sometimes) capabilities if the engineer opened the *Arlingtons'* throttle all the way, that was all the kick you had when you were backing. So, you had best not misjudge your distance entering the slip!

Meadville, as discussed previously, handled well against the tide, just the opposite of the other boats; she was an excellent backer, fast, and highly maneuverable, provided the captain was knowledgable of her capabilities. About 10 ft. longer than the other boats, she had scissor gates that rolled along the deck on casters, thus keeping the gates out of the way so that trucks would not pull them down, as was the case on occasion with the conventional gates. Meadville was not liked by the older deckhands because of her speed, gates, and length. Yet, once you got to know how to work her, you did not want to work the other boats.

Tuxedo, like the *Arlington,* was light and would slide on the tide. The worst backer of all the Erie boats, she carried only 143 lbs. of steam pressure, meaning that most engineers would have to open her bypass on the first back and use live steam to start her backing. By far in the worst condition of all five Erie boats, the *Tuxedo* had apparently been worked hard during her 51-year career on the Erie.

Three of the Erie boats had been designed by J. W. Millard around the turn of the century, and all were built between 1903 and 1905. These boats were *Arlington, Goshen,* and *Tuxedo.* (When I started working in 1947, *Goshen* was already gone.) Even though built along the same plan, these three had some slight differences: The color of the *Arlington's* engineroom vent was green, while *Tuxedo's* vent was white; *Arlington's* whistle was on the starboard side of the stack, while *Tuxedo's* was on the port side, each whistle with different tones; the *Arlington* had two fireroom vents, just aft of the stateroom on the Jersey end. *Tuxedo's* Jersey-end deck was ramped to facilitate loading heavy trucks. Otherwise, as she was small and low in the water, when trucks would come aboard, the bridge would go up and the boat would go down, sometimes 20 to 24 inches, depending on the truck's load. With the ramped deck, this differential was greatly reduced. No one ever knew why the equally small *Arlington* was never thus equipped.

The *Jamestown* and the *Youngstown* were very similar overall, except for the noticeable port list of the *Jamestown*. Both of these boats had bunkrooms attached to the aft side of the pilothouses. You entered the pilothouse by doors on either side. Both *Arlington* and *Tuxedo* had only one entrance door on the back of the pilothouse. Even though the *Meadville* had two bunkrooms, they were separated from the pilothouses with a stairway between them. You could always tell the *Meadville* when you came down Pavonia Avenue, because the stacks of the boats were visible above the ferryhouse, and the white heat ring from the forced-draft was plainly visible. *Jamestown*, of course, was distinguishable by her list.

18.   CAPTAIN SI BRODHEAD AND THE COAST GUARD INSPECTORS

Si was the captain of the night boat, *Youngstown*, around 1949. He was an excellent boatman. Si had worked on the New Haven Railroad tugboats before coming to the Erie Railroad. He told me that he preferred ferryboating to tugboating and that was why he had left the New Haven. I believe that most of the skippers, such as Tom Hogan and Si Brodhead, who had tugboat experience were much more flexible in their ability to find alternate solutions to the many problems of maneuvering on the busy lower Hudson of the mid-1940s and '50s. I have been with both of these men when they have been forced to deviate from normal procedure and rely on their former tugboat experience to get them out of a situation and still maintain their time schedule.

The night boat worked until after the morning rush hour and, naturally, having worked all night, the captain was tired. So, after he had finished steering across the river, Si would sit down in the high-backed pilothouse chair, put his feet up on the hand-wheel drum, and close his eyes. One morning, Si assumed his normal resting position when he heard a knock on the pilothouse door. Joe Glennon was Si's wheelsman and Joe was at his usual post at the pilothouse window near the telegraph and observing the vessels loading. Hearing the knock, Si looked toward the door and saw a stranger standing there. He motioned for him to enter. The stranger thanked Captain Brodhead for allowing him to enter the pilothouse. (It was customary to receive permission to enter a pilothouse.*) The stranger introduced himself as a steamboat inspector. (I never found out his name.)

---

*In fact, Coast Guard regulations prohibited anyone except authorized persons in the pilothouse or on the bridge. The captain was the master and he could refuse to allow the president of the railroad, the superintendent, or any other person in his pilothouse or upon his bridge, if he so chose.

The inspector stated to Si that his vessel was overloaded and he would not allow it to depart from the slip. With that remark, the fun started.

Si, by this time, was standing at the pilothouse window; he reached up and blew a short toot on the whistle, yelling to "Toots," the day ferrymaster, to close the gates. Now began a very serious problem: On the one hand, you had the commuter who made the same boat morning after morning, seeing the gates being closed; by nature, that commuter starts to run and crowd to get on his or her regular boat; on the other hand, you had a captain, being pushed by an inspector, yelling to his ferrymaster to close the gates, although Toots was yelling, "It's not *time*, what's going on?" Finally, you had the bridge gates closed and the boat still tied to the bridge. About 1,600 passengers were beginning to wonder what was going on, as were the deck and dock forces of the Erie company. Jess Baker, the port captain and Toots came up on the boat and went upstairs where they had a little conference with Si and the inspector. The outcome of this conference was that some of the people had to debark before the inspector would let the boat leave for Chambers Street. Telling the commuters that was next to impossible, but after several suggestions, it was decided that if we could get some people to leave and take the next boat, the inspector would allow us to sail. After some grumbling, about two hundred passengers on the Jersey end accepted the ruling that the boat would not move until the load was reduced and agreed to take the next boat.

This incident created a whole new way of rush-hour life for everyone on the Erie marine department's ferryboat division. For Jess Baker, the port captain, it meant that he was on the dock every morning for the entire rush hour, no matter the weather. Many mornings, he was joined by Marcy B. Roderick, the department superintendent. Even the Erie attorneys were involved, since they had to protect the company's interest at the Coast Guard and come up with some type of solution.

A.   Effects of the Overload Incident

The company increased the life-preserver capacity as each boat went into the marine yard for its annual inspection. The Coast Guard worked out the formula of increased allowable number of life preservers based on passengers using the vehicle space with no vehicles to be transported during the peak rush-hour trips. Erie boats now had their life-preserver capacity increased to over 1,600 per boat. I still believe that we carried much more than that number during the heaviest rush-hour trips.

The crew of the boats had to start taking head counts, which the captain would enter on the vessel's log. It worked this way: Each deckhand took the bridge gang-

Ferryboat *Youngstown* a 1922 product of the Staten Island Ship Building Co. of Mariners' Harbor, New York heads down river from Jersey City to Chambers Street in this post World War II photograph. — Dan Biernacki Collection

way count on his respective side, and the captain and wheelsman took the center gangway count together. In this way, it was hoped that we could at least get an approximate count of the number of passengers on board. No vehicles were carried from 7:30 A.M. to 9:10 A.M., nor from 4:50 P.M. to 5:55 P.M., Mondays thru Fridays, excluding holidays.

This made it rather difficult for the deckhand who had to drop the pin since he had to walk the entire length of the boat and be back in time to count passengers as they started to board the boat. What I used to do was go down through the vehicle gangway and return through the ladies' cabin and count the passengers who passed me. I was friendly with the big Jamaican porter, Herb Headley, so when he worked, he would drop the pin for me on the two heaviest trips.

The skipper would approximate the number of people boarding by his count and when he figured that he was approaching the maximum load point, he would blow the whistle. The ferrymaster had ordered that when that whistle sounded, he was to start closing the gates.

B.   Bridge and Dock Problems Created

The morning after the surprise visit by the Coast Guard, three Erie policemen, in uniform, plus the regular station patrolman, Mike Daly, were assigned to assist the bridgemen close the gates.

The gates of the lower and middle slips in Jersey City were full-length flexible ones, attached to a runner running across the entire front of the ferry slip. The ferrymaster and two policemen would take one side and the bridgeman and the other two policemen, the other one. Jess Baker, the port captain, stood on the side observing

the general operations. The boat captain became the key figure. When he blew the whistle, this six-man force started to close the gates. It was quite a sight to watch six men infiltrate several hundred commuters and form a human chain to get those gates closed.

The upper slip was a little more difficult, as it had two pipe gates, which were open in the middle and hinged in the middle of the bridge at the center of the hog frame.* Each gate closed from the center, swinging in to the center of the bridge teamway, and the outer edge swinging into the passenger gangway on their respective sides. Because of this gate, it was much harder to close in the rush hour as the commuters would gang up in the team gangway and just push, while the other commuters in the passenger gangways would pull on the gates. Also, since the gates were open in the middle, commuters would duck and go through the wide area of the gates. The ferrymaster would take the teamway end of one gate, while the bridgeman took the end of the other teamway gate, and each deckhand would come from the boat and take the passenger gangway on his respective side. In the meantime, the four policemen would station themselves at the foot of the bridge and direct the commuters to the next boat.

Once the system was finally worked out, the policemen would start to divert the people shortly before the bridgemen started to close the gates. Once a slight gap was made in the flow of commuters, it became fairly easy to get these gates closed. With four boats running, there was always a boat in the slip starting to load while the other one was finishing loading. Also, the captains

---

*The hog frame was that large, wooden, semi-circular piece that ran from each end of the bridge and rose to some eight feet in the center. It provided the main supports for the bridge and gave it its strength and flexibility.

Bridge with police at gates: Jersey City Terminal ferry bridge during morning rush hour. Port Captain Jesse Baker observes operation, as Ferrymaster Claude Turse is assisted by company police officers closing the gates. Circa 1954.

helped to confuse the issue, once in a while, by coming into a different slip than their assigned one.

After about a week of this operation, one of the bridgemen commented that, on one particular trip for a couple of days in a row, he got a well-placed knee in his backside. His partner said, "What, you too?" It became apparent that one of our commuters did not like the idea of being shut out of his regular boat and was taking it out on the bridgemen. So they told Mike Daly, our rather large, strong, friendly, red-faced Irish cop. It took Mike a couple of days until, one morning, the long arm of Mike's law struck and Mike had himself one commuter at its end. With commuter in hand, Mike went to the ferrymaster's office, where he gave him a long lecture about respecting the rights of his fellow man. The young commuter apologized and was allowed to continue on his way to New York, never to knee another bridgeman. Occasionally, other commuters would try something like that, but the younger extra men, who had faster reflexes, would respond with a fast backward thrust of an elbow as they closed the gates and could usually discourage further problems from the commuter.

This gate-closing war continued right up to the time the Erie ceased rush-hour operations with the consolida-

tion with the Lackawanna at its terminal in Hoboken, NJ. With the majority of the trains then going to Hoboken, this left only the Northern Branch and New York, Susquehanna, & Western trains running into Pavonia Avenue.

19. THE WHEELSMEN HAVE MORE DUTIES

The wheelsmen on the Erie boats were licensed men. Each Erie wheelsman had to have a first class pilot's license. Even though the Coast Guard did not require a licensed mate in the pilothouse, the Erie did. This was one way that the Erie figured it would never be caught short of qualified captains. If it kept a man working on getting his pilot's license, it felt that he should have the preference in the pilothouse over a nonlicensed person. Within two years after a man got his pilot's license, he would generally have the required time in the pilothouse to sit for his master's license, meaning that the Erie could qualify him to steer almost immediately.

This proved valid for a while but, unfortunately, someone forgot about the reverse principle: men who no longer steered, but who were too young to retire.

THE STORIES OF A DECKHAND

These men claimed their seniority right to remain in the pilothouse as wheelsmen. The Erie, in 1947, had four men who no longer steered but were wheelsmen. In fact, Al Wilson would not even touch a wheel for his friend, Tom Hogan. One man, in fact, would steer only his own boat, the overtime boat.

Later, the TWU became the bargaining agent for the deck crew, which included the wheelsmen, and forced the Erie to rescind the "licensed man rule." After I left the Erie marine department, they did run out of sufficient licensed pilots. I know of one occasion when they used the afternoon captain of the *Jamestown* on the *Arlington* the day boats, and tied the *Jamestown* up for the entire 3 P.M. to 11 P.M. tour. But they had to pay the rest of the *Jamestowns'* crew for sitting idle in the slip for eight hours.

Besides acting as a lookout on the river, the wheelsman had to count the vehicles that came aboard, separating cars and trucks. He would enter the count on the log of how many cars and trucks were to be carried per trip. When the boat was rung off, it was the wheelsman's responsibility to see that both bridge lines were off, the rudder pin was pulled, each deckhand was aboard, that the bridge gates were closed, and no passengers were on the bridge. Once this was done, he would notify the captain in the offshore pilothouse that the boat was clear of the bridge by pulling the pilothouse clearance bell twice and then throw the boat-direction indicator to the opposite direction. Then, the wheelsman would remain at the pilothouse window near the clear-bell pull until the vessel was several feet away from the bridge. If an emergency arose, such as a passenger running down the bridge, he would pull the clear bell several times in rapid succession to alert the captain. Once the telegraphs were installed, he could stop the boat by bringing the lever up to the stop position. The major fear every wheelsman had was that a passenger would get on the bridge, think that he or she could make the boat run up the bridge, then realize that it couldn't be done. In an attempt to stop abruptly, such would-be passengers could easily lose their balance and fall overboard. If this were to happen, they surely would be crushed by the churning wake pushing them against the pontoon of the bridge.

Once the boat was safely away from the bridge, the wheelsman would then go to the forward pilothouse and act as a lookout for the skipper. Another duty of the wheelsman was to keep the pilothouse clean. It was company policy that the day crews maintained the Jersey-end pilothouses and the afternoon crews, the New York ends. The relief crew did not have to clean any, as they did not have an assigned boat.

The wheelsman would mop the floor, wash the windows, inside and out, wipe down all the woodwork, and polish the brass. Each crew was responsible to keep its own bunkroom clean. Because certain metals affect the compass but brass does not, ninety percent of all the metal in the pilothouses was brass. Here's an idea of how much brass was in the average pilothouse: the steam steering gear stanchion; the window rods, between the windows; the light shades; the telegraph stanchion; the bell pulls; the bell-pull identification plates; the speaking tubes; the sound-return tubes; and the doorknobs. The *Meadville* also had an all brass hand-steering-gear stanchion. They say that, when the *Meadville* first came up from the shipyard, it took over three hours to clean and polish all the brass in just one pilothouse. The wheelsmen wanted it painted, but the company would not hear of it. But, in 1947, when I first started there, the pilothouses had a lot of the brass painted: Both steering-gear stanchions and the telegraph base had been painted.

Usually, when you were cleaning the pilothouse, the captain would let you stay back and keep working; then, once the boat was let go, he would ring it off and you would start the boat out for him.

The wheelsman would also assist the captain in steering when he missed the slip for one reason or another. The Erie and the other ferry companies had a system of bell signals developed to be used by the captain when he had a wheelsman operating the opposite steering wheel. The Erie's maneuvering bells were:

Clear	2 bells
Left or port wheel	1 bell
Right or starboard wheel	2 bells
Wheel amidships	3 bells
Pin down or stuck	1 bell
Alarm	5 bells

These bells would work something like this: When the wheelsman got in the pilothouse, he would ring two bells, to notify the captain. When the forward rudder pin was pulled by the deckhand, the captain would ring two bells to indicate "all clear" to the wheelsman. The next command that the captain would ring would be to turn the wheel in the desired direction. When the captain was finished with his steering commands, he would ring three bells for the wheelsman to center the wheel. In most cases, he would let the forward rudder pin up as they would be running only a short distance to get into the slips. If the captain had a steering wheelsman, he would just tell him which way to head and, in most cases, a bell was never rung other than the first clear bell.

20. PILOTHOUSE EQUIPMENT

The typical equipment of an Erie ferryboat pilothouse included these five major elements:

1. *The telegraph.* This is the main method of communication for engine speed requested by the captain. As

Captain Jesse Baker at the helm of the ferryboat *Youngstown* after the retirement of Harry Weaver in 1948, Baker became the Port Captain of the Erie. — Dan Biernacki Collection

Pilothouse of the Ferryboat *Youngstown* with Captain Jess Baker at the wheel. Some of the equipment looking from left to right is:

1. Auxiliary whistle cord

2. Main whistle cord

3. Binnacle light — used to light the compass at night or in bad weather

4. Compass

5. Annunicator/telegraph to engine room

6. Main steam steering wheel

7. Beckett — turns running lights on when position shown. When yoke is in downward position it locks the wheel in place and turns off the running lights (red and green)

8. On large wheel hub, left to right:
   a. cowbell handle, just under name plate
   b. deckbell name plate — handle is not shown, but was about even with the bottom of the large nut in the center of the hub
   c. Fire gong name plate, handle is large loop right below.

9. Engine room speaking tube, just over Baker's left shoulder between the windows

10. Large hand steering wheel

11. Pilothouse door

Items not shown:

Directly in front of the telegraph was the speaking tube to the other pilothouse. On the underside of the second window was the handbell pull (a small loop for the "jingle bell" and a larger loop for the gong. There was an identical set of handbell pulls on the wheelsman's side, just under the window that you are looking through). The speaking tube to the main deck was in the same location as the engine room speaking tube, but on the opposite side. The captain's desk was directly behind the large handwheel in the center of the pilothouse. Just visible behind the large wheel is a small window; there were two more which ran across the back of the pilothouse. Over the outer two windows hung fire axes. Just over the desk was a compartment which contained the ship's papers. Over the desk was the pilothouse light.

Both the *Arlington* and *Tuxedo* had only one entrance door which was located by the small window in this picture. The remainder of the rear wall of the pilothouse had a long, couch-like bench; the captain's desk was located on the right wall next to this bench.

This photograph gives the reader a fair idea of what an Erie Railroad ferryboat pilothouse was like: compact enough to have all the necessary equipment at your fingertips, but large enough to be comfortable. Even with all those windows, some of which did not fit exactly tight after years of raising and lowering, these pilothouses were warm. Fortunately, these pilothouses had a large radiator under the desk.

THE STORIES OF A DECKHAND

the captain moves the handle on the telegraph past each indicated position, a series of chains, cables, and pulleys cause a bell to ring and an arrow to move on a dial in the engineroom at the engineer's station. Erie boats had a seven-position telegraph, with the following indicators: Top center was *Stop;* Ahead speeds were *Slow, Half Speed,* and *Full Speed;* Astern speeds were *Slow, Half Speed,* and *Full Speed.* When you moved the handle forward and downward, your speed was *Ahead;* and, when you moved the handle backward and downward, your speed was *Astern.* Each and every time you passed the *Stop* position, an alarm bell sounded in the engineroom. This alarm continued to sound until one of two things happened: Either the captain's final indication was one of the three positions and the engine was set for that direction, or the engineer changed the engine's direction to correspond to the captain's command.

2. *The compass.* Each pilothouse was equipped with a good marine compass and binnacle light. The binnacle was a hood-shaped cover with a glass front which was placed over the compass at night, with a light in the top so that the compass could be seen. All pilothouses are dark at night to increase visibility; consequently, the compass required artificial light to be read. In fog, mist, falling snow, heavy rainstorms, or other weather conditions which make visual navigation impossible, a captain must steer by compass course. Each captain had the compass course from Jersey City to Chambers Street, and return, for each stage of the tide. They would take these readings in clear weather so that, in bad weather, they would be able to refer to them, and the courses would put them just about right off of the slip. When a captain was breaking in a new pilot, he would make him steer compass courses in clear weather, so that he would be used to them if and when he started steering on his own and was caught in bad weather.

3. *Steam steering wheel and column.* The steam-steering wheel was connected by a system of gears and rods which ran under the pilothouse and through a column to the steering compartment down into the hold of the vessel. These rods, in turn, were connected to the steam-steering engine, which was directly under this open column. As the captain turned the steering wheel, each connecting part turned until a gear opened and closed an eccentric on the steering engine. This eccentric allowed steam to pass into the engine cylinder and move the drum, to which the steering cable was connected. The steering cable ran from the engine drum up to pulleys attached to the hull, thence along the upper side of the hull to the rudder quadrant, which was attached to the rudder. The rudder quadrant was in a watertight compartment which could be opened only by a special wrench in the engineroom. The rudder quadrant was attached to the rudder post, which ran through the hull encased in a watertight seal, commonly called a "glan." This glan could be tightened up with nuts and bolts that compressed a collar on both sides of the hull. The rudder compartments were the endmost compartments of the boat.

4. *Hand steering wheel.* The hand-steering wheel was also connected to the steering engine and, as you turned the steam wheel, the hand wheel also turned (except on the *Meadville*). If and when it became necessary to use the hand wheel in emergencies, a friction, or tension, wheel and ratchet on the side of the pilothouse had to be released and backed off. This disconnected the steam-steering engine portion of the steering gear so that you could move the drum and rudder cables. It took at least two men to move the hand-steering wheel. For this reason, when we had a steering problem on the Erie, the captain would turn the boat around and use the good end to get back to Jersey, then tie the boat up and take one of the other boats until his boat could be repaired.

The Erie had a rigger and helper working in the marine yard. The rigger, named Jack Derks, was proud of the fact that his stepson, John Grogan, was mayor of Hoboken. He would always tell stories about Johnny Grogan. Jack spent a lot of time at the ferry terminal, so if a problem arose, Jack was usually there to solve it. In all the years that I worked for the Erie, I do not recall any captain steering with the hand wheel.

5. *Boat direction indicator.* This, too, was a chain, cable, and pulley arrangement which ran between both pilothouses and the engineroom. There was a round dial with a handle on it in each pilothouse, which corresponded to a dial in the engineroom with an arrow on it, a coordinate arrangement thrown back and forth during the day by the wheelsman. Its purpose was to indicate the forward direction of the vessel to the engineer, as well as to indicate that the boat had been cleared to move. The engineer would not move the boat when we had an annunciator if this direction indicator did not point in the proper direction.

A.   Auxiliary Equipment

All of the boats had certain auxiliary equipment which could be used if the main unit failed, such as the hand-steering wheel – the large wheel in the center of the pilothouse which operated in conjunction with the steam-steering wheel. If for some reason or other the steam-steering gear failed, it could be disengaged and the boat steered by hand.

Next in auxiliary equipment importance would be the signal system to the engineroom. The telegraph was the main unit for transmitting commands to the engineroom. Most ferryboats used a basic telegraph, which was simpler than the ships' telegraphs on seagoing vessels. (These are the ones you see decorating fancy seafood restaurants with such signals as "finished with engines" or "stand by" on them.)

On a double-end ferryboat, the vessel's direction is always governed by the vessel's direction indicator, which is controlled from the two pilothouses, and always in the ahead position, which is facing the bridge when tied up. Ahead is always in the direction of the arrow indicated on the engineroom dial and the handle position in the pilothouse. The engine is always set to operate in the ahead position unless a command for an astern movement is displayed on the telegraph.

As was mentioned earlier, once the new telegraphs were installed, an alarm sounded every time the engine's direction contradicted the command shown on the telegraph. This made for a rather fool-proof system.

But how were commands given to the engineroom when the telegraph failed? Each master had to fill out a *Monthly Equipment Condition Report*, as required by Coast Guard regulations. That report required that all equipment be periodically tested—at least once a month. Auxiliary equipment which had to be tested were the "hand bells," used to signal engineroom commands. There were two basic bells—the jingle bell and the gong. The *Pilot Rules for Inland Waters* of the U.S. Coast Guard set down a standard set of bells to be used. These bells' commands were a guide and could be modified, if desired:

From *All Stopped* to *Slow Ahead*	1 Jingle bell
From *Slow Ahead* to *Full Ahead*	1 gong
From *Full Ahead* to *Slow Ahead*	1 gong
From *Slow Ahead* to *Stop*	1 gong
From *Stop* to *Slow Astern*	2 gongs
From *Slow Astern* to *Full Astern*	1 jingle
From *Full Astern* to *Stop*	1 gong

The Erie ferryboat handbell signals were modified slightly:

From *All Stop* to *Full Ahead*	1 jingle
From *Full Ahead* to *Slow Ahead*	1 gong
From *Slow Ahead* to *Stop*	1 gong
From *Stop* to *Full Astern*	2 gongs
From *Full Astern* to *Stop*	1 gong
From *Stop* to *Slow Ahead*	1 jingle & 1 gong.
From *Dead Stop*	1 cow bell

When the engineer heard the "cowbell" rung, regardless of what the telegraph or any other signal indication was, he was required to stop the engine. The only time the cowbell would be rung during a moving situation was in an emergency.

Another piece of interesting auxiliary equipment that was mandatory on Erie ferryboats, but never used, was a large boxlike object measuring aboiut 24 in. × 18 in. × 8 in. with a handle on the side and an opening on one end. It was a hand-operated foghorn. When you pumped the handle back and forth, it pumped a bellows arrangement inside which created air and made a foghorn sound. All fog signals were blown on the main whistle.

Erie boats also had an auxiliary whistle, so while it was doubtful that the hand foghorn was ever used, it must have been required Coast Guard regulation equipment.

21. BOAT DRILLS

Each year, all steam vessels had to be taken to the marine yard for their annual inspection. At this time, major repairs were made, as well as boilers and hull plates inspected, tested, and replaced or repaired. The Coast Guard had a team of inspectors who supervised this operation. The Erie scheduled each boat into the yard for at least a two-month stay. When the boat was ready, the company would notify the Coast Guard which would send its inspection team to the marine yard (except the hull inspection, which was done when the vessel was in dry dock). Generally, the Erie boats were sent to Rodermond's Dry Dock at the foot of Henderson Street, Jersey City on the Old Morris Canal Basin.

One day, I was in the marine yard where I watched an inspector perform a life-preserver test. He took each life preserver and held it by the shoulder straps, then applied an outward pressure. If the life preserver tore, it was discarded. Later, one of the marine-yard workers told me that the inspector ripped up almost a thousand life preservers that day.

Shortly after a boat was put back in service, the inspectors would order a fire and boat drill. That was the day it didn't pay to work on that boat. There were certain regular deckhands who apparently had a contact in the main office, for they never seemed to work on the day a boat drill was ordered. They took that day off and an extra man would work in their place.

The boat that was scheduled to have the drill would work its regular run during the rush hour, usually around 9:30 A.M., after which they would be ordered to tie up in the upper slip at Jersey City to wait for the inspector. When the inspector came aboard, you would back out of the slip and go to the marine yard, where the drill was held. The north side of Pier #1 was the regular tie-up place for the ferryboats. We had to know which side we were tying up on because of the way the lines had to be placed. Normal practice was with the Jersey end into the dock bulkhead. This meant that the bow and breast lines had to be placed on the downtown side of that end and the single stern line on the downtown side of the New York end. These lines were 1½-in. towing hawsers and there was no way that you were going to throw them over the dock clump. Therefore, a ¼-in. heaving line was attached, with a half-hitch, through the eye of the line. These lines were kept in the team gangway coiled up between the steering column and the barber's pole.*

---

*A black and white painted stripped support column which was directly forward of the steering column.

After our last trip, with the passengers all unloaded, each deckhand would go to his respective end and drag out this dirty old line. We would lay the line across the deck and place the eye through the boat's cleat and lay the eye over the quarterdeck rail. We would then take the heaving line, secure it to the tie-up line with a half-hitch, then coil the heaving line so that we could throw it to the yard worker on the dock, when so ordered.

The bow lines were placed with the breast line through the forward cleat and the bow line through the aft cleat. With the inspector aboard, the order came to cast off and head for the yard. The captain would remain in the Jersey-end pilothouse and send the wheelsman to the opposite end. As we left the slip, he would sound the usual slip whistle of one blast, followed by backing whistles—three short blasts. By using the standard maneuvering bells, he would instruct the wheelsman which way to turn the wheel. Some skippers were fortunate enough to have a steering wheelsman, who could take the boat out the normal way and then just switch ends. Si Brodhead did this with Joe Glennon. Joe would go to the New York end and Si would stay in the Jersey end. When the boat was in the right position, Si would just stop the boat, wait for Joe to center the wheel, have the deckhand drop the Jersey-end pin, and then go in the yard.

With wheelsmen who did not steer, the captain handled the engineroom telegraph; wheelsmen only centered the wheel. Then, when the deckhand dropped the pin, the captain would proceed in the yard. (It was not good policy to run with the forward pin up as it could damage the rudder cables.) On approaching the dock, the skipper would sound the Erie dock call of three long blasts, followed by two short, on the whistle. This was to notify the yard that we were coming in and to warn anyone working between floating objects and equipment to stand clear, else when we backed the boat, the quick water from the forward propeller could knock them overboard or rock the float and injure the worker.

The yard would station two men, one at each end of the dock, to catch the heaving lines and place the tie-up line over the dock clumps. The breast line was the first one to go out, followed by the bow line. The breast line would be made fast and then the bow line. Then the deckhand would go back to the breast line and ease it off until the boat was up against the dock. As the stern came toward the dock, the stern line was put out and secured. The breast line was used to hold the boat off of the bulkhead. The skipper would tell you when he wanted it out, and when he wanted it made fast. The breast line was also used to work the boat around on, so as to bring the stern up close to the dock. With the boat tied up to the dock, the yard crew would drop the gangplank. The yard would then do the many minor jobs that had to be done, so long as they did not interfere with the boat drill.

We were now ready for the drill. During the first part of the drill, a fire drill, the fire pump was started when the captain rang and the gangway firehoses were pulled out and water was sprayed overboard. Usually, the inspector asked only for these hoses to be tested. You never opened the valve all the way as the pressure from the pump could flip you all over the place and you could get hurt. This happened once to an extra deckhand and he struck the gangway bulkhead and was hospitalized. It was lucky for him that the inspector had ordered the fire drill in the slip as we were able to get the doctor from the station right away.

Instructions to start the fire drill come with the ringing of the fire gong, located in the center of the team gangway. Each deckhand would take his respective firehose, straddle it, and throw his weight slightly forward. In this way, he would be well braced for the first surge of water. All of our boats had a steam-driven fire pump capable of pumping better than 1,000 gallons of water a minute. These pumps were set up so that they could be used as an emergency bilge pump in the event the vessel was involved in an accident and the hull was ruptured. (This did happen to the *Youngstown* in 1960, after she was sold to the Lackawanna, when she was struck by the *Seatrain Georgia*.)

Once the inspector was satisfied with the fire drill, the next phase was the boat drill. The skipper would sound the "abandon ship" signal on the main whistle, at which all hands went topside to lower the lifeboat. While the deckhands had been tying the boat up to the dock, the porter had opened a window in the center of the cabin on the side that the lifeobat was going to be lowered. He placed a ladder through the window and tied it off onto a seat leg. With all hands safely topside, the wheelsman was in charge of lowering the lifeboat. He and one deckhand took one davit, while the other deckhand and the porter took the remaining one. The wheelsman always took the after davit. We would untie the cover, remove the cover supports, untie the davit's guylines and secure the lifeboat drain plugs. Once this was done, the boat was ready to be swung out on its davits which were then secured by the guylines to their respective deck cleats. Then the boat was lowered as evenly as possible. The davits had a cleat on which you would lay the line, with a turn, then slide the line over the cleat by slacking off on it. Once the boat was in the water, all of us had to go back to the main deck to get into the boat. There were a couple of ways to do this—either go through the window, or walk along the 18-in. wide guardrail, which most of us chose.

The wheelsman was the first to get in the boat as he had to place the tiller in position, then the porter, who took up a position in the bow. Each deckhand then took one of the middle seats and placed an oar in the oarlock. The porter would release the forward davit lines as the wheelsman released the aft one. The deckhands would then row away from the vessel with the wheelsman steering the boat by means of the tiller. Generally, the porter had to use a pike pole to push the boat away from the hull of the ferryboat. Then, off we went for a nice row out into the marine yard canal.

Once the inspector saw that we were not Volga boatmen, he would tell the skipper to recall us and we would return to the side of the ferry. The porter would use the pike pole to hold the boat near the hull and then place the davits block into the eyelet. Once this was done, we all climbed up the ladder and back on the ferryboat. Our part of the boat drill was over for a few minutes. The yard men were told to pull the boat back up to the hurricane deck, which took about thirty or forty men to do. They would then secure the boat back in the davit and recover it, so that we could go back on our run. Thank God we did not have to put that boat up. I remember commenting to one of my partners after a boat drill that if anyone jumped or fell overboard he'd be dead before we could get the boat anywhere near the water. In those days, there were a lot of railroad and privately owned tugs in the North River, unlike today.

The New York City Staten Island ferries carry a lifeboat on the main deck on each end. I have heard of them lowering boats in the Upper Bay to rescue people. The difference is that their boats are only a few feet off the water and not all the way up on the hurricane deck as ours were.

22. WHEELING – NOT EVERYONE LIKED IT

It was common practice on the Erie that, when a wheelsman was off, the senior man would take his place in the pilothouse. Yet the cardinal rule of the sea prevailed on the river: "The Captain is Master and he makes all final decisions."

I remember Ernie Rodgers, the captain of the *Jamestown* days, coming up to me one day when I was going to work on the *Jamestown* afternoons and asking me to come back the next morning at 7:00 A.M. to wheel for him. It seems that one of Ernie's regular deckhands was on vacation, the other one did not like to work in the pilothouse, and his regular wheelsman had been called upon to steer for another captain. Ernie could not stand the extra deckhand who was next in line to work upstairs, so he had asked "Toots," the day ferrymaster, if I could work the job. I liked old "Chin," as he was called, so we went to see Toots and I was assigned the *Jamestown*.

The next morning, we were all in the ferrymaster's office and the senior extra deckhand said, "I said I guess I'm wheeling, since Charlie don't go upstairs?" Eddie Bednarski, the night ferrymaster, said, "That's up to the captain." Ernie no sooner opened the office door when the senior deckhand blurted out, "Hey, Capt. Nick's off – I guess I'm wheeling today!" All Ernie did was reach in his pocket and pull out the bunkroom keys; throwing

them to me, he said, "Put the coffee on, kid." With that, I signed in as wheelsman and left the office. The senior extra was left standing there with his mouth wide open and a look on his face that said, "How come this happened to me?" I worked the job for the remainder of the week. The first morning, after the rush hour, Ernie asked me, "You've been steering for Hogan, right?" I replied that I had. So, when we got to New York, he would put the boat to the bridge and walk away, saying, "Finish'er up." Before the day was out, I was taking over after the first back and putting the boat to the bridge for him. Ernie would go to the other pilothouse and read his paper. My "friendly" senior extra was so mad he could have bitten the end off the rudder pin.

23. *JIMMY* BREAKS A WHEEL

We had just completed the morning rush-hour trips on my second day of wheeling with Ernie Rodgers. We had left Jersey City with a full load of cars and trucks and were just off the Chambers Street slip when we heard a loud thump and the *Jimmy* seemed to vibrate. Ernie looked at me and asked, "Did we hit something?" I told him that I had not seen anything. He immediately rang "slow ahead" and slowed the boat down, saying, "I don't like the way that sounded." He intentionally let the *Jamestown* ease up to the rack and left the stern low. In this way, she could slide along the rack and bind on the center clump, thus breaking her way. It's a good thing he did, because when he rang to go back was when we noticed that the *Jimmy* wasn't backing. Jake Petri, the engineer, whistled up to the pilothouse and told Ernie that the engine was vibrating so badly that he thought it would pull loose from its mounts. Slow astern was all that he could run the engine. The binding between the rack and clump broke our headway and the *Jamestown* was docked without damage.

Ernie told the bridgeman not to load the boat until we told him to. Once in the slip, Jake Petri started to check the boat out, looking for the problem. Tom McGrane, the gateman at Chambers Street, was not too happy, as he had sold tickets ahead and the dock was loaded with trucks. Jake found the trouble – apparently the *Jamestown* had struck a submerged object and broken her tailshaft* on the New York end. The *Jamestown* was not going anywhere. McGrane was told that she was not going out and that we had to contact Jersey City. He had to void all the tickets that he sold ahead and then back all of

---

*The propeller shaft is built in sections that are coupled together with a flat, threaded coupling that is screwed on the end of the shaft, placed against its counterpart on the next section and the two then finally bolted together. As the tailshaft section is the last section which goes through the hull, the stern gland and the propeller is placed upon it and secured.

Tailshaft – that section of the propeller shaft which goes through the hull to the propeller.

New York City Staten Island ferry *American Legion* on drydock at Rodermond's Yard, Morris Canal, Jersey City. First of New York City diesel series.

the trucks off the dock. Chambers Street was going to be operating out of one slip for a while. Ernie and Jake went out on the dock and called Jersey City. We left the *Jamestown* in New York and took the next boat to Jersey City. We ran the remainder of our tour on the *Youngstown*. Tom Hogan's afternoon crew was called out and they took the *Jamestown* to Rodermond's shipyard in Jersey City where she was drydocked and the repairs made. The next day, we found out that the propeller was also lost. Apparently, we had struck a submerged log that became jammed between the hull and rudder and, as the propeller turned, its blade caught the log, breaking the propeller off at the hub and the tailshaft.

The Erie was forced to order the crew out and get the *Jamestown* repaired as soon as possible because it had no spare boat — the one boat that was in the marine yard for repairs was in no shape to be put in service. We were lucky that Rodermond had an open drydock for the *Jamestown*. (I have seen the time when the Erie was forced to get a temporary certificate of inspection for the boat in the yard . This was done when one of the other boats had an accident and had to be taken out of service and sent to the yard for repairs.) I believe it was the *Meadville* when she was struck by the *Veedam* of the Holland-American Lines.

24.   *WASHINGTON IRVING* TALE

Ernie Rodgers was the one who told me about the excursion boat that was hit by an oil barge and sank on top of the Holland Tunnel. Ernie put the bow of his boat up against the sinking excursion boat and transferred her passengers to his boat.

At the time, I did not believe him, so I discounted the story. Many years later, I had the pleasure of making the acquaintance of Alfred Van Santvoord Olcott, Jr., whose family owned the Hudson River Day Lines for over a hundred years. "Van" verified that one of the Day Line's prize vessels, the *Washington Irving*, did indeed sink in the North River just off the end of Pier #9, Jersey City, and that the passengers were transferred to other river craft that came to her assistance. Pier #9 also houses the Holland Tunnel ventilator shaft on the end of the pier, so Ernie was telling the truth.

25.   CHARLIE COURTIERS – CLEAN SWEEP DOWN FORE AND AFT

Charlie Courtiers and Cliff Vreeland were the two deckhands on the *Jamestown* days. Cliff was an extra man's friend, because he used to take a lot of time off.

What I remember the most about Charlie was that he was always brushing off his pants. Charlie's uniform was always as neat as a pin. He called everyone "Pal." Each deckhand had to sweep his own gangway, once each watch. So, when you got a chance, or had a small load of vehicles, you would grab a broom and start to sweep. But with Charlie, and with whoever was working with him, it was a little different. Since Charlie did not want the dust that you created when you swept to blow on him, he had you sweep one way and he would sweep the other way. Charlie worked the Jersey end so he would sweep going to New York and his partner would sweep coming from New York.

26. SPECIAL TRIPS

During the course of the year, the boats were used for special trips. One such annual trip that the *Youngstown* made every year was the New York State Apple Grower's Association outing up the Hudson. The *Youngstown* would make the 9:30 A.M. trip out of Chambers Street, Manhattan, then come back in the upper slip in Jersey city to await the special party's arrival. On the way over to Jersey City from Chambers Street, the yard crew would remove the New York-end sheer pole (because the Erie boats had a longer pole than New York Central boats and it would strike the roof of the 42nd Street ferryhouse and break off). Once the *Youngstown* had the apple growers aboard, she took them to the New York Central West Shore ferry slip at 42nd Street, Manhattan. The party then would disembark and walk the short distance to Pier #81 North River where they would board a Day Line river steamer for their trip up the Hudson River. In the evening, the *Youngstown* would return to 42nd Street, pick up the party, and return them to Jersey City for their trip home. The sheer pole would be replaced on the way back down the river.

Each year, the Erie had a large group of camp trains which would serve the many resort camps in the Delaware and Sullivan County areas as well as in Pennsylvania's Pike and Wayne Counties. Each summer, several hundred kids, bag and baggage, would converge on the Chambers Street ferryhouse. After the morning rush hour, one of the boats would be taken off its regular run and tied up in the lower slip to pick up camp kids. No special boat was used. It was mainly a question of timing as to which boat got the trip. To be truthful, very few of us wanted the trip, because it meant more work cleaning up after the trip, as well as other headaches. Once loaded, you would leave Chambers Street and use the upper slip in Jersey City which could be more easily blocked off from the regular traffic. Mr. Dooley, the stationmaster in Jersey City, would be on the dock wearing his white hat with its highly polished gold "Stationmaster" badge, along with our ferrymaster. It was a major project to keep the kids in some kind of order and keep the parents from the trains. The only way that the company could do this was to have the kids get on the boats in Chambers Street and depart before the regularly scheduled boat. This way, they were on the trains before the parents could get transportation to Jersey City. Sometimes it worked and sometimes it did not. We managed to get through it somehow.

One special trip that was more a rumor than a reality was when we heard that a radio broadcast was going to be made from an Erie ferryboat. Many years ago, there had been a morning radio program called "Don Mc-Neal's Breakfast Club," broadcast from various different places. It was rumored that the program's sponsors were going to charter the Erie ferryboat *Meadville* for a program from the river around New York. Unfortunately, this very interesting charter never took place. One of the reasons given was that Willie Wolfer, the *Meadville's* captain, got a good case of stage fright. Another was that the all-metal structure of the *Meadville* would have blocked the radio signal—but we all knew this was not true.

Another special trip that came up were movie company assignments. One of the most famous ones was "On the Waterfront," starring Marlon Brando. It was filmed on location in Hoboken and Lackawanna ferryboats were used. I believe that the Lackawanna terminal in Hoboken has had many films made in it over the years. The Erie is no exception—They, too, had films shot on their property. Tom Hogan and Larry Caruso once spent hours backing the *Youngstown* away from the bridge as a stuntman ran up the bridge and jumped on the boat as she was leaving the slip. After a long day and a few near misses, the director was finally satisfied.

27. JOE GLENNON AND THE HOT DOGS

Joe Glennon was an extra captain and the regular wheelsman on the *Youngstown* nights. Joe and I struck up a friendship and, on days when there was no work, I would make a couple of trips with him rather than travel back home in the rush hour.

Joe and I both liked the hot dogs that the vendor outside of the Lackawanna-Barclay Street terminal sold. A couple of times I walked down to Barclay Street to get a half-dozen. One morning, we decided that we wanted hot dogs, so I walked down to Barlcay Street and arrived back at Chambers Street just as the *Youngstown* was coming in the slip. I had forgotten what time it was and this was the *Youngstown's* heaviest rush-hour trip. Here I was, with both hands full of hot dogs and several hundred people coming at me on their way to work. I felt like the lone cowhand facing the stampeding herd, but I made it without dropping any sauerkraut or onions.

28. FERRYBOAT RACES

Arlington vs. *Niagara.* Both the Lackawanna and New York Central boats had to cross the Erie route to reach Barclay Street and Cortlandt Street.

One morning, I was decking on the *Arlington.* Ernie Rogers was steering and Walter Wright was the engineer. It was a late rush trip and we had several hundred passengers on board. As was my custom, I walked through one of the cabins before going to the deck-hands' room in the centerhouse. This particular trip, I was walking through the Ladies' cabin when I happened to notice the New York Central *Niagara* coming down-river. We were rapidly approaching a collision course and someone would have to take some type of corrective action soon. Ernie continued on his course and maintained his speed since, under the rule, he was the privileged vessel. Shortly, the captain of the *Niagara* altered his course by turning to port, which now put us on a parallel course; but there was one big problem. The *Niagara* was now on the wrong side. She was upriver of her slip and the *Arlington* was in between. Her captain had two choices: slow down and let us pass, which was the logical one, or try to outrun us. He chose the latter. We were neck and neck and there was only about twenty feet from guard to guard (the one-foot rail that the boat rides against the slip racks with). Knowing Ernie Rogers, there was no way that he was going to slow down and let the Central boat by him, especially not when he had the "right of way" *and* the edge. Both boats matched up fairly well with respect to weight, horse-power, speed, and maneuverability, though the *Niagara* was some 75 to 100 tons lighter than the *Arlington*. The biggest difference was that the *Niagara* was oil fired, whereas the *Arlington* was coal fired. This gave the *Niagara* the edge in that she could maintain constant steam pressure over the long haul. The *Arlington*, being coal burning and fired by hand, would start to lose steam pressure on the long haul, but this was a short race.

The passengers got just as involved in the race as the captains. You could hear comments like, "He's getting ahead of us." "No he's not, now *we're* gaining." I stood just about amidships near the stairs, talking to the porter. I could see the *Niagara* inching ahead. All of a sudden, I heard the jingle bell ring in the *Arlington's* engine room and she started to vibrate as Walter removed the chock from the engine links. (Some of the boats had a two-inch-wide, U-shaped piece of metal with a handle on it. This was placed on the engine reversing link shaft to adjust the engine's piston-stroke length. The bigger the chock, the shorter the stroke. This was done to conserve steam.) Now, with the chock removed, the *Arlington* started to move ahead and Chambers Street came closer and closer. It was now apparent that the *Niagara* had run out of room to maneuver as she slowly slipped back and passed under our stern and on to Cortlandt Street.

Meadville vs. *Niagara*. Several years later, I was steering with Tom Hogan on the *Meadville* afternoons. One of our regular evening rush trips was the 5:08 P.M. from the upper slip in Chambers Street. The New York Central *Niagara* used to make a 5:05 P.M. trip out of Cortlandt Street. Willie Smith, the regular skipper of the *Niagara,* used to come out of Cortlandt Street and swing out into the river before heading upstream towards Weehawken. By doing this, he left room for the other

ferries to get out of their respective slips. This all changed when Al Lozier, who had steered the *Albany* for years, bumped Willie Smith out of the *Niagara*. Lozier believed that the weaker tides were along the dock and you made better time there. This was a dangerous practice, as you had to watch for tugs and barges coming out from the docks, as well as other ferryboats leaving their slips. A tug and float was the most dangerous combination as the floats averaged about three hundred feet in length and the tugs were usually tied to the floats near the middle. The mate would go to the end of the float and watch to see if it was clear. If something was coming, he would have to yell to the tug captain to stop and, on a cloudy day, with the wind blowing, it was hard to hear the mate.

Besides the Erie and New York Central, the Lacka-wanna also had a trip out of Barclay Street around the same time. Thus you had the 5:05 P.M. *Niagara*, the DL & W boat right behind her, and the *Meadville* leaving the slip at Chambers Street. All of this congestion was so timed that it bunched up off the Chambers Street slip, if everyone went up along the docks. As I said before, Captain Smith would head the *Niagara* toward midstream to let the DL & W boat out, whose captain, in turn, would head out so that we, too, could get out. But, once Lozier took over the *Niagara* and came up hugging the docks, this changed and problems began.

One day, I had just blown the slip whistle when I heard two shorts toots on the *Niagara* whistle. I thought that Willie Smith was still steering the *Niagara* so I started to reach for the telegraph to slow down when I heard Tom yell, "Don't stop, throw her hard over and head upriver." The race was on, so to speak. Lozier and the *Niagara* were on our port side and her bow was just slightly aft of our forward pilothouse. So we had the edge. By now, Tom had taken the *Meadville* from me and he had her straightened up. Her rudder was almost amidships, and you could feel her starting to pick up speed by the rhythmic vibration under your feet. As we increased our lead, Tom started to give just a little port wheel and the upriver race now became a crossriver one, with the *Meadville* taking the lead. As we approached Jersey City, it was apparent that Tom and the *Meadville* had won and Lozier took our stern and headed up river for Weehawken.

When we got to Jersey City, I asked Tom, "What happened to Willie Smith?" Tom said, "Maybe that was him on the *Albany* who saluted me the other night." Al Lozier was the senior captain on the New York Central and he did, in fact, outbid Willie for the *Niagara*.

The next night on the 5:08 P.M. trip, as I left the slip, I did not blow the slip whistle until I was almost at the mouth of the slip. Looking over the pier roofs, I could see the *Niagara's* stack coming up along the docks. I followed the slip whistle with one short blast and kept going. The *Niagara* acknowledged and pulled out in the river. Lozier never bothered the *Meadville* again.

29. OVER THE YEARS, FOG HAS ALWAYS BEEN A PROBLEM

The majority of the railroad boats did not have radar after WW II, when I started working on the Erie.

The Erie and New York Central boats never did have radar. The Pennsylvania Railroad ferry was discontinued in 1949. In later years, the Central Railroad of New Jersey equipped all its boats with radar and the DL & W experimented with it on the *Lackawanna*. The basic fog equipment were keen lookouts, sharp eyes and ears, the vessel's compass and whistle, coupled with the skill of the captain.

Each Erie skipper knew the compass heading to our New York terminal and Pavonia Avenue, Jersey City, for the various stages of the tide. Many a morning, I came to work to find the terminal "socked in." As soon as I came up out of the subway at Church and Chambers Streets in Manhattan, and heard the Governor's Island bullhorn, our fog siren and the boat whistles, I knew that it was going to be a long, hard day. I was involved in numerous close calls in the fog, but I was never on a boat involved in a fog accident. I believe the closest I came was the incident between the *Jamestown* and *Catskill*.

It is very easy to become disoriented in the fog, especially when you are forced to slow your boat down. When a boat is slowed down and steerage way is lost, it tends to drift with the tide. In order to compensate, when you are laying and waiting for a slip, you head your boat into the tide. Yet in doing this, you have turned your vessel off its original course. In normal weather, when you hear the whistle of the departing boat leaving the slip, all you have to do is ring for full speed and turn your boat back on course and watch the slip shape up. But, in the fog, you cannot see the slip and all you have to go by is the compass course and the sound of the departing boat's whistle. Once the whistle sound is gone, all you have then is the fog signal at the mouth of the slip.

One evening, while Tom and I were waiting for the boat to be loaded, we kept hearing this very distant whistle of a Jersey Central ferry boat coming closer and closer. Before we knew it, we were looking at a Jersey Central boat coming in the slip. Tom yelled out the window "Hey, Capt., you're in the Erie slips!" The skipper of the CNJ boat yelled back, "Thanks, Capt.!" as he backed out and headed downriver, disappearing in the fog.

Tugboats always tried to tie up in the fog. But, once in a while, they would get caught in the river. When a tug had a tow, her skipper would sound one long whistle blast, followed by two short blasts, every minute. If a tug got caught in the fog it would head for shore and tie up on the end of a pier. Ferryboats, on the other hand, could not do this, as they had to keep running.

People always wanted to help you in the fog, when you were on bow watches, though most of them did not know what you were looking for. Some even saw things that were not there.

John "Bip" Walsh was decking on the *Arlington* in a real heavy fog one day and he had just such a "helpful" commuter next to him. Finally, Bip could take no more of the friendly assistant. Bip said, "It's not very safe up here. If I were you, I'd go to the back of the boat." The commuter took Bip's advice and retired to the stern of the *Arlington*. A short time later, the Lackawanna's *Scranton* struck the *Arlington* and stove in the after-quarter deck railing. As the commuter left the boat, he looked at Bip and said, "I thought you said it was safe back there."

Of the many interesting fog stories, some involved little damage, while others were more serious.

The Erie 23rd Street ferry route was operated until 1942. One such fog story had to do with the 23rd Street route. All during WW II, the North River was used as an anchorage for ships waiting their convoys to be made up. At times, these ships were anchored in the busy downriver area. The fog signal for a vessel at anchor is the rapid ringing of the ship's bell for about five seconds every minute. Ole Man Stein was steering the *Chautauqua* on 23rd Street and Gink Wolfer (Willie's brother) was steering the *Jamestown* downtown. Coming across the river, Gink had an accident and tore a hole in the downtown (Men's cabin) side of the *Jamestown*. He tied her up in the middle slip at Jersey City to unload. As Ole Man Stein was coming into the 23rd Street slip at Jersey City, Gink walked out on the *Jamestown's* hurricane deck and yelled over to him, "Hey, John, I guess you'll have to run for me, I just tore the *Jimmy's* side out." Ole Man Stein yelled back, "You should see the uptown side of this boat—I just left half of it wrapped around some ship's anchor chain." So, in less than one hour, the Erie had two boats headed for the marine yard for repairs.

All of these railroads had excellent marine yard forces. In most cases, they would rebuild the boats so well you would not be able to detect where the damage had been.

30. CAPTAIN JOHN STEIN, *MEADVILLE* AND THE HOLLAND-AMERICAN LINE'S *VEEDAM*

During the years that I worked on the river, I knew of only one serious accident involving an Erie ferryboat and a ship underway. Early in the morning, John Stein's relief crew had made the 5:45 A.M. trip out of Chambers Street with the *Meadville*. I was working on the night boat and we had made the 5:45 A.M. trip out of Jersey City with the *Youngstown*. We passed in midriver, giving each other the usual "good morning" salute of a low whistle toot followed by one short blast. About three-quarters of the way across, we heard Steinie blow one long blast of the whistle, which was answered by the ship coming up along the Jersey shore, the Holland-American *Veedam*. A short time later, we heard the *Meadville* blowing the alarm and the ship blowing backing whistles (three blasts). This was soon followed by a loud crash. The *Veedam* had struck the *Meadville* aft about thirty-five or forty feet from the stern on the port side. It turned the *Meadville* right up against its starboard side, doing extensive superstructure damage, but fortunately, none below the waterline.

After the Coast Guard hearing, John Stein told us that the *Veedams'* pilot, an American member of the Sandy Hook Pilot's Association, stated that when he saw that the *Veedam* was not stopping rapidly enough and he determined that danger existed, he ordered the starboard anchor dropped to pull the ship away from the *Meadville*. In the confusion (plus the language problem), the crewmen dropped the port anchor, thus pulling the ship into the *Meadville*.

31. *JAMESTOWN* AND AMERICAN PRESIDENT LINE'S QUICK WATER

The American President Line leased Pier #9, Jersey City, from the Erie Railroad Co. For many years, the President Line docked its ships at that pier. All of the captains knew that, on occasion, the ships' engineers would turn over the ships' engines prior to sailing or when they were working on them. This standstill engine action would churn up the water, producing what is called "quick water." This particular day, the quick water coming from the ship was extra heavy.

Steve Rogers was steering the *Arlington* and running ahead of the *Jamestown*. He managed to get into the middle slip in Jersey City without much trouble, due mainly to the fact that the middle slip had an extra wide mouth that you just dropped into. Tom Hogan would have to make the upper, or 23rd Street, slip and it was a little more difficult to negotiate in the ebbtide. Rogers knew the quick-water condition that existed with the ship working its engine, and he chose to wait for the *Jamestown* to come into the slip before he went out. For Steve Rogers, this was highly unusual, as most times he could not wait to get out before the other boat. Just about the time that the *Jamestown* reached the end of dock #4, the ship's quick water caught the *Jamestown* full force, forcing it into the end of the dock. The result was that the *Jamestown* lost the starboard quarter-deck superstructure, right back to the cabin doors. The part of the dock that was damaged was the Railway Express Agency's Men's locker room, and for several days they were without a john. The end of dock #4 became known as "Hogan's Point."

32. SURPRISED BY THE SUPERINTENDENT

I would steer for Tom Hogan every chance that I got and was told that I should study for my license. Tom let me steer whenever I came on board, since his wheelsman, Al Wilson, would not touch the boat because the company had set him back after an accident for which Al refused to accept responsibility as he felt that it was because of equipment. This afternoon, we had been rung off and Tom and I walked to the New York-end pilot-house. Tom said that he was going to pour the coffee and that I should take the boat out, but watch out for the *Meadville*. I had just blown the slip whistle when I heard the door close. Without looking around, I said, "How's the coffee, Tom?" There was no answer. Turning around, I saw the superintendent, Mr. Roderick, walking toward the wheelsman's chair. We exchanged "hellos" and I went on steering the boat. Just then, Tom came in and saw Roderick. I kind of moved out of the way so that Tom could take the wheel, but all Tom said was, "You have ebbtide and the upper slips, Son," and parked his behind on the hand-wheel stanchion.

Much to my surprise, it was my trip to steer and Tom was not going to take the boat. I made a good trip across the river without any problems. Coming in the slip, I don't think we even touched the rack. I gave the boat three good backs and she settled up to the bridge, nice and easy. Looking over to me, Mr. Roderick said, "That was a good job," and he and Tom left the pilothouse. By the time Al and I got to the New Jersey-end pilothouse, Roderick was gone. Tom told me what Roderick had come to see him about: me. Apparently, Gus Matasak, the afternoon ferrymaster, thought I was taking too long to make a trip across the river and he told Roderick that I was causing the delays on the *Jamestown*. Roderick told Tom that he had no objection to my steering but he wanted Tom to steer the rush hour. In my defense, Tom told Roderick that I was making better time than he was with the boat because he was letting me work closer or tighter than he normally did, since I needed the practice. In fact, the reason that the *Jamestown* was not making good time was that she was due to go into the yard for her annual inspection and hull painting. So, to prove his point, Tommy just took a minute or two longer than I did to make a crossing. All Gus did was get madder and madder. Tom's steering during the rush hour lasted about one week and, before you knew it, I was back steering every trip that I was on the boat.

I had a couple of problems arise while I was steering. Every trip that you steered was different in those days, and you never knew what was going to happen next. As I said before, there was a lot of traffic on the river. You would be coming out of the slip and the next think you knew, a tug was backing a float down across the slip. Most of the time, our tugboat captains were not the best when it came to blowing a slip whistle or backing whistles, so you had to guess what they were going to do.

33. TOOLS USED ON THE FERRYBOATS

It may seem peculiar that I should discuss tools being used on the ferryboats. Because the upper decks of the boats were canvas and painted over, we had to be very careful not to puncture the decking. For that reason, steel shovels and other such items could not be used. The company marine yard made most of the tools used on the boats and they were made of wood, including a wooden shovel to move snow from the upper decks.

There was a wooden snow pusher which was used to push snow from the decks, as well as to push the coal down the coal hole on the main deck. It was a lot easier pushing the coal down the hole than shoveling it.

The third tool which the marine yard made for the boats was the porter's "grass mop," as we called it. It looked like any other mop, except that, the mop strands were made from pieces of hemp instead of cotton. The mop handles were made in the yard and the porters would get pieces of hawser about three to four feet long, then separate each length into single strands and place them in the mop head. They now had a grass mop with strands from eighteen to twenty-four inches in length. A long, quarter-inch line was tied to the mop from the head to the tip of the handle. This line was used to allow the mop to be thrown overboard and tied to the stern gates of the boat. The mop would flop along in the wake of the boat and clean itself. The porter would then pull the mop back on board and proceed to mop the cabin decks with it.

These were the basic tools that the shop in the marine yard made for the boats. Of course we did use some factory-made tools, such as brooms, shovels, pails, etc.

34. SURPRISING STEERING PROBLEMS

It was a hot summer evening and it seemed that every commuter on the Erie Railroad decided to use the ferries rather than the Hudson Tubes. We had a swinging load of passengers leaving Chambers Street this night. The Jamestown – the "Jimmy," as we called her – seemed to be responding well to the wheel as I maneuvered through the heavy, evening river traffic. The middle slip in Jersey City was open and I started to shape up for it. Satisfied that the boat was in good shape, I slowed her down. Since it was ebbtide, I had the boat in an upriver position heading down into the slip. The Arlington was in the lower slip. As I started to give the Jamestown starboard wheel to bring her around to the mouth of the slip, she kept heading toward the Arlington's stern. Quickly, I rang for full speed ahead to give the Jimmy a hook on

(extra power to improve steerage way), and she responded to the wheel. When I went to use port (left) wheel to bring her off the upper clump of the rack, she did the same thing and I had to hook her on again. Now I was in the slip and closer to the bridge than I liked. Stopping the engine, I rang for an immediate back, full speed astern, and left the Jimmy backing until I was satisfied that she would not hit the bridge. After a very interesting couple of minutes, the Jamestown was safely tied up to the bridge. I turned to Tom and said, "What the hell happened?" He explained that because it was a nice evening and we had so many people on the boat as we approached the slip they moved forward and, in so doing, the weight shift brought the Jamestown's stern higher out of the water. When I slowed the boat down, the quick water or wake flattened out and the rudder was partly out of the water. This caused it to lose effectiveness and the only way to correct this was with a hook on. Tom said that I had taken the right corrective action without his telling me.

By this time, I had been doing a lot of steering for Tom and, unless he saw some real danger, he would sit back and let me figure out my problems in the river. I would look over to him and say, "What do you think I should do?" Most times, his reply was, "You are steering, not me, you must work out your problems," and go right on reading his newspaper.

We left Jersey City one evening and Fritz Kompers, the engineer, whistled up the speaking tube to tell us that his firemen were going to clean fires and that we should take it easy coming back to Jersey. Fritz always ordered fires cleaned just before the rush hour and in the direction favoring the tide. In this way, he was not bucking the tide with low steam pressure and thus would have a reserve for an emergency. The Jamestown had developed a steaming problem. She was a good steaming boat if she had good coal, but the railroads were noted for burning the cheapest coal they could find. The Erie was forced to order a special car of coal for the Jamestown. The ferryboat coal cars were set out on the old dock #2 track on the south side of Pavonia Avenue, with "Jimmy" or Jamestown marked on one car in chalk.

As I left Chambers Street, I could see that the Jimmy was laboring across the river and that it was going to be a long trip. There was no question but that I would be going behind everything and anything going up or down the river. Shaping up for the slip, the Jimmy was looking good, so I slowed her down. She was in perfect shape – a clear shot right to the bridge. It looked as if I wouldn't even hit the rack until almost up against the bridge. I stopped the engine and rang to go back. Then it happened: The Jametown did not appear to be backing. In sheer amazement, I stood watching the bridge and station getting closer and closer. Both Tommy and I had the same thought in mind and, almost in unison, we reached for the jingle bell on our respective sides of the pilothouse. The *Jamestown* started to throw a quick water up in front of us that looked wonderful. I left her backing and Tom left me behind the wheel. When the *Jamestown* stopped, with one back to the bridge, there was not ten feet between her bow and the bridge. If I had waited one more second, the *Jamestown* would have ripped up a new ferry slip a lot closer to the trainsheds. Tom Hogan would have had a lot of explaining to do and I would never get to touch a ferryboat wheel again.

35.   SOMETIMES THE BOAT HAS A MIND OF ITS OWN

I had never steered the *Arlington* much and, as I have mentioned, she was over a hundred tons lighter than the *Jamestown*. Because of this, the tide and wind affected her differently. For some reason, the *Jamestown* had to be tied up and her crew transferred to the *Arlington* after the rush hour. The tide was running ebb and it was running down pretty good. I left Chambers Street with the *Arlington* and was shaping up for the middle slip in Jersey City. I thought that I had her in good shape when, all of a sudden, she hit the broad slack caused by Dock 4 which extended out beyond the ferry slips and the tide caught the stern, pushing it down and causing the bow to go up. My "pretty good shape" was rapidly turning into a missed slip. The more the tide pushed on the stern, the more left wheel I gave the *Arlington*. Before I knew it, I had struck the clump between the middle and the upper slips dead center. Tom said that I should have hooked her on and gone for the upper slip and then worked along the long rack. He could not figure out why I kept trying to make the middle slip. I backed off the clump and then did what Tom said. After we made the slip, Tom bawled the living daylights out of me for making such a stupid decision. He told me that I was too flat for that stage of the tide and that when I saw my stern dropping, I should have gone for the upper slip. It is always better to take the slip with the long rack and work in on it than to miss a slip and maybe do some damage to your boat or injure a passenger. I learned a bitter lesson that evening: Never underestimate the tides of the North River.

36.   *ARLINGTON'S* 5:15 P.M. TRIP – HEAVIEST OF THE EVENING RUSH

I had spent the day in New York City and was standing on the dock talking to Jimmy Ramagelli as he was loading the *Arlington* for her 5:15 P.M. trip. I knew that the *Jamestown* would be in to make the 5:20 P.M. and I could still make my train. Suddenly, we heard a toot on the *Arlington's* whistle. I looked at Jimmy and asked, "What's wrong with Steve Rogers – it's not leaving time

yet?" As I looked up at the pilothouse, I saw Tom Hogan at the window waving for me to come on board. I had not known that he was steering the *Arlington*. (Sometimes when a day-boat captain took off and the ferry-master could not get an extra captain, they would call Hogan, because he lived within about a half-hour of the ferry in Jersey City. Then they would fill his regular job on the *Jamestown* with the extra man.) When I got to the pilothouse, Tom told me that he was sick and that he wanted me to take the boat over. I looked at him, saying, "You must be kidding – me take the *Arlington* into the lower slip in Jersey City with the heaviest rush hour crowd of the day?" With a real you-can-do-it pat on the back, we headed for the Jersey-end pilothouse. As we got to the bunkroom, Tom said, "I'll be in here if you need me." I told him that I would start her out and when we got near the slip I'd call him.

The wheelsman rang the clear bell and I started across; as I reached the mouth of the slip, all I could see was other boats where I wanted to be. "Well, here goes nothing," I thought, as I started to wiggle the *Arlington* through the traffic – in front of this tug, astern of that one and, before I knew it, I was shaping up for the lower slip in Jersey City. I called to Tom tell him that we were off of the slip. We kept getting closer and closer and still no Tom. I thought to myself, "Well, Ray, you only get one chance and it better be good or you'll wipe out the whole place." As I said before, the *Arlington* was a light boat, which I was not used to and had never run into the lower slip before. The wheelsman, as I remember, was not much help, as he did not steer and that was why Tom was glad to see me. The principle was the same: Open your slip up and hold your boat high in the ebbtide and this is what I was doing. The only difference with the lower slip is that you had to be just a little higher. The company had replaced the long rack with a group of clumps after the Dock 2 fire, so you did not have that nice long rack to slide on, like the upper slip. If you missed, you could go right through the clumps, as they gave and you would hit the car floats that were tied up next to the ferry slips. If the tide got your stern, your bow could swing around and you would hit the boat in the middle slip. These were the alternatives that I had as I shaped up for the slip. Looking at the good side, if I got in trouble I knew that the engineer, Walter Wright, was one of the best. You never had to wait for him to respond to any signal that you sent to the engineroom. He always stayed by the throttle from the first slow bell to the final cowbell (although, yes, we did have some awful slow engineers on the Erie). Slowing the boat down, she looked good. I was just a little high, but I was keeping her bow pointed inside of the end clumps of the rack. As I stopped the boat and turned the wheel to starboard, the *Arlington* started to straighten out. Her bow was just about opposite the upper clump and just a little high. I rang to go back and, with the back, she started to straighten up the rest of the way. I knew now that she would not bind against the upper clump and the lower rack. I had made a good landing, the *Arlington* was in the slip, and I had made it! Centering the wheel, I rang the pin bell so that the deckhand could drop the pin and get up forward to tie up his side. Putting the *Arlington* to the bridge, I finished the job by ringing the stop and finished with engine bells. I rang the final two cowbells letting Walter Wright know that we were all finished for the night and that he could put her to bed. As the vessel's light went out and the emergency standby lights were lit, Tom came out of the bunkroom thanking me for coming along, and saying, "I don't think I could have made it across."

37. "SHOW YOUR SISTER-IN-LAW HOW GOOD YOU CAN STEER A BOAT"

My late sister-in-law, Barbara, lived on Long Island. One day, she was returning from Florida, but the flight that she was coming in on landed at Newark Airport. She called and asked me if I could pick her up and drive her to the island. Of course, I agreed, so on the way from Newark Airport, I said, "Let's take the ferry over—you like boats."

As luck would have it, we caught the *Meadville* on her next-to-last trip out of Jersey City. I asked Barbara if she would like to ride across in the pilothouse. After introductions were made and the boat was rung off, Tom, Barbara, and I went to the New York-end pilothouse. As we entered, Tom said, "Go ahead and show Barbara how good you can handle a boat." I looked out the window to see that the rudder pin was down, pushed up the wheel beckett, ringing for "full ahead," and headed out of the slip. Everything was done perfectly, right down to a good slip whistle. The river was moderately crowded for that time of the night and I had no problems. I shaped up for the mouth of the slips and thought I had everything just right, when Tom said to me, "What slip are you going into?" I replied, "The lower." He shot back, "No! We're supposed to be in the upper this trip, go back and throw the wheel hard to starboard to bring the head up." I did, but this was one time when the ole *Meadville* did not live up to her reputation. Her head stayed down and I could not get her to come up. So Tom had to send Al Wilson, the wheelsman, to the Jersey end, have the deckhands pull the other rudder pin, and he drilled for the slip. I felt bad that I had messed up and had to have Tom finish the trip. But I learned a good lesson that night, because I realized just what had happened. In order for any boat to handle properly, she must have room. Apparently, the *Meadville's* stern was laying next to the clumps along the dock and they prevented her from pulling up in such a short distance.

That was the only time in all the years that I steered for

Tom Hogan that a wheelsman had to drill for a slip because of me. Every other scrape that I got into, I managed to get out of.

38. ANOTHER CAPTAIN USED TO LET ME STEER

When I first started to work on the Erie, Tom Hogan was the captain of the night boat and his wheelsman was Joe Yacono. Joe later became captain of the *Youngstown* afternoons, or the "late boat," as it was known. Joe used to see me steering for Tom. One evening, I was sitting with him in the Jersey-end pilothouse and, when the wheelsman rang the boat off, Joe said, "Start her out, Ray." So I got up and took the *Youngstown* out of the slip. Joe came over and stood behind me, leaning on the hand-wheel hub. He let me take the *Youngstown* to Jersey City. I was now steering for two captains. As a result, I got a lot of steering, but all captains handle their boats differently. Earlier, I mentioned that Tom Hogan was one captain who did not use a lot of wheel. He learned to steer on the Pennsylvania Railroad ferries and, from the stories he told me, the Penn boats were not always in the best shape, so you had to be right on the money. Joe Yacono, on the other hand, had learned to steer on the Erie and used a lot of wheel going across the river. I, in turn, must have gotten into the same habit. One afternoon I was steering the *Jamestown*, working the wheel back and forth. Ole Man Stein used to stay back in the opposite-end pilothouse and read his paper, so Tom would sit in the wheelsman's chair when I was steering. Tom was watching me over his *Jersey Journal* and he could hear the steering engine working like mad as I kept the *Jimmys'* wheel going back and forth. I was watching another boat coming up the river and I did not notice the surprise that was in store for me, for the next thing I knew, a rolled-up *Journal* smacked across the knuckles of my left hand and Tom said, "What the hell are you doing with that wheel?" Would you believe that I never realized the way I was rolling the wheel back and forth?

Tom promptly started to tell me why you don't use a lot of wheel. By turning the wheel back and forth, you are turning the rudder across the quick water caused by the propeller and this creates a drag or strain on the engine. So, once you get your boat shaped up to where you want it to go, then you straighten the wheel out and let the engine pick up its natural momentum. In this way, your engine works better and your boat runs better. You let things work for you and not against you.

Tom said, "We are lucky on the Erie, because when a boat has a steering or a boiler problem, they let us take another boat. You know Al Wilson and I used to work on the Penn ferries. Over there," he continued, "you kept your boat no matter what. One night I came to work and the ferrymaster said, 'Captain, we turned the *Wash-*

ington around because the steering engine on the Jersey end broke down, and this way you have the long rack at Desbrosses Street to slide in on.' Another night, I went to work the night boat and found that the *Washington* not only had hand gear on the New York end, but one boiler was shut down." After those stories, I knew what Tom meant by using as little wheel as possible. By my working the wheel back and forth, I was using extra steam, both to operate the steering engine and to make the engine work that much harder crossing the river. This also meant that the firemen had to work that much harder.

39. I LEARNED TO HANDLE THE *MEADVILLE'S* ENGINE

The *Meadville* had a Skinner-Uniflow steam engine which was somewhat different than the conventional, compound reciprocating engine. Where the double-compound engine, used on the average ferryboat, had two high-pressure and two low-pressure cylinders, where the steam passed from the high-pressure to the low-pressure cylinders, the Uniflow had only high-pressure cylinders. The *Meadville's* engine was a five-cylinder 1,700 hp unit. The basic design of the Uniflow engine was similar to an inline internal combustion engine used in automobiles. It had two sets of intake and exhaust valves which operated off of cam shafts. The cam shafts, in turn, were controlled by three levers: one ahead, one astern, and one main-throttle lever. It was said that a good engineer could go from full ahead to full astern without moving the throttle lever, just by using the ahead and astern levers. This was achieved by centering these two levers simultaneously, so that the lever stops were in the open position.

The *Meadville* was by far one of the best handling and fastest railroad-owned ferryboats in New York Harbor. Sam Burns, her day engineer, was on her from the time she was built. In fact, I understand that he went to Chester, PA before she came up from the Delaware River. She was his pride and joy. Sam knew the boat and just how to make her do the job.

For a short time I worked on the afternoon *Meadville* job. John Brywa was the engineer and John liked to ride in the pilothouse with Tom Hogan after the rush hour. Tom did not really like this too much, but rather than say anything, he just went along with Brywa. One day, I said to Tom, "Doesn't it bother you that John is up in the pilothouse and he leaves Manuel Villa alone in the engineroom?" (We both knew that Manuel had a heart condition.) "Frankly, Ray, it does," said Tom, "but I don't want to cause any problems with Brywa." I decided that maybe I would ride down in the engineroom, which was okay with Tom. Manuel and I became pretty good friends and Manuel taught me how to handle the *Meadville's* engine. Thereafter, as soon as we would let

the boat go, I would go down into the engineroom. The throttles were situated on the Jersey end of the engine. The ladder leading from the main deck to the engineroom was also situated near that end of the engine. Many a trip, I would be at the throttle before the bells were rung to start out of the slip, because, with a three-boat schedule, the incoming boat was too close to the mouth of the slip for you to leave safely. (Remember, the "rules of the road," as the pilot rules were known, gave the inbound vessel the right of way.)

It was really interesting to learn a little bit about the boat's engine. When you see something like a steam engine in operation you take for granted that it's doing the best job possible. But there is more to it than that. This, I started to find out. When I used to travel home by bus or train, I used various routes. I never really liked the subway and bus route via New York City that I was forced to take, so I decided to take alternate routes. By far the best route was the Northern Branch trains, which got me home to Tenafly in about forty minutes. Unfortunately, there were only three trains in each direction a day. The route that I enjoyed most was the West Shore ferry to Weehawken, then the train to Bergenfield or Dumont, and then a short bus ride to Tenafly. Using this route, I got to meet many of the West Shore ferryboat men, such as Willie Smith, captain of the *Niagara*, Al Lozier, captain of the *Albany*, and Tom Lyons, a deckhand on the *Albany*. During one of my trips upriver on the *Niagara*, I was permitted in the engineroom and the fireroom, both of which, were as neat and clean as one's home. The brass and bright work were highly polished, and each oil and grease fitting wiped clean of excess lubricant.

Everywhere that I went, I started to study the different things about a boat. I was eager to learn the differences between one company's equipment and another's. One thing that I noticed on the *Niagara*, that I did not see on the Erie boats, was a group of U-shaped brass objects with a handle on the end. I asked the engineer what they were. He told me that they were "chokes," their purpose to shorten the stroke of the engine. By varying the stroke of the engine, you could improve the efficiency of the engine. Then I remembered that the Erie boats did have one choke which was set up on the engine reversing link. The *Jamestown* and *Youngstown* had their reversing eccentrics on the opposite side of the engineer and, because of this, the choke was connected to a long, spring-loaded handle. The engineer would engage the choke when he started the engine in the forward direction and it would automatically disengage when the engine was reversed. The *Arlington* and *Tuxedo* had one like the *Niagara*, which was taken in and out by the engineer.

The *Meadville*, on the other hand, had no chokes whatsoever. Her engine did not have the conventional link arrangement. All of the steam to her cylinders was controlled by three levers (as mentioned earlier). The two ahead and astern levers controlled the valve opening by regulating the cam adjustments. So, when you received the vessel's direction indication from the pilothouse, and the skipper rang for "full speed" ahead on the telegraph, you would move these two levers to the desired engine direction, then open the throttle. Once the *Meadville's* engine had turned several hundred revolutions, the engineer would then adjust the cam levers to the desired, predetermined setting. The engine direction was never changed, unless ordered by the pilothouse. When the vessel is tied up to the ferry bridge, the direction is always toward the bridge.

40. TRIP IN AN ENGINEROOM

Let's take an imaginary trip across the North River in the engineroom of the *Meadville*. There is often controversy as to which end of a double-end ferryboat is the bow and which, the stern. So, we are going to say that the New York end is the bow and the Jersey end is the stern. You board the boat in Jersey City going to New York. Walking in the team gangway, you will see a hatch at the end of the centerhouse with a ladder descending into the fireroom. This is an open hatch, protected by an iron railing and a chain across the ladder side. Looking down into the fireroom, you can see part of the boilers, as well as the ash and coal bunkers. You walk past the hatch until you are at the center of the centerhouse, where there is a door similar to a Dutch door in a house, where the upper half can be opened while the lower half stays closed and locked. As you look through it, you see the top of the engine, a grating around the engine with an opening, and a ladder at the end of the engine nearest the doors. Opening the door, you descend the ladder to the first landing, which is another grating, running around the engine and protected by a brass railing. All of the handrails on the sides of the ladders and the walk-

Standing on the engine grating just inside of the centerhouse the photographer has taken this photograph to show the public the confined quarters of a ferry boat engine room. The vessels generators are just behind the engineer, who is leaning on the desk, while the electrical panel is just to the left of the desk. — Dan Biernacki Collection

way gratings are made of highly polished brass. These gratings and walkways enable the engineer and oiler to inspect and work on the engine and other machinery in the engineroom.

Descending the second ladder, you are now down on the main engineroom deck, standing next to the engine itself: a large, gray, fully enclosed machine. The Skinner-Uniflow marine engine was fully encased, with the crankshaft immersed in oil, just like your car's engine. Its five glass inspection ports allow the engineer and oiler to inspect the inside of the engine. The engineer turns on the lights inside the crankcase (so that you can see the connecting rods and, since we are still tied up to the bridge, they are just about turning over). Looking around, you see the two generators: main and auxiliary, directly opposite the engine; right behind the engineer, against the fireroom bulkhead, are the two feedpumps which regulate the water going into the boilers. Only one is slowly working, with a steady click, click, click as the piston reaches the end of its stroke and starts back again. Over in the opposite corner, over the shoulder of the engineer, you can see the large condenser which converts steam back into water for reuse or discharge. The *Meadville's* condenser discharges the water overboard. You can hear it working at a steady pace. Between the two generators, there is a panel of gauges at which the engineer is continually looking. These gauges monitor the operating condition of the various pieces of machinery in the engineroom. The only sounds you hear are the steady clicks and whines of the various auxiliary pieces of equipment and the voices of the men. Then, you hear the clang of a small bell, rapidly followed by a similar clang. The wheelsman has just thrown the vessel's direction indicator over to the other end. The engineer walks over to the throttles at the end of the engine and stands by. Then, there is the sound of a larger bell, clanging in rapid succession, along with the rasping of chains and cable moving. The telegraph has moved from "stop" to "full ahead." The engineer reaches up and, placing his hands on the two smaller ahead and astern levers, he reverses them and quickly places his right hand on the throttle to ease it open to a premarked notch on the throttle rachet. You feel the deck under your feet start to vibrate gently as the *Meadville's* engine starts to pick up momentum.

Once the engineer is satisfied that the *Meadville* has picked up speed, he then reaches for the two smaller levers and starts to adjust them to a point which he has come to know as her best operating position. You can hear the sound of steam entering the cylinders change its pitch as the vibration under your feet seems to settle down to a steady rhythm. You glance down at the rpm indicator just above the shaft and notice it starting to climb to 100, 105, 110, 115, 120 and, finally, it evens off at around 125 rpms.

You can hear the steering cables sliding along the ca-

ble housings on each side of the hull as the captain maneuvers the *Meadville* expertly across the river towards Chambers Street. Then just when you have gotten into the swing of things; the steady whisp of steam entering the cylinders and the various noises of the auxilaries there is a sudden clanging of bells again which tell you that the telegraph has a new order for the engineer "SLOW AHEAD." You look at the engineer saying, "are we in New York already?" Looking at the ships clock he replies we should be just off the slip. The engineer is now standing right by the throttle. The telegraph sweeps again with the sounding of bells. This time it reads "STOP". Reaching up the engineer pushes the throttle completely in towards the engine and quickly reverses the two smaller levers and opens the throttle briefly to stop the roll over of the engine. Again the telegraph bells clang ordering a command "FULL SPEED ASTERN". As the engineer opens the throttle about half way you can feel the vibration under you really heavy now as the *Meadville* engine start conteracting the forward way of her 1599 tons. To you it seems like an enternity that we are backing. Not being able to see where you are you begin to think "Are we going in too fast? Is she going to hit the bridge?" Once again the telegraph bells sing out "STOP" Now you feel relieved. Clang, clang, clang and the telegraph once again repeats "FULL SPEED ASTERN" as your engineer quickly responds. Now the bells come down faster clang, clang, clang "STOP" then quickly clang, clang, clang "FULL ASTERN" and almost immediately clanging out "STOP" then just as suddenly clanging "FULL SPEED AHEAD" and a sudden bump as the *Meadville's* bow noses up to the bridge. Once the boat is tied up to the bridge there is a normal clanging of the telegraph as the Captain rings "STOP" followed by the flat sound of the Cow Bell which indicates that he is finished with the engine. Thanking our engineer we ascend the ladder and depart.

41. THE BRIDGEMAN

Another important part of a successful ferry operation is that played by the bridgeman. The Erie Railroad, like most of the other railroads which operated ferry routes on the North River, used wooden bridges with either wooden or steel pontoons at the river end to make them float. The exception was the New York Central, which had all electrically hoisted bridges. The Erie did have one electric bridge in the upper slip at Chambers Street.

It was the bridgeman's job to always have his bridge in proper shape so that a boat could come into any slip at any time. The Erie had one bridgeman for each bridge in operation during a particular tour or shift. If two bridges were in operation, then there were two bridgemen. The only exception to this was Jersey City, in the morning and evening rush hours. All three bridges were kept

Ferryboat *Arlington* loading at Jersey City. Coal gang awaits coal truck coming on board to pull ashes. Circa 1954.

ready, but only two were used. The reason for this was that, after the rush hour, one of the boats would be tying up in the spare slip, so it had to be ready.

The tide played a major role in the daily routine of the bridgeman. Since the bridges were pontoon bridges, they rose and fell with the tide. So, naturally, a smart bridgeman learned about the tides. I found this out early in my career as a marine department employee. Having worked for the Erie just a short time, I was assigned the day bridge in Jersey City. John Di Nuto had the middle bridge, I had the lower bridge, and the upper was the spare, in which the *Youngstown* would tie up at 9:45 A.M.

The first boat out of the lower slip was the *Arlington*, shortly after 7:30 A.M. I did not know the score yet, as I was still new. But I found out quickly that some deckhands were better than others. The *Arlington* was the lowest boat of the fleet, the *Meadville* was the highest, and the *Jamestown* had a port list. And, as fate would have it, the *Meadville* always followed the *Arlington* in the slip, since the boats alternated slips on a three-boat schedule.

One morning, the tide had changed completely, which meant that the bridge-hoisting chains were played out and laying on the deck of the bridge. The deckhand is supposed to take the chain slack up before the boat leaves. Well, this morning, there was a lot of slack out on the deck and the deckhand took up most of it. Being new, I did not realize that the smart thing to do was go up on the bridge after the boat was let go and take up as much on the hoisting wheel as I could before the boat left. When the *Arlington* pulled away from the bridge, and I saw my bridge drop about two feet, I knew I was in trouble. So I went up to the take-up winch and started pulling on it for all I was worth. What I did not know was that, in the rush hour, the boats were liable to come in any slip. For some unknown reason, the next boat came in the lower slip rather than one of the others. So there I was, pulling my arms off trying to get this bridge high enough for the boat to slide under the toggles, because I knew what was going to happen. I almost made it, but not quite. Just as the boat backed for the last time, her bow went down and then came up, catching the upper-bridge toggle and pushing it all the way in.

This made it difficult to unload the boat. And, to tell you the truth, I did not know just what to do. The deckhands saw I was totally confused and they came to my assistance. In order to avoid creating a problem in unloading the boat, they told me I had to keep a drag on the foot brake as the cars and trucks came off. I was lucky that day, because we did not have any really heavy trucks. Once the boat left, I had to start working. The toggles were held in place by two large nuts and bolts attached to a metal piece running overtop. The bolts ran through the bridge. When the nuts were tightened on the metal piece, they tightened down on the toggle, holding it in place. I loosened the nuts with a wrench that was about three feet long. Once this was done, I had to take a long, wooden, pinchbar type of tool about eight feet long and force the toggle back out to normal position and then tighten it back down again. It sounds easy, but the bridges are out in the elements and weather, dust, mud, and other debris get in between the toggle and the bridge. To make things even harder, you could not get in good position to pull on the bar, since, if it slipped, you would go over backwards into the river. So, the only way you could work on it was by pushing. The toggle had a metal plate on the top of it where the other metal plate fit. This metal-to-metal apparatus was so rusted I had to get some oil to loosen it. After a lot of hard work, I finally got the toggle back in place, vowing that it would never happen to me again!

42. THERE ARE PERSONALITY CLASHES IN EVERY BUSINESS

Inevitably, in any large company where there are various types of people working, there are going to be differences of opinion and personality clashes. I was no different from anyone else and so not immune to problems with certain deckhands. One such person was the man who held the seniority spot right before me on the roster. His name was John and, for some unknown reason – that I no longer remember – John and I just did not see eye to eye. Of course, there was the fact that Ernie Rogers preferred me in the pilothouse to John, but I seem to think that our problem went back further than that.

One day, I was working the afternoon Jersey City bridge and John was on his regular job on the Youngstown afternoons. His partner was little Joe Smith. Joe put up with John, but he, too did not get along too well with John. Since they worked together, they kind of kept things in balance for the general good of all. Smithie was the senior man and his job was to take up the bridge slack in Jersey City. Each man had to help the other when it was time to eat or sweep the gangways and cabins, since one man had to be on deck at all times while in

the slip. Anyway, Smithie was off on one of his chores, and John took the slack up and let the boat go. As the Youngstown left the slip, the bridge take-up winch wheel started to spin madly. I knew that John had not put the winch pawl on. I ran up the bridge and stood on the brake as hard as I could until the wheel stopped, then put the pawl on, and started to take up the bridge. If I were lucky, the next boat would clear the toggles. I knew that John had done it to bust my chops. I was still working on the bridge as Tom Hogan came into view with the Jamestown. I knew that the Jimmy had that damn port list and a knack for catching the upper-bridge toggles. I did have one thing in my favor, though – Tom Hogan was good at toggle ducking. As the Jamestown started to back, the quick water helped me by causing the bridge pontoon to raise in the water. With each back, I got a bit more slack and the bridge hung higher. There was a short toot on the whistle and Tom yelled, "That's good, Ray, I'll do the rest." He disappeared from the pilothouse window for a second, then he started to back the Jamestown away from the bridge. She was about fifteen feet from the bridge. Then I heard the front propeller grab at the water and the Jamestown started to move ahead. About this time, thoughts ran through my mind of seeing both me and the bridge go right up Pavonia Avenue. All of a sudden, the bow of the Jamestown dipped right under my toggles and all I got was a little bumping around as she hit the bridge a little harder than usual. To be sure, my extra labors were due to John, but he who laughs last, laughs best.

It took some time, but one night, the shoe was on the other foot. John had bid the afternoon bridge in Jersey City and I was now working on the Meadville afternoons with Tom Hogan. My knowledge of the tide was coming into play. As things would have it, during that evening, the tide was ebb, or going out. I looked in a tide book to see when mean low water (when the tide is at its lowest point) was, for then the toggles and the bridge would be lower than the dock. If the bridge was not in just the right position, no boat would get under it. I took up the slack, but did not put the pawl on. As we left the slip, the bridge wheel started to spin. John spotted the wheel and ran up to stop it, but I knew that it was no use: That bridge was down. As we crossed the river, I heard the boat in the slip, because John's bridge was out of service. When we returned to Jersey City, John and Gus Matasak, the afternoon ferrymaster, came storming up the bridge. John returned to Jersey City, John and Gus Matosak, the afternoon ferrymaster, came storming up the bridge. John started to tell me that he was going to knock my block off. Gus was yelling that I did it intentionally and that he wanted no such problems. I told Gus that anyone could make a mistake. Anyway, I got my revenge and it took John until we returned for our next trip to get the bridge ready.

43. TOGGLE DUCKING WAS TRICKY, BUT A LITTLE FUN

I always remembered when Tom ducked the toggles for me. I was thankful for several other good captains who helped out when you needed them. Other captains who used to duck toggles for bridgemen were Willie Wolfer, Frank Windknuckel, Walter Huess, Joe Yacono, and Si Brodhead. They helped not only the bridgeman, but themselves. If they had to wait for the bridgemen to raise the bridge, it would take away from the time that they were tied up in the slip. The less time that you have to load can make you run later and later, thus you have to work harder to keep on time.

When I started to steer for Tom Hogan, I always wanted to learn to duck toggles. One way to practice was to hold off with the last back so you could see just how much the boat's bow would dip. As I mentioned, the *Jimmy* had that darn port list which created several problems – one being that the starboard side was always higher going into the slip. This meant that you had to watch that she did not catch the upper toggle. One evening, I was coming in the slip and I noticed the bridgeman working to get the bridge up. I told Tom and he said, "Now, you learn to duck toggles and you better do it right or you'll be down there helping to push it out!" He walked over to the speaking tube and whistled down to Fritz Kompers to tell him what was going to be done. Fritz was right there, boy you would have thought the *Jamestown* was pilothouse controlled the way she responded. As soon as I rang to go back, the *Jimmy* was throwing quick water out in front of the bow. Tom told me to keep some forward way on the boat. I let her drift toward the bridge and, just at the last minute, at Tom's command, I rang a quick back, followed by "Full speed ahead;" the *Jamestown's* bow dipped down with Fritz's quick response on the full ahead and the *Jimmy* worked her blunt nose into the bridge facing just a little bit hard. After that, it became a regular thing. I helped out many fellow bridgemen and made their day just a little bit easier.

44. HAND BELLS – LET'S USE THEM

The Lackawanna ferries operated for years on hand bells. In fact, they did not install telegraphs on their boats until after the *Meadville's* hit the bridge in Chambers Street as described earlier. I believe the Coast Guard ordered telegraphs on all ferry vessels that were not so equipped.

Coast Guard regulations require that a vessel's master file a report of a vessel's equipment condition once a month. I kept bugging Tom about operating for a trip or so on hand bells. One night, he called down to Fritz and told him that we were going to run on bells to Chambers Street. When we were rung off, he told me "Okay, pull

the jingle." Now, you must remember just what bells you have pulled, once you start. A jingle bell was full speed ahead. As we approached the slip and I had my boat in shape, I pulled one gong to slow down; when I was ready to stop the boat, I pulled one more gong and, to go in reverse, two gongs together, then one to stop, and so on. After the last back, with the boat almost to the bridge, I needed a slow ahead to work up to the bridge, but full speed would have been too much as we would have hit the bridge too hard. Rather confused, I looked at Tom and he knew what I was going to ask before I asked it. "Pull the jingle and a gong right behind it," was his reply. I did, and the *Jimmy* worked her way to the bridge, nice and easy. Up against the bridge, I rang a jingle for full speed. Once the boat was tied up, all I had to do was pull the cowbell for "Finished with engine." After I had finished, Tom said, "Okay, now you know how to run a boat on bells."

45. JOE CONNELLY AND THE TUGS

While I was on the extra list, it got quite expensive going back and forth from home to shapes. I found myself spending more time and money on travel than it was worth. Rather than go home between shapes, I started to go to New York City shows and other places of interest, but this, too, was costly. I had to find some way to spend the time between shapes, yet still save money. This came by way of the friendship of a cigar-chewing, tugboat relief captain named Joe Connelly. Joe would work the job of a regular tug captain who was on vacation. Joe and I used to take the same boat over in the morning. Joe would go to Dock #4 or the marine yard for his boat and I would go to the ferrymaster's office for the shape. One day, Joe said, "Hey, Kid, if there's no work, come on down to Dock #4. I'm working on the *Cleveland* – you can take a ride on a tug." As luck would have it, there was no work, so I took Joe up on his offer. The *Cleveland*, the queen of the Erie tug fleet, was the first tugboat I had ever set foot on. She was one of four diesel/electric tugs that the Erie purchased between 1930 and 1931. Her three sisters were the *Rochester*, *Scranton*, and *Olean*. These boats were diesel/electric pilothouse controlled. They were powered by a McIntosh–Seymour constant-speed diesel connected to an electric generator which powered an electric motor. You could move the pilothouse controller from "Full speed ahead" to "Full speed astern" and it would not kick out the circuit breakers, something that could not be done on the later Erie diesels.

Joe taught me how to steer a tugboat and I had many an interesting day with him and the various tug crews with whom I rode. I could dock a pair of car floats, berth and spot a lighter or scow, tow a string of barges on a hawser, or just run light. I got to handle almost every boat on the Erie. Of all the boats I handled, I liked the steam tugs with their hand bells best. Sure, pilothouse-controlled boats are good and, in many cases, safer because the pilot has control of the engine. Yet, there is something about a steamboat that is fascinating. The smell of steam, coal smoke, the power that is released as a boiler reaches it maximum and the safety, or pop-off, valve send the steam up the relief tube behind the stack. All you have with a diesel is the smell of diesel fuel and a noisy engine. Most times the engineer is up on deck because he can't stand the noise of the engine in the confining engineroom.

I never did steer the steam lighter *Elmira* or diesel lighter *Corning.* I did, however, steer the *Corning's* sister, the *Dayton,* which I might say was an experience. These two boats were direct-drive diesels which were steered by a little hand lever. They had no steering wheel or quadrant to indicate what position your rudder was in. If you kept your hand on the handle, the engine kept turning the rudder and you would go in a circle. I really enjoyed my trips with Joe. I learned more about New York Harbor on his tugboat trips than I could on the ferries. I never rode a Circle Line boat around Manhattan, but I did one better than that: I had a private cruise on the tugboat, *Johnson City.* The Harlem job was one of the choice jobs on the Erie tugs. The *Johnson City* was a wooden-hulled steamboat, built around the time of WW I. Because of this, her class of boat was called "Shipping Board boats," as they were built during the period when the railroads were under the control of the U.S. Government. The Erie marine yard had cut down her pilothouse and stack for the Harlem service. Because of the large number of low bridges across the Harlem River, a tugboat of normal height could not get under them and it required that these bridges be opened. The solution came with the concept of low-stack and low-pilothouse boats.

The *Johnson City* came out of the marine yard five days a week, from Monday to Friday. Your first job was to tie up at the ash dock on the north side of the marine yard canal, just east of Mid-Hudson Warehouse, to blow ashes. Then you would go to the end of Dock #4 for water and orders. The tug dispatcher would tell you where your float was. After picking up the float, the *Johnson City* would head down the North River towards the Battery; rounding the Battery, she would head up the East River towards the Harlem River, favoring the west side of the river as she would be heading up the west channel past Welfare Island. Just off Wards Island, the Harlem River branches left and the East River branches right. Although there was sufficient water just south of Wards Island, the preferred channel was the west one, keeping Mill Rock to your right, since the west channel had the better tides. The current in the Harlem was extremely strong and, on occasion, the Lackawanna Railroad tug, *Bronx,* would help the *Johnson City* with her float.

As we head northward up the Harlem, we start to go under the many bridges which cross the river. Some of them are highway and some are railroad bridges. At 149th Street, the Bronx, the Erie had its freight terminal. The float is docked and pinned to the float bridge and our job is over. Now, the train crew takes over. Erie Box Cab diesel #19, a 300-hp engine built in 1928, squeals as her wheel rubs the rails of the tight curves on the yard as she comes to pull the cars from the float. The mate goes to the yard office to call Jersey City to see if the dispatcher has any jobs for the tug. If there are none, the *Johnson City* will lay at 149th Street until the float is loaded and then return to Jersey City.

This day was an unlucky one for the crew, but I was happy, because we had a job. The 103, a stick lighter, which we saw downriver, was ready and had to be towed to the Long Island Rail Road's pine dock where it would be picked up by another tug. Joe let out a low curse, because the 103 is a stick lighter and we will have to have every bridge on the Harlem opened for us. It would be a long, slow trip downriver. "Okay," Joe said to me, "you saw her as we came up, so you might as well go and pick 'er up."

The *Johnson City* was a steam tug, so the engine was handled by an engineer rather than pilothouse controls. I started to pull bells and backed away from the float. Heading downriver, I spotted the 103; coming up behind her, I asked Joe what side he wanted her on. He wanted the lighter on the starboard side, which meant that the tug had to go on the inside between the lighter and the dock. The floatman got up on the lighter and let her stern line go as the mate threw a line around the inside cleat. With a quick back, the *Johnson* pulled the lighter off the dock and I worked her ahead as the mate let the line go. Once we were made up to the lighter, I started to head downriver. Approaching the first bridge, I sounded the required three blasts of the whistle to indicate that I wanted the bridge opened to pass. The bridge tender responded with a similar three blasts and, a short time later, the bridge was opened. Everything went smoothly until I blew for the New York Central Bridge. This time, the tender answered our three blasts with two blasts, which meant to wait, that he had traffic due. I stopped the boat and the current started to set us down on the bridge. I rang two bells and backed the boat a safe distance away. I could not back too far as I would back into the last bridge that we had passed. Once again, the tide started to set us down onto the bridge. This went on for about twenty minutes and each time the tide set us down towards the bridge, I would back off. Finally, a passenger train went rattling over the bridge. A few minutes later, the bridge tender blew three blasts, signalling that he was opening the bridge. The railroad bridge tender was stationed on a catwalk underneath the bridge and, as I passed, I noticed this big black man with a smile on his face that seemed to say, "Made you wait, didn't I, Mr. Tugboat?" Reaching up, I took hold of the *Johnson City's* whistle cord and pulled it back as far as it would go. The *Johnson's* whistle let out a real loud, deep "whoooooooop!" that must have sounded like the *Queen Mary* to him, because, as I looked over my shoulder at him, his feet were about two feet off the catwalk. I sailed down the river with a smile on my face.

On the return trip upriver, I did not see the New York Central bridge tender, as we came up on the opposite side of the bridge. When we got back to 149th Street, the float was ready and we picked her up. Joe told me that he was going to take her back to Jersey City by another route and that we would not be going past the New York Central bridge. We headed upriver, cruising around the north end of Manhattan Island and out through the Spuyten Duyvil, then headed down the Hudson River for Jersey City.

46. MORAN'S NEW TUGS

The Moran Towing Company had just bought some new diesel tugboats. Moran, like McAllister, Dalzell, and many other towing companies, had a large ship-docking business. Light tugboats were always running up and down the river from one job to another. Two Moran tugs were coming down the river as I was crossing the river from Chambers Street to Jersey City. There was no way that the old *Jamestown* could outdistance these two new, fast diesel boats. So I decided to take their sterns. Tom warned me to be careful how I hit the wake. As the *Jamestown* turned to cross the wake, she hit it just a little off. To the surprise of many commuters who were standing on the bow, the *Jamestown* had hit the wake at just the right angle and a large volume of water came up over the bow, engulfing gatepost and commuters alike. Women screamed and men cursed. The Hudson River did a fair job on many commuters that night. When I went off to catch my train, I noticed that the deck was wet all the way back to the centerhouse—almost half the boat's length.

47. CAN YOU STEER FOR A WHILE?

Frequently, when I came aboard, Tom would say "Boy, am I glad to see you. Can you steer for a while?" Since that was one of the reasons I was there, the answer was always "Yes." Don't get me wrong; Tom was very good to me and I used to wait for my train riding with him, but I did enjoy steering the boats. I would go to the New York end with him. Tom would go into the New York-end bunkroom to change his clothes and I would go to the pilothouse and take the first trip out. Tom continually warned me that there were two trips you had to be extra careful on: the first trip, because you were never sure of

what the tide was doing, and the last, because, if you had an accident, the company would say that you were in a hurry to tieup. We looked at the tide calendar to get an idea of what the tide was doing or was supposed to be doing. You had no way of telling just how strong it was running or just how the wind was going to affect your boat in relationship to the tide. So you had to estimate these factors on the first trip, since your only assistance came from the tide calendar and your knowledge of the river. When you got near the docks, you could get a fair idea of the tide by looking at the end of the dock to see just how fast it was flowing by the piles. Then, you could correct for it. The safest way was to be just a little high on the ebbtide, as you could always open the slip up a little more, if necessary. In other words, if the tide was not pushing you down as fast as you thought it would, you would turn your wheel to swing your boat away from the upper clump towards the lower clump, so as to show more of the slip. Then, you simply turned your wheel back towards the slip. On the floodtide, it was a little simpler, as you did not have your boat in such a sharp angle to enter the slip on that stage of the tide. But, if you were too low on the ebbtide, it was almost impossible to bring your boat up against the tide. It could be done, but it was much more difficult.

I started the afternoon shift for Tom, on the *Jamestown*. The first Northern Branch train came and went; before I knew it, the second one was gone, and it was 6:20 P.M. Our 6:20 P.M. was the train boat trip for the last Northern Branch train, which was the 6:35 P.M. out of Jersey City. Tom asked, "Would it be possible for you to steer a while longer?" Looking at him, I said, "I guess so." Before I realized it, the watch was almost over, so I decided to finish it. Everything was going along just fine. I had managed to get through the rush hour with no problems and that was most of the battle. Most of the fruit was in New York, so the tug traffic was getting lighter. About the only thing on the river were the Lackawanna boats and ours.

Since we had an ebbtide during most of the watch, I was letting the Lackawanna's ferryboat *Scranton* go downriver across my bow and I would go on to New York behind her. This seemed like the smart thing to do as the tide was pushing her downriver, anyway. Out of Chambers Street, we both left at the same time and I would be out of the slip and heading upriver before the *Scranton* reached Chambers Street. Everything had worked out fine until the last trip.

Gus Matasek had let us go about two minutes early for the 10:30 P.M. trip from Jersey City. I got the clear bell and started out of the slip. I saw the *Scranton* coming downriver. I knew that I had the right of way, as well as the edge on her, so I kept going, but watching her course. I told Tom that I knew I could beat her and that I was going to keep going. It was okay with him. I reached up for the whistle and blew one whistle. Much to my surprise, the *Scranton* came back with two short whistles which, I might add, she was not in position to take. I looked at Tom, saying, "He's got one hell of a nerve, after us giving him the right of way all night." Quickly, Tom said, "What are you gonna do? You're the skipper. It's your boat." Reaching for the whistle cord, I said, "I'll show you." I answered his two whistles with a quick alarm and one whistle, which the *Scranton* meekly answered with a similar "one whistle." Crossing the *Scranton's* bow with a lot of room to spare, I went on to Chambers Street for our last trip of the night. On the return trip from Chambers Street, I was out of the slip and three-quarters of the way across the river before the *Scranton* left Barclay Street. I tied the *Jamestown* up that night; Tom had never touched the wheel for the entire tour.

48. EVEN A COP CAN STEER A FERRYBOAT

I mentioned earlier that, early in 1954, the Erie started to reduce crews and I wound up back on the extra list. I decided that I had better look for a more secure position. One day, while working the Chambers Street bridge, I was approached by Erie Railroad Police Lieutenant Herman Limsky about transferring to the Erie Railroad police. Herman told me that they had an opening. So, the next day, I went over to Chief Stern's Office and applied for the job. I was accepted and, early in April 1954, I left the Erie Railroad marine department. Unfortunately, the police department was also going through some changes and I was laid off shortly after starting. But I did not leave the Erie.

A friend of the family got me a job in the signal department and, within a month or two, I was right back in the Jersey City terminal, only this time as a signalman. By October 1954, I was back in the police department and working in the terminal and the yards around it. One of the most interesting yards was the north yard, which handled all of the float freight to all parts of New York Harbor. Certain special-class shipments had to be escorted by police officers. I made many trips on Erie tugs doing this duty. Some of these special shipments were whiskey, cigarettes, and other high-priority freight. After the float was delivered, we would return to Jersey City overland (public transit) and then check the ferryboats and the Chambers Street station. So I managed to still ride the tugs and ferries for some time.

When I got my uniform, I was assigned to the afternoon station job in the Jersey City terminal. This job was mainly a ferry traffic and station security job. So I was right back where I had started in 1947 on the ferry dock. Part of my job was to inspect the train equipment for the Chicago trains after it was brought down from the yard.

On Sunday nights, the terminal lunchroom closed early and finding lunch was a problem. I had befriended the dining car crews on my inspection trips just by doing them the small favor of taking the dining car department's mail to the baggage room. So, each Sunday night, they had a bag lunch made up for me. I had an hour lunch period, so I would take my nice bag lunch and go ride on the *Youngstown* with Joe Yacono. Joe's wheelsman did not steer and, one night when I got in the pilothouse, Joe said, "Do you think you can still steer a ferryboat?" Naturally, my reply was, "Sure I can." Then, he said, "Take her out – I don't feel good." I steered two trips that night for Joe. I continued to steer with Joe Yacono as long as I held the station job.

49. DECLINE OF THE ERIE FERRY SERVICE

In the summer of 1956, the Erie Railroad had a reduction of forces. All departments, including the police department, had to reduce its work force. I was among those furloughed. After a short stay with the New Jersey Bell Telephone Co., as an installer, I was hired as a railroad policeman with the Delaware, Lackawanna & Western Railroad out of Hoboken, NJ. With this job, I found myself right back on the waterfront. With the Lackawanna police, I was still working in terminal jobs and directing ferry traffic. I mentioned earlier that, in 1956, the Erie consolidated its trains with the Lackawanna Railroad at the latter's Hoboken, NJ terminal. On the morning of March 25, 1956, I was working the Hoboken terminal uniformed police job. Many of my old friends from the Erie were now using the Lackawanna ferries to New York. My tenure on the Lackawanna police department was not to last, either. By December 1956, I was furloughed and working a shape job on the Lackawanna ferries.

But the Lackawanna Ferries were not like the Erie's. The men on the Lackawanna did not take time off as they did on the Erie, and extra deck work was scarce as they had a strict seniority list and the top couple of extras got all the work. So, in April 1957, I went to work as a police officer for the Lehigh Valley. The Lehigh Valley Railroad was a good company to work for, and I regretted leaving its employ. While working on the Erie in late 1955, I was talked into taking the New Jersey Civil Service test for the Jersey City Police Department. The list lay dormant for just over two years and then, in May 1958, they started appointing off it. About the middle of November, I was notified to report to the Jersey City Police Academy for a preappointment interview and, on December 16, 1958, I was appointed, thus ending my career in railroading and marine crafts.

But my association with the waterfront continued, for, on February 20, 1959, I reported to the Second Precinct on Seventh Street, Jersey City. Believe it or not, the Second Precinct was the one that encompassed all of the Erie Railroad's Jersey City waterfront yards, as well as a large portion of the Lackawanna's and a big Pennsylvania yard. There were many times that my knowledge of both the Erie and Lackawanna yards helped me during my job as a radio-car patrolman for the Jersey City police department.

50. DECLINE OF RAILROAD MARINE TRAFFIC IN NEW YORK HARBOR

When I retired from the Jersey City Police Department on February 1, 1985, the Jersey City waterfront property owned by all the major railroads was completely gone. To give you a brief idea: The large Erie-Pavonia Avenue complex from the Harmsimus Cove Canal north to 12th Street was completely demolished, except for the diesel shop building and the marine yard, both of which were sold to private businesses. They, too, will be demolished shortly, as they have been taken over by the Jersey City Redevelopment Agency. South of the cove was a large Pennsylvania Railroad facility of which Conrail operated only a few tracks, servicing Colgate Palmolive Co. and the Harborside Terminal Complex. North of Twelfth Street to the Hoboken City line, the large Lackawanna freight complex has also been removed.

The remaining tracks in Hoboken yard are owned by New Jersey Transit and used for its passenger-train operations.

Of the large marine operations started back in the early 1800s, by men such as Robert Fulton, John Stevens, and Homer Ramsdell, there is, today, only the memories of those of us who worked on the boats and loved every minute of it. The North River itself is a counterpart of the western ghost towns of the Gold Rush days.

As one rides through downtown Jersey City or Manhattan on a foggy morning, the only sound of the past is the mournful sound of the Governor's Island foghorn which still blows to warn the few mariners approaching the island that it is there. Even Governor's Island is not the same as it was in the 1940s and '50s. In those days, it was the headquarters of the First Army of the United States; today, it is the district headquarters for the United States Coast Guard.

Times do change. There are times when I wonder if they are for the better or worse.

51. LABOR UNIONS: SOMETIMES, THE SMALLER, THE BETTER

Labor unions were created to improve working and safety conditions for the various crafts and industry of American blue-collar workers. All one has to do is read one or two books on the conditions which American workers had to endure before the turn of the century to see how sorely they were needed. As the conditions changed, so, too, did the unions. The first unions were divided by crafts, i.e., the captains and engineers, who were licensed, both had their own unions, while the unlicensed men of the deck and fireroom forces had theirs. The best-known union representing the captains is the Master's, Mate's and Pilot's. The local which represented the railroad captains was Local #1. The deck and fireroom forces were represented by such unions as the Transport Worker's Union, the Seafarer's International, and Local #333 of The International Longshoremen's Association ILA. The latter represented most of the nonrailroad boats, which were owned by companies like Moran Towing, McAllister Towing and Meseck Brothers, which handled large shipdocking, local pier barge shifting, and oceantowing.

But, in 1947, when I started on the Erie, these unions were different. Their men had broken with tradition. All of the Erie's Marine Department—licensed and unlicensed men—were represented by the United Marine Worker's, District 50, a splinter union of John L. Lewis' United Mine Workers of America. Tom Hogan, a ferryboat captain, was the president and Fred Koleberg, a tugboat captain, was the vice president. These men, together with the other officers, had proven themselves in acquiring for the Erie Marine Department one of the best contracts of any railroad in the harbor. Just a few advantages the Erie men had over the other railroads were: no split-watch boats (whereas the Lackawanna had three boats which laid up for two hours in the middle of the day during which time the crew was not paid, as was also true for the non-relieved bridge jobs at Hoboken and Barclay Street. This meant that you spent at least ten hours around the terminal or job area while only getting paid for an eight-hour day.) Erie deckhands did not wash windows, as Lackawanna deckhands did. Porters did porter work on the Erie. Erie wheelsman stayed in the pilothouse, unlike the Lackawanna wheelsmen who had to walk down to the main deck and drop the rudder pin after each trip, while deckhands also walked back to the outboard end to chock the vehicles.

Around 1950, the United Marine Workers held a special meeting at Bednarko's Hall in Jersey City to discuss a possible merger with the Transport Workers' Union, which represented the Lackawanna men (I believe they also represented the Central Railroad of New Jersey Marine Department men). The position placed before the membership was to present a stronger, more united front in the harbor, and to negotiate better contracts for all men.

After many concerns were discussed, it was agreed that Erie men would retain their same contract and the TWU would represent us. Some minor changes were implemented on the extra list: The afternoon shape was abolished, as was the rotating list. The extra list would be based on strict seniority, except in cases of emergency, when the first person to be contacted would get the job. This worked out better, because now, a man who did not work didn't have to break up his day and return in the middle of the afternoon. I think I was only on the list for a short time, but I was very high up and thus worked almost every day.

Several years later, the Erie men were to regret this merger. For, in 1954, when the *Tuxedo* was taken out of service, the TWU did little to help the men. Then, in 1956, with the completion of the Erie consolidated passenger agreement with the Lackawanna, where all Erie trains operated out of Hoboken, Erie senior men were not granted any seniority rights on the consolidated ferry service.

It was a black Erie porter, Ulysses Shell, who elected to bid a position on Lackawanna rather than take a lump-sum severance settlement, which finally broke the long tradition of split watches on Lackawanna ferries. Shell would not accept the terms of the Lackawanna contract, claiming he was working under the Erie consolidation guarantee, and thus was entitled to the terms of the Erie contract which stated that he was to be paid time-and-a-half after eight hours' daily work. He filed a labor-relation grievance with the National Railway Labor Relations Board, against both the Erie and Lackawanna railroads. After a long battle, the Lackawanna lost and the split watches were abolished. Shell was paid his back time, but all the Lackawanna men got was pay from the time the order took effect.

In 1958, when I worked on the Lackawanna Ferry, for a short time, I would find out just how much the TWU was a true "company union," doing little to improve the working conditions of the men. While I was on vacation, which I had coming to me from another department on the railroad, the company made some changes, with the consent of the union. These changes cost the men two bridge jobs, one at Hoboken and the other at Barclay Street. This placed two junior men back on the extra list where, as the two lowest men on the list, got very little work.

When the boat that I was working on pulled into the slip and there was no bridgeman to tie up the boat, I refused to leave my assigned position to perform another man's job, because to do so would have violated a company safety rule. When the boat was secured to the bridge, I went to the other ferry slip and questioned the president of the TWU Local as to why this was allowed by the union. His response was, "If you don't like it, you should complain to Captain Davis, assistant superintendent of the company." After we left Barclay Street for Hoboken and the boat was about halfway up the river, I was informed by the captain that I was to report to Captain Davis. When I got to his office, I was given a good tongue-lashing for questioning company policy with the president of the union.

Subsequently, I was very slowly eased out of the Lackawanna Marine Department. I had to file for unemployment, but the Lackawanna kept me working just enough hours so that while I could not live on the pay, it was a couple of dollars over the maximum to be eligible for any benefits. The one good thing that came out of my filing for unemployment was that I was offered a job, which I accepted, with the Lehigh Valley Police Department. The irony was that the position was created when the Lehigh Valley replaced the Lackawanna Railroad as the carrier for Acme Fast Freight!

I came to realize that the small, hardworking and -fighting, District 50 Local of the United Marine Workers was far superior to the larger Transport Workers' Union of America. As a very young man, I learned that, when the union removes the yoke of labor from one's back, it replaces it with the whip of the union shop agreement, which amounts to paying more for less protection.

Thankfully, this is not true with all unions.

52. PARTIAL ROSTER OF ERIE MARINE DEPARTMENT DECK EMPLOYEES

Ferrymaster

Claude Turse	Days, Chief
August Matasak	Afternoon
Edward Benarski	Nights
Alfred Dorr	Night Relief

Captains

Stephen Rogers	*Arlington*
Ernest Rogers	*Jamestown*
William Wolfer	*Meadville*
Frank Windknuckel	*Meadville*
Thomas Hogan	*Jamestown*
John Stein	Relief Crew
Joseph Yacono	*Youngstown*
Silas Brodhead	*Youngstown*
Jess Baker	Port Captain

Wheelsmen

Al Rowe	*Arlington*
Nicholas Ferriolia	*Jamestown*
Walter Huess	*Meadville*
Alfred Wilson	*Meadville*
John Stein Sr.	*Jamestown*
Lawrence Caruso	*Youngstown*
Joseph Glennon	*Youngstown*
Harold Cunningham	Relief Crew

Deckhands and Bridgemen, Days

Bridges

John Walsh	Jersey City #1
John Di Nuto	Jersey City #2

| Frank Bleam | Chambers Street #2 |
| William Grace | Chambers Street #1 |

Deckhands and Bridgemen, Evenings

Bridges

Jack Pierson	Jersey City #1
Joseph Iwanowski	Jersey City #2
James Ramagelli	Chambers Street #1
Ross Esposito	Chambers Street #2

Nights

Dave Collins	Jersey City
Joseph Pandolf	Chambers Street
Relief?	

Boats

Arlington	Al Fulton & Joseph Marino
Jamestown	Cliff Vreeland & Charles Cortess
Meadville	Tom Heaney & Eddie Hamm
Meadville	Hugo Krauss & Emil Troncy
Jamestown	Walter Swan & James McEntee
Youngstown	Joseph Smith & John J. Sullivan
Youngstown	Henry Footer
Relief Crew	Bill Heaney & Bob Webster

Porters

Arlington	Moses Simmons
Jamestown	Elmer Price
Youngstown	Ullysses Shell
Meadville	Herbert Headley
Relief:	Cunningham (never knew his first name as no one ever used it)

Some of the Extramen with whom I worked
Fred Wessels
John Chupak
John Dunn
John Brusca

Gatemen

Eddie Holmes	Days, Jersey City
Tom McGrane	Days, Chambers Street
Al Hoffman	Evenings, Jersey City
Red Devlin	Evenings, Chambers Street
Al Dorr	Nights, Jersey City
Tom Sullivan	Nights, Chambers Street
Bill Heany	Extra
Ray Baxter	Extra

PART III

APPENDIX

~~~~~~

Bibliography

Adams, Arthur G. *The Hudson, A guide book to the River,* SUNY, 1981.

Adams, Arthur G. *The Hudson River in Literature, An Anthology and History.* Albany: State University of New York Press, 1981.

Adams, Arthur G. *The Hudson Through the Years,* Lind Graphics, 1983.

American Ferryboats – by John Perry – William Funk Inc. New York 1957.

Archer, Robert F. *The Lehigh Valley Railroad,* "The Route of the Black Diamond" Howell-North, 1978.

Block Line, Tri-State Chapter Newsmagazine, National Railway Historical Society, Dover, New Jersey, October, 1981.

Casey, Robert J., and Douglas, W. A. S. *The Lackawanna Story,* McGraw-Hill, 1951.

Cassier's Magazine Vol. VI, No. 34 August 1894 – an article *The Ferryboat of Today* by Col. Edwin A. Stevens

Conniff, James C. G., and Richard *The Energy People, A History of PSE&G Public Service Electric and Gas Company,* 1978.

Cunningham, John T. *Railroading in New Jersey,* Associated Railroads in New Jersey, 1951.

Erie Railroad Magazine, various issues, 1905-1960, Cleveland, Ohio.

Floating Equipment, An article from the Archives of the National Museum of American History, Division of Transportation, Smithsonian Institute, Washington, D.C.

Haines, Henry S. *Efficient Railway Operation.* New York: The Macmillan Company, 1919.

Hardy, A. C. *American Ship Types.* New York: D. Van Nostrand Company, Inc., 1927.

Harper's Weekly, Supplement, January 5, 1889.

Helmer, William F. *O. & W.: The Long Life and Slow Death of the New York, Ontario & Western Ry.* Berkeley, California: Howell-North, 1959.

Hilton, George W. *The Staten Island Ferry,* Berkeley, California: Howell-North Books, 1964.

Hungerford, Edward. *Men of Erie,* Random House, 1946.

A History of New York – From the Beginning of the World to the End of the Dutch Dynasty, by Diedrich Knickerbocker. The Kinderhook Edition of *The Works of Washington Irving.* New York: G. P. Putnam's Sons, 1880.

Lossing, Benson J. *Field Book of the American Revolution.* New York: Harper & Brothers, 1852.

Lossing, Benson J. *From Wilderness to the Sea.* Troy, N.Y.: H. L. Nims & Co., 1866.

Lyon, Peter. *To Hell In A Day Coach: An Exasperated Look At American Railroads.* Philadelphia: J. B. Lippincott Company, 1968.

Lucas, Walter Arndt. *The History of the New York, Susquehanna & Western Railroad, Second Edition,* Railroadians of America, 1980.

Merchant Steam Vessels of the U.S. 1790 to 1868 – The Lytle-Holdcamper List – Steamboat Historical Society – 1978

Morris, George Pope. *Poems by George P. Morris.* New York: Charles Scribner, 1853.

Morrison, John Harrison. *History of American Steam Navigation.* New York: W. F. Sametz, 1903.

New York Walk Book. New York-New Jersey Trail Conference and The American Geographical Society. Garden City, N.Y.: Doubleday-Natural History Press, 1971.

Paulding, James Kirke. *New Mirror For Travellers; and Guide To The Springs.* New York: G. & C. Carvill, 1828.

Register of American Bureau of Shipping – various Years.

Rifkind, Carole, and Levine, Carol. *Mansions, Mills and Main Streets.* New York: Schocken Books, 1975.

Ringwald, Donald C. *Hudson River Day Line: The Story of a Great American Steamboat Company.* Berkeley, California: Howell-North Books, 1965.

Roberts, Franklin B., and Gillespie, John. *The Boats We Rode,* Quadrant Press, 1974.

Romance of the Hoboken Ferry, by Harry J. Smith, Prentice-Hall – 1931 Excerpts and update by George Eastland Public Relations Department Erie Lackawanna Railroad Co.

Stevens, Col. Edwin A., President of the Hoboken, N.J. Ferry Company, Cassier's Magazine, Vol. VI, No. 34, August 1894.

Swanberg, W. A. *Jim Fisk: The Career of an Improbably Rascal.* New York: Charles Scribner's Sons, 1959.

Taber, Thomas Townsend, *The Delaware, Lackawanna & West-*

ern Railroad in the Nineteenth Century, Thomas Townsend Taber III, 1977.

Taber, Thomas Townsend, *The Delaware, Lackawanna & Western Railroad in the Twentieth Centurry,* Thomas Townsend Taber III, 1980–81 (in two volumes).

The Delaware, Lackawanna & Western Railroad in the Twentieth Century, Volume 2. Taber, Thomas T. & Thomas T. Taber, III.

The Hudson A Guide Book of the River – Arthur G. Adams

The Lackawanna Story Casey & Douglas – McGraw Hill – New York 1951

Van Zandt, Roland. *Chronicles of the Hudson: Three Centuries of Travellers' Accounts.* New Brunswick, N.J.: Rutgers University Press, 1971.

Vessell Documents from The National Archives, Washington, D.C.

Wakefield, Manville B. *To The Mountains By Rail.* Grahamsville, N.Y.: Wakefair Press, 1970.

Whitson, Skip. *The Hudson River One Hundred Years Ago.* Albuquerque, N.M.: Sun Publishing Company, 1975.

Whittier, Bob. *Paddle Wheel Steamers and Their Giant Engines,* Seamaster Books, Inc. 1983.

Willis, Nathaniel Parker. *American Scenery.* London: George Virtue, 1836.

Willis, Nathaniel Parker. *Rural Letters.* Auburn, N.Y.: Alden, Beardsley & Co. 1853.

Wilstach, Paul. *Hudson River Landings.* Port Washington, N.Y.: Ira J. Friedman, Inc. 1969. Original edition: New York: The Bobbs-Merrill Company, 1933.

Central Railroad of New Jersey
Ferryboats

NAME OF VESSEL & OFFICIAL NUMBER:	DIMENSIONS:	TONS:	YEAR: BUILT:	WHERE BUILT:	REMARKS:
Sidewheel Vessels					
Central 4877[a]	217×33×12	1023	1863	Brooklyn, NY	1st Documented 5/11/65. Abandoned 1903
Communipaw 4876[a]	217×33×12	1023	1863	Brooklyn, NY	1st Documented 5/11/65. Abandoned 1905
Elizabeth I 8281[a]	217×33×12	1079	1867	Brooklyn, NY	Burned J.C. Shops 10/22/1901
Plainfield I	213×33×12	1051	1869	Brooklyn, NY	Burned 9/8/1900
Fanwood [a]	213×33×12	1092	1876		Burned 7/4/1906
Screw Propeller Vessels					
Easton 136350[a]	145×32×14	643	1893	Wilmington, DE	Sold 1901 to 125th St. Line, renamed *Leonia*
Mauch Chunk[a]	145×32×14	642	1893	Wilmington, DE	Sold 1901, renamed *Margate*
Lakewood[b]	200×44×17	1016	1901	Wilmington, DE	Burned 1949, rebuilt 1950, renamed *Elizabeth III*
Bound Brook 3909	200×44×17	1016	1901	Wilmington, DE	Scrapped 1967
Red Bank 111411	200×44×17	1016	1902	Wilmington, DE	Scrapped
Plainfield II 200879	200×43×15	1225	1904	Elizabethport, NJ	Scrapped
Elizabeth II 201490[c]	191×44×15	1197	1904	Wilmington, DE	Scrapped 1947
Wilkes-Barre 201355[c]	191×44×15	1197	1904	Wilmington, DE	Scrapped 1967
Cranford 202704	191×44×15	1197	1906	Wilmington, DE	Scrapped 1965
Somerville 202713	191×44×15	1197	1906	Wilmington, DE	Scrapped 1965
Westfield 208674	191×46×17	1238	1911	Wilmington, DE	Scrapped
Bayonne 211559	182×46×17	1334	1913	Wilmington, DE	Scrapped 1947
Elizabeth III[d]	200×44×17	Unknown	1901	Wilmington, DE	Rebuilt 1950, sold 1967—PSE&G, renamed *Second Sun*

Notes: [a] Single Decked Vessels.
    [b] All vessels built after 1900 were double decked vessels.
    [c] Built with upper deck unloading capabilities for W. 23rd Street.
    [d] All steel superstructure replaced wood after fire destroyed it while in the Jersey City Shops in 1949. Sold in 1967 to the Public Service Electric & Gas Company and is moored at Somers Point, N.J. Nuclear Station as a display vessel and renamed *Second Sun*.

Pennsylvania Railroad Ferryboats
And Predecessor Companies

NAME OF VESSEL & OFFICIAL NUMBER:	DIMENSIONS:	TONS:	YEAR: BUILT:	WHERE BUILT:	REMARKS:
Jersey[a]	78×32	118	1811	New York	Robert Fultons 1st ferryboat. Abandoned 1818
York[a]	78×32	118	1813	New York	Disposition unknown
New Jersey[b]	Unknown	Unknown	1818	Unknown	Exploded 7/12/1824, Paulus Hook
George Washington[c]	Unknown	Unknown	1827	Unknown	
Jersey City[c]	Unknown	Unknown	1827	Unknown	
Washington[c]	Unknown	258	1833	Newburgh, NY	Converted to barge 12/9/1859
Sussex[c]	Unknown	184	1834	New York	1st documented 2/21/1839. Abandoned 1849
Essex[c]	Unknown	242	1835	New York	1st documented 3/31/1839. Abandoned 1859
New Jersey[c]	Unknown	288	1836	New York	1st documented 3/21/1839. Abandoned 1862
Hudson 11937[c]	Unknown	345	1845	Brooklyn, NY	Chartered to NY & Lake Erie RR in 1861. Abandoned 1882
Philadelphia I 20295[c]	Unknown	341	1852	Hoboken, NJ	Chartered to NY & Lake Erie in 1861. Sold to US Government in 1863. Abandoned 1869
John S. Darcy 13192[c]	191×34×11	850	1857	Brooklyn, NY	Rebuilt after fire in 1859. Abandoned 1903
John P. Jackson 12982[c]	Unknown	777	1860	Brooklyn, NY	Sold to US Government in 1861. Redocumented in 1865. J. P. Jackson. Abandoned 1871
Jersey City 13158[c]	192×34×13	982	1862	Brooklyn, NY	Abandoned 1917
New York 18277[c]	192×34×13	793	1863	Brooklyn, NY	Abandoned 1902
		Sidewheel Vessels			
Newark I 18278[c]	192×34×13	661	1865	Brooklyn, NY	Sold 11/9/1901, renamed *America* (Amenia)
New Brunswick I 18295[e]	193×36×13	909	1866	Brooklyn, NY	Burned 4/19/1889, rebuilt 1890, double decked. Destroyed by fire 12/28/1896
Hudson City 11927[c]	203×35×12	1008	1867	Brooklyn, NY	Abandoned 1913
New Jersey II 18785[c]	212×36×12	1062	1873	Brooklyn, NY	Abandoned 1912

NAME OF VESSEL & OFFICIAL NUMBER:	DIMENSIONS:	TONS:	YEAR: BUILT:	WHERE BUILT:	REMARKS:
Princeton 150187[c]	192 × 36 × 12	888	1879	Brooklyn, NY	
Baltimore 3207[c]	192 × 36 × 12	1007	1882	Wilmington, DE	
Chicago I[c]	192 × 36 × 12	1006	1882	Wilmington, DE	Double decked in 1890. Sunk 10/31/1899
Annex 3[c]	128 × 29 × 9.7	367.57	1879	Wilmington, DE	Annex boat to Brooklyn[g]
Annex 4 106795[c]	138 × 31 × 11	501	1890	Wilmington, DE	Annex boat[g]
Annex 5 106860[c]	136 × 31 × 12	507	1891	Wilmington, DE	Annex boat[g]
Annex 107187[c]	139 × 31 × 11	529.13	1895	Tomkins Cove, NY	Annex boat[g]
Cincinnati 126803[d]	193 × 46 × 15	1255	1891	Elizabethport, NJ	1st double decked screwboat in NY Harbor. 3rd screwboat on North River
Washington 81366[d]	193 × 46 × 15	1247	1892	Chester, PA	Sold 1947 to Delaware & NJ Ferry Company.
St. Louis 116755[f]	200 × 46 × 15	1273	1896	Philadelphia, PA	1st twin screw ferryboat in NY
Pittsburgh 150741[f]	200 × 46 × 15	1273	1897	Philadelphia, PA	Ex Pittsburg
New Brunswick II 131757[f]	200 × 46 × 15	1273	1897	Philadelphia, PA	Last boat to operate to Cortlandt St., NY
Philadelphia II[f]	191 × 46 × 15	1273	1899	Chester, PA	Sold to Delaware & NJ Ferry Company in 1950
Chicago II[d]	193 × 46 × 15	1334	1901	Port Richmond, NY	Sold to Delaware & NJ Ferry Company in 1950
Newark II[d]	192 × 46 × 15	1308	1902	Newburgh, NY	

Notes:

[a] Centerwheel boats

[b] Very likely a centerwheel boat and the same dimensions as the Jersey

[c] Sidewheel vessels

[d] Double decked screw propeller boats

[e] First double decked ferryboat in New York Harbor

[f] Twin screw double decked vessels (only four vessels of this type were ever built for New York Harbor)

[g] Diposed of after opening of Penn Station in New York in 1910.

Pavonia Ferry Company
Erie Railroad Company

NAME OF VESSEL & OFFICIAL NUMBER:	DIMENSIONS:	TONS:	YEAR: BUILT:	WHERE BUILT:	REMARKS:
Iron witch[b]	Unknown	614	1846	Unknown	Steamer. Note: Renamed Erie in 1846. Abandoned 1862
New Haven[b]	178×22×15	342	1835	New York	Steamer. Abandoned 1869
Onalaska 19037[b]	130×32×11	411	1849	New York	Purchased 1861 from Union Ferry Company. Dismantled 1877
Niagara 18282[b]	130×32×11	411	1849	New York	Purchased 1861 from Union Ferry Company. Burned Jersey City 1/26/1868
Pavonia 19903[b]	193×34×13	831	1861	Brooklyn, NY	Renamed Rutherford 1907
Susquehanna 22797[b]	208×32×14	921	1865	Greenpoint, NY	Renamed Arden 1912
Delaware 6634[b]	198×35×13	985	1868	New York	Renamed Sterlington 1902
Jay Gould 75118[b]	160×34×12	663	1868	Brooklyn, NY	Renamed Chautauqua 1894
James Fisk 75120[b]	170×34×12	745	1869	New York	Renamed Passaic I 1879
Erie II 8930[b]	180×36×14	981	1873	Chester, PA	1st Iron hull double-ender on Erie. Renamed Ridgewood 1902
Passaic I 75120[b]	170×34×12	745	1879[a]	New York	Sold 1910 ex James Fisk
John King 76632[b]	190×36×13	1057	1886	Philadelphia, PA	Renamed Paterson 1899
John G. McCullough 76922[c]	200×38×16	1309	1891	Philadelphia, PA	2nd screwboat in N.Y. 1st to use compound engine
Chautauqua I 75118[b]	160×34×12	663	1894[a]	Brooklyn, NY	ex Jay Gould
Paterson 76632[b]	190×36×13	1057	1899[a]	Philadelphia, PA	Sunk December 29, 1906
Ridgewood 8930[b]	180×36×14	981	1902[a]	Chester, PA	ex Erie
Rutherford I 199903[b]	193×34×13	831	1907[a]	Brooklyn, NY	ex Pavonia dismantled 1911
Sterlington 6634[b]	198×35×13	985	1902[a]	New York	ex Delaware
Arlington 200661[c]	206×43×16	1446	1903	Port Richmond, NY	1st double decker on Erie. Last to run Chambers St. 1958
Tuxedo 200636[c]	205×43×16	1483	1904	Wilmington, DE	Scrapped 1955
Chautauqua II 76922[c]	200×45×14	1372	1906[a]	Philadelphia, PA	ex John G. McCullough double decked and rebuilt and renamed.
Goshen 201685[c]	205×43×16	1459	1905	Wilmington, DE	Sold to US Navy 1943 YFB 47
Jamestown 204817[c]	206×44×17	1538	1907	Port Richmond, NY	Dismantled 11/27/62
Suffern 6634[b]	198×35×13	985	1908[a]	New York	ex Delaware ex Sterlington, rebuilt 1908 and renamed. Dismantled 1926

NAME OF VESSEL & OFFICIAL NUMBER:	DIMENSIONS:	TONS:	YEAR: BUILT:	WHERE BUILT:	REMARKS:
Arden 22797[b]	196×35×12	921	1912[a]	Greenpoint, NY	ex *Susquehanna.* Dismantled 1924
Passaic II 130644[b]	193×36×13	1056	1883 1917[a]	Newburgh, NY	West Shore *Oswego* purchased 1916 dismantled 1936
Newburgh 130262[b]	193×36×13	1056	1883	Newburgh, NY	West Shore *Newburgh* purchased 1916
Youngstown 222704[c]	206×44×17	1553	1922	Mariner's Harbor, NY	Sold to DL&W 1957
Rutherford II 76922[c]	200×45×14	1372	1936[a]	Philadelphia, PA	ex *John G. McCullough,* ex *Chautauqua.* Sold to US Navy 1943 YFB 48
Meadville 234618[d]	221×45×17	1599	1936	Chester, PA	Sold DL&W 1957

Notes:

[a] Year vessel renamed

[b] Paddlewheel vessels

[c] Screwboats

[d] Skinner Unaflow engine screwboat. First ferryboat in New York Harbor to use this type engine. Last completely new ferryboat built for any New York Harbor railroad ferry company.

Delaware, Lackawanna & Western Railroad Co.
Hoboken Ferry Company Ferryboats

NAME OF VESSEL & OFFICIAL NUMBER:	DIMENSIONS:	TONS:	YEAR: BUILT:	WHERE BUILT:	REMARKS:
				Sidewheelers	
Juliana	Unknown	Unknown	1811	Hoboken, NJ	Abandoned 1813
Hoboken I	98 × 26 × 3.5	100	1822	Hoboken, NJ	Abandoned 1856
Pioneer	Unknown	143	1823	Hoboken, NJ	Abandoned 1860
Fairy Queen	Unknown	173	1825	New York	1st documented 8/23/1842. Renamed *Phoenix* 1851
Newark 18288	Unknown	162	1828	New York	Single end steamer. Abandoned 1873
Bergen 2313	Unknown	211	1834	New York	Abandoned 1875
Passaic	Unknown	Unknown	1844	Unknown	Sold 1869. Abandoned 1873
John Fitch 13164	Unknown	125	1846	Hoboken, NJ	Abandoned 1878
James Rumsey I	Unknown	341	1846	Hoboken, NJ	Burned NY 11/4/1853
James Watt	Unknown	372	1851	Hoboken, NJ	Burned Hoboken 8/1/1870
Phoenix	Unknown	173	1851[a]	New York	ex *Fairy Queen*, abandoned 1860
Chancellor Livingston 4863	Unknown	457	1853	Hoboken, NJ	Abandoned 1886
Patterson 19907	Unknown	360	1854	Hoboken, NJ	Had engine from *James Rumsey I*. Abandoned 1874
Hoboken II	Unknown	530	1861	Hoboken, NJ	Sold U.S. Government 1862. Lost January or February/1862
Hoboken III 11468	Unknown	551	1863	Hoboken, NJ	Abandoned 1880
Morristown 6988	Unknown	682	1864	Unknown	Abandoned 1898
John Stewart	Unknown	Unknown	1864	Unknown	Abandoned 1890
James Rumsey II 13828	Unknown	671	1867	Unknown	Sold 1889. Sunk 2/20/91
Weehawken 26900	Unknown	724	1868	Unknown	Sold 1887. Abandoned 1907
Hackensack	Unknown	Unknown	1871	Unknown	Sold 1893
Secaucus	Unknown	Unknown	1873	Unknown	2nd deck added 1892. 2nd deck removed 1906. Sold 1920
Moonachie	Unknown	Unknown	1877	Unknown	Sold 1907
Lackawanna I	Unknown	Unknown	1881	Newburgh, NY	Sold 1888. Abandoned 1936
Hoboken IV	200 × 35 × 13	831	1881	Newburgh, NY	Sold 1888. Abandoned 1936
Paunpeck	197 × 35 × 13	Unknown	1882	Newburgh, NY	Sold 1923. Abandoned 1939
Hopatcong I	Unknown	Unknown	1885	Unknown	Burned 8/7/1905, converted to barge, sunk 12/6/1910

NAME OF VESSEL & OFFICIAL NUMBER:	DIMENSIONS:	TONS:	YEAR: BUILT:	WHERE BUILT:	REMARKS:
Musconetcong 91813	197×35×13	846	1885	Newburgh, NY	Sold 1923, renamed *F.R. Pierson*, abandoned 1946
Orange 155132	218×35×13	1096	1885	Newburgh, NY	2nd deck added 1906. Sold 1944. Adandoned 1946
Montclair 91903	218×35×13	1096	1885	Newburgh, NY	Last sidewheeler built for company and last to run. Sold 1944. Abandoned 1947
		Screwboats			
Bergen II 3418	200×37×16	1120	1888	Newburgh, NY	1st screwboat on the North River. Abandoned 1953
Bremen 3523	219×40×16	1252	1891	Newburgh, NY	1st double decker in company. Renamed *Maplewood* in 1918. Sold 1946
Hamburg 96148	219×40×16	1266	1891	Newburgh, NY	Renamed *Chatham* in 1918. Rebuilt after fire 1920
Netherlands 130644	190×43×16	1129	1893	Newburgh, NY	Renamed *Oswego* 1935. Abandoned 1956
Scranton 201628	187×43×16	1462	1904	Newport News, VA	Sold 1967. Sunk 1968. Abandoned 1972
Binghamton 201734	187×43×16	1462	1905	Newport News, VA	Sold 1967. Restaurant at Edgewater
Elmira 201684	187×43×16	1462	1905	Newport News, VA	Last boat to operate 11/22/67. Sold 1968
Scandinavia 201816	187×43×16	1462	1905	Newport News, VA	Renamed *Pocono* in 1930. Sold 1967. Scrapped 1978.
Ithaca 203492	187×43×16	1462	1905	Newport News, VA	Burned Brighton Yard August 1946. Scrapped
Lackawanna II	206×39×14[a]	1079	1905 1907[b]	Wilmington, DE	ex *Woodbury*, Norfolk & Washington Ferry Company. Sold 1948.[c]
Hopatcong II	206×39×14[a]	1079	1906 1907[b]	Wilmington, DE	ex *Callahan*, Norfolk & Washington Ferry Company. Sold 1949.[c]
Maplewood I 3523	219×40×16	1252	1891	Newburgh, NY	ex *Bremen*, renamed in 1918
Chatham I 96148	219×40×16	1266	1891	Newburgh, NY	ex *Hamburg*, renamed in 1918, burrned 1920, rebuilt. Taken out of service 1949
Buffalo 222703	210×43×18	1292	1922	Elizabethport, NJ	Single deck. Sold 1957
Hoboken V 222638	210×43×18	1292	1922	Elizabethport, NJ	Single deck. Sold 1957
Pocono 201816	187×43×16	1462	1905	Newport News, VA	ex *Scandinavia*, renamed in 1930. Scrapped 1968

(continued)

Delaware, Lackawanna & Western Railroad Co.
Hoboken Ferry Company Ferryboats (*continued*)

NAME OF VESSEL & OFFICIAL NUMBER:	DIMENSIONS:	TONS:	YEAR: BUILT:	WHERE BUILT:	REMARKS:
Oswego 130644	190 × 43 × 16	1129	1893	Newburgh, NY	ex *Netherlands*, renamed 1935. Scrapped 1956
Lackawanna III 96148	219 × 40 × 16	1309	1891	Newburgh, NY	ex *Chatham I* rebuilt as diesel-electric 1949. Next to last boat to operate 11/22/67. Sold 1967. Scrapped in 1980.
Maplewood II 234618	221 × 45 × 17	1617	1936 1957[b]	Chester, PA	ex *Erie* RR *Meadville*. Had 15' added to each bow overall length 264'. Sold 1967. Scrapped 1979.
Chatham II	206 × 44 × 17	1571	1921 1957[b]	Mariners Harbor, NY Port Richmond, NY	ex *Erie* RR *Youngstown*. Scrapped 1960 after accident had 15' added to each bow, overall length 255'

Notes:

[a] Year renamed.

[b] Year purchased by the Delaware, Lackawanna & Western Railroad.

[c] Lengthened 20 feet in 1926.

New York Central System Ferries

NAME OF VESSEL & OFFICIAL NUMBER:	DIMENSIONS:	TONS:	YEAR: BUILT:	WHERE BUILT:	REMARKS:
Sidewheelers					
Abbie 1819	Unknown	Unknown	1852	Greenpoint, NY	Sold Albany & Bath Ferry Company. Abandoned 1884
Lydia 14938	Unknown	299	1853	Greenpoint, NY	Abandoned 1872
Rosyln 21440	Unknown	462	1860	New York	Purchased from Union Ferry Company 1873. Converted to derrick in 1888
Midland 90729	Unknown	Unknown	Unknown	Greenpoint, NY	Sold 1903 to Thames Ferry Company
Chester W. Chapin 126456	Unknown	Unknown	1875	Kingston, NY	Purchased in 1881 from Boston & Albany RR. Sold 1901
Albany I 106246	193 × 36 × 13	1056	1883	Newburgh, NY	Purchased from NYO & W in 1883. Sold to Carteret Ferry Company in 1917
Kingston 14420	193 × 36 × 13	1056	1883	Newburgh, NY	Purchased from NYO & W in 1883. Sold to Chesapeake Ferry in 1917
Newburgh 130262	193 × 36 × 13	1056	1883	Newburgh, NY	Purchased from NYO & W in 1883. Sold to Pavonia Ferry (Erie RR) in 1916
Oswego 155090	193 × 36 × 13	1056	1883	Newburgh, NY	Purchased from NYO & W in 1883. Sold to the Pavonia Ferry (Erie RR) in 1916. Renamed *Passaic* in 1917. Scrapped 1936.
Buffalo 3704	Unknown	Unknown	1897	Wilmington, DE	Last West Shore sidewheel ferryboat built. Sold in 1925 to Chesapeake Ferry Company. Renamed *Chesapeake*
Steel Hulled Propeller Boats:					
West Point 81737	192 × 40 × 16	1328	1900	Newburgh, NY	Sold 1941 to Norfolk Ferry Company
Syracuse 117261	193 × 40 × 17	1344	1903	Newburgh, NY	Scrapped 1959[a]
Rochester 202712	194 × 40 × 17	1338	1905	Newburgh, NY	Scrapped 1959[a]
Utica 207842	182 × 40 × 16	1351	1910	Newburgh, NY	Sold 1959 Dismantled Wildwood N.J. in 1970's.[a]

(continued)

New York Central System Ferries *(continued)*

NAME OF VESSEL & OFFICIAL NUMBER:	DIMENSIONS:	TONS:	YEAR: BUILT:	WHERE BUILT:	REMARKS:
Niagara 210464	183×40×17	1250	1912	Newburgh, NY	Sold 1959 to PSE&G for floating workshop. Dismantled at Marion Generating Station Jersey City in 1980's.[a]
Weehawken 212806	187×38×16	14022	1914	Wilmington, DE	Sold 1959 Derelict at Black Tom, Jersey City. Dismantled in 1970's Liberty Park restoration.[a]
Catskill 212027	184×39×16	1400	1914	Newburgh, NY	Burnt July, 1952 at Rodermond's Yard Morris Canal, Jersey City. Scrapped 1955
Stony Point 215069	197×39×16	1391	1917	Wilmington, DE	Sold 1959 Later sunk in Florida.[a]
Albany II 225146	203×45×16	1389	1925	Mariner's Harbor, NY Port Richmond, NY	Scrapped 1959[a]

Notes:

[a] In 1959 after the abandonment of its ferry service the New York Central sold all their boats to Mowbray Tug and Barge Co. of New York. Mowbray had two yards in Jersey City; one at Morris Canal and one at Black Tom. Mowbray did resell a few of the boats like the *Niagara* and *Utica*. I believe that *Stony Point* was also sold. The remaining boats Mowbray scrapped at Black Tom except *Weehawken* which for some reason was left abandoned in the mud for many years. She was finally dismantled when the State of New Jersey built Liberty Park in the 1970's.

The Fort Lee & Riverside Ferry Co.
of the
Public Service Street Railway Co.

NAME OF VESSEL & OFFICIAL NUMBER:	DIMENSIONS:	TONS:	YEAR: BUILT:	WHERE BUILT:	REMARKS:
Leonia 136350	145×32×14	643	1893	Wilmington, DE	ex *Easton* purchased from CNJ in 1905. Scrapped 1943
Englewood 127167	135×31×12	347	1896	Wilmington, DE	ex *City of Englewood*. Abandoned 1942
Paterson 207961	160×37×13	579	1898	Boston, MA	ex *Governor Russell*. Abandoned 1942
Edgewater 136971	146×39×15	687	1902	Wilmington, DE	Abandoned 1947
Tenafly 203468	185×45×16	1310	1906	Wilmington, DE	ex *Baylon* purchased from Long Island RR Co. Abandoned 1947
Hackensack 203563	185×45×16	1310	1906	Wilmington, DE	ex *Hempstead* purchased from Long Island RR. Abandoned 1946
Fort Lee	177×39×16	923	1915	Wilmington, DE	Sold to Norfolk Ferry Co. Dismantled in 1952
Thomas N. McCarter	189.5×36.2×14.5	1028	1926	Bethlehem Ship Building Company. Harlan Plant	ex *Philadelphia* Reading Co. Purchased June 1938. Sold 1943 to Norfolk Ferry Co. Renamed *Newport News*

The Electric Ferry Company

NAME OF VESSEL & OFFICIAL NUMBER:	DIMENSIONS:	TONS:	YEAR: BUILT:	WHERE BUILT:	REMARKS:
E.G. Diefenbach	184×45×14	565	1940	Orange, TX	Sold 1965 renamed *Fonseca*
Hamilton	117×45×13	569	1940	Orange, TX	Sold 1965. Renamed *Nicayano*
Hudson	117×45×13	569	1941	E. Boston, MA	Sold 1964 to Delaware River Port Authority. Renamed *Chester*
Gotham	172×42×13	545	1941	Oyster Bay, NY	Sold 1965 to Delaware River Port Authority. Renamed *Delaware*
Palisades	177×45×13	569	1942	E. Boston, MA	Sold 1965 to Delaware River Port Authority. Renamed *Bridgeport*
The Narrows	178×45×13	546	1946	Oyster Bay, NY	Sold 1968 to U.S. Coast Guard. Stripped for parts.
The Tides	178×45×13	545	1947	Oyster Bay, NY	Sold 1968 to U.S. Coast Guard. Still in service.

INDEX

GENERAL FERRY INDEX
key

BFF	=	Brooklyn Fulton Ferry
BUF	=	Brooklyn Union Ferry Co.
CAF	=	Claiborne & Annapolis Ferry Co.
CAR	=	Carteret Ferry Co.
CFC	=	Chesapeake Ferry Co.
CNJ	=	Central Railroad of New Jersey – Communipaw Ferry
DLW	=	Delaware, Lackawanna & Western Rwy. – Hoboken Ferry
DRF	=	Delaware Ferry Co.
DRPA	=	Delaware River Port Authority
ELEC	=	Electric Ferries
ERIE	=	Erie Railroad – Pavonia Ferry
GOVI	=	Governor's Island Ferry
HOB	=	Hoboken Ferry – Pre-railroad ownership
LIRR	=	Long Island Rail Road
NAVY	=	United States Navy
NFC	=	Norfolk Ferry Co.
NWFC	=	Norfolk & Washington Ferry Co.
125th	=	Edgewater to 125th Street Ferry
PHF	=	Paulus Hook Ferry – Pre-railroad ownership
PRR	=	Pennsylvania Railroad – Paulus Hook Ferry
RDG	=	Reading Company Railroad
SI	=	Staten Island Ferry – Whitehall to St. George
SIRT	=	Staten Island Rapid Transit – Tottenville to Perth Amboy
TFC	=	Thames Ferry Co.
WS	=	West Shore Ferry – New York Central – Weehawken Ferry

GENERAL FERRY INDEX

COMMUNIPAW – JERSEY CENTRAL

PAULUS HOOK – PENNSYLVANIA

PAVONIA – ERIE

HOBOKEN – LACKAWANNA

WEEHAWKEN – NEW YORK CENTRAL

EDGEWATER – 125th STREET

ELECTRIC FERRIES

MISCELLANEOUS VESSELS

OCEAN, COASTAL AND SOUND LINERS

STEAMSHIP COMPANIES

RAILROAD COMPANIES

INDEX OF PERSONS

GENERAL INDEX